ABOUT THE AUTHOR

Roger LeRoy Miller graduated Phi Beta Kappa from the University of California at Berkeley, where he also won the Department Prize in Economics. He was a Woodrow Wilson Honor Fellow, National Science Foundation Fellow, and Lilly Honor Fellow at the University of Chicago, where he received his Ph.D. in economics in 1968. Now at the Institute for University Studies, Dr. Miller has taught at the University of Washington, the University of Miami, Clemson University, and the University of Texas. He has also taught methodology to teachers of high school economics for the National Council on Economic Education. Among the more than 200 books he has written or co-authored are works on economics, statistics, law, consumer finance, and government. Dr. Miller also has operated several businesses and served as a consultant to government agencies, private corporations, and law firms.

Glencoe/McGraw-Hill

A Division of The McGraw-Hill Companies

Send all inquiries to:
Glencoe/McGraw-Hill
8787 Orion Place
Columbus, OH 43240

ISBN 0-02-823592-4 (Student Edition) ISBN 0-02-823596-7 (Teacher's Wraparound Edition)
Printed in the United States of America

6 7 8 9 10 071/043 03

CONTENTS

UNIT

5 MACROECONOMICS: MANAGING THE NATION'S ECONOMY

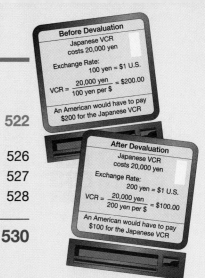

NIGHTLY BUSINESS REPORT

MULTIMEDIA ACTIVITIES

SKILLS

Personal Perspective

News Clip

Point ▶◀ Counterpoint

CASE STUDY Focus on Free Enterprise

ECONOMICS LAB

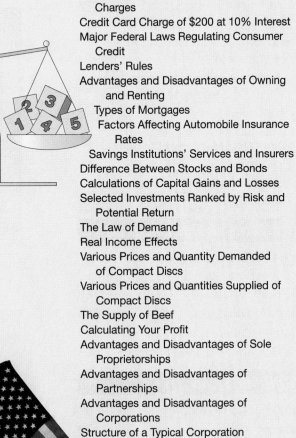

Home Equity Loan
40% Interest

PROFITS

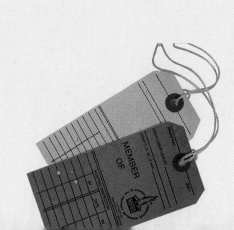

Basic Economic Concepts

Economics: Today and Tomorrow incorporates the 21 Basic Concepts established in "A Framework for Teaching the Basic Concepts," published by the National Council on Economic Education.

FUNDAMENTAL ECONOMIC CONCEPTS

1 Scarcity and Choice

Scarcity is the universal problem that faces all societies because there are not enough resources to produce everything people want. Scarcity requires people to make choices about the goods and services they use.

2 Opportunity Cost and Trade-Offs

Opportunity cost is the foregone benefit of the next best alternative when scarce resources are used for one purpose rather than another. **Trade-offs** involve accepting or choosing less of one thing to get more of something else.

3 Productivity

Productivity is the amount of output (goods and services) produced per unit of input (productive resources) used.

4 Economic Systems

Economic Systems are the ways in which people organize economic life to deal with the basic economics problem of scarcity.

5 Economic Institutions and Incentives

Economic institutions include households and families and formal organizations such as corporations, government agencies, banks, labor unions, and cooperatives. **Incentives** are factors that motivate and influence human behavior.

6 Exchange, Money, and Interdependence

Exchange is a voluntary transaction between buyers and sellers. It is the trading of a good or service for another good or service, or for money. **Money** is anything that is generally accepted as final payment for goods and services, and thus serves as a medium of exchange. **Interdependence** means that decisions or events in one part of the world or in one sector of the economy affect decisions and events in other parts of the world or sector of the economy.

MICROECONOMIC CONCEPTS

7 Markets and Prices

Markets are arrangements that enable buyers and sellers to exchange goods and services. **Prices** are the amounts of money that people pay for a unit of a particular good or service.

8 Supply and Demand

Supply is defined as the different quantities of a resource, good, or service that will be offered for sale at various possible prices during a specific time period. **Demand** is defined as the different quantities of a resource, good, or service that will be purchased at various possible prices during a specific time period.

9 Competition and Market Structure

Competition is the struggle between businesses that strive for the same customer or market. Competition depends on **market structure**—the number of buyers and sellers, the extent to which firms can control price, the nature of the product, the accuracy and timeliness of information, and the ease with which firms can enter and exit the market.

10 Income Distribution

Income distribution refers to the way the nation's income is distributed by function—to those who provide productive resources—and by recipient, primarily individuals and families.

11 Market Failures	**Market failures** occur when there is inadequate competition, lack of access to reliable information, resource immobility, externalities, and the need for public goods.
12 The Role of Government	The **role of government** includes establishing a framework of law and order in which a market economy functions.

MACROECONOMIC CONCEPTS

13 Gross Domestic Product	**Gross Domestic Product** (GDP) is defined as the market value of the total output of all final goods and services produced within a country's boundaries during one year.
14 Aggregate Supply and Aggregate Demand	**Aggregate supply** is the total amount of goods and services produced by the economy in a period of time. **Aggregate demand** is the total amount of spending on goods and services in the economy during a period of time.
15 Unemployment	**Unemployment** is defined in United States statistics as the number of people without jobs who are actively seeking work.
16 Inflation and Deflation	**Inflation** is a sustained increase in the average price level of the entire economy. **Deflation** is a sustained decrease in the average price level of an entire economy.
17 Monetary Policy	**Monetary policy** consists of actions initiated by a nation's central bank that affect the amount of money available in the economy and its cost (interest rates).
18 Fiscal Policy	**Fiscal policy** consists of changes in taxes, in government expenditures on goods and services, and in transfer payments that are designed to affect the level of aggregate demand in the economy.

INTERNATIONAL ECONOMIC CONCEPTS

19 Absolute and Comparative Advantage and Barriers to Trade	**Absolute advantage** and **comparative advantage** are concepts that are used to explain why trade takes place. **Barriers to trade** include tariffs, quotas, import licenses, and cartels.
20 Exchange Rate and the Balance of Payments	An **exchange rate** is the price of one nation's currency in terms of another nation's currency. The **balance of payments** of a country is a statistical accounting that records, for a given period, all payments that the residents, businesses, and governments of one country make to the rest of the world as well as the receipts they receive from the rest of the world.
21 International Aspects of Growth and Stability	**Growth** and **stability** are more important today than in the past because all nations are much more interdependent.

Adapted from the National Council on Economic Education's *A Framework for Teaching the Basic Concepts, 1996.*

U N I T

AN INTRODUCTION TO ECONOMICS

Did You Know

- Your choice of jeans as a consumer determines how many will be produced.
- Most new jobs will be in the services and professional specialties.
- Taxes account for about 60 percent of the price of fuel in the United States.
- Experts predict that the amount of travel will double in the next 25 years.
- China plans to turn over most state factories to private individuals.

In this unit you will learn what economics is, and how different societies have chosen what goods and services should be produced and how they should be distributed.

1 WHAT IS ECONOMICS?

What benefit are these students receiving from this activity?

What would be the benefit of studying instead of watching television?

What are the long-term effects of watching too much television?

How do students make the choice between studying and watching television?

What are these students doing?

Your Economics Journal

During a one-week period, keep track of how you spend your time. At the end of the week, list the most frequent activities in which you engage and how many hours you spent on each.

SECTION 1 The Basic Problem in Economics

SECTION 1 FOCUS

Terms to Know economics, resource, scarcity, wants, land, labor, capital, productivity, entrepreneurship, factors of production, goods and services, technology

Objectives *After reading this section, you should be able to:*

1. Explain why scarcity faces all people at all times.
2. Distinguish between wants and needs.
3. List and summarize the four types of resources.

Economics—The Study of Choices

Economics is the study of how individuals and nations make choices about how to use scarce resources to fulfill their wants. A **resource** is anything that people can use to make or obtain what they want.

As a student, you probably have a small amount of income—from an allowance or a part-time job—to spend. As a result, you have to make choices about its use. Whenever you make such a spending decision, each available choice competes with every other available choice. Suppose you have $20 to spend. You could use it to buy lunch for four days or two budget compact discs or a sweatshirt and so on as shown in Figure 1.1.

The Problem of Scarcity

The need to make choices arises because everything that exists is limited, even though some items may appear to be in overabundant supply. At any one moment in the United States, or anywhere, a fixed, or set, amount of resources is available. At the same time, people may have competing uses

◄ **Figure 1.1 Economic Choices**
When you decide whether to spend your money on clothes or a new CD, you are making an economic choice. The basic economic problem of scarcity makes the choice necessary.

for these resources. This situation results in the problem of scarcity—the basic problem of economics.

Scarcity means that people do not and cannot have enough income, time, or other resources to satisfy their every desire. What you can buy with your income as a student is limited by the amount of income you have. In this case, your income is the scarce resource. Scarcity is not the same as *shortage*, as **Figure 1.2** shows.

Choices The problem of scarcity faces businesses as well as individuals. Businesspeople make decisions daily about what to produce now, what to produce later, and what to stop producing. These decisions in turn affect people's income and their ability to buy. Nations, too, face the problem of choosing how to spend their scarce resources. The United States, for example, must decide how much to spend on Social Security benefits and aid to higher education. How people make these choices is the subject of economics.

Wants versus Needs

How many times have you said that you "need" something? How often do you think about what you "want"? When you say, "I need some new clothes," are you stating a want, or a real need? Typically the term *need* is used very casually. When most people use the word *need*, they really mean that they want something they do not have.

The difference between wants and needs is not a clear one. Everyone needs certain basic things—enough food, clothing, and shelter to survive. Americans also consider a good education and adequate health care as needs.

Economists call everything other than these basic needs **wants.** People want such items as new cars and personal computers. Although more and more people have these items, this does not mean that anyone actually needs them.

▲

B Temporary shortages of products such as gasoline may be caused when imports are dramatically decreased for any reason.

Figure 1.2
Shortage vs Scarcity
It is important not to confuse shortage and scarcity. Scarcity always exists, whereas shortages are always temporary.

A Shortages often exist after major hurricanes or floods that destroy goods and property.

For example, people entertained themselves and informed themselves of news long before the invention of the radio. As the wonders of radio were advertised, more people began to believe they needed one. What began as a luxury, or want, became to many people a necessity. This cycle of wants and perceived needs is repeated over and over. In economics, however, only a few true needs, such as minimal food and shelter, exist.

Types of Resources

Besides the question of whether you need or want a VCR, there is the issue of whether there will be enough VCRs to allow every person to own one. Also, not everyone would have enough money to buy one. Only a certain amount of resources exist, regardless of wants and needs. Traditionally, economists have classified resources as land, labor, capital, or entrepreneurship.

Land As an economic term, **land** refers to natural resources, as shown in Figure 1.3, not just to surface land. Among the most important natural resources in economic terms are land and mineral deposits such as iron ore. In economics, the location of land is also important in establishing its value as a resource.

Labor The work people do is **labor**—often called a human resource. The labor resource includes anyone who works.

Capital All the property people use to make other goods and services is **capital**. For example, the machines used to make automobiles are capital. The cars are not considered capital unless they are used, for example, as taxicabs, to produce services. Combining capital with land and labor increases the value of all resources by increasing their productivity. **Productivity** is the ability to produce greater quantities of goods and services in better and faster ways.

When you read references to "capital" in newspapers, they generally mean *financial capital,* such as the funds made available in the stock market for starting a new business. In this book, if we mean such funds, we will always say *financial* or *money* capital.

**Figure 1.3
Natural
Resources**
Natural resources are all the things found in nature—on or in water and the earth—such as fish, animals, forests, and minerals as well as land and water.

▼

Entrepreneurship The fourth type of resource is **entrepreneurship** (AHN-truh-pruh-NUHR-ship), which refers to the ability of individuals to start new businesses, to introduce new products and techniques, and to improve management techniques.

All changes in business organization are part of entrepreneurship. It involves initiative and individual willingness to take risks to make profit. Entrepreneurs succeed when they produce new products, improve an existing product or produce it more efficiently, or reorganize a business to run more smoothly.

Together, the resources of land, labor, capital, and entrepreneurship are called the **factors of production.** They are used to produce **goods and services.** Goods are the items that people buy. Services are the activities done for others for a fee.

Technology Some economists add technology to the list of resources. Any use of land, labor, and capital that produces goods and services more efficiently is technology. For example, a computer keyboard is a technological advance over the typewriter.

Today, however, **technology** usually describes the use of science to develop new products and new methods for producing and distributing goods and services. Figure 1.4 illustrates a modern application of technology.

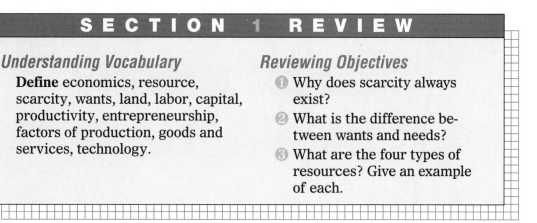

Figure 1.4 ▲
Technology in Action
Advanced machinery and new production and distribution methods increase the productivity of the other resources. For example, without modern drilling machinery, it would be impossible to tap the oil resources of the ocean.

SECTION 1 REVIEW

Understanding Vocabulary
Define economics, resource, scarcity, wants, land, labor, capital, productivity, entrepreneurship, factors of production, goods and services, technology.

Reviewing Objectives
1. Why does scarcity always exist?
2. What is the difference between wants and needs?
3. What are the four types of resources? Give an example of each.

LEARNING ECONOMIC SKILLS

Reading Tables and Graphs

Tables and graphs are easy to read and show much information in a small space. Do you know how to interpret them?

Tables

Tables, such as Figure A below, represent data in rows and columns according to topics.

Figure A. Understanding How Americans Traveled in a Recent Year

Forms of Transportation	Miles in Billions	Percent Distribution
Automobiles	1,287	83.4
Airlines	213	13.8
Other	43	2.8

Graphs

Graphs are a visual representation of statistical data and are often easier to read than tables. The three types of graphs include circle ("pie") graphs, bar graphs, and line graphs.

Circle Graph Circle graphs show the proportions of the elements of a whole. Figure B shows the percentage distribution of forms of transportation from Figure A in a circle graph.

Bar Graph The bar graph in Figure C shows teenage unemployment over four years.

Line Graph Line graphs are often used to show the same information as a bar graph. Figure D, for example, is a line graph representation of the information in Figure C.

Figure B. Understanding How Americans Traveled in a Recent Year

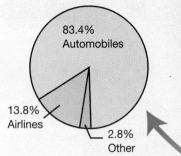

83.4% Automobiles

13.8% Airlines

2.8% Other

Figure C. Teenage Unemployment Rates (1994-1997)

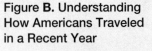
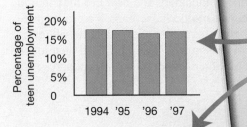

Figure D. Teenage Unemployment Rates (1994-1997)

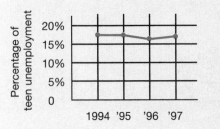

Practicing the Skill

① What information does Figure A provide that Figure B does not?

② According to Figure C, when was teenage unemployment highest?

12

SECTION 2 Trade-Offs

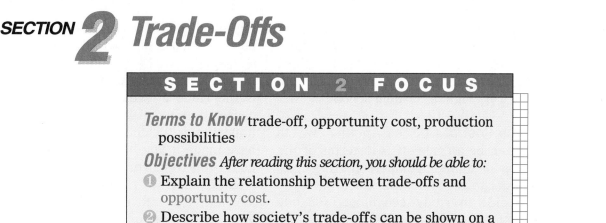

SECTION 2 FOCUS

Terms to Know trade-off, opportunity cost, production possibilities

Objectives *After reading this section, you should be able to:*

1. Explain the relationship between trade-offs and opportunity cost.
2. Describe how society's trade-offs can be shown on a production possibilities curve.

Choices Involve Opportunity Costs

Scarcity forces people to make choices about how they will use their resources. Those choices affect not only how people live today, but how people will live in the future. It is important to realize that the economic choices people make involve exchanging one good or service for another. If you choose to buy a video for your VCR, you are exchanging your money for the right to own the video. Exchanging one thing for the use of another is called a **trade-off.**

Opportunity Costs

As Figure 1.5 shows, individuals, businesses, and nations are forced to make trade-offs every time they use their resources in one way and not

Figure 1.5 Trade-Offs

Trade-offs involve making choices that are unavoidable because of the problem of scarcity. Having high levels of automobile pollution or higher car manufacturing costs (to reduce pollution) is an example. ▼

GO TO

Lesson 1 of **Interactive Economics!** to learn more about "Opportunity Costs."

another. For example, as a student you may be faced with a decision about going to college or vocational school to increase future earnings, or going to work right after high school.

The Cost of Choices Another way to describe a trade-off is in terms of the cost of something a person gives up in order to get something else. When you decide to study economics for one hour, you are making a choice. You are giving up any other activities you could choose to do. Because time is a scarce resource—there are only so many hours in a day—you must decide how to use it.

In other words, there is a cost involved in time spent studying this book. Economists call it an **opportunity cost**—the value of the next best alternative that had to be given up for the alternative that was chosen. Whatever you consider as the value of the next best alternative to studying—watch-ing television, for example—is the opportunity cost of your studying for one hour.

The opportunity cost of any action is the value of what is given up because the choice was made. What is important is the choice that you would have made if you had not studied one hour. Your opportunity cost is generated from the next-highest-ranked alternative, not all alternatives. Therefore, in economics, cost is always a forgone opportunity.

A good way to think about opportunity cost is to realize that when you choose to do something, you lose. What do you lose? You lose the ability to engage in your next-highest-valued alternative.

A Practical Example Consider an example at the national level. Suppose Congress votes $2 billion for projects to clean up polluted rivers. The opportunity cost of its vote is the next best alternative use of those same tax dollars. For example, Congress could have voted for increased spending on space research. Then the opportunity cost of clean rivers would be fewer space flights.

Considering Opportunity Costs

Being aware of opportunity costs and trade-offs is important in making economic decisions of all kinds. For example, you will be able to make wiser use of your own resources if you know the opportunity costs and trade-offs involved. You will be able to vote more intelligently if you are aware of the choices your elected officials face. Businesspeople, too, must consider opportunity costs and trade-offs.

Production Possibilities

The term *mix* brings up another fact about resources. How do people determine how much of each item to produce? What are the trade-offs and opportunity costs involved in each decision? The concept of production possibilities is useful in examining this problem.

Production possibilities are all the combinations of goods and services that can be produced from a fixed amount of resources in a given period of time. For each situation, only a limited number of factors are considered. A fixed amount of resources and a given period of time exist.

The Classic Example The classic example for explaining production possibilities in economics is the trade-off between military defense and civilian goods, sometimes referred to as *guns* versus *butter*. The extremes for a nation would be using all its resources to produce only one or the other. Figure 1.6 shows the two extremes as points A and E.

The federal government determines where on the production-possibilities curve the nation will be. The government takes income from citizens through taxes. It uses this revenue, which could have been used for butter, to produce guns. "The nation" on the curve is Congress and the

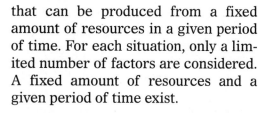

▼ Figure 1.6
Guns or Butter?

Point A on the graph represents all resources being used to produce only guns (military defense). Point E represents the other extreme—all resources being used to produce only butter (civilian goods).

Countries produce combinations, or mixes, of goods. That is shown by the curve between points A and E. The curve represents the production possibilities between guns and butter in a nation during one year.

The maximum quantity of guns made per year is shown by the vertical distance from point 0 to point A. What is shown by the horizontal distance from point 0 to point E?

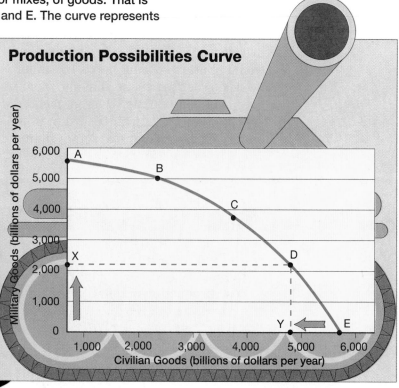

Production Possibilities Curve

Military Goods (billions of dollars per year)

Civilian Goods (billions of dollars per year)

**Figure 1.7 ▲
From Military to
Civilian Goods**
A small defense contractor, Harris, was able to outbid AT&T to obtain a $1.66 billion contract to manufacture a new civilian air-traffic control system such as the one shown.

President, who make decisions for the American public.

Production-possibilities curves are a good way to show trade-offs and opportunity costs visually. As you can see from Figure 1.6 (page 15), a nation or a business cannot produce more of one thing without giving up something. For example, if a nation starts with all civilian goods production and no military production—point E—it can only get to point D—some weapons production—by giving up some butter production. In other words, the price of having some weapons production (represented by the vertical distance from 0 to point X) is giving up some butter

production (represented by the horizontal distance from point E to point Y). The amount of civilian goods production given up in the year is the opportunity cost for increasing military production.

By using a production-possibilities curve, a nation or a business can decide how best to use its resources. By "best" is meant using resources most efficiently for economic growth. Such a curve is useful in locating the opportunity costs if a particular course of action is followed.

A Real-World Example: Military Downsizing in the 1990s From the 1950s until the early 1990s, the United States was engaged in a so-called cold war with the Soviet Union, and we produced more and more military goods. When that country split up into 15 separate republics, our major military adversary seemingly disappeared. Consequently, we needed to move from, say, point C to point D in Figure 1.6.

The real world and our graphs are not always quite the same, however. In the real world, it takes time to move from point C to point D. For example, our military had been purchasing guns, bombs, and planes from such major contractors as McDonnell-Douglas and Hughes. In the 1990s, much of their military business evaporated. Some former military-hardware companies started making civilian goods as Figure 1.7 shows.

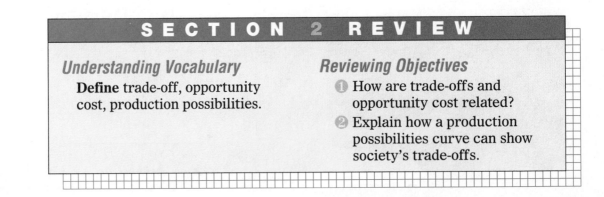

SECTION 2 REVIEW

Understanding Vocabulary
Define trade-off, opportunity cost, production possibilities.

Reviewing Objectives
1. How are trade-offs and opportunity cost related?
2. Explain how a production possibilities curve can show society's trade-offs.

Robert L. Heilbroner on the Great Economists

Profile

- 1919–
- attended Harvard University and the New School for Social Research in New York City
- has taught at the New School for Social Research since 1972
- published works include *The Worldly Philosophers* (1953), *The Future as History* (1960), *The Great Ascent* (1963), *Between Capitalism and Socialism* (1970), and *The Nature and Logic of Capitalism* (1985)

Robert L. Heilbroner's book *The Worldly Philosophers* gives a unique and insightful look into the lives and works of the great economists of the past. In his introduction, Heilbroner explains the importance of these great economists to history.

By all the rules of schoolboy history books, they were nonentities: they commanded no armies, sent no men to their deaths, ruled no empires, took little part in history-making decisions.... Yet what they did was more decisive for history than many acts of statesmen who basked in brighter glory, often more profoundly disturbing than the shuttling of armies back and forth across frontiers, more powerful for good and bad than the edicts of kings and legislatures. It was this: they shaped and swayed men's minds.

Heilbroner expresses his belief that economists have a major impact on the world:

And because he who enlists a man's mind wields a power even greater than the sword or the scepter, these men shaped and swayed the world. Few of them ever lifted a finger in action; ... But they left in their train shattered empires and exploded continents, they buttressed and undermined regimes, they set class against class and even nation against nation— not because they plotted mischief, but because of the extraordinary power of their ideas.

He disagrees with the perception that the work of economists is dull and boring:

... A man who thinks that economics is only a matter for professors forgets that this is the science that has sent men to the barricades.... No, the great economists pursued an inquiry as exciting—and as dangerous—as any the world has ever known.... The notions of the great economists were world-shaking, and their mistakes nothing short of calamitous.

Checking for Understanding

❶ Why is it important to study the great economists of the past?

❷ Have economists made a real difference in the world?

❸ What does Heilbroner believe about the power of economists' ideas?

SECTION 3 FOCUS

Terms to Know economy, economic model, hypotheses, values, generalization

Objectives *After reading this section, you should be able to:*

1. Describe and give examples of economic models.
2. Explain the purpose of economic models.
3. Explain why there are different schools of economic thought.
4. Tell why economists do not normally work with values.

Economists Use Models to Study the Real World

Economics is concerned with the ways individuals and nations choose to use their scarce resources. For example, economists might analyze teenagers' spending and its effect on the economy. See Figure 1.8. To economists, **economy** means all the activity in a nation that together affects the production, distribution, and use of goods and services.

To carry out their investigations, economists often gather information from the real world. These data then become the basis for testing theories that explain an event, such as rising unemployment. The theories or solutions then become the basis for actual decisions by private business or government agencies.

Figure 1.8
Teen Buying Power
United States teenagers spend billions of dollars each year on clothing and other items. Their buying patterns definitely affect the types of goods that are produced.

▼

Economic Models

In their work, economists use economic models, or theories. An **economic model** is a simplified representation of the real world. Physicists, chemists, biologists, and other scientists also use models to explain in simple terms the complex workings of the world.

What Models Show Economic models show the way people react to changes in the economy. The most frequently used model explains how people react to changes in the prices of goods and services they want to purchase. An economist has three ways of presenting such a model: through an explanation in words, in a graph, or with a mathematical equation. Whichever method is chosen, the information in the model is the same, as shown in Figure 1.9.

Limits of Models No economic model records every detail and relationship that exists about a problem to be studied. A model will show only the basic factors needed to analyze the problem. For example, economists have found that they need to analyze only three basic factors to determine buyer reaction to price changes. These factors are the price of the item, the income of the average buyer, and the price of alternative items.

The Purpose of Models

As you study economics, it is important to keep in mind the purpose of economic models. They are not supposed to account for all the possible factors that might influence a problem. They take into account only the most important ones.

Creating An economist considers a model *good* if it provides useful material for analyzing the way the real world works. As in forming a hypothesis, an economist begins with some idea about the way things work, then collects facts and discards those that are not relevant. Once a conclusion is reached, the only way an economist can find out whether a model works is to test it.

Testing Suppose an economist has developed the model shown in Figure 1.10 (page 20). The economist tests the model in the same way that other scientists test **hypotheses,** educated guesses, or predictions, used as the starting points for investigations, as shown in Figure 1.11 (page 21).

For the model in Figure 1.10 (page 20), an economist would collect data on the amount of teenage unemployment every year for the last 30 years.

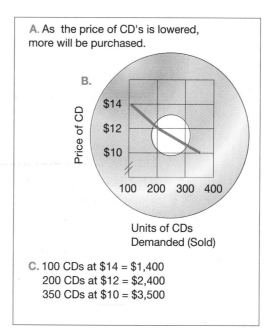

A. As the price of CD's is lowered, more will be purchased.

B.

Price of CD

$14
$12
$10

100 200 300 400

Units of CDs
Demanded (Sold)

C. 100 CDs at $14 = $1,400
   200 CDs at $12 = $2,400
   350 CDs at $10 = $3,500

◀

Figure 1.9 Economic Models of CD Prices
In the case of prices, these three ways of presenting the model all show that consumers respond to lower prices by purchasing more of less expensive items.

He or she also would gather information on the frequency of federal legislation increasing the legal minimum wage paid to teenagers.

Suppose the economist finds that every time the minimum wage rate increased, teenage unemployment increased. The economist can be fairly satisfied with the model. See Figure 1.10, graph A.

Suppose that the data does not seem to show a relationship between teenage unemployment and increases in the legal minimum wage. See Figure 1.10, graph B. The economist then will have to develop another model to explain changes in teenage unemployment.

Applying Much of the work of economists involves predicting how people will react in a particular situation. Individual human behavior is not always predictable, however. As a result, an economist's answer to a specific problem may turn out not to work for everyone.

For example, to stimulate the economy, some economists believe that taxes should be cut and government spending increased. These economists believe that cutting taxes will raise personal spending, which, in turn, will increase total production.

However, some people's fears concerning possible higher taxes in the future might cause them to save the extra money rather than spend it. As this illustrates, economists cannot predict all the factors that may influence people's behavior.

Schools of Economic Thought

Economists deal with facts. Their personal opinions and beliefs may nonetheless influence how they view those facts and fit them to theories. The government under which an economist lives also shapes how he or she views the world. As a result, all economists will not agree that a partic-

ular theory offers the best solution to a problem. Often, economists from competing schools of thought claim that their theories alone will predict a certain result.

At a particular time, a nation's political leaders may agree with one school of economic thought and develop policies based on it. Later, leaders may agree with another group of economists. For example, during the 1980s, many economists stressed the role of businesses and consumers rather than of the government in preventing increased unemployment and inflation. In the 1990s, however, many influential national leaders proposed that the federal government should intervene in the economy to reduce unemployment.

Values and Economics

Economics will help you to predict what may happen if certain events occur or certain policies are followed. Economics will not, however, tell you whether the result will be good or bad. That judgment will depend on your values.

Values are the beliefs or characteristics that a person or group considers important, such as religious freedom,

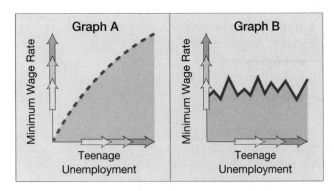

Figure 1.10 ▲ Testing an Economic Model
Economists, like scientists, must collect data to prove or disprove their theories. Graph A supports the direct relationship between increases in the legal minimum wage rate and increases in teenage unemployment. Graph B does not support that relationship.

Figure 1.11 Using a Hypothesis

The list below reviews the steps involved in making and testing hypotheses. In working with models, economists use these same steps.

1. Define the problem.

2. From the possible alternatives, state a hypothesis that appears to offer the best solution to a problem or explanation of an event.

3. Gather data to test the hypothesis. Besides using facts from the real world, an economist must identify economic principles involved.

4. Evaluate the data and discard any that are not relevant, or related to the immediate situation, or that are not objective (those that are based on fact).

5. Make sure there are enough data to test the hypothesis thoroughly.

6. Develop a conclusion based on the data. To do this, an economist evaluates whether the alternative is the best, in view of its consequences and trade-offs.

7. If the hypothesis appears to be proved, retest it with new data to see if the same results can be obtained again.

8. If the hypothesis appears to be proved, form a generalization that can be applied to other cases. A **generalization** pulls together common ideas among facts and is true in most cases. For an economist, this step involves developing an economic policy based on the best alternative.

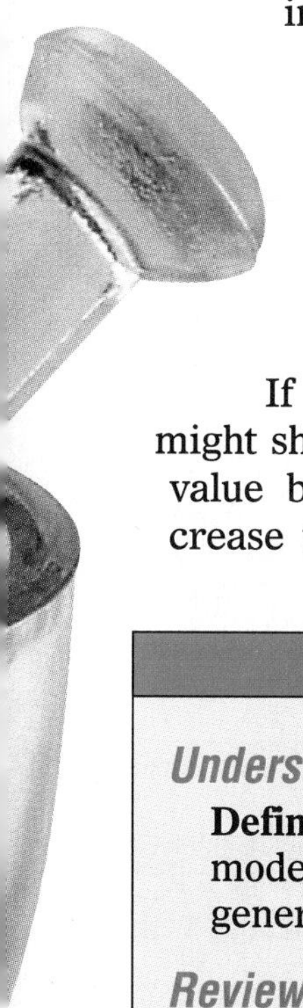

equal opportunity, individual initiative, freedom from want, and so on. Suppose, for example, that you believe the nation should do something to lower unemployment among teenagers. This belief is a value judgment on your part.

If you were a legislator, you might show your commitment to this value by introducing a bill to decrease teenage unemployment. The economists who help you research the causes of teenage unemployment may not tell you whether your bill is good or bad. They will tell you whether the proposed solution may be workable or not.

Having the same values does not mean that people will agree about solutions, strategies, or interpretation of data. For example, those in favor of decreasing teenage unemployment may disagree about the best way to solve this problem.

SECTION 3 REVIEW

Understanding Vocabulary
Define economy, economic model, hypotheses, values, generalization.

Reviewing Objectives
① What are three ways of presenting an economic model?

② What is the purpose of economic models?

③ Why do not all economists agree on the same solutions to problems?

④ Briefly explain why economists do not deal with values.

Readings in Economics

TIME · AUGUST 4, 1997

THE KING LIVES
by S.C. Gywnne

Let's say . . . that you have been bitten by the Elvis bug. . . . You start the world's 481st Elvis fan club. You print up personalized Elvis stationery and Elvis T shirts, and start a Web page with photos of Graceland [Elvis's home]. You throw Elvis-themed parties.

Having your way with the image of a long-dead superstar—it may sound like innocent if somewhat obsessive fun. Legally speaking, however, virtually everything you are doing is a form of copyright infringement. If you keep it up, you are likely to receive . . . something called a cease-and-desist order from a company in Memphis, Tenn., telling you that . . . you may not use the name and image of the King without the company's permission. . . .

The name of this tenacious corporation, not coincidentally, is Elvis Presley Enterprises [EPE]. . . .

Unlike the story of Elvis' rise, . . . the story of what happened after his death is both more unfamiliar and nearly as compelling. . . . Its unlikely heroine turns out to be none other than Elvis' "child bride," Priscilla Beaulieu Presley, who divorced him in 1973 but took over EPE six years later as trustee for their young daughter Lisa Marie. . . .

The estate was heading toward the red when Priscilla took over. . . . While their bankers looked on aghast, she and Soden [her business manager] blew the last of the estate's cash, $560,000, on their own plan to open Graceland to the public. . . . Today the mansion has some 750,000 visitors a year and generates revenues in excess of $20 million. . . .

• THINK ABOUT IT •

1. **Who took over Elvis Presley Enterprises in 1979?**

2. **Why do you need permission to start an Elvis fan club?**

ECONOMICS IN ACTION

What Is Economics?

Setting up the Video

With your classmates, view "What Is Economics?" on the videodisc *Economics in Action*. The video focuses on the economic concept of scarcity. The program points out that all resources are inherently limited. As a result, society as a whole must decide how it wants to allocate them.

‖‖‖‖‖‖‖‖‖‖‖‖‖	**Chapter 2**
	Disc 1, Side 1

View the video by scanning the bar code or by entering the chapter number on your keypad and pressing Search. (Also available in VHS format.)

Hands-On Activity

Recognize the economic trade-offs in your own life. Make two columns on a piece of paper. In one column, list the things you feel you **need** to buy each week. In the other column, list the things you **want** to buy. Which column has more items? What is the difference between a need and a want? About how much money is required to satisfy your weekly needs and wants?

INTERACTIVE ECONOMICS!

Opportunity Costs

Introduction

Lesson 1 of *Interactive Economics!* describes the concept of opportunity costs, which is the cost of the next best alternative use of money, time, or resources when one choice is made rather than another. Economists use a popular model called a production possibilities frontier to illustrate the concept of opportunity cost. The frontier is a diagram representing various combinations of goods and/or services that can be produced when all productive resources are fully and efficiently employed.

Lesson 1 of *Interactive Economics!* takes you to the mythical Ourland where you will help determine the best mix of producing automobiles and wheat.

Using the Software

1. Select "Opportunity Costs" from the Main Menu.

2. Read the introduction to "Opportunity Costs," then click on "Amalgamated."
3. After reading the "Tutorial," go back to the introduction and click on "Consolidated." Repeat this process for "Federated."
4. Finally, click on the "Advanced Topics Menu" and read about Ourland's production possibilities frontier, the cost of unemployed and underemployed resources, and economic growth and development.
5. Then click on "Economics Lab." Complete the lab by clicking and dragging the appropriate symbols and numbers to their proper locations on the two tables and the graph.
6. Print your completed lab.

Identifying Key Terms

Use the correct terms to fill in the blanks in the paragraph below:

scarcity (p. 9)
wants (p. 9)
factors of production (p. 11)
goods and services (p. 11)
technology (p. 11)
trade-off (p. 13)

opportunity cost (p. 14)
production possibilities (p. 15)
economic models (p. 18)
hypotheses (p. 19)
values (p. 20)
generalization (p. 21)

Human (1) are unlimited. Consequently, the problem of (2) faces even the richest person on earth, particularly because that person has a limited amount of time on earth. When (3) are used together to produce (4) , human wants can be satisfied. The use of (5) can help us increase the amount of production we get from the resources in our economy. No matter how many resources we have, though, we always face a (6) . The production of one good always involves giving up the production of some other good or goods. This is called a(n) (7) . The graphic representation of this trade-off is called a (8) curve. Economists use (9) to represent how the economy works. They set up a (10) that they test with real-world information. If their tests work well, they come up with a (11) , but economists never can tell us about (12) .

Write a short paragraph about the factors of production in the United States using the following terms:

land (p. 10)
labor (p. 10)
capital (p. 10)
entrepreneurship (p. 11)

Recalling Facts and Ideas

Section 1
1. What is the condition that results because wants are unlimited, yet people cannot satisfy every desire?
2. What is the difference between scarcity and shortages?
3. Your friend says, "I need some new clothes." Under what conditions would this be expressing a need? A want?
4. List the four factors of production.

Section 2
5. What does making a trade-off require you to do?
6. What do economists call the next best alternative that had to be given up for the one chosen?
7. In economics, what is cost?
8. What do economists call a graph showing the combination of goods and services that can be produced from a fixed amount of resources in a given time period?

Section 3
9. For what purposes do economists use real-world data in building models?
10. An economic theory is another name for what?
11. When will an economist consider an economic model useful?

Critical Thinking

Section 1
Identifying Central Issues Tell why entrepreneurship is considered a factor of production.

Section 2

Synthesizing Information Look again at the Production Possibilities Curve in **Figure 1.6** (page 15). What is the balance between military and civilian production that is represented by point C on the graph?

Section 3

Analyzing Information What is the reason that economists will not tell you whether a possible solution to a problem will be good or bad?

Applying Economic Concepts

Trade-Offs and Opportunity Costs Because your time is scarce, you are constantly facing trade-offs. Make a list of the trade-offs you have made in choosing how you used your time during a one-week period. What activities did you choose to do? What were the opportunity costs involved in your choices?

Chapter Projects

1. **Individual Project** Watch the TV news and read newspapers for one week. Make a list of proposed actions on the part of federal, state, or local governments that may involve opportunity costs.
2. **Cooperative Learning Project** Working in groups of four, choose a consumer product such as a VCR, pencil, or automobile. Try to determine the elements of each of the four factors of production that went into making that consumer product. Consider, for example, that in making a VCR, there has to be land on which to put a factory. Consider also that in making a VCR, somebody has to take the risk of putting together the other three factors of production to form a company that will produce the VCR, and so on.

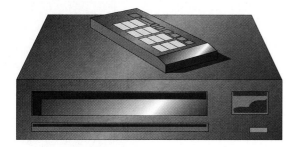

Reviewing Skills

Reading Tables and Graphs

1. The following graph shows the number of men and women in the U.S. labor force from 1980 to 2005. Approximately how many men were in the labor force in 1990? How many women? What is the estimated total number of people in the labor force in 2000?

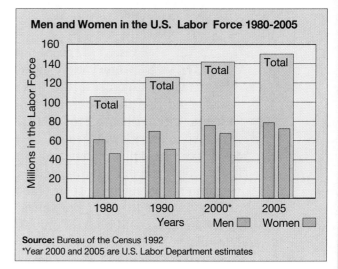

Men and Women in the U.S. Labor Force 1980-2005

Millions in the Labor Force

Source: Bureau of the Census 1992
*Year 2000 and 2005 are U.S. Labor Department estimates

2. Make a bar graph of the following information.

   Age of School Teachers in a Recent Year

Under 30 years old	66,000
30 to 39 years old	104,000
40 to 49 years old	83,000
over 50 years old	49,000

Technology Activity
Using a Word Processor

Refer to the activities you listed in Your Economics Journal on page 7. Then use a word processor to write one or more paragraphs describing how you spent your time during that week. Be sure to consider the following question when you write: Why did you choose to spend more time on certain activities than on others?

ISSUE: Should the Government Require Domestic National Service?

During times of war, many Americans have been required to join the military. Until 1973, males over the age of 18 could be drafted into the military for a two-year period, even in peacetime. Never, however, has this nation required its young people to perform any other type of public service. Nonetheless, the idea of national service has been around for at least 100 years.

PRO One proposal by the Democratic Leadership Council in the late 1980s suggested that the government should form a "citizens' corps" of up to a million "volunteers" who would be paid $100 per week plus room and board. They would then be rewarded with government vouchers worth about $10,000 for each year of service. These vouchers could be used only for education or for buying a home.

Sociologist Charles C. Moskos claims that we need more national service programs because of the nation's unmet needs. Moskos contends that 3.5 million tasks that should be done are presently left undone in our society. These include many environmental and health-related tasks.

Nicola Clark, an editorial writer for the *Wall Street Journal*, believes strongly in the use of a national service corps. She argues that many countries use such a method:

The Danes, for example, dispatch their national servants as civilian public works laborers and foresters. French and Portuguese [national servants] are funneled to various humanitarian organizations or are sent to do development work in their former colonies. And in 1992 . . . doctors in Switzerland actually proposed supplementing the newly introduced Swiss national service with a corps devoted to providing low-cost ambulatory care for the elderly.

[President] Clinton has inundated Americans with proposals for expanded government programs in public works, environmental conservation, child care, health care, community policing—many of which are the kinds of things that are done by extremely low-paid conscripted national servants in other advanced industrialized countries. Why? Because it's the only way these governments can afford to make good on the generous welfare promises they have made to voters without burying their nations in debt. . . .

Counterpoint

CON Opponents of domestic national service stress that except in times of war, no one should be required to participate in any work that that person does not wish to do. They also contend that there is no way to define or quantify a nation's "unmet" needs because they are in fact infinite— there is no limit.

Opponents of domestic national service also use the opportunity cost concept. If a skilled individual holds a job for which he or she has no particular expertise, the opportunity cost is the lost production for the nation. We would be operating inside the production possibilities curve in Figure 1.6 (page 15) and would, therefore, be using resources inefficiently. Critics contend that requiring people to work in jobs that pay less than the market wage rate they could obtain elsewhere involves tremendous opportunity costs.

Another issue is the impact on private charities that would not receive funds. Bruce Chapman, president of Discovery Institution (a public policy center in Seattle, Washington), says:

Congressional hearings on President Clinton's national service plan and the public relations campaign advancing it almost always bring forward as spokesmen young, ingenuous participants in private charities. . . . But these admirable youngsters are not the organizers of the scheme, and they are not likely to understand its long-term implications for the voluntary sector as a whole. Nei-ther, apparently, does much of the disorganized opposition.

One sees this especially in respect to religious organizations, now the source of roughly half of all charitable activities. Because of understandable concerns over separation of church and state, national service will not support any programs that provide "religious instruction, conduct worship services or proselytize." But, effectively, that means that a church or synagogue running a youth leadership program or day-care center will be at a disadvantage against comparable national service programs.

Exploring the Issue

Reviewing Facts

1. What types of jobs would be done by people in a domestic national service program?
2. Explain the opportunity cost argument against having a domestic national service.

Critical Thinking

3. Who would most benefit from a mandatory domestic national service program? Who would lose the most?

Who produced these jeans?

How were they produced?

How did they know how many to make?

Does the producer or the government guarantee the quality of these jeans?

What factors determined the price of these jeans?

How much do these jeans cost?

Who will buy this product?

Your Economics Journal

Keep track of the consumer goods and services you purchase in a week. List these items and their prices in your journal. Next to each item explain why you made the purchase.

SECTION 1 Economic Systems

Economic Systems Determine Use of Resources

As a young adult, you probably have set some goals for your life, even if they are short-term. They might be no more distant than finishing this year in school or getting a part-time job. You may have long-term goals such as going to vocational school or to college, learning a trade or profession, or opening a business.

If you were to make a list of your personal goals and compare it with a list a person of your age made in another part of the world, the lists might be very different. One of the reasons the lists might be very different is that some nations have a different **economic system,** or way in which they use their resources to satisfy their people's needs and wants.

Four Basic Questions

Every nation's economic system is faced with answering the same four basic questions: What goods and services and how much of each should be produced? Who should produce them? How should they be produced? Who should share in their use? Figure 2.1 examines these questions.

Businesses must determine the most efficient mix of the factors of production. Prices affect decisions about what and how much to produce. The type of economic system determines who should produce what.

Figure 2.1 The Four Basic Economic Questions

The way each economic system answers these questions affects how every person within that system uses goods and services.

A How Should Goods and Services Be Produced? ▶

For each good and service produced, there is always a trade-off possible among the available factors of production. For example, a farmer could use 10 laborers with horse-drawn plows to plow a field or 1 tractor and driver. Owners and/or managers of businesses must decide what combination of available resources will get the job done for the least cost.

B What and How Much Should Be Produced?

◀ We live in a world of scarcity and trade-offs. If more of one item is produced, then less of something else will be produced. For example, an automobile manufacturer must decide how to use its limited supply of labor, steel, rubber, and so on. Should it produce pickup trucks or full-sized automobiles? How much of each?

C Who Should Produce What?

Within each economic system, different people do different jobs. Who decides which people will produce which goods and services? This question relates directly to choice of career—auto mechanic, teacher, musician, and so forth. ▼

D Who Should Share in What is Produced?

Money payment for work, the amount of health care, education, food, and so on, that each person receives are all part of the **distribution of income.** This last question relates to how goods and services are distributed among all members of ◀ an economic system.

Types of Economic Systems

Each society answers the four basic questions according to its view of how best to satisfy the needs and wants of its people. The values and goals that a society sets for itself determine the kind of economic system it will have. Economists have identified four types of economic systems: traditional; command, or controlled; market, or capitalist; and mixed. Remember as you read this section that the economic systems described are pure, or ideal, types. They are economic models, not examples of the real world.

Traditional System A pure **traditional economic system** answers the four basic questions according to tradition. **Figure 2.2** illustrates one such system in which tradition dictates the role each individual plays. In such a system, things are done "the way they have always been done." Economic decisions are based on customs, beliefs—often religious—and ways of doing things that have been handed down from generation to generation. Traditional economic systems exist today in very limited parts of Asia, the Middle East, Africa, and Latin America.

Figure 2.2 Traditional Economy

Nomadic herders retain many elements of a traditional economy although this is changing rapidly. In general, when the food for their herds in an area is used up, the group moves on in search of new food supplies. ▶

Command, or Controlled, System

The traditional economic system is in some ways similar to a pure command economic system. In a pure **command economic system,** the individual has little, if any, influence over how the basic economic questions are answered. See **Figure 2.3.** Government controls the factors of production and, therefore, makes all decisions about their use. This is why this form of economic system is also called a controlled economy.

The government may be one person, a small group of leaders, or a group of central planners in a government agency. These people choose how resources are to be used at each stage in production and decide the distribution of goods and services. They even decide who will do what. The government, through a series of regulations about the kinds and amount of education available to different groups, guides people into certain jobs.

Market, or Capitalist, System

The opposite of a pure command economic system is a pure **market economic system**—or capitalism. In a pure market economic system, government does not intervene. Individuals own the factors of production, and they decide for themselves the answers to the four basic economic questions.

Economic decisions are made through the free interaction of individuals looking out for their own best interests in the market. **Market** in this sense is not a place. Rather, it is the freely chosen activity between buyers and sellers of goods and services.

Buyers and sellers freely choose to do business with those who best satisfy their needs and wants. The exchange of goods and services may take place in a worldwide market for a good such as crude oil. It may also take place in a neighborhood market for the services of someone to mow lawns, deliver papers, or shovel the snow.

In a pure market economic system, producers of goods and services decide how to use their resources based solely on signals from the market. Government planning has no part in the decisions. Whether people buy a certain good or service or not indicates to producers the various ways to use or not use their resources, as shown in **Figure 2.4** (page 34).

People are also free in a pure market economic system to sell their

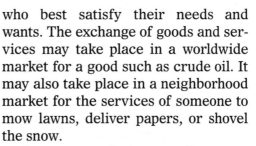

Figure 2.3 ▲ Command Economy
Only a couple of countries in the entire world still have much of a command economy—North Korea and parts of the People's Republic of China are the two main examples because so much economic activity there is government-planned.

labor as they wish. They may take, refuse, or change jobs whenever they choose. This assumes, of course, that there is a demand for their labor. Figure 2.5 illustrates the flow of economic activity through the market in the capitalist system.

Mixed Economic System With the exception of the traditional economic system, it is doubtful whether these pure or ideal systems ever existed. They are useful models for analyzing existing systems, however. Today, almost all economic systems are what economists call mixed

economies. A **mixed economy** contains characteristics of a command economy and a pure market economy. Figure 2.6 shows the two most prominent examples of mixed economies— one leans heavily toward the market model, the other toward the command model.

Lesson 2 of Interactive Economics! to learn more about "Circular Flows."

Figure 2.4 Demand Affects Production

Suppose that in a specific market economy more people begin buying the compact discs (CDs) of a particular rap group. This increase in demand signals the record company to invest more resources—time, money, effort—into producing CDs by that group. If, however, few people are buying CDs by another rap group, the CD company will not sign that group again. Buyers have signaled that they do not want more CDs by that group. ▼

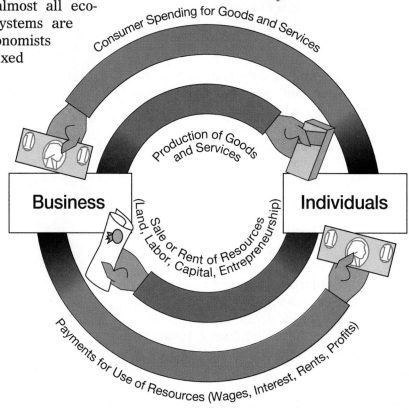

Consumer Spending for Goods and Services

Production of Goods and Services

Business

Individuals

Sale or Rent of Resources (Land, Labor, Capital, Entrepreneurship)

Payments for Use of Resources (Wages, Interest, Rents, Profits)

Figure 2.5 ▲ Circular Flow of Economic Activity in a Market Economy

The inside arrows on the graph show individuals selling the factors of production to businesses, who use them to produce goods and services. The flow of money income from businesses to individuals in the form of rent, wages, interest, and profits and its return to business as consumer spending, is illustrated on the outside of the graph.

Figure 2.6
Two Mixed Economies

In mixed economies, the mix will vary so that any one economic system leans more toward one pure type than another.

A The United States tends much more toward the market system than toward the command system. Not all decisions, however, are made by individuals reacting to the market. Federal, state, and local governments make laws regulating some areas of business. Among these, for instance, are the rates that certain cable companies may charge.

▶

B Although the People's Republic of China still tends much more toward the command than toward the pure market system, the economy is changing. Many factories in China are owned by the government. Government officials tell the managers of those factories what to produce and how much. They also tell the factory managers at what price they should sell their output. There is a growing unrestricted market sector within that country, however. In some "special economic zones," citizens in the People's Republic of China make economic decisions without interference by the government.

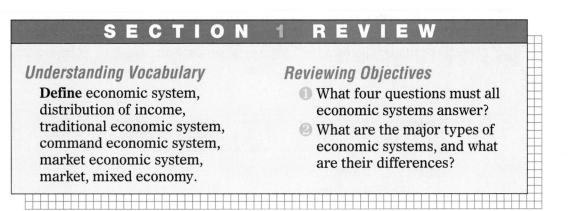

SECTION 1 REVIEW

Understanding Vocabulary
Define economic system, distribution of income, traditional economic system, command economic system, market economic system, market, mixed economy.

Reviewing Objectives
1. What four questions must all economic systems answer?
2. What are the major types of economic systems, and what are their differences?

Understanding Percentages and Discounts

Economists use statistics to describe different population characteristics—occupations, income, and so on. Percentages are a useful form of statistics. Do you know how to use them?

Percentages

Percent means "parts per hundred." Sales taxes are figured in percents. Suppose a skirt costs $24 and the sales tax is 6 percent. As Figure A shows, the tax adds $.06 for every dollar of the price.

Figuring Percentages

Suppose a pair of shoes is 30 percent off the regular price. If the regular price was $57, what will the new price be? You can find the price by multiplying percent off by the original price and subtracting the discount. Or, as Figure B shows, you can multiply the original price by the percent you will pay (70 percent).

If the $57 shoes are on sale for $39.90, you can find the percent you are paying by dividing the amount you pay by the original price. See Figure C.

Percent and Actual Number

Is it a better discount if the store says you can buy the first pair for $57 and get the second pair for half price? You would pay 100 percent for the first pair of shoes and 50 percent (half) of the second. Total these percentages and divide by the number of pairs of shoes. You would pay 75 percent. Figure D shows that the discount is only 25 percent.

Figure A
6% = .06
$24.00
X .06
$ 1.44 sales tax

Figure B
$57.00 $57.00
 X .30   −17.10
$17.10 $39.90

or

$57.00
 X .70
$39.90

Figure C
$39.90 ÷ $57 = .70 X 100 =70%

Figure D
100% + 50% = 150%
150% ÷ 2 = 75%
100% − 75% = 25%

Practicing the Skill

❶ A store advertises jeans at 33 percent off the original price of $37. What is the new price?

2 Characteristics of the American Economy

S E C T I O N 2 F O C U S

Terms to Know invisible hand, capitalism, free enterprise system, private property, profit, profit incentive, competition

Objectives *After reading this section, you should be able to:*

① Describe the **role of government** in the free enterprise system.

② Explain the importance of **freedom of enterprise** in the American economy.

③ Define **freedom of choice** as it applies to the American free enterprise system.

④ List the advantages of **private property**.

⑤ Identify the role of the **profit incentive**.

⑥ Evaluate **competition** in the American free enterprise system.

Free Enterprise with Some Regulations

A pure market economic system has six major characteristics: (1) little or no government control, (2) freedom of enterprise, (3) freedom of choice, (4) private property, (5) profit incentive, and (6) competition. These characteristics are interrelated, and to varying degrees all are present in the American economy.

In his book, *The Wealth of Nations*, Adam Smith in 1776 described a system in which government has little to do with a nation's economic activity. He said that individuals left on their own would work for their own self-interests. In doing this, they would be guided as if by an **invisible hand** of competition to achieve the maximum good for society.

The Role of Government

Smith's idea of the ideal economic system is called capitalism, another name for the market system. Economists argue whether capitalism in its pure form, as Smith described it, has ever existed. **Capitalism** as practiced in the United States today would be best defined as an economic system in which private individuals own the factors of production and decide how to use them within the limits of the law.

Smith's ideas influenced the Founders of the United States, who limited the role of government mainly to national defense and keeping peace. Also, the Constitution as originally written and interpreted, limits the national government's control over economic activities.

Since the 1880s, the role of government—federal, state, and local—has increased significantly in the United States. This is especially true in the areas of regulating business and providing public services, as shown in Figure 2.7.

Freedom of Enterprise

The American economy is also called the **free enterprise system.** This term emphasizes that individuals are free to own and control the factors of production. For example, if you decide to go into business for yourself, your abilities and resources will help you decide the good or service to produce, the quantity, and the methods of production. Of course, you may lose your money. You, or any entrepreneur, have no guarantee of success. In addition, as Figure 2.8 shows, certain legal limits restrict freedom of enterprise.

Freedom of Choice

Freedom of choice is the other side of freedom of enterprise. Freedom of choice means that buyers make the decisions about what should be produced. The success or failure of a good or service in the marketplace depends on individuals freely choosing what they want. The earlier example of people buying or not buying a particular group's CDs and the effects on the CD company illustrates this idea. The music company, in reality, may choose to continue making CDs with the group anyway, even though it knows it will not make much profit.

Although buyers are free to exercise their choice, the marketplace has become increasingly complex. As a result, the government has intervened in various areas of the economy to protect buyers. Laws set safety standards for such things as toys, appliances, and automobiles. In industries in which only a few companies provide services, government regulates the price they may charge. This has happened with public utilities.

Private Property

Private property is simply what is owned by individuals or groups rather than by the federal, state, or local government. The Constitution guarantees an owner's rights to private property and its use. You as an individual are free to buy whatever you can afford whether it is land, a business, a home, an automobile, and so on. You can also control how, when, and by whom your property is used. If you own a business, you can keep any profit you make.

Figure 2.7 U.S. Government Regulation
Today the work of federal agencies includes regulating the quality of various foods and drugs, watching over the nation's money and banking system, inspecting workplaces for hazardous conditions, and guarding against damage to the environment. The federal government also uses tax money to provide social programs such as Medicare. State and local governments have also expanded their role in recent years in such areas as education, job training, recreation, support for the arts, and care for the elderly. ▶

Profit is the money left after all the costs of production have been paid. These costs include wages, rent, interest, and taxes.

Within the United States, government at all levels owns some property. Parks, fire-fighting and police equipment, military bases, municipal buildings, and post offices are some examples of government-owned property. Under no circumstances, though, can any level of government in the United States expand its economic role by simply taking private property. This provision is one of the underlying principles of the Bill of Rights. Part of the Fifth Amendment reads:

> *Nor shall private property be taken for public use, without just compensation.*

That clause simply means that if the federal, state, or local government believes it has to use private property, it must pay the private owners. Also, the government cannot make citizens use their private property to house soldiers.

Profit Incentive

Whenever a person invests time, know-how, money, and other capital resources in a business, that investment is made with the idea of making a profit. The desire to make a profit is called the **profit incentive** (in-SENT-iv), and it is mainly this hope that moves people to produce things that others want to buy. After all, if no one buys what a seller produces, there will be no profit, only losses. See Figure 2.9.

The risk of failing is part of the free enterprise system. Some industries, however, are so large that their failure would seriously damage the economy and throw thousands of people out of work. In the past several decades, the federal government has passed laws providing special private loan guarantees to big corporations such as Lockheed and Chrysler, and even to the city of New York. The federal government has also aided farmers by providing them with loans.

Competition

Competition is the rivalry among producers or sellers of similar goods to win more business by offering the lowest prices or better quality.

Number of Competitors In many industries, effective competition requires a large number of independent buyers and sellers. This large number of competitors means that no one company can noticeably affect the price of a particular product.

Figure 2.9 ▲
Making a Profit
If you went into business decorating and selling T-shirts, you would expect to make enough money to cover your expenses and make some profit. What would some of this seller's expenses be?

Figure 2.8 ▲
Limits on Free Enterprise
In most states, teenagers must be 16 before they can work, and then laws set limits on how many hours they can work.

Figure 2.10 Competition and Price

Suppose that only one business makes a particular product such as a personal computer. It could charge as much as people who really want a personal computer are willing to pay. They have no alternative seller to turn to. Suppose a second company enters the market with a similar computer at a lower price. Then competition for buyers between the two businesses would force the price down. ▼

If one company attempts to raise its prices, potential customers can simply go to one of the many other sellers. In the ideal world, this is how competition would work. In practice, however, the federal government over the past 100 years has regulated some business practices in an attempt to make sure that competition exists. The opportunity to make a profit encourages competition, as **Figure 2.10** shows.

Businesses have to keep prices low enough to attract buyers yet high enough to make a profit. This forces businesses to keep the costs of production as low as possible. Competitors who succeed do so because they are able to produce those goods that people want most at a price that makes people want to buy.

Easy Entry and Exit Competition also requires that companies can enter or exit any industry they choose. Those who feel that they could make more profit in another industry are free to get out of the industry they are in. Some companies expand into new industries while staying in their old one. A company currently producing and selling VCRs may determine that people prefer the added convenience and higher quality of videodiscs. The company may decide to move out of its old business and begin making videodisc players.

Economists say that such an economy has weak barriers to entry and exit from industries. For the most part, the United States has such weak barriers. Some industries, however, have tougher barriers to entry. For example, a person cannot become a doctor until he or she has passed through an approved medical school and received a license from a state government to practice medicine in that state. Government approval is needed to start a public utility or set up a television or radio station.

LOWEST PRICE
$1099!

HURRY!
LIMITED
STOCK

NOW
$629

NEW
LOWER
PRICE

SECTION 2 REVIEW

Understanding Vocabulary

Define invisible hand, capitalism, free enterprise system, private property, profit, profit incentive, competition.

Reviewing Objectives

1. What role does government play in the free enterprise system?
2. Why is freedom of enterprise one of the cornerstones of the American economy?
3. How does freedom of choice apply to the American free enterprise system?
4. What are the advantages of private property?
5. How does the profit incentive encourage business in the American economy?
6. Why is competition important in the American free enterprise system?

Personal Perspective

Adam Smith on Free Enterprise

Profile

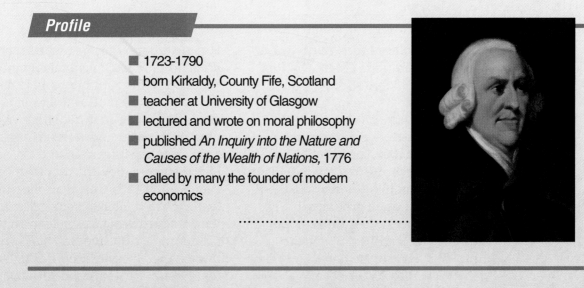

- 1723-1790
- born Kirkaldy, County Fife, Scotland
- teacher at University of Glasgow
- lectured and wrote on moral philosophy
- published *An Inquiry into the Nature and Causes of the Wealth of Nations,* 1776
- called by many the founder of modern economics

In Adam Smith's *An Inquiry into the Nature and Causes of the Wealth of Nations,* he explains why government should not regulate business. He believed that individuals, seeking profit, direct their resources more efficiently than governments.

... No regulation of commerce can increase the quantity of industry in any society beyond what its capital [resources] can maintain. It can only divert a part of it into a direction into which it might not otherwise have gone. ... It is only for the sake of profit that any man employs a capital in support of industry; and he will always, therefore, endeavor to employ it in the support of that industry of which the produce is likely to be of the greatest value.

Smith then describes how the sum of all individual decisions will benefit society as a whole.

... As every individual, therefore, endeavors ... to employ his capital in the support of domestic industry, and so to direct that industry that its produce may be of the greatest value, every individual necessarily labours to render [direct] that annual revenue of the society as great as he can. He ... neither intends to promote the public interest, nor knows how much he is promoting it. By preferring the support of domestic to that of foreign industry, he intends only his own security; ... he intends only his own gain. ...

Smith concludes that government officials who would try to regulate business are overstepping their authority or lack good sense.

The statesman, who would attempt to direct private people in what manner they ought to employ their capitals, would ... assume an authority which could safely be trusted, not only to no single person, but to no council or senate whatever, and which would nowhere be so dangerous as in the hands of a man who had folly and presumption [reckless disregard] enough to fancy himself fit to exercise it.

Checking for Understanding

1. Why do individuals invest their capital?
2. How will the economic choices of the individual benefit society as a whole?
3. According to Smith, which government officials are presumptuous?

Blue Bell Creameries, Inc.

The Main Ingredient In 1907 the Brenham Creamery Company of Texas found a good use for the excess cream in the milk from area farms. They started making butter. Four years later the creamery found another, more delightful use for the cream. They made their first ice cream in a wooden tub filled with ice. Maximum production was two gallons per day. By 1919 Brenham Creamery was still small and struggling. E. F. Kruse, the new plant manager, knew that it was close to going out of business. He kept the company from going under by not cashing his paychecks until the creamery became profitable several months later.

Rising to the Top In 1930 the Brenham Creamery Company changed its name to Blue Bell Creameries, after a Texas wildflower. Like cream, Blue Bell began to rise to the top of the frozen dessert business. One factor that helped the company was the invention of home freezers.

Having freezers in the home created demand for a packaged take-home product. In the summer of 1941, E. F. Kruse's sons Ed and Howard, at ages 13 and 11, came to work, hand-wrapping ice cream sandwiches. Today they are respectively chairman of the board and chief executive officer of Blue Bell. One key move in Blue Bell's history was its decision to replace butter with ice cream as the featured product in 1958. Blue Bell began to branch out, opening facilities in Houston, Austin, Beaumont, and Dallas in the next 20 years.

Advertising and Growth The rapid growth in Texas, plus the potential for distribution in adjacent states, moved Blue Bell to start its own advertising agency. Blue Bell Advertising Associates was launched in 1987. A new corporate headquarters and visitor center in Brenham opened the following year.

42

Diversifying Like other businesses, Blue Bell learned to pay attention to its customers' wants. As a result, the company added many new products. In 1989 Diet Blue Bell, the nation's first frozen dairy dessert made with NutraSweet and marketed in a half-gallon container, was introduced. Blue Bell Nonfat Frozen Yogurt and Blue Bell Diet, a low-fat, no-sugar frozen dietary dessert, followed in 1991. In addition, the dairy now offers ice cream and yogurt in pint and half-gallon sizes and a full line of snacks.

 Crossing the State Line Distribution of Blue Bell products to Louisiana, Kansas, and Mexico began in the 1990s. Strict quality control measures and fresh ingredients have enhanced the company's reputation. *TIME, Sports Illustrated,* and *Forbes* have each touted Blue Bell's products. Perhaps that's because one key ingredient has not changed over the years—care.

Blue Bell Market Share, Texas 1997
Percent Dollars:

	Blue Bell	Private Labels	Dreyers	All Others
	62%	19%	5%	11%

Source: A.C. Nielsen Scantrack
52 weeks ending 3/15/97: Average of Dallas, Houston, San Antonio

 Serving the Community Today Blue Bell Creameries, Inc., employs more than 700 Brenham-area workers. In addition, the company has about 1,000 workers distributing its ice cream in its distribution areas. In a recent year more than 100,000 people toured the facilities in Brenham.

Free Enterprise in Action

1 What was Brenham Creamery's first product?

2 What invention in the 1930s allowed the creamery to expand its take-home business?

3 Why do you think Blue Bell diversified its product line?

43

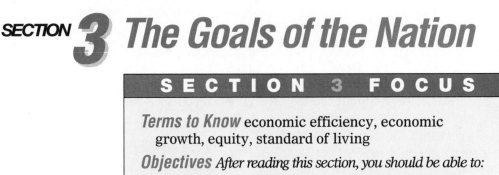

SECTION 3 The Goals of the Nation

SECTION 3 FOCUS

Terms to Know economic efficiency, economic growth, equity, standard of living

Objectives *After reading this section, you should be able to:*
1. Describe the major **aims of a market economy.**
2. List ways in which people can **balance economic rights with economic responsibilities.**

Policies and Goals in a Free Market Economy

Nations—and the United States is no exception—have national values and set goals for themselves based on these values. These goals are evident in government policies and in the actions of people like yourself and those around you. The values and goals of a nation determine which of the several kinds of economic systems that nation will have.

Aims of a Market Economy

The United States tends toward a market, or capitalist, system. Therefore, the major characteristics of a market economy should be evident in its goals. Among the national goals of Americans are efficiency, growth, security, equity, stability, and individual freedom. **Figure 2.11** describes these goals in economic terms because this is an economics text. These goals however, have ethical, social, and religious elements as well.

Turning National Goals into Reality
A plan of action must be developed in order to accomplish the nation's goals. Such a plan often involves economic policy-making by elected or appointed officials who must also deal with the reality of scarcity. Because all resources are scarce, when one person gets something, that something will not be available for anyone else.

Consider the goal of economic (income) security. Many individuals can

afford to buy private insurance policies and retirement plans. The government, however, has public policies such as Social Security, Medicare, and Medicaid that offer income security and health care.

Figure 2.11 Our National Goals

There are many national goals. Differences on how these goals should be accomplished are reasons for the existence of political parties.

A Economic Efficiency ▶
Economic efficiency means using resources wisely so that people will be as well off as possible given our available resources.

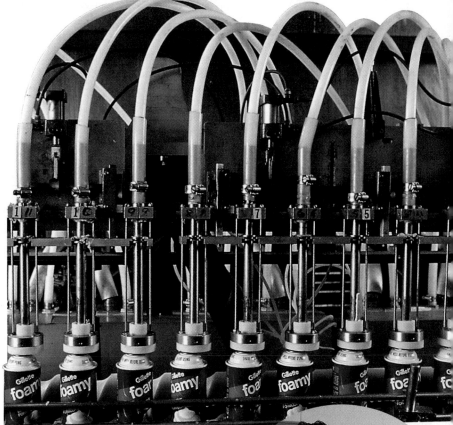

B Economic Growth ▲
Economic growth means an expansion of the economy to produce more goods, jobs, and wealth. Some disagreement exists about whether or not economic growth too often causes problems such as environmental pollution.

C Security and Equity ▶
Security means protecting people against poverty and supplying them with the means to provide for a medical emergency through an increasing number of government social programs directed, among others, to the elderly. The related goal of **equity** means that which is fair and just.

D Individual Freedom
The goal of individual freedom allows each member of society to enjoy the freedoms of enterprise, choice, and private property and to make his or her own decisions in the marketplace. ◀

E Stability
The goal of stability seeks to reduce extreme ups and downs in the standard of living. **Standard of living** is the material well-being of an individual, group, or nation measured by the average value of goods and services used by the average citizen during a given period of time, usually a year.

Figure 2.12
Advantages of Free Enterprise
The American economic system offers many benefits.

A A High Level of Economic and Personal Freedom
Proponents of the free enterprise system point out that of all nationalities, Americans enjoy perhaps the highest degree of freedom in the world to start their own businesses and to pursue their own economic choices. This freedom extends to all aspects of life. With this extreme amount of economic and personal freedom, though, come certain costs. In particular, in our free enterprise system individuals must normally accept the consequences of their decisions.

B A High Standard of Living
Supporters of the American economy explain that the nation has more individuals enjoying a high standard of living than almost anywhere else in the world. They believe that the ability of Americans to enjoy such high standards of living is directly tied to the ability of individuals to work where they want, how they want, and with whom, and to invest in whichever businesses they think will make profits.

C Diverse Lifestyles ▶
The great variety of economic opportunities in the United States allows for a wide range of lifestyles. People may choose to work nights, part-time, at two jobs in different parts of the country for different seasons of the year, and so on. In contrast, command economies result in much less diversity in styles of living.

When the government provides for plans such as Medicare, some people must agree to give up some of their income in order to transfer it to people in need. These people may be in need because they are too poor, too disabled, or too ill to care for themselves, or because they have not saved enough for emergencies or retirement.

In a world of scarcity, achieving national goals requires sacrifices by certain members of society. Any program to provide more economic security, more justice, or more equitable treatment of people involves a trade-off. Once you understand this, you will be well on your way to understanding not only the nation's economic system but also its political system. It is this economic and political system that makes many of the decisions about how resources are used in the nation. Such an understanding will help you realize that not all political desires can be turned into economic reality.

Benefits of the Free Enterprise System Those who support the American free enterprise system emphasize the many benefits that it provides for its citizens. Figure 2.12 illustrates some of these benefits.

Balancing Economic Rights and Responsibilities

The American free enterprise system bestows numerous economic rights and protections on individuals like you, your teachers, your relatives, and your friends. You have the right to enter into just about any profession or business you want. You have the right to work very little or to become a "workaholic." You have the right to buy those products and brands that you like and to reject all others. In short, you have the right to do just about anything that is legal.

A well-functioning free enterprise system will not continue if individuals do not take on certain economic responsibilities. The first, of course, is to be able to support yourself. Additionally, just because education may be offered to you free of charge, it is not free to society. An opportunity cost goes along with it. Consequently, you have a responsibility to use that education in a reasonable manner that helps you become a productive member of the free enterprise system.

Finally, because government has become such an important part of our economy, individuals in our system have the responsibility of electing responsible government officials. This responsibility requires both the knowledge of possible government policies and the ability to analyze the consequences of different government policies.

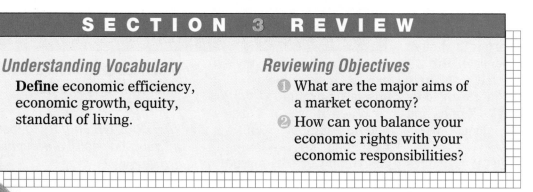

SECTION 3 REVIEW

Understanding Vocabulary
Define economic efficiency, economic growth, equity, standard of living.

Reviewing Objectives
1. What are the major aims of a market economy?
2. How can you balance your economic rights with your economic responsibilities?

Readings in Economics

TIME   JANUARY 25, 1993

PRINCE OF MIDAIR
by Richard Woodbury

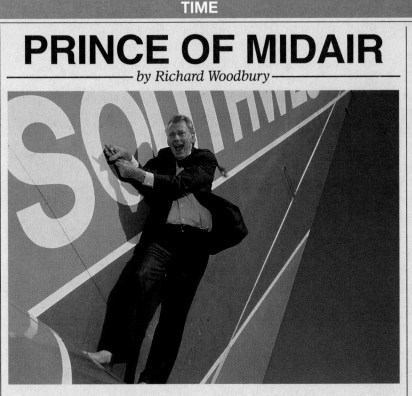

Imagine a major airline that seems to go out of its way to put its passengers in a blind rage: it routinely denies them assigned seats, refuses to transfer their baggage or arrange connections, and crams them three abreast into planes with only crackers and cookies to nibble. It sells no tickets through the industry's computerized reservations system and avoids flying to many large-city airports. As though to compensate for all this, its chief executive dresses in clown suits and Elvis costumes and paints his planes to resemble whales.

Yet Southwest Airlines has used just such perverse tactics to accomplish what no other big carrier has during the current aviation

downturn, the industry's worst: make consistent operating profits. . . .

When it was a Texas puddle jumper, Southwest and its fun-loving chairman were dismissed as an oddity. But now that the Dallas-based airline has made money for 20 straight years and spread to 34 cities in 15 states, the industry is paying it sober respect. . . .

None of this would have happened without [Chief Executive Officer Herb] Kelleher, 61, a folksy ex-San Antonio, Texas, lawyer who runs the company like a carnival sideshow. He schmoozes with employees, who know him as "Uncle Herb"; stages weekly parties at corporate headquarters; and encourages such zany antics by his flight attendants as organizing trivia contests, delivering instructions in rap and awarding prizes for the passengers with the largest holes in their socks. The wackiness has a calculated purpose—to generate a gung-ho spirit that will boost productivity, the key to Southwest's goal of carefully scripted growth.

• THINK ABOUT IT •

1. How does Southwest's service differ from that of other airlines?

2. Why does Kelleher try to instill a "gung-ho" spirit among his employees?

ECONOMICS IN ACTION

Economic Systems and the American Economy

Setting up the Video

With your classmates, view "Economic Systems and the American Economy" on the videodisc *Economics in Action*. The video describes the United States's economic system as a free enterprise economy, one in which the market makes all decisions. A news segment then considers the Cuban economy, which has a command system, completely controlled by the government.

**Chapter 3
Disc 1, Side 1**

View the video by scanning the bar code or by entering the chapter number on your keypad and pressing Search. *(Also available in VHS format.)*

Hands-On Activity

Recognize the amount of government interference in your own economic activities. List 10 items you or your family buy in a typical week. Place a checkmark next to the purchases you think included some level of government involvement. Then reconsider your checkmarks by asking the following questions: Was there a tax? Did the product require any kind of government inspection? Did government regulations affect the price in some way?

As a class, pick one item—pizza, for example—and trace the involvement of government in all stages of the product's development.

INTERACTIVE ECONOMICS!

Circular Flows

Introduction

Lesson 2 of *Interactive Economics!* describes how the basic parts of the economy work together. In the market economy of the United States, people in one part of the country are both affected by and dependent on the actions of other people in different parts of the country.

The circular flow model is a popular tool economists use to show the dynamic workings of a market economy. More than any other tool, it helps to show the economic interdependency of different segments of the economy, and the way in which markets link these components together.

Using the Software

1. Select "Circular Flows" from the Main Menu.
2. Read the introduction to "Circular Flows," then click on "Households and Businesses."
3. After reading the "Tutorial" and clicking on "Overview," go back to the Circular Flows menu and click on "Adding Government to the Circular Flow."
4. Study the information given, then click on "Economics Lab." Complete the lab by clicking and dragging the correct terms to their proper place in the circular flow of economic activity.
5. Print your completed lab.

2 *Review*

Identifying Key Terms

Use terms from the following list to fill in the blanks in the paragraph below.

traditional economic
  system (p. 32)
command economic
  system (p. 33)
mixed economy
  (p. 34)
capitalism (p. 37)
free enterprise
  system (p. 38)
private property
  (p. 38)

profit (p. 39)
competition
  (p. 39)
economic growth
  (p. 45)
equity (p. 45)
standard of living
  (p. 45)

Another term for the market economic system is the (1) , or (2) . Many Americans believe that this system helps to account for the high (3) in the United States. This system is based on concepts such as (4) that allows people to buy and own land, a home, or their own business. A person may keep the (5) earned from selling in (6) with other businesses. Most people, including Americans, actually live in a (7) economic system that contains some characteristics of a (8) . The government promotes both (9) and (10) , or fair and just policies.

Write a short paragraph about the American economy using all of the following terms.

economic system (p. 30)
market (p. 33)
mixed economy (p. 34)
invisible hand (p. 37)
profit incentive (p. 39)
competition (p. 39)

Recalling Facts and Ideas

Section 1
1. "The more of one item that is produced, the less of something else will be produced." What term describes this economic condition?
2. What basic economic question helps determine the career path of individuals?
3. What economic question is being answered if an industry decides to replace some workers with machines?
4. Why do economic systems differ in the way they answer the question "Who should share in what is produced?"
5. How does a traditional economic system answer the question "Who should produce what?"
6. Who answers the basic economic questions in a command system?
7. Who owns the factors of production in a market economic system?
8. Why should the United States economic system be called a mixed system?

Section 2
9. What are six important characteristics of free enterprise?
10. Who wrote *The Wealth of Nations*?
11. What is government's limited role in pure capitalism?
12. Why is private property important in the American economic system?

Section 3
13. What are three benefits of the free enterprise system?
14. What does the United States do to promote economic security for individuals?

Critical Thinking

Section 1

Determining Cause and Effect How might the answers to each of the four basic economic questions affect your personal decisions?

Section 2

Making Comparisons Are recent economic trends in Russia and the United States similar or different? Explain your answer.

Section 3

Identifying Alternatives What are two ways that each of the following services may be provided: health care, mass transit, energy?

Applying Economic Concepts

Economic Systems An economic system within your school determines the answer to the basic question *who should share in what is produced.* Make a list of the goods and services available to students within the school. After each, write whether the distribution of this good or service is determined according to market, command, or traditional economic system principles.

Chapter Projects

1. **Individual Project** Review economic news from national magazines. List the economic decisions of several nations and make a table that classifies them as supporting free markets or command systems.
2. **Cooperative Learning Project** In small groups that will serve as committees, submit proposals for planning a national education system in a command economy. The system should provide answers to such questions as:
   - What level of education should be available without cost to everyone?
   - Should academic achievement or testing be used to qualify students for higher levels of education or specialized fields?

Reviewing Skills

Understanding Percentages and Discounts Study the table below, then apply your skills to fill in the four blank spaces.

original price	percent off	discount	new price
$100.00	30%	$30.00	$70.00
$80.00	15%		
$56.00		$3.92	$52.08
	20%	$12.00	$48.00

Technology Activity
Using a Spreadsheet

Refer to the list of consumer goods and services that you kept track of in Your Economics Journal on page 29. Use your data to create a spreadsheet highlighting your weekly spending habits.

1. In cells B1 through E1, type *Food, Clothing, Entertainment,* and *Other.* In cell F1, type *TOTAL.*
2. In cells A2 through A8, type the days of the week, starting with *Monday* in cell A2. In cell A9, type *TOTAL.*
3. In cells B2 through E2, enter the amount of money you spent in each category on Monday. Repeat this process for the other six days.
4. In cell F2, use the *AutoSum* function (Σ) or a formula such as *=SUM(B2;E2)* to calculate total expenditures on Monday. Click and drag this formula to cells F3 through F8 to find the other weekday sums.
5. Using one of the above summation methods, compute the total *Entertainment* expenditures in cell D9.
6. Insert a new row at the top, put a title in cell B1, and print your results.

Using Economic Models
From the classroom of Michelle Farthing, Alvin High School, Alvin, Texas

In Unit 1 you read about using models, a basic tool of the economist. In this experiment, you will use models to study competition. (You may want to reread the material on pages 18–21 of the text.)

Competition among producers forces businesses to keep prices low enough to attract customers. Some businesses emphasize price when marketing their products. This is called **price competition.** Some businesses choose to emphasize service, product quality, packaging, or factors other than price to distinguish their products. In this lab study, you will try to determine whether certain businesses are using price competition and, if so, how they are using it.

Tools

1. Copies of a local newspaper over a 4-week period
2. Pencils, writing paper, graph paper

Procedures

Step A Depending on the size of your class, choose 5 to 10 products or services from the following list:

1. gasoline
2. hair cuts
3. jeans
4. face soap
5. hamburgers
6. dishwashers
7. motorcycles
8. pizza
9. tennis shoes
10. oranges
11. golf fees
12. motel rooms

Step B Write the names of the brands, stores, distributors, etc., for one product or service that you plan to study in the left column of a table such as the one below.

Example
Gasoline
(87 octane)

Sunoco (Oak St.)				
Ray's Texaco				
Shell (downtown)				
Certified				

Step C Keep a record of the price changes by the supplier of the service or product you are studying over time.

Example

Gasoline (87 octane)	March 5	12	19	26
Sunoco (Oak St.)	$1.09	$1.14	$1.19	$1.13
Ray's Texaco	1.09	1.12	1.15	1.12
Shell (downtown)	1.04	1.10	1.13	1.15
Certified	.99	1.05	1.06	1.04

Step D Make a list of the different kinds of advertising messages used for the competing products or services during this period.

Example

Sunoco	better mileage	more selection	quality
Ray's Texaco	lower price	friendly	contest, prizes

Step E Build a graph similar to the one below that shows the price changes of the products or services you studied.

Example

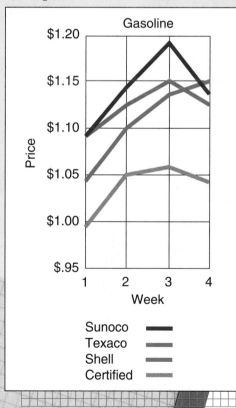

Lab Report

Step F Study the table and graph that you created in Steps D and E and answer the questions below.

1. How frequently did the price of the product or service change?
2. How wide was the price difference among competing brands?
3. What other kinds of competition were evidenced by advertising for this product or service?
4. Is price competition the main kind of competition for this product or service?

Step G Compare the tables and graphs for different products or services that were completed by each member of the class and answer the questions below.

1. What products or services use price competition as their main form of competition? Why?
2. What products use packaging and product quality to distinguish them from their competition? How?

53

U N I T

PRACTICAL ECONOMICS: HOW THEORY WORKS FOR YOU

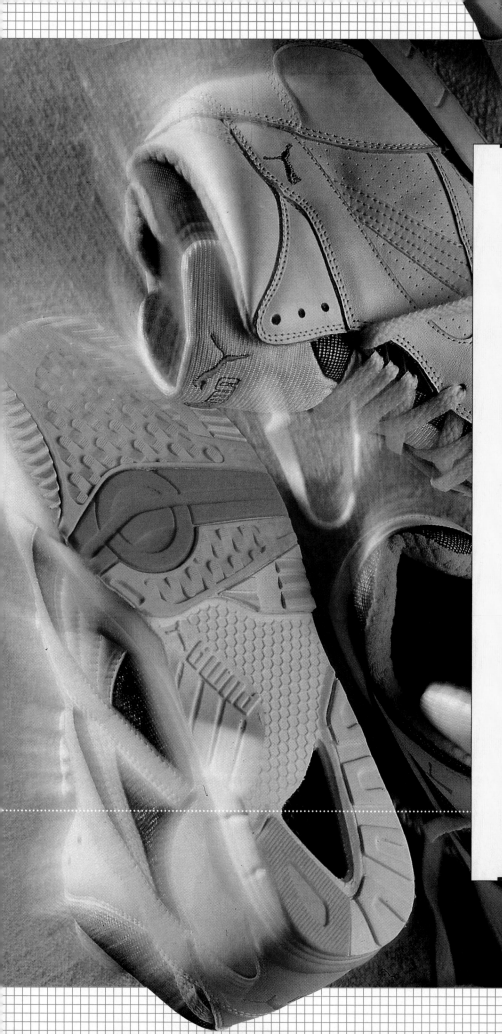

? Did You Know

- The more you compare prices in order to get the "best" deals, the more efficient our economy will be.
- If you are an average American, you will end up owning at least three credit cards (and probably more).
- You will end up spending about 12 percent of your income on food (which is a lower percentage than most other countries in the world).
- You will probably make many of your clothing choices based on your desire for group identification.
- If you someday want to buy the "average" house, it will cost you well over $110,000.
- Americans, both on a per-family and a per-person basis, own more cars than do people anywhere else in the world (with a total of about 175 million in existence).
- Americans save a lower percentage of their income than do people in many other industrial countries.

In this unit, you will see how much of economic theory works for you as an individual consumer, worker, saver, and investor. You will discover how basic economic principles can help you in your daily life.

55

CHAPTER

3 YOUR ROLE AS A CONSUMER

Do you know what is required to make rational decisions when you shop for a computer?

Do you think that when you are shopping for a computer you should visit every store carrying that product in your community?

Do you have alternative sources from which you can buy a computer in addition to stores in your community?

If you and a friend visit the same stores and hear the same sales pitch in each one, will you necessarily decide on the same brand and model computer?

Your Economics Journal

Keep track of the steps used by you, a friend, or one of your parents in buying a small appliance or electronic item. List the number of alternative sources that were considered. Next to each source, write why that store or catalog was or was not chosen.

Consumption, Income, and Decision Making

SECTION 1 FOCUS

Terms to Know consumer, disposable income, discretionary income, warranty, rational choice

Objectives *After reading this section, you should be able to:*

1. Explain the difference between disposable and discretionary income.
2. List three considerations in decision making as a consumer.

Consumers Can Learn to Make Rational Choices

You and everyone around you are consumers and, as such, play important roles in the economic system. A **consumer** is any person or group that buys or uses goods and services to satisfy personal wants. As consumers, people buy a wide variety of things—food, clothing, dental and medical care, automobiles, computers, and so on. To see how typical American consumers spend their money, study the circle graph in Figure 3.1.

Disposable and Discretionary Income

A person's role as a consumer depends on his or her ability to consume. This ability to consume, in turn, depends on the income available and how much of it a person chooses to spend now or save for the future.

Income can be both disposable and discretionary (dis-KRESH-uh-ner-ee). **Disposable income** is the money income a person has left after all taxes have been paid. People spend their disposable income on many kinds of goods and services. First, they buy the necessities: food, clothing, and housing. Once these needs have been met, there may be some income left. This income, which can be spent on extras such as entertainment and luxury items, is called **discretionary income.** See Figure 3.2.

Education, occupation, age, gender, and health can all make differences in a person's earning power and

Figure 3.1 Consumer Spending
The circle graph shows how Americans spend their income. What are the top three categories of consumer spending?

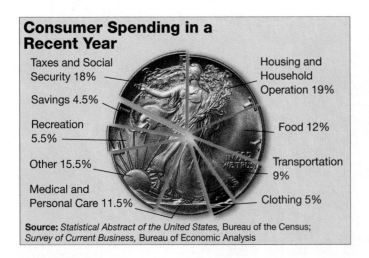

Consumer Spending in a Recent Year

Taxes and Social Security 18%
Savings 4.5%
Recreation 5.5%
Other 15.5%
Medical and Personal Care 11.5%

Housing and Household Operation 19%
Food 12%
Transportation 9%
Clothing 5%

Source: *Statistical Abstract of the United States,* Bureau of the Census; *Survey of Current Business,* Bureau of Economic Analysis

thus in his or her ability to consume. Where a person lives can also influence how much he or she earns. City dwellers tend to earn more than those who live in rural areas. Wages in some regions of the country tend to be higher than those in other regions. How much a person has to spend can also be influenced by inheriting money or property.

Regardless of the size of a person's income, spending that income requires constant decision making. As a consumer, each person has a series of choices to make.

Decision Making as a Consumer

The first decision a consumer must make is whether to buy an item or not. This may sound so basic as to be unnecessary to mention, but how many times do you actually think about the reasons for the purchase you are about to make? Do you think about whether you really need the item? Do you consider the trade-offs involved? Part I of Figure 3.3—Checklist for Consumer Decision Making—on page 60 will help you analyze this first consumer decision.

Scarce Resources Once you have decided to make a purchase, at least two scarce resources are involved—income and time. Once you have decided to spend your money income, you need to invest time in obtaining information about the product you wish to buy. The time you spend making a decision to buy something cannot be used for anything else. Suppose you decide to buy a mountain bike. The time spent visiting stores checking models and prices is a cost to you.

Making consumer decisions involves three parts, each including several steps. The Checklist for

Consumer Decision Making in Figure 3.3 can help to guide you through the entire process.

Opportunity Cost Virtually all of the steps in consumer decision making shown in Figure 3.3 involve an opportunity cost. Opportunity cost is the value of your highest alternative choice that you did not make. In step 1 of Part II of the checklist, for example, your choice between a low-, medium-, or high-quality product involves an opportunity cost.

In general, a high-quality product costs more than a low-quality product. Here is an example: You are trying to decide between new cross-training shoes. One model has a pump system that allows you to get a closer fit on your foot. The other model does not. The pump system model costs $80 more than the other model. If you choose the superior-quality, higher-priced pump system shoe, you will

Figure 3.2 ▲ Using Discretionary Income
The consumer's wants are his or her guide in spending income. Some people have more disposable and discretionary income and can therefore spend more than others on entertainment.

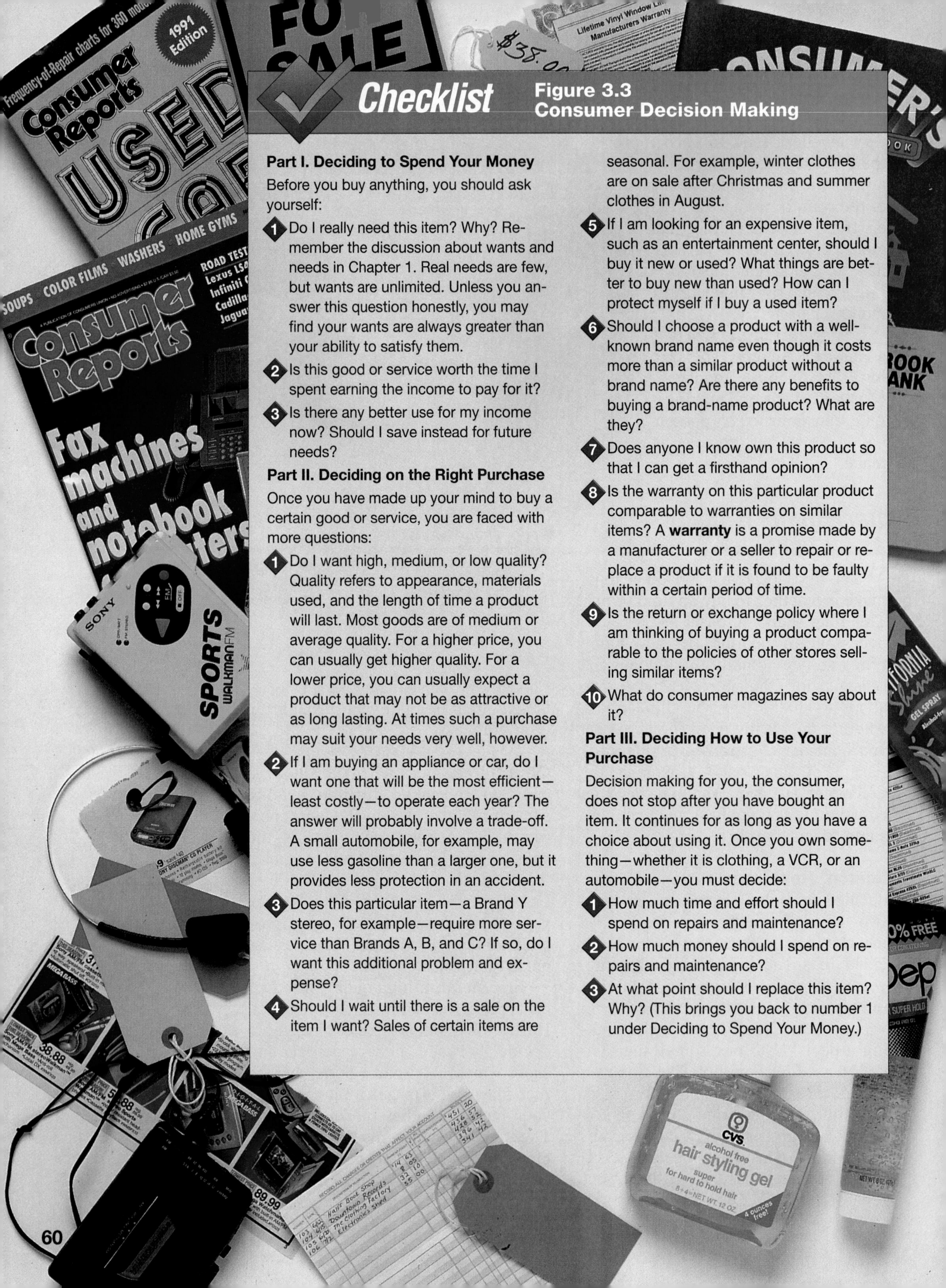

Checklist

Figure 3.3
Consumer Decision Making

Part I. Deciding to Spend Your Money

Before you buy anything, you should ask yourself:

1 Do I really need this item? Why? Remember the discussion about wants and needs in Chapter 1. Real needs are few, but wants are unlimited. Unless you answer this question honestly, you may find your wants are always greater than your ability to satisfy them.

2 Is this good or service worth the time I spent earning the income to pay for it?

3 Is there any better use for my income now? Should I save instead for future needs?

Part II. Deciding on the Right Purchase

Once you have made up your mind to buy a certain good or service, you are faced with more questions:

1 Do I want high, medium, or low quality? Quality refers to appearance, materials used, and the length of time a product will last. Most goods are of medium or average quality. For a higher price, you can usually get higher quality. For a lower price, you can usually expect a product that may not be as attractive or as long lasting. At times such a purchase may suit your needs very well, however.

2 If I am buying an appliance or car, do I want one that will be the most efficient—least costly—to operate each year? The answer will probably involve a trade-off. A small automobile, for example, may use less gasoline than a larger one, but it provides less protection in an accident.

3 Does this particular item—a Brand Y stereo, for example—require more service than Brands A, B, and C? If so, do I want this additional problem and expense?

4 Should I wait until there is a sale on the item I want? Sales of certain items are seasonal. For example, winter clothes are on sale after Christmas and summer clothes in August.

5 If I am looking for an expensive item, such as an entertainment center, should I buy it new or used? What things are better to buy new than used? How can I protect myself if I buy a used item?

6 Should I choose a product with a well-known brand name even though it costs more than a similar product without a brand name? Are there any benefits to buying a brand-name product? What are they?

7 Does anyone I know own this product so that I can get a firsthand opinion?

8 Is the warranty on this particular product comparable to warranties on similar items? A **warranty** is a promise made by a manufacturer or a seller to repair or replace a product if it is found to be faulty within a certain period of time.

9 Is the return or exchange policy where I am thinking of buying a product comparable to the policies of other stores selling similar items?

10 What do consumer magazines say about it?

Part III. Deciding How to Use Your Purchase

Decision making for you, the consumer, does not stop after you have bought an item. It continues for as long as you have a choice about using it. Once you own something—whether it is clothing, a VCR, or an automobile—you must decide:

1 How much time and effort should I spend on repairs and maintenance?

2 How much money should I spend on repairs and maintenance?

3 At what point should I replace this item? Why? (This brings you back to number 1 under Deciding to Spend Your Money.)

Figure 3.4 Buying Decisions

If you choose the higher-priced product, you must believe that the opportunity cost for the higher quality is worth $80—nothing else at that instant will give you as much value. ▼

sacrifice $80. The opportunity cost of the pump model over the lesser-quality model shoe is therefore $80, or what you could have bought with that $80. See Figure 3.4.

Rational Choice When you make consumer decisions based on opportunity cost, you are engaging in **rational choice.** Economists define rational choice as the alternative that has the greatest value.

Rational choice involves choosing the item that is the least expensive from among comparable quality products. As a consumer, you will make rational choices when you purchase the goods and services you believe can best satisfy your wants.

Do not get the impression that rational consumers will all make the same choices. Remember the definition: A rational choice is one that generates the greatest value for any given expenditure. Rational choices that are based on careful consumer decision making will still lead to billions of different consumer choices yearly.

Value is very subjective. You may choose to buy the higher-priced, superior-quality pump cross-training shoes, and your best friend may think you are crazy. If he or she tells you, "That's a rip-off; you shouldn't pay that kind of money for those shoes," your friend is expressing a value judgment about how you are choosing to spend your limited income.

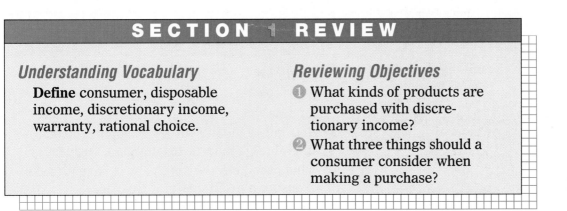

SECTION 1 REVIEW

Understanding Vocabulary
Define consumer, disposable income, discretionary income, warranty, rational choice.

Reviewing Objectives
1. What kinds of products are purchased with discretionary income?
2. What three things should a consumer consider when making a purchase?

Loida Nicolas Lewis on Secrets to Success

Profile

- born 1941 in Sorsogon, Philippines
- graduate of St. Theresa's College and the University of Philippines College of Law
- married Reginald Lewis, CEO of TLC Beatrice International Holdings, Inc.
- assumed control of TLC Beatrice International Holdings, Inc. in 1994 after her husband's death
- author of *How to Get a Green Card*

Loida Nicolas Lewis, the dynamic CEO of TLC Beatrice International Holdings, Inc., took the financial world by storm when she assumed control of the company that her husband, Reginald Lewis, had built. The following excerpt is from a speech that Loida Lewis delivered to the Detroit Economic Club on February 23, 1997. She titled her speech "Secrets to Success, A Woman CEO's Story," and explained her husband's attitudes toward success that she used to guide the company.

I can tell you as CEO of TLC Beatrice for the past 3 years, I have used the three secrets of Reginald Lewis' success. What were these three secrets of his success?

The first secret of RFL's success was that he always set a goal. . . .

The second secret of RFL's success was obedience to an inner code of conduct, a code of ethics. . . .

As for myself, I try to live my life based on the Golden Rule "Don't do to others what you would not have them do unto you," and "Honesty is the best policy." Sometimes when my executives and I are discussing an issue and they recommend a particular course of action, and somehow it does not sit well with me, I say "Wait a minute. If someone did this to us, would

we think it's fair?" If the answer is no, we won't do it. . . .

The third secret of RFL's success was his determination. . . .

In my case, when I decided to take over TLC Beatrice, I was determined for it to succeed. Failure was not an option. And as painful as it was, I was determined to do what needed to be done. I cut costs. As I said earlier, I had to lay off 50% of our headquarters staff. I moved our office to smaller quarters, and cut rent by 70%. I sold the company plane and the company cars. I sold assets to reduce debt. And I assembled my own team to grow the company.

Those are the 3 secrets of success. Set your Goals. Have a Moral Order. Be Determined. Taken together, these three secrets spell God. With God, everything is possible. With God, nothing is impossible.

Checking for Understanding

❶ What was Reginald Lewis's first secret of success?

❷ How does Loida Lewis try to apply ethical and moral standards to running a business?

❸ What sacrifices did Loida Lewis have to make to ensure a profitable TLC Beatrice?

2 Buying Principles, or Strategies

SECTION 2 FOCUS

Terms to Know competitive advertising, informative advertising, bait and switch, generic brands, brand name, comparison shopping

Objectives *After reading this section, you should be able to:*

❶ Evaluate the trade-offs when **gathering information**.

❷ Analyze various **forms of advertising** wisely.

❸ Practice **comparison shopping**.

The Three Basic Buying Principles

Assume that you have decided to make a purchase. Because of the problems of scarce income and time, your goal should be to obtain the most satisfaction from your limited income and time. Three basic buying principles can help you and all consumers achieve this goal. They are: (1) gathering information; (2) using advertising wisely; and (3) comparison shopping.

Figure 3.5 How Much Time and Effort? You can spend time testing out friends' mountain bikes. You could also go to different stores and discuss the good and bad points of various makes and models with salespeople. Actually, as a wise consumer, you would do both. ◀

Gathering Information

Suppose that you are going to buy a mountain bike. Once you have decided that, you have to decide on a brand and a model. How? You first have to obtain information about mountain bikes. See **Figure 3.5**.

Information is costly because obtaining it involves your time. You are faced with the problem of deciding how much information to obtain.

In the case of the mountain bike, the buying principle to follow is: Obtain only as much information as is worthwhile. What does *worthwhile* mean? The value of your time and effort spent gathering information should not be greater than the value you receive from making the best choice of product for yourself.

You would not, for example, want to go to every bike store in your town or city and spend two hours with every salesperson discussing every model. In contrast, you would probably want to spend more than two minutes reading one advertisement about one model. The less valuable a person considers his or her time, the more comparison shopping he or she should do. A nonworking college student generally should spend more time in comparison shopping than a business executive.

As you shop for different products, you will begin to develop a consumer-knowledge base. Information you obtain looking for a mountain bike might help you someday to make decisions about choosing a car or a computer.

Simply getting salespeople to give you accurate information is a skill that you can acquire and hone, or sharpen, over time while you shop for other products.

Using Advertising Wisely

Advertising is all around you. Whenever you turn on the radio or television, you will more than likely hear or see a commercial. Wherever you go, you read advertising on billboards, on posters on buses, and so on. The Checklist for Analyzing Advertisements in **Figure 3.6** gives you some tips for reading these ads, which can generally be classified as competitive or informative.

Competitive Advertising Advertising that attempts to persuade consumers that a product is different from and superior to any other is **competitive advertising.** Its purpose may be to take customers away from competitors or to keep competitors from taking away customers. Ads for well-established brand names and products, such as IBM computers and Nike, are often of this type. The ads are meant to keep the public aware of a company's name and its specific products.

Informative Advertising **Informative advertising** benefits consumers by giving information about a product. From such ads, you can learn about the existence, price, quality, and special features of products without spending much time or effort.

Informative advertising may also be competitive in nature.

Bait and Switch Unfortunately, advertising can be misleading. Although most advertisers try to present their products accurately, some use deceptive, or false, advertising. Sellers may misrepresent the quality, features, or the true (full) price of goods.

One of the most widely used methods of deceptive advertising is **bait and switch.** The bait is an advertised item at an unrealistically low price. When the consumer gets to the store, the item is no longer available, or the salesperson points out all the bad features of the advertised item and how dissatisfied the customer will be with it.

The salesperson then shows higher-priced models and points out all their good features. This is the switch. Instead of being able to buy a $349

DVD player, for example, the customer finds all the available ones are $500 or more. This practice is both deceptive and illegal.

Comparison Shopping

Once you have gathered the information and made a decision about a product you want, you must decide where to buy it. The price you will have to pay will affect your decision. Because you have limited income, a lower price will mean that you will have more income to spend on other purchases. You will be best off as a consumer when you are able to pay the lowest price for what you want. See Figure 3.7.

Figure 3.7
Efficient Comparison Shopping
To efficiently comparison shop for bikes, read newspaper advertisements, make telephone calls, and visit different stores. Remember, however, that finding out price information requires time. ▶

A Some companies produce and sell **generic brands.** The word *generic* means "pertaining to a general class." A generic brand of cereal means there is no brand name at all. It is difficult to know who produced the product.

▼

B A **brand name** is a word, picture, or logo on a product that helps consumers distinguish it from similar products. Brand names are usually sold nation-wide and are backed by major companies.

▼

Figure 3.8 Generic versus Brand Name
Your selection of generic or brand–name products makes a difference in price and sometimes in quality. Wise shoppers can often find non-brand names of equally high quality and reliability.

Shopping around suggests a third buying principle. Whenever you decide to make a purchase, it is generally worthwhile to get information on the types and prices of products available from different stores or companies. This process is known as **comparison shopping.**

Even when you apply rational buying principles to consumer decision making, you may still find that being a wise consumer is not always easy. The marketplace is a complex world with many sellers. Some sellers do not always include complete or reliable information about their products. Others may not readily repair or replace faulty products.

Brand-Name or Generic Products
Another consumer choice is between buying generic and brand-name products. Some consumers find that national brand-name products are worth the higher prices they often command. Figure 3.8 explains more about choosing between brand-name and other products.

SECTION 2 REVIEW

Understanding Vocabulary
Define competitive advertising, informative advertising, bait and switch, generic brands, brand name, comparison shopping.

Reviewing Objectives
1 What trade-offs should a consumer consider when gathering information?

2 How does informative advertising differ from competitive advertising?

3 What is comparison shopping?

LEARNING ECONOMIC SKILLS

Handling a Consumer Problem

Dealing with a faulty product or with a repair that was done incorrectly are two common consumer problems. Getting the results you want requires special communications skills.

Problem-Solving Steps

The Office of Consumer Affairs suggests that you:

1. Report the problem immediately. Do not try to fix a product yourself, because doing so may cancel the warranty.
2. State the problem and suggest a fair and just solution—replacement, refund, etc.
3. Include important details and copies of receipts, guarantees, and contracts to support your case.
4. Describe any action you have taken to try to correct the problem.
5. Keep an accurate record of your efforts to get the problem solved. Include names of people you speak or write to and dates.
6. Allow each person reasonable time, such as three weeks, to solve the problem before contacting another source.
7. Keep cool. The person who will help you solve your problem is probably not responsible for the problem.

If you need to write to the manufacturer, be sure your writing is neat and easy to read. Type your letter, if possible. Keep a copy of the letter for your records and future reference.

Practicing the Skill

1. Using the sample, write a letter to the company that shipped you a computer game CD-ROM that will not operate in your home computer.
2. If you do not receive satisfaction on a complaint in a reasonable time, what might you do next?

Your Address
City, State, Zip Code
Date

Customer Service Department
Company Name
Street Address
City, State, Zip Code

Dear Customer Service
Representative:

I bought a (product name, serial no., model no.) at (location and date of purchase). Unfortunately, (state problem, history of problem, and efforts to solve it).

I would appreciate your (state specific actions to be taken). Enclosed are copies of the following records: (list and enclose all documents connected with the problem).

I am looking forward to your reply and resolution of my problem and will wait (state resonable time period) before seeking third party assistance. Please contact me at the above address or by phone (work and home numbers).

Sincerely,

Your Name

SECTION 3 Consumerism

SECTION 3 FOCUS

Terms to Know consumerism, ethical behavior

Objectives *After reading this section, you should be able to:*

1. List five **consumer rights.**
2. List sources of **private and federal help for consumers.**
3. Define **consumer responsibilities.**
4. Describe **ethical consumer behavior.**

Consumers Have Rights and Responsibilities

Today the decisions Americans face as consumers are increasingly complex. Many Americans are greatly concerned with the safety and reliability of the products and services they use. **Consumerism** is a movement to educate buyers about the purchases they make and to demand better and safer products from manufacturers. Many government agencies and private groups work to ensure the well-being of consumers. Since the early 1960s, consumerism has grown steadily. Business can no longer assume it is the buyer's responsibility to know whether a product is safe, food is healthful, or advertising is accurate. See Figure 3.9.

Figure 3.9 Consumer Protection
Government inspection of many products protects consumers' health and safety and raises quality standards.

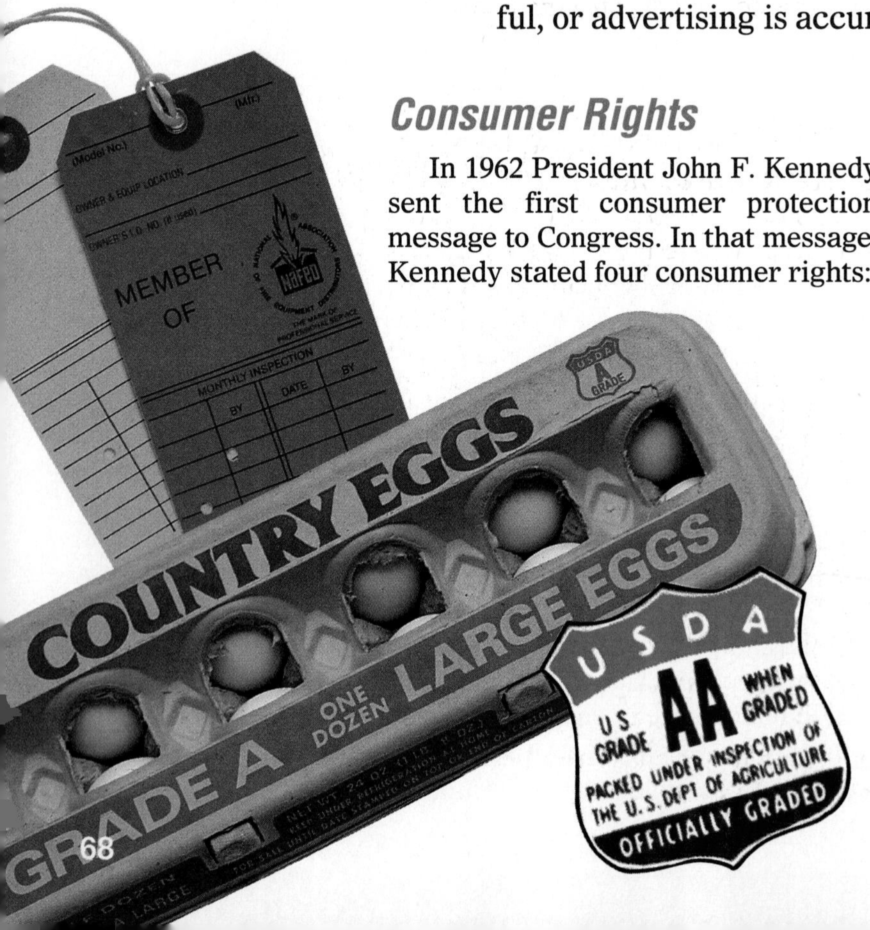

Consumer Rights

In 1962 President John F. Kennedy sent the first consumer protection message to Congress. In that message, Kennedy stated four consumer rights:

- the right to safety—protection against goods that are dangerous to life or health;
- the right to be informed—information for use not only as protection against fraud but also as the basis for reasoned choices;
- the right to choose—the need for markets to be competitive (have many firms) and for protection by government in those other markets, such as electric service, where competition does not exist;
- the right to be heard—the guarantee that consumer interests will be listened to when laws are being written.

Figure 3.10
Informing Yourself

A good consumer reads all contracts and warranties and asks about return and refund policies. After the purchase, he or she reads any instruction booklet and follows the directions for proper use of the product. ▶

To the four listed by President Kennedy, most consumer advocates would add a fifth:

- the right to redress—the ability to obtain from the manufacturers adequate payment in money or goods for financial or physical damages caused by their products.

Following the concepts that President Kennedy listed, Congress passed consumer-protection legislation. Today, consumers dissatisfied with a specific product can complain to the store manager or write to the manufacturer. They can also hire a lawyer or take the case to small claims court. Many private and public agencies can also help consumers.

Consumer Help: Private and Federal

Among the private groups that aid consumers are local citizens' action groups and local chapters of the Better Business Bureau. Many major cities and some smaller ones have better business bureaus. The bureaus provide information on products as well as selling practices to consumers and help settle disagreements between consumers and sellers. Before using these agencies, however, consumers need to learn about the products they wish to purchase as Figure 3.10 shows.

A trade association is a group of companies in the same business that work together to promote that specific industry. Trade associations in some industries also provide consumers with information.

Two national organizations provide excellent sources of consumer information. The Consumers Union of the United States, Inc., publishes a monthly magazine called *Consumer Reports*. An informational magazine, *Consumer Reports* accepts no advertising. A competing publication is *Consumers' Research Magazine*, published by Consumers' Research, Inc.

Numerous federal agencies also have programs to aid consumers. Figure 3.11 (pages 70–71) lists these agencies and what they do. Much of the information that now appears on product labels and in warranties is a result of federal regulations to protect consumers. States also have consumer affairs councils or agencies.

Consumer Responsibilities

Consumers have responsibilities as well as rights. Learning as much as possible about the product or service he or she wishes to buy will enable the consumer to purchase the best product at the best price.

Figure 3.11 Federal Agencies and Consumerism

Agency	How It Helps the Consumer	For More Information
Consumer Information Center Program	Provides free catalog of government publications on consumer topics	*Consumer's Resource Handbook* Consumer Information Center Pueblo, Colorado 81009
Federal Trade Commission	Promotes free and fair competition by enforcing laws against monopolies, price fixing, false advertising, and other illegal business practices; regulates packaging and labeling of products and protects the public against violations of consumer credit laws	Federal Trade Commission 6th St. and Pennsylvania Avenue, N.W. Office of Public Information Washington, D.C. 20580
Consumer Product Safety Commission	Protects the public against unreasonable risk of injury from consumer products; sets product safety requirements, forbids the production and sale of dangerous consumer products, and conducts research and education programs on safety concerns for industry and the public	Office of the Secretary, Consumer Product Safety Commission 4330 EW Highway Bethesda, MD 20207
Government Printing Office	Sells more than 15,000 government publications on a wide variety of topics; lists those of interest to consumers in free booklet: *Consumer Information Subject Bibliography*	Superintendent of Documents Government Printing Office North Capitol and H Streets NW Washington, D.C. 20401
U.S. Postal Service	Through its Inspection Services protects public from mail fraud and other violations of postal laws; through Consumer Advocate's office acts on complaints and suggestions from individual consumers and provides information on past and present schemes used to cheat the public	Consumer Advocate U.S. Postal Service 475 L'Enfant Plaza SW Washington, D.C. 20260
U.S. Department of Agriculture	Inspects and grades meat, fish, poultry, dairy products, and fruits and vegetables through the department's Food Safety and Quality Service; ensures that food production is sanitary and that products are labeled truthfully	Office of the Consumer Adviser Administration Building U.S. Department of Agriculture Independence Avenue Washington, D.C. 20250

Figure 3.11 Federal Agencies and Consumerism

Agency	How It Helps the Consumer	For More Information
U.S. Office of Consumer Affairs (Department of Health and Human Services)	Coordinates all federal activities on behalf of consumers, advises President on consumer affairs, and works for and testifies on behalf of consumer legislation; the Complaint Coordination Center helps solve consumer problems	U.S. Office of Consumer Affairs 4330 EW Highway Bethesda, Maryland 20207
Food and Drug Administration (Department of Health and Human Services)	Protects the public against impure and unsafe foods, drugs, and cosmetics; researches and tests new products in these areas and ensures accurate labeling; publishes *FDA Consumer* magazine and maintains regional consumer affairs offices	Food and Drug Administration 5600 Fishers Lane Rockville, Maryland 20857
National Highway Traffic Safety Administration (Department of Transportation)	Sets requirements for automobile safety, maintenance, and fuel economy and tests products for compliance; researches ways to save fuel and make highways safer and investigates complaints from consumers about vehicle safety	National Highway Traffic Safety Administration Department of Transportation 400 7th St., N.W. Washington, D.C. 20590

Ethical Behavior

Consumers should respect the rights of producers and sellers of goods and services. **Ethical behavior** involves acting in accordance with one's moral and ethical convictions about right and wrong. For example, a responsible consumer will not try to return a used item because it has been advertised elsewhere for a lower price. Nor will a consumer misuse an item and then attempt to return it, saying it was defective—faulty or broken—when bought.

SECTION 3 REVIEW

Understanding Vocabulary
Define consumerism, ethical behavior.

Reviewing Objectives
1. What are the five important rights that consumers have?
2. What private and federal groups aid consumers?
3. Why should consumers learn about products they wish to buy?
4. What role does ethical behavior play in consumers' actions?

Readings in Economics

THE NEW YORK TIMES   JUNE 6, 1993

BEHIND THE 'CLEAR' TREND

by Barnaby J. Feder

From drinks to deodorants to dishwashing liquid, not to mention gasoline and mouthwash, the hot color for new products is no color at all.

Marketers like to have something novel to sell, but the driving force in the trend is an effort to tap into consumers' associations of clarity with health, purity, freshness and no-frills functionality. And if consumers see ... transparent antiperspirant as more "natural" than colored competitors, so much the better.

But clear products are usually as thoroughly processed as any tinted cousins, if not more so. In creating Crystal Pepsi, for example, Pepsi needed 14 months to iron out the formula and production process. Pepsi takes longer and spends more to produce the clear cola, which requires greater quality controls than the brown stuff....

"This isn't rocket science," said Thomas Pirko, president of Bevmark, food and beverage consul-tants based in Los Angeles. "The technology is clearly subservient to the marketing consideration."

...Perhaps the clearest case of technology being subservient to marketing in the trend toward clear products is that of Crystal Clear Amoco Ultimate gasoline. The colorless premium gasoline has been on the market since 1915 in the eastern United States, originally under the White Crown name.

Only in the last five years, though, has the petroleum industry had the tools to analyze auto emissions in great detail. One result was that the Amoco Oil Company discovered that its clear gas—renamed as Crystal Clear last year—has an environmental advantage over its competitors.... [it] cut emissions of hydrocarbons by 13 percent.

• THINK ABOUT IT •

1. *Why are "clear" products gaining popularity?*

2. *What is the environmental advantage of Crystal Clear Amoco?*

ECONOMICS IN ACTION

Your Role as a Consumer

Setting up the Video

With your classmates, view "Your Role as a Consumer" on the videodisc *Economics in Action*. The video focuses on consumer choices and explains the differences between disposable and discretionary income. In a news report on buying a car, the video suggests some basic questions a consumer should ask. The video concludes by pointing out that while the government provides some consumer protection, consumers must also look out for themselves.

Chapter 4
Disc 1, Side 1

View the video by scanning the bar code or by entering the chapter number on your keypad and pressing Search. *(Also available in VHS format.)*

Hands-On Activity

With a group of your classmates, choose a consumer item, such as a stereo system or a new computer, that you would like to purchase. Consider the following questions: Where would you find information about features and quality? How would you find the best price?

Then, as a class choose one item to purchase. Come up with an action plan to ensure that you get the best product for the best price. Ask volunteers from the class to follow through on the plan without actually purchasing the item and report their findings to the rest of the class.

SURFING THE "NET"

Consumerism

In this chapter you learned that many Americans are greatly concerned with the safety and reliability of the products and services they use. Consumerism is a movement to educate buyers about the purchases they make and to demand better and safer products from manufacturers. You can learn more about consumer rights and responsibilities on the Internet.

Getting There

1. Use a search engine. Type in the word *consumer*.
2. After typing in *consumer*, enter words like the following to focus your search: *legislation, protection, complaints, information, safety*.

3. The search engine will provide you with a number of links to follow. Links are "pointers" to different sites on the Internet and often appear as blue, underlined words.

What to Do When You Are There

Click on the links to navigate through the pages of information. Gather your findings. Using the findings, prepare an oral presentation detailing what resources are available to protect consumers who purchase defective products. Your presentation should include a flow chart detailing the steps a dissatisfied consumer can take to ensure that a defective product is repaired or replaced.

Identifying Key Terms

Write the letter of the definition in Column B that correctly defines each term in Column A.

Column A
1. disposable income (p. 58)
2. warranty (p. 60)
3. bait and switch (p. 65)
4. comparison shopping (p. 66)
5. competitive advertising (p. 64)

Column B
a. deceptive advertising intended to defraud the consumer
b. getting information about similar types of products and prices
c. money income left after taxes have been paid
d. attempts to persuade consumers that certain products are different and superior to others
e. written guarantee of a product for a certain period of time

Use terms from the following list to fill in the blanks in the paragraph below.

ethical behavior (p. 71)
informative advertising (p. 64)
generic brand (p. 66)
consumer (p. 58)
discretionary income (p. 58)
brand name (p. 66)

Every one of us is at one time or another a __(6)__ . Sometimes we have __(7)__ to spend on "fun" things. In order to make our purchases, we may use __(8)__ , which tells us about the product. We often have the choice between a __(9)__ and a __(10)__ , which is usually cheaper. In any event, as a consumer, you should always be responsible and be concerned about your __(11)__ .

Recalling Facts and Ideas

Section 1
1. After people have bought necessities, they are left with what type of income?
2. Income is one scarce resource that you use when you are a consumer. What is the other scarce resource?
3. Before you buy anything, what three questions should you ask yourself?
4. Do all rational consumers think alike? Why or why not?

Section 2
5. What are three important buying principles?
6. What are the two major types of commercial advertising?
7. How much information should you obtain before you make a purchase?
8. What type of shopping allows you to be a rational consumer?

Section 3
9. What are the major purposes of consumerism today?
10. What three types of help do federal agencies give to consumers?
11. What are the four consumer rights that President John F. Kennedy stated?
12. What are two consumer responsibilities?

Critical Thinking

Section 1
Determining Cause and Effect How might education, occupation, and health make a difference in a person's earning power (income) and therefore in his or her ability to consume?

Section 2

Analyzing Information Why do some people buy brand–name products and other people buy generic products? What are the trade-offs involved in this decision?

Section 3

Making Comparisons How do consumer rights compare with consumer responsibilities?

Applying Economic Concepts

Competition and Market Structure Choose an advertisement from a newspaper or a magazine, and use the checklist on page 64 to analyze it. Write a sentence to answer each of the questions on the checklist. Do you think it is a competitive ad, an informative ad, or both? Explain the reasons for your choice.

Reviewing Skills

Handling a Consumer Problem

1. List 10 items of information that a person should include in a letter of complaint to a product manufacturer.
2. What should consumers keep in their records when dealing with the problem of a faulty product?
3. What impact do you think your consumer complaint will have on the product manufacturer? Do you think your complaint will result in an improved product?

Chapter Projects

1. **Individual Project** Imagine that you have decided to buy a car, but you still have to decide on the size (not the make and model, but only the size). Go through the steps you would use to research your decision. Keep a record of the information you find.
2. **Cooperative Learning Project** Working in groups of four, take the Checklist for Consumer Decision Making on page 60 and the

three buying principles listed in the text and shop for one of the following: DVD player, portable compact disc player, or personal computer. Each of you should keep a record of the steps you take and the information you gather using a table like the one shown. Compare your information with what others in the class found.

Checklist Number	Step	Information
1.		
2.		
3.		
4.		
5.		
6.		
7.		
8.		
9.		
10.		

Technology Activity
Using E-Mail

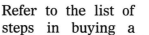

Refer to the list of steps in buying a small appliance or electronic item that you kept track of in Your Economics Journal on page 57. Determine whether or not you are satisfied with the item you purchased. Then E-mail the manufacturer of the product detailing your reactions to the product. You may find the E-mail address in the information included with the product, or you may search the Internet for the E-mail address by using your favorite search engine. Enter the name of the manufacturer or the type of product you purchased to locate the manufacturer's home page on the Internet. Most manufacturers will have E-mail addresses listed on their home pages.

Point

ISSUE: Should "Pollution Taxes" Be Used to Help the Environment and Lower the Deficit?

In 1970 the Environmental Protection Agency (EPA) was set up to combat the growing problem of pollution. After President Clinton took office in 1993, the idea of pollution taxes to help the environment and reduce the federal budget deficit gained popularity and became the subject of debate.

PRO ▷ Some of the groups in favor of pollution taxes seem to think that these taxes will not only help the environment, but will increase productivity and raise individual welfare as well.

According to the World Resources Institute, shifting 10 to 15 percent of the nation's tax burden from "goods" to "bads" could yield an annual economic "dividend" that is greater than 1 percent of annual national output. The National Commission of the Environment argues that such a tax would send the "right economic signals." The Progressive Policy Institute asserts that government regulations to help the environment end up hampering innovation in pollution control methods, while pollution taxes can promote energy efficiency and put the U.S. "on an energy path consistent with sustainable development."

Jonathan Marshall, the economics editor of the *San Francisco Chronicle*, writes in *Reason* that pollution taxes have too much potential *not* to give them a try. He feels that the benefits of such taxes are too great to ignore:

And yet, for all these objections, pollution taxes deserve a hearing among free-market advocates as a viable "second-best" strategy in the absence of some libertarians' utopia. You don't have to be a green zealot to concede that heavy smog impairs lungs and toxic compounds can kill people.... Barring an intellectual or institutional breakthrough, some form of collective action is needed to control pollution. Once that premise is accepted, pollution taxes in principle are cheaper and more effective in most instances than command-and-control regulations.

. . . Like any social policy, pollution taxes must be done right. Given the political system's overwhelming predisposition toward "government failure," that may be wishful thinking. But killing the idea is hardly a superior alternative if it just means accepting the status quo by default.

Counterpoint

CON Those against pollution taxes tend to be political conservatives, who are worried that the costs of such taxes will outweigh their benefits. Unfortunately, both costs and benefits are hard to measure; the benefits even more so than the costs. Fred Smith, president of the Competitive Enterprise Institute, expresses the concern that pollution tax schemes "look a lot better than they may turn out to be in practice."

With one particular type of pollution tax, the carbon tax (a tax based on the carbon content of fossil fuels such as gasoline), Lawrence Goulder of Stanford University questions whether the uncertain benefits will really be greater than the costs. He had been a supporter of carbon taxes, but in his study of the potential effects of the tax, he came up with higher costs and greater economic distortions than expected.

Critics also argue that carbon or energy taxes will hurt U.S. competitiveness in foreign markets, and lead to higher prices for consumers. Economist Anthony Riccardi asserts that taxes on energy are essentially regressive taxes. The working poor would be the group most severely hurt by this type of tax, as a large percentage of their income goes to costs such as gasoline and heating oil.

Writing for the *Asbury Park* (New Jersey) *Press*, Larry McDonnell points out some local criticisms of a carbon tax:

Who could argue with a tax on pollutants threatening the planet? Especially a tax that would take a big bite out of the deficit. As it turns out, many people will argue, particularly the chemical and petroleum industries, two of New Jersey's larger employers.

"Attempting to impose yesterday's costs on today's U.S.-based production undermines our international competitiveness," said Sean T. Crimmins, vice president and general tax counsel for Ashland Oil Inc., testifying before Congress this spring. "To do so at this time—in the face of already large U.S. trade deficits—is the economic equivalent of shooting oneself in the foot."

Exploring the Issue

Reviewing Facts

① What would be the benefits of pollution taxes? What would be the costs?

② What individuals and groups support pollution taxes? What individuals and groups oppose pollution taxes?

Critical Thinking

③ **Identifying Alternatives** What methods, other than pollution taxes, might the government use to encourage the wise use of natural resources?

4 GOING INTO DEBT

What are the costs of using credit cards?

What is this card?

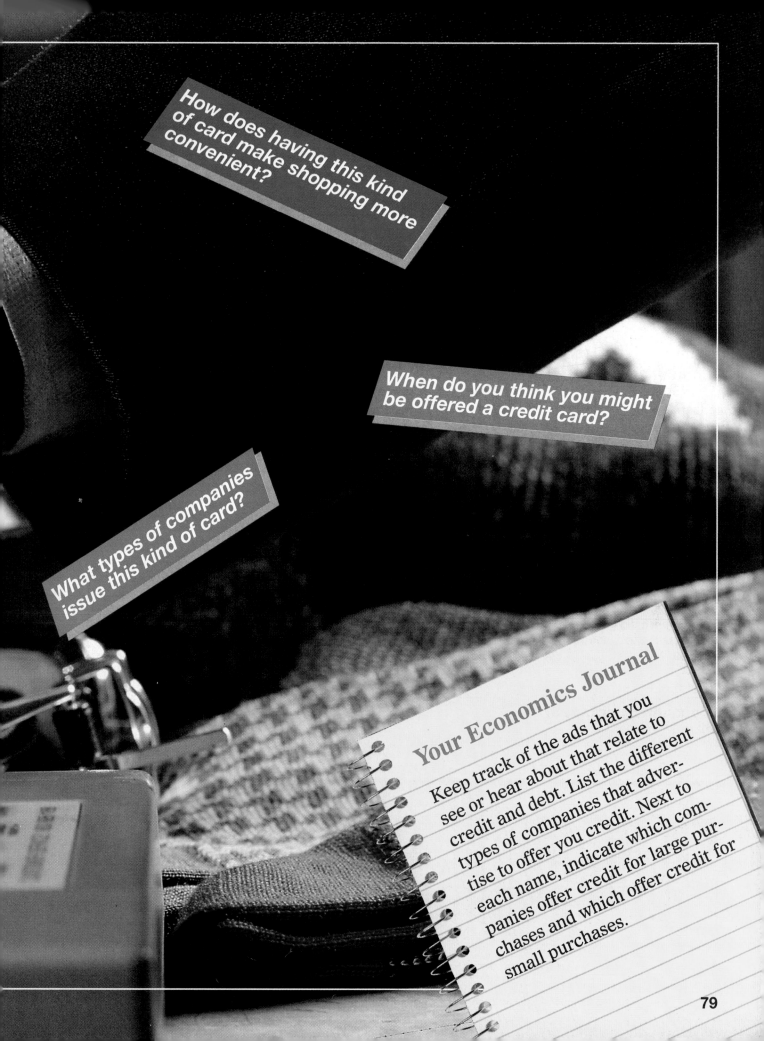

How does having this kind of card make shopping more convenient?

When do you think you might be offered a credit card?

What types of companies issue this kind of card?

Your Economics Journal

Keep track of the ads that you see or hear about that relate to credit and debt. List the different types of companies that advertise to offer you credit. Next to each name, indicate which companies offer credit for large purchases and which offer credit for small purchases.

Americans Use Credit to Make Many Purchases

For the nation as a whole, the total amount of money borrowed and lent each year is enormous. Federal, state, and local governments all borrow each year. The nation's economy depends on individuals and groups being able to buy and borrow on credit. **Credit** is the receiving of money either directly or indirectly to buy goods and services today with the promise to pay for them in the future. The amount owed—the debt—is equal to the principal plus interest. The **principal** is the amount originally borrowed. The **interest** is the amount the borrower must pay for the use of someone else's money. That someone else may be a bank, a credit card company, or a store.

Any time you receive credit, you are borrowing money and going into debt. Taking out a loan is the same as buying an item on credit. In both cases, you must pay interest for the use of someone else's purchasing power.

**Figure 4.1
How Much Debt?**
By how much did consumer debt increase between 1987 and 1997?

▼

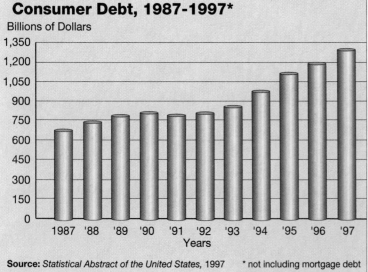

Consumer Debt, 1987-1997*
Billions of Dollars

Source: *Statistical Abstract of the United States,* 1997   * not including mortgage debt

Installment Debt

One of the most common types of debt is **installment debt.** Figure 4.1 shows the change in installment debt owed each year in the United States from 1987 to 1997. Consumers repay this type of loan with equal payments, or installments, over a period of time, for example, 36 months. Many people buy such consumer durables as automobiles, refrigerators, washers, and other appliances on an installment plan. **Consumer durables** are manufactured items that people use for long periods of time before replacing them. People can also borrow cash and pay it back in installments.

The length of the installment period is important in determining the size of the borrower's monthly payments and the total amount of interest he or she must pay. A longer repayment period results in a smaller monthly payment. For example, Figure 4.2 shows that if the repayment of a loan is spread over three years, the monthly payments will be smaller than if the loan were repaid in two years. There is a trade-off, however. The longer it takes to repay an installment loan, the greater the total interest the lender charges.

The largest form of installment debt in this country is the money people owe on mortgages. A **mortgage** is an installment debt owed on real property—houses, buildings, or land. See Figure 4.3.

Figure 4.2
Loan Payments

How much more interest will a borrower pay who spreads loan payments over 36 rather than 24 months? ▼

$1,000   Installment Loan at 9% Interest

Term of Loan	24 months	36 months
Monthly Payments	$45.69	$31.80
Total Interest	$96.56	$114.80
Total Payments	$1,096.56	$1,144.80

▼ **Figure 4.3 Mortgages as Debts**
Most people who owe only a mortgage on their home or farm do not consider themselves deeply in debt. They do not think of a mortgage as being similar to other kinds of debt. A mortgage is a debt, however, because somebody has provided the owner with money to purchase property. In return, the owner must repay the loan with interest in installments over a number of years.

Why People Use Credit

Most Americans are accustomed to borrowing and buying on credit. At times, especially when buying such expensive consumer durables as automobiles and fine furniture, they consider borrowing to be necessary.

Immediate Need In a sense, people feel forced to buy items on credit because they believe they need them immediately. They do not want to wait. Of course, consumers are not really "forced" to buy most goods and services on credit. They could decide instead to save the money needed to make their purchases.

Figure 4.4

If a person saved for 36 months to buy a $15,000 truck, the truck would cost only $13,500. The remaining $1,500 would be made up by the interest paid on the savings over the three years. According to the ad, however, if the person bought the $15,000 truck immediately on a 36-month installment plan, the actual cost would be $18,500. The $3,500 difference would be the interest the person would have to pay on the borrowed money. In addition, the person would not receive any interest on savings.

▼

To illustrate this point, a savings bank once ran a clever advertisement on buying a truck. See **Figure 4.4**. Obviously, there is a big difference between $13,500 and $18,500. As these figures show, it is better to save now and buy later than to buy now and go into debt. The ad, however, omitted an important point. During the three-year saving period, the person would not be able to enjoy the use of the truck. Many people would not wait that long for an important durable good they want. They would rather buy on credit and enjoy the use of the item now rather than later.

Spread Payments Another reason for going into debt is to spread the payments over the life of the item being purchased. For example, people do not buy a truck or car to have it sit in the garage. What they buy is the availability of the vehicle each day, week, month, and year that they own it.

Suppose you buy a car that costs $15,000 and plan to keep it for five years. At the end of that time, it will be worth only $5,000. Over that five-year period, you will get approximately $2,000 worth of use per year, or $166 per month. By buying on the installment plan, a person makes monthly payments that more or less correspond to the value of the use he or she receives.

PICK-UP TRUCK $15,000

BUY NOW SAVE $3,500

Total Costs	
On 36-Month Plan	$18,500
Save, Pay Cash	$15,000
Savings =	$ 3,500

Deciding To Use Credit

Borrowing or using credit is a question of whether the satisfaction the borrower gets from the purchases is greater than the interest payments. It is basically a question of comparing costs and benefits. The benefit of borrowing is being able to buy and enjoy the good or service now rather than later. The cost is whatever the borrower must pay in interest or lost opportunities to buy other items. The benefit of borrowing is something only you can decide for yourself. You and every other borrower, however, should be aware of the costs involved.

The Checklist for Buying on Credit, Figure 4.5 above, can help you decide when to use credit. It can also help you avoid the improper use of credit by overspending. Every day in the United States, thousands of families get into financial trouble because they have ignored the total costs of all their borrowing. They have too many credit cards and too many charge accounts and own a home that is too expensive with too large a mortgage. Just because someone offers you credit or allows you to borrow does not mean that you must accept. Buying on credit is a serious consumer activity. You should keep the information in the checklist in mind before you take the credit plunge.

SECTION 1 REVIEW

Understanding Vocabulary

Define credit, principal, interest, installment debt, consumer durables, mortgage.

Reviewing Objectives

1. What are the advantages of repaying installment debt over a long period?

2. Why do people use credit?

3. What factors should you consider when deciding whether or not to use credit?

Ronald Homer
on Running a Bank

Ronald Homer described his efforts to make the Boston Bank of Commerce successful in *New England Business*, April 1, 1989.

*T*he bank was an embarrassment to the community. It really wasn't serving much of a purpose, other than as a place that didn't charge you if you bounced checks. It was a bank of last resort for people who had difficulty getting checking accounts other places. . . .

At the start, we had to figure out quickly how we would stop the bleeding and make money. But more important, we had to make ourselves relevant to the community. There was an innate sense that there should be a minority-owned bank in town, and everybody wanted it. But for what purpose? Was it there to cash welfare checks, so that the large banks won't have to deal with those people? Or was it supposed to be doing something more?

Homer decided to serve the needs of the local community.

*W*e approached all the major businesses and institutions in Roxbury and said, "We want to be your bank: what will it take?" . . . Gradually, we showed them we could help in a way the other banks weren't equipped or able to do.

. . . We've grown the maximum we can grow with our capital, without raising additional capital. . . .

On the other hand, [the capital situation] has turned out to be a blessing in disguise, because had we raised capital two years ago—a public offering, for example, to raise $5 million—we would probably have been tempted like a lot of these other banks to start doing condo loans and other things. But because we were growing in a controlled area, we found enough business among our core constituency to satisfy us. . . . If we had gotten capital outside of that, we would probably have been lending money outside of our community rather than inside.

Checking for Understanding

❶ What problems did the Boston Bank of Commerce face?

❷ What important questions did Ronald Homer believe his bank had to answer?

❸ How did the bank's financial (capital) situation help it to respond to local needs?

SECTION 2 Sources of Loans and Credit

SECTION 2 FOCUS

Terms to Know commercial bank, savings and loan association, savings banks, credit union, finance company, consumer finance company, charge account, regular charge account, credit limit, revolving charge account, installment charge account, credit card, debit card, finance charge, annual percentage rate

Objectives *After reading this section, you should be able to:*
1. List the six types of financial institutions.
2. Explain the three types of charge accounts.
3. Describe how credit and debit cards are used.
4. Contrast a finance charge and the annual percentage rate.

Lending Institutions Differ

Borrowing money directly by taking out a loan is one of the two major types of credit. Many financial institutions, including commercial banks, savings and loan associations, savings banks, credit unions, and finance and consumer finance companies grant loans. Each of these sources, however, works in the same way, by charging interest on the money it lends. The amount of interest charged can vary widely as Figure 4.6 shows.

Figure 4.6 Interest Rates Vary
On a typical day interest rates may be higher or lower at any given lending institution.

Types of Financial Institutions

As with other items you buy, you should comparison shop when you have decided to apply for a loan. You should check various lending agencies by visiting or phoning them to gather information, because financial institutions differ in several ways as Figure 4.7 (pages 86–87) shows.

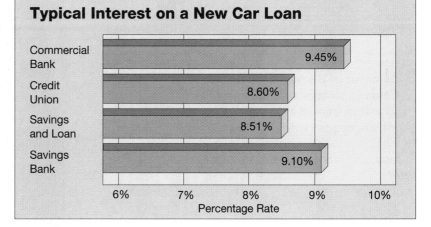

Typical Interest on a New Car Loan

Institution	Percentage Rate
Commercial Bank	9.45%
Credit Union	8.60%
Savings and Loan	8.51%
Savings Bank	9.10%

Percentage Rate: 6% 7% 8% 9% 10%

Commercial Banks The first place you might think to go for a loan is a **commercial bank.** Their main functions are to accept deposits; to lend money; and to transfer funds among banks, individuals, and businesses.

Savings and Loan Associations A **savings and loan association** (S&L), like a commercial bank, accepts deposits and lends money. When S&Ls were first established in the United States in the mid-nineteenth century, they were called "building societies." Members of a society would combine their money over a period of time and take turns borrowing until each mem-

ber was able to build a home. Today, most savings deposits still come from individuals and families.

Savings Banks **Savings banks** are similar to S&Ls in that most of their business comes from savings accounts and home loans. Since 1980, savings banks, like commercial banks, have been able to offer services similar to checking accounts. Savings banks were first set up in the United States in the early nineteenth century. They were meant to serve the small savers who were overlooked by the large commercial banks.

**Figure 4.7
Comparing
Financial
Institutions**
The financial institution you choose will depend on several factors, including differences in interest rates and loan repayment terms.

A   Commercial Banks ▲
Commercial banks today control the largest amount of money and offer the widest range of services. These services include offering checking, savings, and loan services to individual consumers.

B   Savings and Loan Associations
Savings and loan associations make many single-family and multi-family mortgage loans. They also finance commercial mortgages and auto loans. In the 1980s federal laws permitted savings and loans to provide some of the same services as banks. ▼

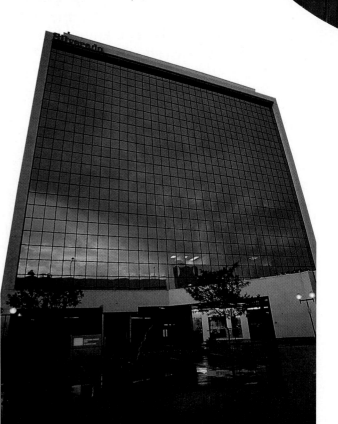

Credit Unions Union members and employees of many companies often have a credit union. A **credit union** is owned and operated by its members to provide savings accounts and low-interest loans only to its members. In general, credit unions offer higher interest rates on savings and charge lower interest rates on loans than other financial institutions.

Finance Companies and Consumer Finance Companies A **finance company** takes over contracts for installment debts from stores and adds a fee for collecting the debt. The consumer pays the fee in the form of slightly higher interest than he or she would pay to the retailer. Retailers use this method to avoid the risks involved in lending money to consumers. Finance companies also make loans directly to consumers.

D Credit Unions
Credit unions primarily make personal, auto, and home improvement loans, though some larger credit unions offer home mortgages as well. They also offer share drafts, which are similar to checking accounts at commercial banks.

▼

C Consumer Finance Companies
People who use consumer finance companies are usually unable to borrow from commercial banks or other sources with lower rates because of nonpayment of loans in the past or an uneven employment record. Consumer finance companies are the largest supplier of installment cash loans for purposes other than buying consumer durables.

▼ E Savings Banks
Names of savings banks often include such words as *farmers'* or *seamen's* to indicate the group for whom the bank was originally intended. The majority of savings banks are located in New England and the Mid-Atlantic states. Most of their loans are for home mortgages, although they do make personal and auto loans. Because of their small number, savings banks account for only a small percentage of the country's home mortgages and other consumer installment debt. Their interest rates for loans, like those of S&Ls, are often slightly less than those for commercial banks.

A **consumer finance company** makes loans directly to consumers at high rates of interest. These rates are often more than 20 percent a year. Some states allow consumer finance companies to charge as much as 36 percent a year on small amounts of money.

Crisis and Changes In the 1980s changes in federal laws expanded the activities of S&Ls, permitting them to offer checking-type accounts and business and consumer loans. While most loans were still used to buy homes, many S&Ls made risky commercial investments. By 1988 many S&Ls were in financial trouble. Congress set up the Resolution Trust Corporation to manage the crisis and save the S&L industry. Experts predicted that the bailout would cost the federal government and taxpayers hundreds of billions of dollars. See Figure 4.8.

The Resolution Trust Corporation sold off assets of failed savings and loans, bailed out other S&Ls with federal money, and stabilized the weaker institutions. The so-called bailout was the way the government began to meet its obligation to insure depositors' accounts.

When it became evident that the Federal Deposit Insurance Corporation had nearly depleted its funds, the agency voted to increase its insurance premiums. This meant that lending institutions would have to pay more for FDIC coverage.

▼ **Figure 4.8**
The Bailout
The Resolution Trust Corporation continued to ask Congress for more and more money to bail out S&Ls. Taxpayers began to wonder whether the bailout would ever end, but by the 1990s the crisis had been resolved.

Charge Accounts

A major type of credit is extended directly to an individual, without that person's having to borrow money first. This credit may be in the form of a charge account or a credit card. A **charge account** allows a customer to buy goods or services from a particular company and pay for them later. Department stores, for example, offer their customers three basic types of charge accounts: regular, revolving, or installment.

Regular Charge Accounts A **regular charge account,** also known as a 30-day charge, has a credit limit such as $500 or $1,000. A **credit limit** is the maximum amount of goods or services a person or business can buy on the promise to pay in the future. The cardholder and usually any member of his or her family can charge items up to this limit. At the end of every 30-day period, the store sends a bill for the entire amount. No interest is charged, but the entire bill must be paid at that time. If it is not, interest is charged on that part of the account.

Revolving Charge Accounts A **revolving charge account** allows you to make additional purchases from the same store even if you have not paid the previous month's bill in full. See Figure 4.9. Usually you must pay a certain portion of your balance each month, for instance one-fifth of the amount due. Interest is charged on the

◀ **Figure 4.9
Store Charge Cards**
Stores allow their customers to choose regular, revolving, or installment accounts. They all allow consumers to purchase more now, but with the latter two customers must normally pay interest.

amount you do not pay. Of course, if you pay everything you owe each month, no interest is charged. This type of account also has a credit limit.

Installment Charge Accounts Major items such as couches, televisions, and refrigerators are often purchased through an **installment charge account.** The items are purchased and paid for through equal payments spread over a period of time. Part of the amount paid each month is applied to the interest, and part is applied to the principal. At the end of the payment period, the borrower owns whatever he or she has made payments on.

Credit and Debit Cards

A **credit card**, like a charge account, allows a person to make purchases without paying cash. The difference is that credit cards can be used at many kinds of stores, restaurants, hotels, and other businesses throughout the United States and even foreign countries. Visa, MasterCard, and others issue cards through banks. These cards can be used to purchase items in stores that accept them, or they may be used to borrow money, up to a certain limit. This gives consumers access to loans at all times without having to apply for them. So many cards have been marketed that it is not unusual for a person to have several different kinds. Figure 4.10 illustrates sample credit and charge cards.

Credit cards usually charge high interest. Throughout the 1990s, banks charged an average of 18 percent on

Figure 4.10
The Credit Card Trade-Off

Individual stores, such as Pier I and Home Depot, issue their own charge cards, which consumers may use to purchase goods. Consumers may also use credit cards, such as MasterCard and Optima. Although using credit cards is convenient, it is also costly. Stores must pay a certain percentage of credit purchases to the credit card company or bank that issued the card. The stores include this cost in the price they charge customers, making prices higher for everyone.

▼

MasterCard and Visa. The high interest rates eventually brought additional issuers into the market. Sears, Roebuck & Co. issued its Discover Card. General Electric Co. and General Motors joined American Telephone & Telegraph in issuing cards with more attractive interest rates and other benefits.

Gradually the competition brought credit card interest rates down, but one factor kept rates from dropping very low—bad loans. Visa and MasterCard issuers charge off almost 25 percent of the revenues collected in bad loans. Because of this some issuers began to offer lower rates to special categories of customers who they believed were more reliable.

A **debit card** does not provide a loan. Instead it makes cashless purchases easier by enabling the customer to transfer funds electronically. Debit cards were first available in the 1970s, but they did not catch on with the public. Popular use of automated teller machines (ATMs) has paved the way for acceptance of debit cards. In 1992 Visa and MasterCard launched a campaign to sign up banks combining their credit cards with debit cards. Today, these cards have gained widespread consumer acceptance.

Finance Charges and Annual Percentage Rates

The terms *finance charge* and *annual percentage rate* tell the consumer the same thing—the cost of credit—but each is expressed in a different way.

Finance Charges The **finance charge** is the cost of credit expressed in dollars and cents. It must take into account interest costs plus any other charges connected with credit. For example, yearly membership fees for the use of a credit card are included in the finance charge.

Computing Finance Charges The way finance charges are computed is an important factor in determining the cost of credit. The method can vary from creditor to creditor. Store charge accounts and credit cards use one of four methods to determine how much people will pay for credit: previous balance, average daily balance,

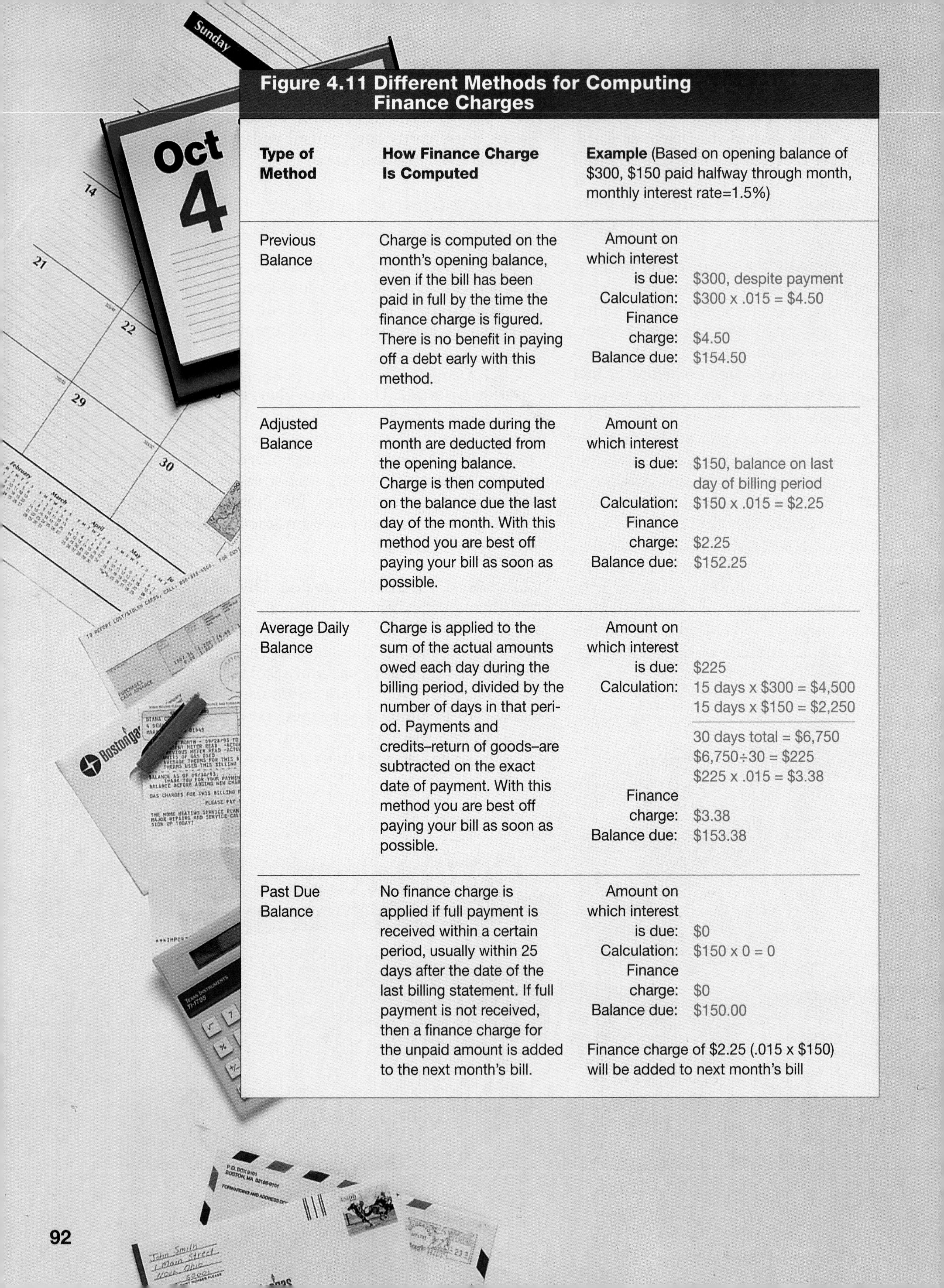

Figure 4.11 Different Methods for Computing Finance Charges

Type of Method	How Finance Charge Is Computed	Example (Based on opening balance of $300, $150 paid halfway through month, monthly interest rate=1.5%)	
Previous Balance	Charge is computed on the month's opening balance, even if the bill has been paid in full by the time the finance charge is figured. There is no benefit in paying off a debt early with this method.	Amount on which interest is due: Calculation: Finance charge: Balance due:	$300, despite payment $300 x .015 = $4.50 $4.50 $154.50
Adjusted Balance	Payments made during the month are deducted from the opening balance. Charge is then computed on the balance due the last day of the month. With this method you are best off paying your bill as soon as possible.	Amount on which interest is due: Calculation: Finance charge: Balance due:	$150, balance on last day of billing period $150 x .015 = $2.25 $2.25 $152.25
Average Daily Balance	Charge is applied to the sum of the actual amounts owed each day during the billing period, divided by the number of days in that period. Payments and credits–return of goods–are subtracted on the exact date of payment. With this method you are best off paying your bill as soon as possible.	Amount on which interest is due: Calculation: Finance charge: Balance due:	$225 15 days x $300 = $4,500 15 days x $150 = $2,250 30 days total = $6,750 $6,750÷30 = $225 $225 x .015 = $3.38 $3.38 $153.38
Past Due Balance	No finance charge is applied if full payment is received within a certain period, usually within 25 days after the date of the last billing statement. If full payment is not received, then a finance charge for the unpaid amount is added to the next month's bill.	Amount on which interest is due: Calculation: Finance charge: Balance due:	$0 $150 x 0 = 0 $0 $150.00 Finance charge of $2.25 (.015 x $150) will be added to next month's bill

adjusted balance, or past due balance. Each method applies the interest rate to an account's balance at a different point during the month. The different methods can result in widely varying finance charges. Figure 4.11 describes these four methods for computing and shows the difference in finance charges that can result. Creditors must inform their customers in writing of which method they use for computing finance charges.

Annual Percentage Rates The **annual percentage rate** (APR) is the cost of credit expressed as a yearly percentage. Like the finance charge, the APR must take into account any non-interest costs of credit such as a membership fee. Figure 4.12 shows how a sample APR affects the cost of credit.

Understanding and using APRs makes it easier to shop around for the best deal on credit. For example, if you are looking for a car, creditor A might ask for a large down payment and offer in return small monthly payments. Creditor B might not require a down payment at all, but charge large monthly payments instead. Creditor C might ask for small payments over a much longer period of time.

Knowing which creditor is charging the most for credit would be very difficult without some guide for comparison. The APR provides that guide by allowing consumers to compare costs regardless of the dollar amount of those costs or the length of the credit agreement. Suppose creditor A is charging an APR of 16 percent, while creditor B is charging 17 percent, and creditor C is charging 18½ percent. On a yearly basis, creditor C is charging the most for credit and creditor A the least.

Figure 4.12 ▶
Annual Percentage Rates
Say you charge $200 worth of clothes. The interest rate charged to you, let's say, is 10 percent, but the annual fee for the credit card is $5. Your APR will be $20 of interest plus the $5 fee, or 12½ percent. The APR is normally larger than the interest because it includes the noninterest cost of extending credit.

Credit Card Charge of $200 at 10% Interest		
Amount Charged	$200.00	$200.00
Interest at 10%	$20.00	$20.00
Annual Membership Fee	none	$5.00
APR	10%	12.5%

SECTION 2 REVIEW

Understanding Vocabulary

Define commercial bank, savings and loan association, savings banks, credit union, finance company, consumer finance company, charge account, regular charge account, credit limit, revolving charge account, installment charge account, credit card, debit card, finance charge, annual percentage rate.

Reviewing Objectives

1. What are the six types of financial institutions?
2. How do regular, revolving, and installment charge accounts differ?
3. How are credit and debit cards used?
4. How is a finance charge different from an annual percentage rate?

3 *Applying for Credit*

Several Factors Determine a Person's Credit Worthiness

When you apply for credit, you usually will be asked to fill out a credit application. Once you have filled out the application, the store, bank, or other lending agency will hire a **credit bureau,** a private business, to do a **credit check.** This investigation will reveal your income, any current debts, details about your personal life, and how well you have repaid debts in the past.

The Credit Rating

The information supplied by the credit bureau provides the creditor with a **credit rating** for you. This is a rating of the risk—good, average, or poor—involved in lending money to a specific person or business. If a person has a history of poor credit

Figure 4.13
Three Credit Check Factors

A **Capacity to Pay**
Capacity to pay is related to income and debt. If your employment has been spotty, your capacity to pay will be considered questionable. The amount of debt that you are already carrying is also a factor. If your debts are large, creditors will be reluctant to loan you more.

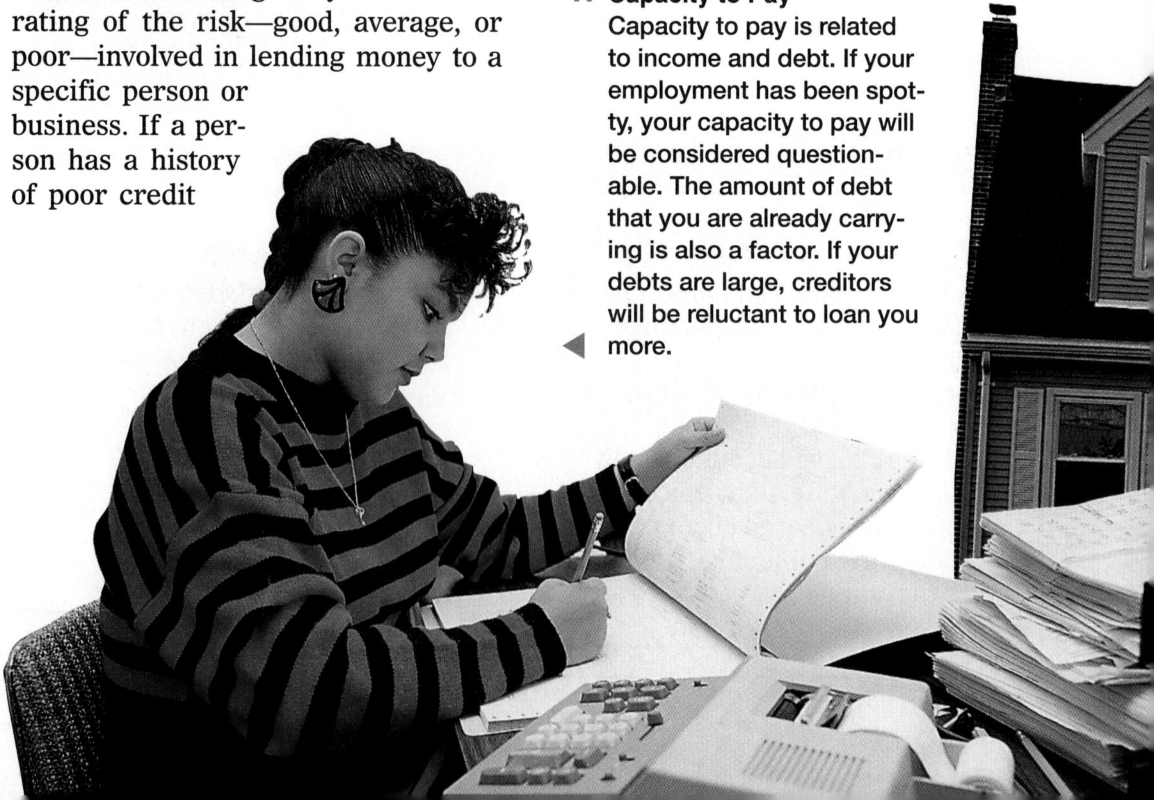

use—usually late in paying debts—he or she will receive a poor credit rating. As a result, the creditor reviewing the credit check will be less willing to lend that person money.

Though past history of credit use is important in deciding a person's creditworthiness, the creditor also looks at three other factors that a credit check reveals. These are: capacity to pay, character, and collateral (kuh-LAT-uh-ruhl). Figure 4.13 examines these three factors.

Secured Loans Usually when a bank, S&L, or other financial institution makes a loan, it will ask for collateral from the borrower. The **collateral** may be the item purchased with the loan money, such as a house or car. It may be something of value the borrower already owns. For example, a borrower might offer his or her car as collateral to obtain cash for home improvements. The borrower then signs a legal agreement allowing the lender to claim the collateral if the loan is not repaid. A loan that is backed up with collateral in this way is called a **secured loan.**

Unsecured Loans Usually a young person will have little to offer as collateral. When dealing with a trusted customer, financial institutions will sometimes lend money on the person's reputation alone. Such a loan is called an **unsecured loan.** It is not guaranteed by anything other than a promise to repay it. Most young people have not had enough experience

B Character ▶
Character refers to a person's reputation as a reliable and trustworthy person—educational background, whether or not he or she has had any problems with the law, and any other factors that might indicate something questionable.

◀ C Collateral
Lenders also consider collateral. The size of your capital, or personal wealth, is important because it indicates your past ability to save and accumulate. It also indicates your present ability to pay off a loan, even if you lose your job, because you could sell some of your belongings in order to make the payments.

◀ **Figure 4.14**
Cosigning a Loan
A bank will sometimes lend money to a
person without a financial reputation if
he or she has a cosigner. A **cosigner** is
a person who signs a loan contract
along with the borrower and promises to
repay the loan if the borrower does not.

with borrowing and repaying money to have established this type of trust. See Figure 4.14.

Your Responsibilities as a Borrower

Once you have applied for credit and obtained it, you have also taken on responsibilities. After all, the businesses that gave you credit expect to earn a profit, although in earning that profit they are helping you satisfy your consumer needs by allowing you to buy goods and services on credit.

Paying on Time If you do not pay your debts on time, the costs to businesses are higher. At the very least, there will be extra mailing costs to send **past-due notices.** The business that lends you money may have to hire a collection agency to help get back the money loaned to you. If you never pay off your debt, the lending institution has to write it off and take a loss.

When lending institutions end up paying higher costs, they have to pass these costs on to all consumers in the form of higher prices—higher interest rates charged. Ethical consumers pay their debts on time except under extraordinary circumstances.

Another thing happens when you do not pay your debts. You get a bad credit history. You may then have a difficult or impossible time when you really need credit for something else, say, to purchase a house. Consumers who cannot obtain credit sometimes find it difficult to achieve their personal goals.

Keeping Records If you applied for a credit card and got one, you have additional responsibilities. You need to keep a complete record of all the charges you made. This way you will not go over your credit limit in any one month. You also have the responsibility of notifying the credit-card issuer immediately if your card is lost or stolen.

SECTION 3 REVIEW

Understanding Vocabulary
Define credit bureau, credit check, credit rating, collateral, secured loan, unsecured loan, cosigner, past-due notices.

Reviewing Objectives
1. What four factors determine a person's credit rating?
2. What are your responsibilities as a borrower?

Technology Skills

Using a Word Processor

Has your teacher ever asked you to turn in a report that had to be typed and formatted correctly? Word processing software can help you.

The Functions of the Programs

Most word processing programs perform the same basic functions. A few simple commands are all you really need to know to begin.

- **Creating a Document (File)** When you start your word processor, the screen will probably show either a blank document or a main menu. If you see a blank document, you are ready to enter text. If you see a main menu, select the option that says "Create a document" or "Open a file."
- **Inserting and Deleting Text** To insert new text, move the cursor to the space where you want to place new text. Then, you type it in. If you want to remove text, highlight the unwanted text and press the command key(s) for deleting copy.
- **Formatting Text** Press the "Format" button and follow the directions to tell the computer how you want your text to look.
- **Saving Your Document** Before you turn off your word processor, save your text either onto the computer's hard drive or onto a floppy disc. Name the document in such a way so you can later identify what the file contains.

Practicing the Skill

❶ Open a new word processing file, change the line spacing to double, and type a heading using your own name, your teacher's name, and today's date.
❷ Type the title of the excerpt in **Figure A** in all caps, centered. Then type the body of the excerpt.
❸ Proofread. Then save your document as TRUST, print the document, and close it.

Figure A
THE PRIVATE SECTOR: ITS ROLE IN RESTORING TRUST IN GOVERNMENT

Our economy is going through a profound transition, a sea of change from a product/manufacturing economy to a knowledge-based economy. The transition is cataclysmic—affecting millions of jobs, futures, quality of life, and even our social cohesion.

. . . The challenge for government is how it should make the transition that it is just beginning. First, to catch up and, then, to keep pace with the knowledge economy. About half of the improvements in business productivity during the past 20 years are due to computerization and automation. But the transition was very painful. It involved redesigning jobs, eliminating jobs, changing virtually all of the business processes.

In a fundamental way, government leaders at all levels should take advantage of what we learned to avoid some blind alleys as they seek to create similar changes in government.

–Dan G. Mead,
CEO Tenneco, 1997

SECTION 4 Government Regulation of Credit

SECTION 4 FOCUS

Terms to Know usury law, bankruptcy

Objectives *After reading this section, you should be able to:*

1. State how the **Equal Credit Opportunity Act** affected consumer credit.
2. Describe **state usury laws**.
3. Explain why a person might declare **personal bankruptcy**.

The Government Regulates Credit to Protect Consumers

Both the federal and state governments regulate the credit industry. Most states, for example, have set a maximum on the interest rates charged for certain types of credit. The federal government has also passed laws designed to increase the flow of credit information to consumers and to protect consumers from unfair credit practices.

The Truth in Lending Act of 1968 was the first of a series of major federal laws that greatly expanded the government's role in protecting users of consumer credit. An important aspect of the government regulation of credit is to make sure that everyone has equal access.

The Equal Credit Opportunity Act

In 1974 Congress enacted the Equal Credit Opportunity Act (ECOA) as an addition to the Truth in Lending Act of 1968. Among other things, those who provide credit cannot deny you such credit solely on the basis of your race, religion, national origin, gender, marital status, or age. In addition, no one is allowed to discriminate against you in offering you credit simply because your income might come from public assistance benefits.

Because there had been so much credit discrimination against married women, the 1974 Credit Act made it illegal for a creditor to require an applicant's spouse to sign unless an application for credit was made jointly by husband and wife. See Figure 4.15. If a woman on her own qualifies for the amount and terms of credit requested, she does not have to get her husband to sign the credit application. Figure 4.16 (pages 100–101) presents the important points about five major federal government laws that regulate credit.

State Usury Laws

A law restricting the amount of interest that can be charged for credit is called a **usury** (YOOZH-uh-ree) **law.** Often states set up different maximum rates for different types of consumer credit. Maximum rates on charge accounts and credit cards, for example, are often about 18 percent a year, or 1½ percent per month. Consumer finance agencies, in contrast, are often allowed to charge higher rates because their loans involve higher risks.

Interest Ceilings The ceilings for usury laws were controversial in past years when interest ceilings in many states were as low as 6 or 10 percent. When interest rates in general began to rise in the early 1970s, many lenders complained that they could not keep within such ceilings and still make a profit. In states that were slow to raise interest ceilings, some lenders cut back on the amount of credit they offered. Others stopped lending money completely. Many consumers, particularly those who were poor credit risks, found it hard to obtain credit. People opposed to raising interest ceilings claimed people with lower incomes would not be able to afford credit. Supporters of higher ceilings claimed that low rates made credit less available because it was less profitable for lenders. Low rates actually hurt those they were supposed to help.

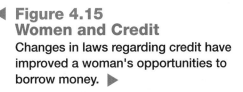

◀ **Figure 4.15**
Women and Credit
Changes in laws regarding credit have improved a woman's opportunities to borrow money. ▶

Figure 4.16 Major Federal Laws Regulating Consumer Credit

Name of Law	Main Purpose	Major Provisions
Truth in Lending Act (1968)	Ensures that consumers are fully informed about the costs and conditions of borrowing	• Creditors must keep borrowers informed in writing of a credit agreement's annual percentage rate, the way charges and fees are calculated, and the payment schedule. • Consumers have a 3-day cooling-off period in which to cancel certain contracts. • Consumers are liable for only the first $50 in unauthorized purchases made on a credit card before it is reported lost or stolen.
Fair Credit Reporting Act (1970)	Protects the privacy and accuracy of information in a credit check	• If refused credit, a consumer can request from the lender the name and address of the credit bureau issuing the report. • The credit bureau, if requested, must provide at least a summary of a consumer's credit file. • If the consumer claims part of the file is in error, the bureau must correct the record or explain why it thinks the information is correct. • A consumer can have a statement of disagreement placed in his or her file about the item. • Outdated information must be removed from a consumer's file. • Credit records can be shown only to those with a true business need.
Equal Credit Opportunity Act (1974)	Prohibits discrimination in giving credit on the basis of sex, race, color, religion, national	• The same guidelines for credit worthiness must be applied to all borrowers. • Lenders cannot extend credit to an individual on terms different from those given another individual in a similar economic situation.

Personal Bankruptcy

If you take out too many loans, use too many credit cards, and pile up debts that you cannot pay off, you may have to file personal **bankruptcy.** In bankruptcy, debtors give most of what they own to be distributed to their creditors. The Constitution authorizes Congress to establish bankruptcy laws. Certain debts, such as taxes, cannot be discharged.

If you declare personal bankruptcy, you may have a fresh start. Be aware, however, that it is very difficult to reestablish credit as long as the bankruptcy proceedings remain on your credit record. That is why choosing bankruptcy to get out of your credit "mess" should be a last resort. Also, when you declare bankruptcy, you are making sure that your creditors will never be paid off (at least not in full) for what they loaned you.

Figure 4.16 Major Federal Laws Regulating Consumer Credit

Name of Law	Main Purpose	Major Provisions
Equal Credit Opportunity Act (1974) (cont.)	origin, marital status, age, or receipt of public assistance	▪ Questions about age, sex, and marital status can be asked only if those questions relate directly to a person's ability to repay a loan. ▪ Loan applicants must receive notice of a decision within 30 days. If the loan is denied, the lender must give the reasons or inform the applicant of the right to request the information.
Fair Credit Billing Act (1974)	Sets up a procedure for the quick correction of mistakes that appear on consumer credit accounts	▪ Consumers may challenge a billing statement for errors. ▪ Consumers have 60 days to notify a creditor of a disputed item. The creditor must investigate and either correct the mistake or explain why the charge is not an error. ▪ While the mistake is checked, the consumer can withhold payment of the disputed sum but must pay for other items on the account. ▪ Under certain circumstances, a consumer can withhold payment for merchandise that has been purchased and found defective. ▪ Creditors must supply consumers with a statement of their rights under the act.
Fair Debt Collection Practices Act (1977)	Prevents abuse by professional debt collectors; applies to anyone employed to collect debts owed to others; does not apply to banks or other businesses that collect their own accounts	▪ Collectors can contact a person other than the debtor only to discover the debtor's location. ▪ The debtor cannot be contacted at an inconvenient time or place. ▪ All harassing behavior is prohibited. This includes the use or threat of violence, the use of annoying or repetitive phone calls, etc.

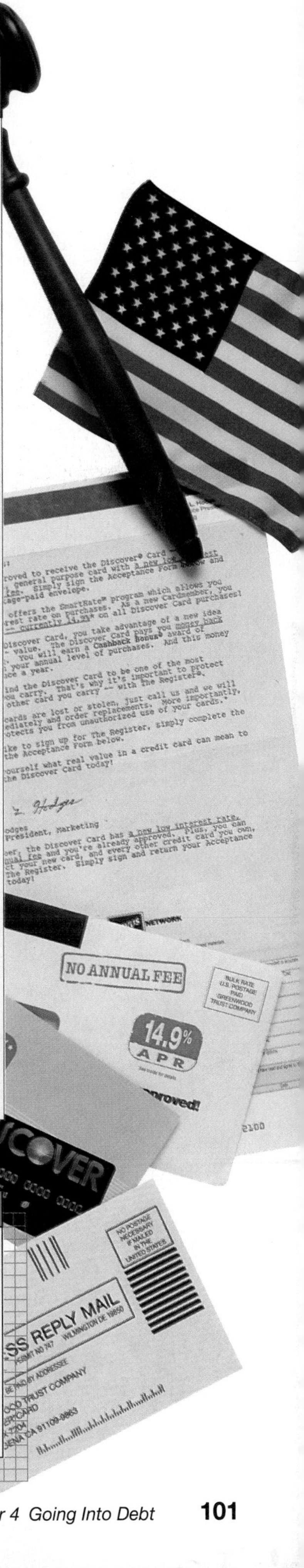

SECTION 4 REVIEW

Understanding Vocabulary
Define usury law, bankruptcy.

Reviewing Objectives
1. What are the major provisions of the Equal Credit Opportunity Act?

2. Why do many states have usury laws?

3. Why might a person declare personal bankruptcy?

Readings in Economics

DATELINE: CHANGING TIMES | MARCH 1991

DIGGING OUT OF THE DEBT TRAP

by Kristin Davis and Rebecca Little

It's no surprise that consumer credit counselors say they're getting busier. Here's what they advise for consumers overwhelmed with debt.

Don't avoid creditors. Instead of skipping a payment, contact creditors to explain why you can't pay. "Creditors will fall off their chairs if you contact them first," says Tom Hufford, executive director of the Consumer Credit Counseling Service (CCCS) of Northeastern Indiana. They have a lot of latitude early on, he says, to temporarily waive or reduce payments.

Beware of consolidation loans. Many people hope to stretch out payments over a

Home Equity Loan
40% Interest

longer period with a consolidation loan. But the finance companies that offer those loans typically charge high interest rates. Using a home-equity loan for this purpose may seem an ideal solution—interest rates are relatively low and inter-

est on up to $100,000 is tax-deductible. But your home is collateral and you risk losing it if you fall behind. Warns Hufford: "You start again with zero balances on your credit cards, and old habits die hard."

Work out your own plan. Although secured creditors may not be as flexible, unsecured creditors may be receptive to a revised payment plan. William Kent Brunette, author of *Conquer Your Debt*, suggests figuring out how much you can afford to pay toward all debts monthly and prorating payments based on how much you owe each creditor. Assure creditors that they're all being treated equally and that you won't take on new debt until the accounts are paid, he advises. . . .

Seek credit counseling. If bill collectors' calls get unpleasant, contact a CCCS. These nonprofit agencies can serve as a buffer between you and anxious creditors.

• THINK ABOUT IT •

1. *What four major things do the authors urge indebted consumers to do?*

2. *What is the drawback of a consolidation loan?*

ECONOMICS IN ACTION

Going Into Debt

Setting up the Video

With your classmates, view "Going Into Debt" on the videodisc *Economics in Action.* The video focuses on different methods of using credit. It explains that credit card companies charge interest on unpaid balances, and a news segment considers the interest rates charged for credit card purchases. It then describes loans, which have lower interest rates than credit cards, and differentiates between secured and unsecured loans.

**Chapter 5
Disc 1, Side 1**

View the video by scanning the bar code or by entering the chapter number on your keypad and pressing Search. *(Also available in VHS format.)*

Hands-On Activity

Work with a group of your classmates to compare the cost of purchasing a $100 item with a credit card with the cost of obtaining a $100 loan to purchase the same item. Assume that it will take you one year to pay off the loan. You should study ads to find typical credit card and loan rates and terms at financial institutions in your community. Use the information you find to calculate the total cost of the purchase. After your group has completed the comparison, share your findings with the rest of the class. Then participate in a class discussion on the merits of each type of borrowing.

SURFING THE "NET"

Credit Cards

In this chapter you learned about consumer loans and credit. A major type of credit is extended directly to an individual, without that person's having to borrow money first. This credit may be in the form of a credit card. In recent years, more Americans have begun using credit cards regularly. You can learn more about credit cards and the interest they charge on the Internet.

Getting There

1. Use a search engine. Type in the word *credit card.*
2. After typing in *credit card,* enter words like the following to focus your search: *rates, compa-*
nies, interest, visa, discovercard, mastercard, bravo, American Express.
3. The search engine will provide you with a number of links to follow. Links are "pointers" to different sites on the Internet and often appear as blue, underlined words.

What to Do When You Are There

Click on the links to navigate through the pages of information. Gather your findings. Using your word processor, create a document showing at least five credit card companies and their addresses along with the interest each charges. Compute how much interest a consumer would pay each year on a $5,000 balance.

4 Review

Identifying Key Terms

Write a short paragraph about the different types of lending institutions and their differences using all of the following terms.

commercial bank (p. 86)   credit union (p. 87)
savings banks (p. 86)   consumer finance
                               company (p. 88)

Write the letter of the definition in Column B below that correctly defines each term in Column A.

Column A
1. principal (p. 80)
2. usury law (p. 99)
3. collateral (p. 95)
4. annual percentage rate (p. 93)
5. unsecured loan (p. 95)

Column B
a. restricts the amount of interest that can be charged for credit
b. requires only a promise to repay
c. amount of money borrowed in a loan
d. something of value that a borrower uses as a promise of loan repayment
e. cost of credit expressed as a yearly percentage

Recalling Facts and Ideas

Section 1
1. What do you have to pay when you borrow?
2. How is taking out a loan similar to buying an item on credit?
3. People typically use installment debt to buy what type of goods?
4. Why do people use credit?

Section 2
5. What are the six types of basic lending insti-

tutions in our economy?
6. What are some of the most common types of credit cards used today?
7. When you take out a loan, what do you call the total cost of credit expressed in dollars and cents?

Section 3
8. When you make an application for a loan, what are four factors that a creditor looks at to determine whether you are creditworthy?
9. What is the difference between a secured and unsecured loan?
10. What are your responsibilities as a borrower?

Section 4
11. What does the Equal Credit Opportunity Act of 1974 prohibit?
12. States often restrict the maximum amount of interest that can be charged on loans. What are such laws called?
13. What are the three important federal laws regulating consumer credit?

Critical Thinking

Section 1
Evaluating Information In deciding whether to pay cash or use credit for a personal purchase, what are the costs involved and the benefits of each choice?

Section 2
Identifying Alternatives How would you decide which of the six types of lending institutions discussed in this section would be most appropriate for a particular loan?

Section 3

Making Comparisons What are the differences between a secured and an unsecured loan?

Section 4

Demonstrating Reasoned Judgment If you declare personal bankruptcy, your creditors clearly lose. What ethical concerns should you have before ever taking this action?

Applying Economic Concepts

The Role of Government Sometimes credit cards are lost or stolen. The owner must take steps to keep his or her card from being used by an unauthorized person. Find out by researching the Truth in Lending Act what a credit card holder must do when his or her card is lost or stolen.

Chapter Projects

1. **Individual Project** Call various retail stores in your area as well as some gas stations and ask them to send you a credit card application. Write a list of the questions asked that are virtually the same on each application.
2. **Cooperative Learning Project** Work in small groups to create a loan application that is appropriate for high school students and circulate it in class. Based on the application, discuss why it is or is not difficult to decide who should receive loans. Is it difficult to decide who should *not* receive loans?

Reviewing Skills

Using a Word Processor

Computing Finance Charges Reread the information in Figure 4.11 on page 92. Then review the material on using a word processor on page 97. Use what you have learned to reconstruct the table in Figure 4.11 on your word processor. Follow these steps to construct your table:

1. Select "Create a document" from your computer's main menu.
2. Select "Table" from the options appearing on your screen and insert a table with three columns and five rows.
3. Key the information from Figure 4.11 into your document.
4. Proofread your final document.
5. Save your document as "Credit Card Rates."
6. Print your final document.

Technology Activity
Using the Internet

Refer to the ads for credit that you collected in Your Economics Journal on page 79. Choose one of these ads and design a consumer-oriented brochure advertising the specific company's services. Be certain to use the persuasive style of writing in the brochure because the goal of the brochure is to attract new business. Use the Internet to gather information on brochures or to view brochures from financial institutions. If the company that you choose for your brochure has its own Internet address, be certain to visit the site for more information and to include the address in your completed brochure.

5 BUYING THE NECESSITIES: FOOD AND CLOTHING

How often do you buy a jacket?

How long will the jacket last?

Does each jacket's price have anything to do with how long it will last?

Why does the style of jackets change?

What happens to the value of a jacket when it is out of style?

Your Economics Journal

Keep track of where your parents purchase food over a period of one week. List the types of food stores and the items purchased for each type. Next to each type of food store indicate why your parents went there.

Grocery Shopping Is a Skill You Can Learn

Because of our diverse ethnic groups, Americans consume a great variety of foods. They can choose from thousands of different food products and buy them at thousands of stores. Hundreds of brands offer numerous choices: sliced carrots, whole carrots, carrots with peas—canned or frozen. In all, American consumers spend hundreds of billions of dollars a year on food.

Comparison Shopping

Because American families spend so much for food, comparison shopping is important. A consumer should, however, do only as much comparison shopping as is worthwhile to that person. It does not pay a shopper to go far out of his or her way to shop at a store that has only a few needed items at low prices. Such savings would be outweighed by the additional costs of time and transportation.

Reading advertisements is a good, inexpensive way to comparison shop. Food store ads describe sales and often contain cents-off coupons.

Comparison shopping involves making comparisons among brands and sizes as well as stores. You need to decide not only where to shop but what to shop for. Figure 5.1 will also be a useful guide.

Food Stores

Figure 5.2 shows the three major types of stores. Each has its own characteristics.

Figure 5.2
Major Types of Food Stores
Where you choose to shop for food regularly can have a major impact on your budget.

B Warehouse Food Store
The **warehouse food store** has only a *limited number of brands and items*. They are less expensive than in supermarkets, however. In many warehouse stores, goods are *sold only by the case.* Therefore, warehouse food stores are best for consumers who can buy in large quantities. ▼

C Convenience Stores
Convenience stores seem to be everywhere. They are usually open 16 to 24 hours a day and carry a limited selection of items. The price per unit of almost anything is higher than in a supermarket or warehouse store because consumers are paying for the cost of convenience. ▼

A Supermarkets
Just about anything in the way of meats, fresh vegetables, paper products, canned goods, and so on, can be bought in a supermarket. Prices may be relatively high, however, so it is important to be aware of supermarket sales.

Brand-Name Products Versus Private-Labeled Products When you go shopping in virtually any food store, many of the food items have well-known brand names. Some food stores also carry regional brands that are found only in certain areas of the country.

As an alternative to expensive national brands, some big supermarket chains as well as club wholesale chains carry their own store-brand products. These are also called **private-labeled products.** According to some consumer surveys, it is possible to save as much as 40 percent by buying store-brand (private-labeled) products. As Figure 5.3 shows, you can save even more when you buy generic or bulk items.

The Trade-Off Between Price, Quantity, and Quality There is often a trade-off between quality and price in the products you buy. A lower-priced generic dishwasher soap might leave a slight film on your drinking glasses compared to a more expensive national-brand alternative.

Often you will find that the larger the quantity of any item you buy in a supermarket, the lower the per-unit price. Most states require stores to provide unit pricing for food and other products. That makes it easy to compare prices not only for different brands, but for different sizes of the same brand. For example, the price of milk might be expressed in terms of cents per ounce. You can then tell how much you save per ounce if you buy milk in larger containers.

Cents-Off Coupons Many manufacturers give cents-off coupons as shown in Figure 5.4. To take advantage of them, a consumer has to buy the brand, size, and quantity named on the coupon. The store then reduces the price paid by the amount printed on the coupon. The manufacturer, in turn, pays the store.

Convenience Foods In most food stores, you can buy either foods that require preparation, such as fresh meat and vegetables, or foods that require little or no preparation, such as complete frozen dinners. The latter are called convenience foods and usually require no work other than heating. Some nutritionists (noo-TRISH-uh-nists)—experts on food and health—believe that convenience foods are

Figure 5.3
Generic and Bulk Foods
Some food products are available in brand-name, store-label, generic, or bulk form. Generally, price decreases in that order. ▼

unhealthful. They believe they contain too many added chemicals, too much sugar, and too many preservatives. The economic issue involved is time.

The purchase of a convenience food involves a trade-off. Convenience foods are more expensive than foods that you must prepare. Because of the higher price you pay when you buy convenience foods, you sacrifice the purchase of other goods and services. You are gaining more time for leisure or making extra money, however, because convenience foods require less work. Convenience foods illustrate one of the situations in which the consumer must choose between having more free time or having more money to spend on other items.

◀ **Figure 5.4**
Coupon Trade-Off
If you make a habit of using coupons, you can reduce your food bill by more than 10 percent over a one-year period. The use of such coupons, however, requires time—the time to collect and match them to items when shopping. Because time is a scarce resource, you have to decide if the money you save using coupons is worth the time you spend.

SECTION 1 REVIEW

Understanding Vocabulary
Define warehouse food store, convenience stores, private-labeled products.

Reviewing Objectives
❶ What are the advantages of comparison food shopping?
❷ How do the three kinds of food stores differ?

Personal Perspective

Barbara Ward on Saving Our Resources for the Future

Profile

- 1914-1981
- born in England
- educated in France, Germany, and England
- lectured on the growing gap between the rich nations and the poor nations
- authored many books, including *The West at Bay* (1948), *Nationalism and Ideology* (1967), *The Rich Nations and the Poor Nations* (1962), *Spaceship Earth* (1966), and *Only One Earth* (1972) with René Dubos

Ward's earlier works, such as *The Rich Nations and the Poor Nations*, emphasized the growing gap between the wealth of different countries. Her later works, including *Only One Earth* excerpted below, extended her ideas to look at the availability of resources such as energy for the future.

. . . But the really new risk, foreseen in the past by only a few of the world's economists, is that such a pressure of rising demand may begin to put intolerable strains on what had appeared to be the planet's limitless resources. This risk had been masked in the thrusting nineteenth century by the opening up of all the planet's temperate lands to European settlement and later by the extraordinary productivity of new forms of energy and chemical transformations.

Ward offers ideas for planning for the future.

. . . The first step toward devising a strategy for planet Earth is for the nations to accept a collective responsibility for discovering more—much more—about the natural system and how it is affected by man's activities and vice versa. This implies cooperative monitoring, research, and study on an unprecedented scale. It implies an intensive world-wide network for the systematic exchange of knowledge and experience.

. . . Here again, no one nation, not even groups of nations, can, acting separately, avoid the tragedy of increasing divisions between wealthy north and poverty-stricken south in our planet. No nations, on their own, can offset the risk of deepening disorder. . . . Either they will move on to a community based upon a more systematic sharing of wealth—through progressive income tax, through general policies for education, shelter, health, and housing—or they will break down in revolt and anarchy.

Checking for Understanding

1. Why does Ward believe that resources once regarded as unlimited are proving to be limited?
2. What does she believe should be done now to prepare for the future?
3. According to Ward's view of the world, what should happen to the availability of such necessary items as food and clothing in the future? Do you agree or disagree?

SECTION 2 Clothing Choices

SECTION 2 FOCUS

Terms to Know durability, service flow

Objectives *After reading this section, you should be able to:*

① Explain how **personal values affect clothing choices**.

② List three factors that determine **clothing value**.

③ Decide when to take advantage of **clothing sales**.

Factors to Consider When Buying Clothing

Americans spend about $400 billion annually on clothing and other personal products, as Figure 5.5 shows. Most people could buy a few very durable, sturdy, and even good-looking pieces of clothing that would last much longer than their owners might want to keep them. By purchasing such clothing, consumers could reduce their clothing budget considerably. These clothes would protect them from the cold, sun, wind, and so on. The clothes, however, would not serve another purpose—variety. Variety is just one factor involved in clothing choice. Custom, attitude about one's self, and values are other factors that cannot be judged statistically.

Figure 5.5 Sales of Clothing and Personal Products
Personal care and clothing are huge industries. How many dollars does each category on this graph represent? ▼

Clothing and Personal Values

Historically, people's dress reflected their social position, or status. When the American colonies were founded, the influence of social class on clothing began to break down. In this country today, clothing is more a reflection of personal values than of position. In this sense, the clothing that a person buys makes a statement about his or her values. For example, it may not be important to you to have special clothes to wear for a date, while it may be important to someone else. An individual's values are linked to the larger value system—family, friends, and culture. See **Figure 5.6** (pages 114–115).

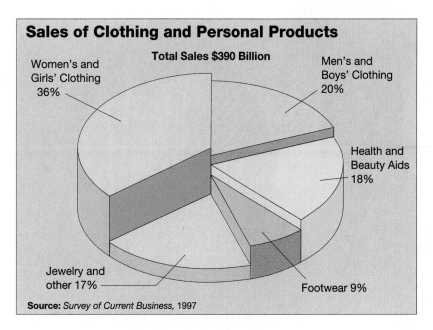

Sales of Clothing and Personal Products

Total Sales $390 Billion

Women's and Girls' Clothing 36%

Men's and Boys' Clothing 20%

Health and Beauty Aids 18%

Jewelry and other 17%

Footwear 9%

Source: *Survey of Current Business,* 1997

Comparing Clothing Value

Comparison shopping is an important part of buying wisely. Comparing value in clothing means more than simply purchasing an item from the store that offers the best price. Clothing value depends on at least three other factors: style, durability, and cost of care.

Style You may be able to buy the minimum amount of clothing you need at a very low cost. You will, however, generally give up style to do it. Wearing clothes that are stylish—up-to-date—is usually expensive because you need to buy new clothes each year.

Wearing current styles costs more than wearing what are called classic styles, which are the more basic clothing designs and colors that do not change much through the years. Again, you are faced with a trade-off. Should you buy stylish clothes each year to keep up with fashion and have

Figure 5.6
Why So Many Clothes?
Several major factors combine to influence the types and styles of clothing we choose to wear.

A Customs
- Customs sometimes determine styles of clothing.
- Customs change slowly.
- Among some traditional cultures, self-adornment is a strong motivation.

B Self-Image ▲
- Clothing conveys a message to others about what you do, what you believe, and what you are.
- We dress to preserve our self-image. This is aesthetic; it has to do solely with our ideas of beauty.

less money to spend on other items? Or should you buy less stylish clothes that you can wear from year to year and have more money?

Durability The ability of an item to last is known as **durability.** The longer a piece of clothing—or any item—lasts, the more durable it is. When you purchase an item of clothing, you are purchasing it for the service flow that it yields per time period. This **service flow** is how much you get to use it over time and the value you place on this use. If you buy a jacket that will last three years and costs $300, the cost per service flow per year is $100.

A consumer would not really be comparing similar value if he or she automatically bought the less expensive coat, dress, or shirt. In the long run, it might be more expensive. An inexpensive but poorly made pair of pants, for example, might have to be replaced after one season. A slightly more expensive but more durable pair might last for several seasons.

In comparison shopping for clothing, you should try to determine how long an item will last and how long you will need it. Then you should compare prices. Suppose you think Coat A will last twice as long as Coat B, and Coat A costs only 20 percent more. Then Coat A is a better buy. You should also try to decide, however, if the coat will still be in style in a year.

D Variety
- Many people want to have different "looks" for different occasions.
- People in different climates need different wardrobes for summer and winter. ▶

C Values
- Values determine choice of clothes because such choice is a statement of what we consider important.
- Clothing reflects values instilled in us by society as well as our own individual attitudes and values.
- Values inherent in clothes are self-expression, esteem, and comfort.
- Unconventional dress often identifies a person as part of a small group. ▼

In deciding on clothing purchases, ask yourself the following questions:

1. What do I already have? Check the condition of the clothes you have, and see what you need to replace.
2. What clothes do I need for:
   - school?
   - job?
   - social life?
   - recreational activities?
3. How many changes of clothes do I need to meet my minimum requirements for:
   - cleanliness?
   - variety?
   - social status, or standing in society?
4. How do my answers to questions 1 through 3 compare with the amount of money I have to spend?
5. Should I pay cash or charge my purchases? Consider the trade-offs involved in paying cash or using credit.

Cost of Care Finally, the cost of care is another important factor in deciding value. Two shirts or blouses may cost the same, but one may need dry cleaning, an expensive alternative to hand or machine washing. When deciding on the best choice in a clothing purchase you must consider maintenance costs.

Figure 5.8 ▶
Seasonal Sales
In many cases when you buy clothes on sale, you will not be able to wear them until the following year. For example, you might be buying winter clothes at the end of the winter or summer clothes in late August.

Clothing Sales

Clothing sales are numerous throughout the year, and it is easy to become a bargain fanatic, buying sale items just because they are on sale. Before going shopping, wise consumers make a list of the clothing they have and decide what they need. Figure 5.7 can help you evaluate your needs. Take your list with you when you go shopping. It will help you keep your spending within limits. Remember, too, that finding the best deal involves using time.

You should be aware of the timing factor in clothing sales. Generally, a clothing sale occurs when a store owner is trying to get rid of goods that he or she could not sell during the regular selling season. See Figure 5.8.

SECTION 2 REVIEW

Understanding Vocabulary
Define durability, service flow.

Reviewing Objectives
1. How do personal values affect clothing choices?
2. What three factors determine clothing value?
3. When should you buy clothing that is on sale?

LEARNING ECONOMIC SKILLS

Learning About Percentage Changes

Many important economic statistics change every year. Economists use *percentages* to describe such changes. Can you express a change in percentage terms?

Calculating Arithmetic Changes

The calculation of an arithmetic change is a simple task of subtraction. This year Americans consumed 1.6 billion pounds of butter. Last year they consumed 1.5 billion pounds. As **Figure A** shows, the difference is 0.1 billion pounds. This seems large. Is it?

Computing Percentage Change

It is often more meaningful to compare the arithmetic change in a statistic with what that statistic was before it changed. In this example, how does the arithmetic change in pounds of butter consumed from last year to this year (0.1 billion) compare to the total amount consumed last year (1.5 billion pounds)? After all, 0.1 billion pounds of butter sounds like a tremendous amount. Expressed as a percentage of last year, however, it is not so much.

Figure B shows how to determine the percentage change in the amount of butter consumed. First calculate the arithmetic difference, which in this case is 0.1 billion pounds of butter. Then divide the difference by the original quantity (1.5) and multiply by 100.

Figure A

1.6 billion pounds
– 1.5 billion pounds
0.1 billion pounds

Figure B

Increase in butter =
0.1 billion pounds
Original quantity =
1.5 billion pounds
Percentage change =

$\frac{0.1}{1.5} = .067 \times 100 = 6.7$ percent

Figure C
(expressed in thousands)

Year	Men's Suits	Men's Shirts
1999	9,559	90,439
2000	10,062	106,855

Practicing the Skill

1. Last month 3,300,000 women's coats were sold. This month 3,450,000 women's coats were sold. What was the percentage increase in coat sales?
2. Look at **Figure C**. It shows hypothetical annual sales of men's suits and shirts in 1999 and 2000. Which had a greater percentage increase?

Readings in Economics

U.S. NEWS AND WORLD REPORT — **JULY 7, 1997**

LET THEM EAT AHI JERKY

by Kerry Hannon

In Cambridge, Mass., a long line of shoppers formed outside Trader Joe's an hour before the door slid open on its first day of business not long ago. As the locks clicked free, a perfectly sane looking woman, in all likelihood a onetime Los Angeles-area resident, broke ranks, grabbed a cart, and began running down the store's center aisle, shouting, "Yahoo!"

A combination discount warehouse, upscale gourmet deli, and health food store, Trader Joe's has long enjoyed cult-like status in Southern California, where most customers gladly put up with long waits and choked aisles at many of the chain's locations. . . .

Analysts estimate that sales in the stores average about $1,000 per square foot per year, roughly double that of conventional supermarkets and more than triple that of other specialty-food stores. . . .

Part of Trader Joe's appeal is that despite its fancy fare, it doesn't take itself too seriously. The motif, if you can call it that, is vaguely reminiscent of *Gilligan's Island*. The store manager is referred to as "the Captain" and the staff, "Crew Members." . . . Brightly colored plastic fish hang from the ceiling. Seafaring tunes play throughout the day.

Even the food selection is kind of goofy. There's ahi jerky, chili and lime tortilla chips, vegetarian dog biscuits, and pineapple salsa, to name a few. "Trader Joe's has turned shopping from a chore into a culinary treasure hunt," says Gary Hamel, a professor of international

management at the London Business School. "We want our products to be whimsical, tactile, informative, and just plain fun."

• THINK ABOUT IT •

1. *How do sales at Trader Joe's compare with sales at conventional supermarkets?*

2. *How does Trader Joe's try to make shopping fun?*

ECONOMICS IN ACTION

Buying the Necessities: Food and Clothing

Setting up the Video

With your classmates, view "Buying the Necessities: Food and Clothing" on the videodisc *Economics in Action*. The video focuses on guidelines to help a consumer save money on food or clothing purchases, including planning and comparison shopping. It also compares specialty stores, which sell only one type of goods, and department stores, which stock a wide range of goods.

Chapter 7
Disc 1, Side 1

View the video by scanning the bar code or by entering the chapter number on your keypad and pressing Search. *(Also available in VHS format.)*

Hands-On Activity

Work with one of your classmates to prepare a shopping list of five items. You may choose either grocery items that your family uses each week or clothing that you would like to purchase. Using newspaper ads, compare quality and prices of your shopping list items at four or more stores. Identify which store in your community offers the best value on the items you wish to purchase, and explain how you made your choice. Share your findings with the rest of the class.

SURFING THE "NET"

Internet Shopping

In this chapter you learned about shopping for food and clothing. In recent years, many people have begun to use the Internet to shop because of the convenience of shopping without leaving their homes. The products they order are delivered to them within a few days. You can learn more about using your computer to shop for necessities on the Internet

Getting There

1. Use your favorite search engine. Type in the word *shopping*.

2. After typing in *shopping*, enter words like the following to focus your search: *food, clothing, online*.

3. The search engine will provide you with a number of links to follow. Links are "pointers" to different sites on the Internet and often appear as blue, underlined words.

What to Do When You Are There

Select a few items that you would like to purchase. Then click on the links to navigate through the pages of information to find those items. Gather your findings. Using the findings, prepare a short oral presentation describing what items you were seeking and how you found them on the Internet.

5 Review

Identifying Key Terms

Use terms from the following list to fill in the blanks in the sentences below.

service flow (p. 115)   durability (p. 115)
private-labeled   warehouse food
  products (p. 110)   store (p. 109)
convenience stores (p. 109)

    When you are shopping for food, the most expensive place to buy is in __(1)__ . The cheapest place to buy is usually in a __(2)__ . When you are in a store, you will see national brands, generic brands, and __(3)__ . This last kind of food products usually carries the name of the store.

    You can buy clothes that are attractive, but fall apart after a while. They lack the quality of __(4)__ . If you buy a coat that you think will last five years, it will give you a __(5)__ per year.

Recalling Facts and Ideas

Section 1

1. What is one of the best ways to engage in comparison shopping for food products?
2. What are the most expensive and the least expensive places to buy food?
3. What is the trade-off involved when you buy a generic brand rather than a brand-name product?
4. What trade-off does buying convenience food involve?

Section 2

5. What four factors influence the kind of clothing choices people make?
6. What is the normal relationship between how long an article of clothing will last and its price?

7. State two things consumers should remember about clothing sales.

Critical Thinking

Section 1

Identifying Alternatives Warehouse food stores almost always sell food at a lower price than any other place from which you can buy food. Why do some consumers, nonetheless, shop at supermarkets instead of at warehouse stores?

Section 2

Recognizing Bias "I went clothes shopping with Ingrid last weekend. You won't believe what she bought. She went to one of the most expensive stores in the neighborhood and paid way too much for the blouses that she got. I don't know what's wrong with her." Could the opinion this person is expressing ever be valid? Why or why not?

Applying Economic Concepts

Competition and Market Structure Examine the food ads in your local newspaper for one week. Write down those food items that are common to each ad. For example, milk is usually advertised by all supermarkets on a specific day of the week. Compare the prices from the different food stores for the common items advertised. What is the largest percentage difference between the highest and lowest price for an advertised common food item? Are any of the food items advertised at exactly the same price for the same brand and the same size?

Chapter Projects

1. **Individual Project** Go to your favorite clothing store or department store. Look at all of the suits, coats, or dresses. Write down the prices for one type of clothing item, such as a raincoat. With your list in hand, ask a salesperson to show you the most durable and least durable brand. Is there a relationship between the price and what the salesperson believes is the most durable brand? What is that relationship?

2. **Cooperative Learning Project** You now know that the type of clothes that we choose to buy and wear depends on many things such as customs, aesthetic considerations, values, and group identification. Work in small groups to analyze what is most important in determining the clothes that you buy and wear.

   Write down the list of determinants in order of importance. In a class discussion, see if there is a consensus—a meeting of the minds—about which determinant is most important for the class. During the discussion, make sure that you distinguish between what is truly an aesthetic consideration that you, as an individual, and your classmates, as individuals, really believe and what is the result of "peer pressure."

   At the end of this exercise, you might want to discuss the importance of clothing you have seen on television in terms of what you and your friends think is "in style." Are you influenced by clothing styles seen on television? If so, why?

Reviewing Skills

Learning About Percentage Changes

1. **Figuring Percentage Changes** Last year stores in your city sold 26,450 T-shirts. This year those same stores sold 23,160. Describe what happened in terms of percentage of T-shirts sold.

2. **Using Percentages** Study the table below and then apply your skills to determine the numbers that fit in the blank spaces and complete the table.

Price Last Year	Price This Year	Percentage Change in Price
$1.00		53.7%
	$2,000	100%
$5,721.00	$6,821.00	
$2.00	$1.00	

Technology Activity
Using a Spreadsheet

Refer to the list of food purchases you kept track of in Your Economics Journal on page 107. Use this list as the basis of a spreadsheet on grocery prices in your community. Choose at least 5 food stores and at least 10 food products to enter on your spreadsheet. The food stores should be at the top of your spreadsheet. The products should be along the side. Be certain to calculate the price of your "market basket" of products at each store. Then, using a word processor, write a persuasive essay encouraging others to shop at the least expensive store.

6 BUYING THE NECESSITIES: HOUSING AND TRANSPORTATION

Why are Americans so fascinated with cars?

What are the costs of owning a car?

Do you automatically think that you "need" a car?

How much insurance does a car owner need?

What are your alternatives to using a car?

How much does a car depreciate in one year?

Your Economics Journal

Make a record of the number of times that you go from one location to another during a week's period. Each time, list the distances and the mode of transportation. Next to each occasion write reasonable alternative modes of transportation that you could have used.

SECTION 1 FOCUS

Terms to Know real estate taxes, condominium, cooperative, lease, depreciate

Objectives *After reading this section, you should be able to:*

① List five **types of housing** available.

② Explain **the pros and cons of sharing an apartment or house**.

American Consumers Have Many Housing Alternatives

Besides food and clothing, housing and transportation are the two important necessities in virtually everybody's budget. If you are living at home with your parents, you are probably not too concerned with housing. Some day, however, you are going to have to make the decision about renting an apartment or a house. At some time you may have to make the decision about buying a house. As Figure 6.1 shows, construction begins on an average of 1 to 2 million new houses each year. Americans also spend billions of dollars remodeling existing houses.

Figure 6.1 Housing Construction New housing starts peaked in the early 1970s. Although they have decreased since then, Americans still demand about 1.5 million new homes each year.

▼

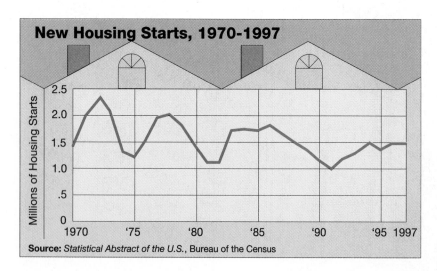

New Housing Starts, 1970-1997

Millions of Housing Starts

2.5
2.0
1.5
1.0
.5
0

1970   '75   '80   '85   '90   '95 1997

Source: *Statistical Abstract of the U.S.*, Bureau of the Census

Types of Housing

The average American family spends about one-fourth of its annual income on housing. The United States has more than 115 million housing units, of which about 60 percent are owned by the people living in them. The rest are rented. Families or individuals are not just buying or renting a place to live. They are also paying for the satisfaction gained by living in a place called "home." The amount of satisfaction depends on many things. Among them are the size of the dwelling, the neighborhood, the quality of construction and furnishings, and how well the house suits the family's or individual's needs. Figure 6.2 explains some types of housing.

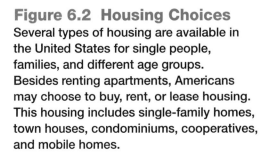

Figure 6.2 Housing Choices
Several types of housing are available in the United States for single people, families, and different age groups. Besides renting apartments, Americans may choose to buy, rent, or lease housing. This housing includes single-family homes, town houses, condominiums, cooperatives, and mobile homes.

A Single-Family Houses
The single-family house is one that is separate from neighboring homes and has some land around it. This type of housing usually is the most expensive type to buy and maintain. Owners are responsible for insurance and real estate taxes. **Real estate taxes** are taxes paid on land and buildings. The single-family house perhaps is also the type of housing that most Americans hope to own. It is part of the American dream and here, more than in any other country, it is a symbol of success and happiness.

◀

B Town Houses ▶
A town house is a house of two or more floors with a front yard and backyard but with common sidewalls. The advantage of a town house is its economy of construction. Its style saves on the amount of land, insulation, windows, foundation, roof, and walls needed, which makes it less expensive to buy and maintain. Unfortunately, noise often carries through the common walls.

125

Figure 6.2 Housing Choices (cont.)

C Condominiums ▶

Some town houses are condominiums. A **condominium** (KAHN-duh-MIN-ee-uhm) is a single unit in an apartment building or in a series of town houses that is owned separately. Common areas such as hallways and the land on which the building is built are owned in common by the owners of the single units. Owners pay a monthly maintenance fee for upkeep of these common areas. Ownership rights in a condominium are similar to those in a single-family house, with some exceptions. Owners are free to make any changes they wish within their own units. However, the need for repairs to common areas is usually determined by a majority vote of the owners of all the units.

D Cooperatives ▶

Owners of **cooperative** apartments, in contrast, own equal shares in the company that owns the apartment building and the land on which the building stands. They do not own their apartments but rather hold leases on them. A **lease** is a long-term agreement describing the terms under which the property is being rented. All operating costs such as real estate taxes and maintenance are divided among the owners according to the number of shares each owns. A major problem with cooperative apartments is that individual members usually must obtain approval from the co-op before remodeling, renting, or selling their units.

E Mobile Homes

Mobile homes are a popular form of low-cost housing in the United States. One reason is that mobile homes are often taxed as motor vehicles rather than as real estate. Another reason is that they often are the least expensive form of housing to buy and maintain. However, owners of mobile homes face unique problems. The purchase of a mobile home does not always guarantee a space in a mobile home park. Mobile homes are also more likely to suffer damage during storms than are other types of housing. Third, mobile homes, like automobiles and boats, **depreciate** (di-PREE-shee-AYT)—decline in value over time—as the mobile homes or the fixtures that are part of them wear out or become ◀ outdated in style.

The Pros and Cons of Sharing an Apartment or House

If you go on to college or start working right out of high school, you may find that sharing a rented house or apartment with one or more friends makes sense. Sharing involves a number of human problems and a number of economic problems as shown in Figure 6.3.

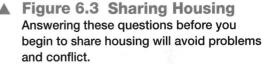

▲ **Figure 6.3 Sharing Housing**
Answering these questions before you begin to share housing will avoid problems and conflict.

- How will responsibilities be shared? Are you splitting the rent in exactly the same amounts? If something needs to be repaired, will you share in the expenses?
- Will one person be responsible to the landlord, or will each of you put money in a special bank account from which the rent can be paid?
- How will you share the payment of telephone and utility bills?
- Who is going to be responsible for household expenses such as cleaning supplies and light bulbs?
- What about furniture? What if a nice sofa that your parents gave you gets stained by someone else? Who is responsible?
- Who is responsible for cleaning up what and when?

SECTION 1 REVIEW

Understanding Vocabulary
Define real estate taxes, condominium, cooperative, lease, depreciate.

Reviewing Objectives
1. What are the five types of housing available to consumers?
2. What pros and cons should persons consider if they plan to share an apartment or house?

Thorstein Veblen on Conspicuous Consumption

Profile

- 1857-1929
- lectured at University of Chicago
- harsh critic of American capitalism
- major published work: *The Theory of the Leisure Class,* 1899

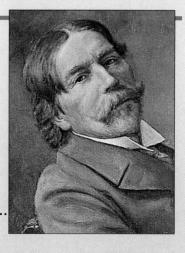

In *The Theory of the Leisure Class,* Veblen criticized the rich, or leisure, class and its spending habits. He talked about conspicuous consumption, which is buying goods and services to impress others.

The quasi-peaceable gentleman of leisure, then, not only consumes of the staff of life beyond the minimum required for subsistence and physical efficiency, but his consumption also undergoes a specialization as regards the quality of good consumed.... Since the consumption of these more excellent goods is an evidence of wealth, it becomes honorific [conferring honor]; and conversely, the failure to consume in due quantity and quality becomes a mark of inferiority and demerit.

Veblen adds that conspicuous consumption is more common in an urban population than in a rural one.

...Conspicuous consumption claims a relatively larger portion of the income of the urban than of the rural population, and the claim is also more imperative.... In the struggle to outdo one another the city population push their normal standard of conspicuous consumption to a higher point.

Veblen calls conspicuous consumption waste because it does not serve human life well. He concludes that it does not have the approval of the conscience—it is not ethical.

In the view of economic theory the expenditure ... is here called "waste" because this expenditure does not serve human life or human well-being on the whole.

...The popular reprobation [disapproval] of waste goes to say that in order to be at peace with himself the common man must be able to see in any and all human effort and human enjoyment an enhancement of life and well-being on the whole.... Relative or competitive advantage of one individual in comparison with another does not satisfy the economic conscience, and therefore competitive expenditure has not the approval of this conscience.

Checking for Understanding

1. What is conspicuous consumption?
2. What groups tend to engage more in conspicuous consumption?
3. According to Veblen, what is wrong with conspicuous consumption or with competitive expenditures?

SECTION 2 FOCUS

Terms to Know closing costs, points, equity, security deposit

Objectives *After reading this section, you should be able to:*

❶ List three rules that determine how much you should spend for a house.

❷ Explain the rights and responsibilities of renters.

Deciding to Buy Housing Is a Big Step, But Renters Also Have Responsibilities

Some people will save for years and scrimp on food and clothing their whole lives in order to buy a nice house. Others simply rent most of their lives.

No matter what type of housing you decide to live in, you have to make the decision whether to rent or buy. Figure 6.5 (page 130) compares the advantages and disadvantages—both economic and psychological—of owning and renting. Wise consumers should consider both when deciding whether to buy or to rent housing.

If You Buy, How Much Should You Spend?

When you decide to buy housing, it is important that you do not take on financial obligations that are beyond your budget. As Figure 6.4 shows, lenders use certain rules to help buyers determine how much housing they can afford.

In addition to the cash down payment, you will need money for **closing costs.** These are costs involved in arranging for a mortgage or in transferring ownership of the property. Closing costs can include fees for such items as the title search, legal costs, loan application, credit report, house inspections, and taxes. Although the person buying the house usually pays these fees, the seller may agree to pay part or all of them if this will make it easier to sell the house.

In arranging for a mortgage, it is important to know about **points,** which are included in closing costs. Points are the fee paid to the lender and computed as percentage points of the

**Figure 6.4
What Can You Borrow?**
Why would it be unwise for both you and the lender if you spent more than a third of your income on the mortgage?

▼

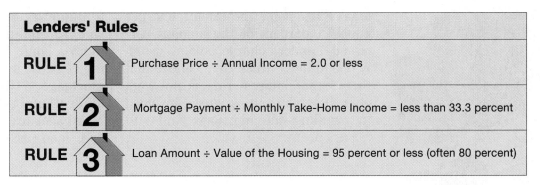

Lenders' Rules
RULE 1 Purchase Price ÷ Annual Income = 2.0 or less
RULE 2 Mortgage Payment ÷ Monthly Take-Home Income = less than 33.3 percent
RULE 3 Loan Amount ÷ Value of the Housing = 95 percent or less (often 80 percent)

Figure 6.5 Advantages and Disadvantages of Owning and Renting

Advantages	Disadvantages
Ownership provides the following for a family or individual:	**Ownership has the following drawbacks:**
■ freedom of use; owners can remodel whenever or however they choose	■ less mobility, especially in years when interest rates on mortgages are high and housing is difficult to sell
■ the pride of ownership; people tend to take better care of things they own	■ less feeling of being able to move to another property because the present one is too small, too big, and so on
■ greater privacy	
■ usually a good investment that in the past has risen in value as much as, or more than, the general rise in prices	■ necessity of a large outlay of money for a down payment
■ significant income tax benefits	■ maintenance costs, real estate taxes, and possible depreciation
■ creation of **equity** (EK-wuht-ee), the amount of money invested in the property minus the debt—mortgage payments—still owed	■ less money for other purchases because of high monthly mortgage payments
■ a good credit rating if mortgage payments are made on time	■ possibility of overextending a family's debt load to make home improvements or repairs
■ property to use as collateral for other loans	
Renting provides an individual or family:	**Renting has the following drawbacks:**
■ greater mobility; a renter does not have to worry about trying to sell property quickly if he or she must move	■ no freedom of use; renters may not remodel or even paint without the owner's permission
■ a feeling of freedom to choose another place to live if dissatisfied with current rental unit	■ no return on rental money; a renter will never own the property regardless of how much rent he or she pays, regardless of the length of this period of time
■ having to pay only a small security deposit rather than a large outlay of money for a down payment. A **security deposit** is money the renter gives to the owner to hold in case the rent is not paid or the apartment is damaged.	■ little or no tax benefits
	■ often less privacy
■ no direct maintenance costs, real estate taxes, or depreciation	■ little feeling of responsibility for seeing that the property is well taken care of
■ a good credit rating if rent is paid on time	■ no property for use as collateral
■ more money for other purchases because monthly rental payments are often less than monthly mortgage payments	■ need to wait for maintenance work at the convenience of the owner
■ no temptation to overspend on home improvements	

loan. Each point the lender charges equals 1 percent of the amount borrowed. Lenders charge points—usually one to four—when they believe that the current interest rate is not high enough to pay the expenses involved in handling the mortgage and still make a profit.

Financing a Housing Purchase
One of the major problems facing today's home buyer is that of financing. Almost every home buyer has a mortgage. **Figure 6.6** shows several kinds of mortgages that are available. Mortgages are available from savings and loan associations, savings and

Figure 6.6 Types of Mortgages

Type of Mortgage	Interest Rate Changes	Monthly Payment Changes	Term Changes	Description
Standard Fixed-Rate Mortgage	No	No	No	Interest rate and monthly payments remain the same over the term of the mortgage. Term is fixed, usually at 15 to 30 years.
Flexible Rate Mortgage	Yes	Yes	Yes	The interest rate and monthly payments float up or down along with interest rates in general. Rates can increase by no more than a few percentage points over the life of a mortgage, while there is often no limit on the amount of decrease. Three such plans are variable rate mortgage (VRM), adjustable rate mortgage (ARM), and renegotiable rate mortgage (RRM).
Federal Housing Administration (FHA) Mortgage	No	No	No	The FHA will insure the entire amount of its mortgages. This added security makes it possible for borrowers to obtain a larger loan than they could with an uninsured mortgage.
Graduated Payment Mortgage (GPM)	No	Yes	No	Interest rate and term are usually fixed for the life of the mortgage. Monthly payments are small at the beginning and increase gradually over the years. GPMs are used by people who expect their incomes to increase steadily from year to year.
Veteran's Administration (VA) Mortgage	No	No	No	These loans can be obtained only by qualified veterans or their widows. The interest rate is generally lower than for other mortgages. The VA guarantees a large percentage of the loan. Loans with no down payment are possible under the VA program.

commercial banks, and sometimes from the seller of the house, co-op, or condominium.

A mortgage usually involves a down payment and interest. If you buy a house for $100,000 and make a $20,000 down payment, you will need to obtain a mortgage for the remaining $80,000. The mortgage will then be repaid in monthly installments that include interest on the loan.

If You Rent: Rights and Responsibilities

Most renters sign a lease that contains several clauses. A prospective tenant should read the lease carefully. See **Figure 6.7**. Most leases are for one to three years.

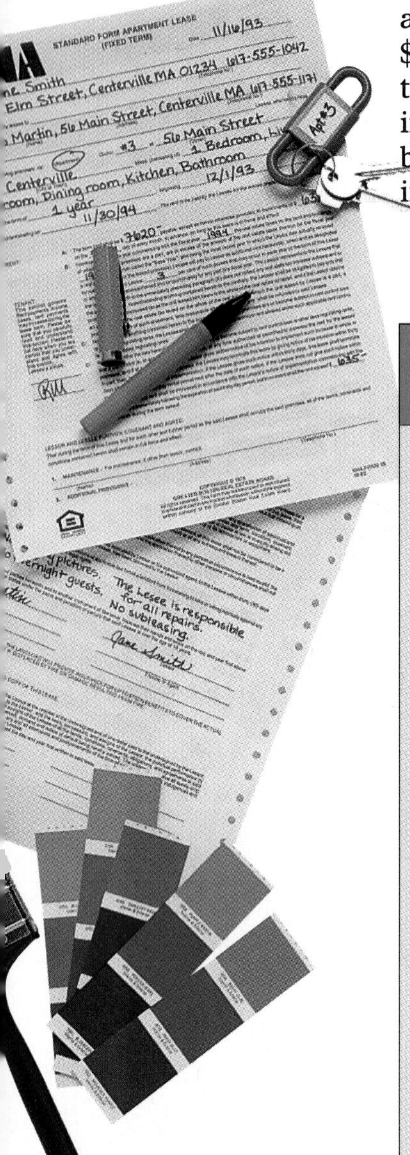

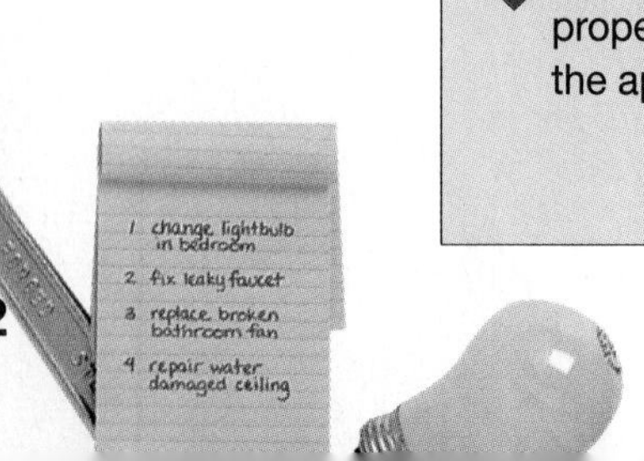

Checklist
**Figure 6.7
Clauses in Housing Leases**

You should be aware of several types of clauses to avoid in leases.

1 According to a confession-of-judgment clause, the lawyer for the owner of the rental unit has the right to plead guilty for you in court in the event the owner thinks his or her rights have been violated. If you sign a lease with a confession-of-judgment clause, you are admitting guilt before committing any act. Such a clause is, in fact, illegal in some states.

2 According to the inability-to-sue clause, you give up your right to sue the owner if you suffer injury or damage through some fault of the owner, such as neglected repair work.

3 Leases may include arbitrary clauses, or those based on one's wishes rather than a rule or law. These give the owner the right to cancel the lease because he or she is dissatisfied with your behavior. Some leases include clauses that:
- forbid hanging pictures.
- forbid overnight guests. This is usually done to make sure the apartment is occupied only by the renter and members of the renter's immediate family.
- forbid subleasing, or the leasing of the apartment by the tenant to someone else.
- allow the owner to cancel the lease if you are only one day late in paying the rent but hold you legally responsible to pay the rent for the rest of the lease.
- allow the owner or a representative, such as a plumber, to enter your apartment when you are not home.
- make you legally responsible for all repairs.
- make you obey rules that have not yet been written.

If you have the opportunity, these are some clauses that you should have added to your lease.

1 If the person renting the unit to you says that it comes with dishwasher, garbage disposal, and air conditioner, make sure the lease lists them.

2 If you have been promised the use of a recreation room, a parking lot, or a swimming pool, make sure that the lease states this. Also have it indicate whether or not you must pay extra for their use.

3 If the owner has promised to have the apartment painted, have this stated in the lease. If you wish to be able to choose the color, also have this stated in the lease.

4 In certain cases, you may be able to cancel your lease if you are transferred to a job in another city or state. Usually, however, you must agree to pay a certain amount to do this. The amount should be stated in the lease.

5 If you plan to put in lighting fixtures, shelves, and so on, and wish them to remain your property when you move, have this stated in the lease. Otherwise they become part of the apartment and you may not take them with you.

Tenant Rights Among the rights of tenants is the use of the property for the purpose stated in the lease. Tenants also have the right to a certain amount of privacy. A landlord usually cannot enter an apartment any time he or she chooses. A landlord may enter only to make necessary repairs or to show the apartment to a potential renter.

Tenant Responsibilities In turn, the tenant must pay the rent on time and take reasonable care of the property. If major repairs such as replacing a leaky roof are needed, the tenant is responsible for notifying the landlord. Often a lease will limit how an apartment can be used. The lease may forbid pets, for example, or forbid anyone other than the person named on the lease from living there. In signing a lease, the tenant is usually required to give a security deposit equal to one month's rent. The deposit is returned after the tenant has moved. The purpose of the security deposit is to pay for repairing any damages that the tenant caused, such as cracked plaster from hanging pictures. The amount returned depends on the condition of the apartment, as determined by the landlord. Figure 6.8 offers tips on ensuring that your deposit is returned.

The tenant is also required to give notice, or a formal warning, if he or she plans to move before the term of the lease is up. In this event, the landlord may ask for several month's rent to pay for any time the apartment is empty before a new tenant moves in.

Landlord Responsibilities In many states, landlords must make sure apartments have certain minimum services, such as heat, and that their apartments are fit to live in. Landlords may also have to obey building safety laws. For example, fire escapes and smoke detectors may be required. Leases usually call for the landlord to make repairs within a reasonable amount of time. In many states, a tenant has the right to pay for the repairs and withhold that amount of rent if the landlord does not make the repairs.

Figure 6.8 ▲ Making Sure You Get Your Security Deposit Returned

1. Do a "walk through" with the manager or owner to record any damage that already exists.
2. Take photos (with dates shown) of the apartment when you move in and when you leave.
3. Keep copies of all the bills that you paid for repairs, improvements, or cleaning.
4. Find out what the local regulations are. They might require that an apartment be "broom cleaned" before you move out.

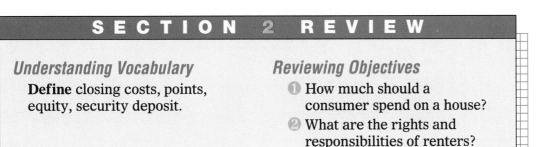

SECTION 2 REVIEW

Understanding Vocabulary
Define closing costs, points, equity, security deposit.

Reviewing Objectives
1. How much should a consumer spend on a house?
2. What are the rights and responsibilities of renters?

Technology Skills

Using the Internet

Are you one of the many people worldwide who would like to surf the Net? Using the Internet can give you the chance to find information on many subjects.

Local Real Estate

1. Log on to the Internet and access one of the World Wide Web search tools, such as Yahoo!, Lycos, or WebCrawler.

2. Search by category or by name. If you search by category in Yahoo!, for example, click on *Business and Economy*. To search by name, type in *Real Estate* and your town's name.

3. Scroll the list of Web pages that appears when the search is complete. Select a page to bring up and read or print. Repeat the process until you have enough information to develop a short report on housing prices in your community.

Internet Basics

The Internet is a global computer network that offers many features, including electronic mail, information, and on-line shopping. Before you can connect to the Internet and use the services it offers, however, you must have three things: a computer (or WEB-TV), a modem (the device that lets your computer send and receive data over a telephone line), and a service provider. A service provider is a company that, for a fee, gives you entry to the Internet.

Once you are connected, the easiest and fastest way to access sites and information is to use a "Web browser," a program that lets you view and explore information on the World Wide Web. The Web consists of many documents called "Web pages," each of which has its own address, or Uniform Resource Locator (URL). Many URLs start with the keystrokes

http://

Surfing the Net

This chapter focuses on housing and transportation. Surf the Internet to learn about housing opportunities in your community.

Practicing the Skill

Go through the steps just described to search the Internet for information on prices of used automobiles in your area. Based on the information, write a brief report detailing what type of used automobile interests you, what features it might have, and what price would be fair in your community.

3 Buying and Operating an Automobile

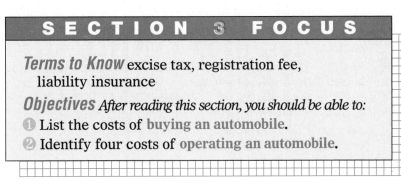

Automobiles Cost More Than a Monthly Loan Payment

In many places in the United States, an automobile is a necessity. Some Americans rent or lease cars because they do not have the down payment or because they wish to gain a tax advantage by leasing or renting for business purposes. Nevertheless, most people prefer to own their own automobiles. Therefore, it is probable that at some point in your life you will buy a car. You should be aware of certain factors as you shop for a car. Your choice of an automobile, like all other decisions, involves trade-offs. See **Figure 6.9** for some of the major trade-offs you should consider.

The Costs of Buying an Automobile

Buying a car involves opportunity costs. One is the amount of money and time spent shopping for the car. Another is the amount of money and time spent in actually purchasing the car. Because people have limited resources, most people have to borrow to buy a car. The costs of the loan are the interest, the down payment, and the monthly payments on the principal. Interest is an important cost of buying an automobile on credit, but buying a car with cash has a cost, too. By paying cash, a person loses the ability to purchase other goods and services. See **Figure 6.10** (page 136) for tips on choosing a new or used car.

Figure 6.9 Car Buying Trade-Offs

- Usually, the smaller the engine, the less gas an automobile burns. This makes a car with a smaller engine less costly to operate, but the car will accelerate less quickly.
- Newer automobiles cost more, but they require fewer repairs than older ones.
- The smaller the automobile, the more energy efficient it is and the easier it is to park and turn. In an accident, however, larger automobiles usually protect passengers better than smaller automobiles.

◀

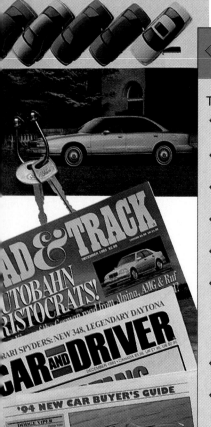

These tips will help you in making a good choice of a new car or used car:

1. Ask friends and relatives about their satisfaction or dissatisfaction with their cars.

2. Read articles about different makes and models in car magazines such as *Car and Driver* and *Road and Track*.

3. Read *Consumer Reports* and *Consumers' Research Magazine* for reviews of new automobiles. Read their reports on repair records of different models carefully.

4. Visit various dealers and read the material they hand out about their automobiles. Remember that these pamphlets are advertisements that promote the best features.

5. Personally inspect various makes and models. Automobile showrooms are open to provide you the chance to complete your inspection.

6. Check what is covered by the service warranty for each make and model as you compare automobiles. Warranties may vary from manufacturer to manufacturer. If you are buying a used car that is only a year or two old, check to see if it is still covered under the original manufacturer's warranty. Also, some dealers offer their own limited warranties for used cars.

7. Once you decide on the particular make and model that you want, compare the prices offered by several dealers.

8. If you are buying an automobile off the lot rather than ordering one, check the options on the car and their prices. Options are the extra features and equipment on a car—such as air conditioning, a compact disc player, special paint, and so on—that you must pay for in addition to the basic price. If you do not want any of the options, such as white sidewall tires, you may be able to get the dealer to take some additional money off the price.

9. If you are buying a used car, have an automobile diagnostic (DY-ig-NAHS-tik) center or a mechanic not connected with the dealer check it. Add to the dealer's price the cost of any repairs the mechanic thinks the car will need. This is the real cost of the automobile to you.

10. Make sure the price given includes federal excise tax and dealer preparation charges. An **excise** (EK-syz) **tax** is a tax on the manufacture, sale, or use within the country of specific products, such as liquor, gasoline, and automobiles. Dealer preparation charges cover the costs of taking a car as it arrives from the factory and preparing it to be driven away. This can include the costs of cleaning, installing certain options, and checking the car's engine. The price given by the dealer will not include state and local sales taxes. These will be added later.

11. Check various dealers for the reputation of their service departments. Your warranty usually allows you to take your car to any dealer selling that make of car. However, it may be most convenient to return to the service department of the dealer who sold you the car for maintenance and repair work.

12. Do not put a deposit on a car unless you are sure you are going to buy it. You may have a problem getting your deposit back if you change your mind.

The Costs of Operating an Automobile

As with other purchases, a consumer's responsibilities do not end with the purchase of the automobile; nor do the costs. Ongoing costs include a registration fee, normal maintenance, major repairs, depreciation, and insurance.

Registration Fee The owner of an automobile must pay a state licensing fee, or a **registration fee,** to use the car. Usually the fee must be paid annually. In many states, the amount of the fee varies depending on the car's age, weight, type, and value.

Normal Maintenance and Major Repairs The amount of normal maintenance—oil and filter changes and minor tune-ups—that an owner gives a car depends on the amount the car is driven and how carefully the owner maintains the car. The more maintenance an owner gives a car, the better service it will give and the longer it will last. The trade-off is that the owner will have less money available for other things.

Major repairs are those that are normally unexpected and expensive. They include rebuilding the transmission and replacing the exhaust system. No one can guarantee that an automobile will not require major repairs while you own it, but you can follow certain steps to reduce the probability.

As you read in Figure 6.10, you should check the repair records of different cars before deciding on a particular make and model. If you are considering a used car, you should also take it to a diagnostic center, or have a mechanic check it. Sometimes dealers offer warranties for used cars for a limited time period, such as 30 days, or you can purchase a warranty covering a longer period for a used car. See Figure 6.11.

Extended Warranty One way to guard against having to pay for major repairs is to buy extended warranty coverage. New-car warranties generally protect owners for all major repairs except tune-ups and damage resulting from improper use of the automobile. New-car warranties usually last only a few years, or up to a certain limit of miles or kilometers. These warranties, however, can often

**Figure 6.11
Used Car
Warranties**
Used car dealers' warranties often provide for the buyer and the dealer to share the cost of repairs. The warranty coverage may be an indication of the used car's quality.

▶

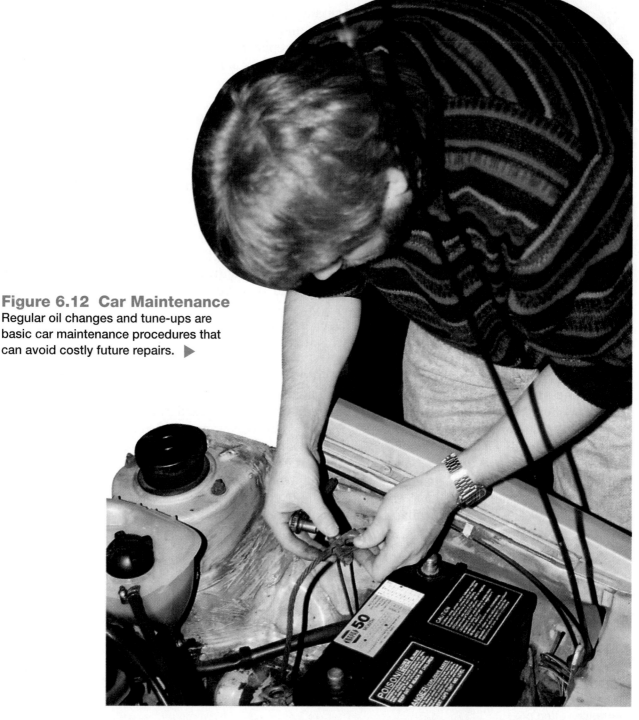

Figure 6.12 Car Maintenance
Regular oil changes and tune-ups are basic car maintenance procedures that can avoid costly future repairs. ▶

be extended for another one, two, or three years by paying additional money when the car is purchased.

Depreciation Depreciation—a decline in value over time—takes place as an item wears out or becomes outdated. Age, obsolescence, and wear and tear cause a car to depreciate. Age is the major factor. A car loses value every year even if it is not driven because an automobile is a con-

sumer durable. All consumer durables deteriorate, or become worse. Second, new makes and models include current technology and new features. These changes make older models obsolete—out of date and out of style.

Physical wear and tear depends on how hard a car is driven, how many miles or kilometers it is driven, and how well it is maintained. See Figure 6.12. Generally, cars depreciate about 20 percent each year.

Figure 6.13 Factors Affecting Automobile Insurance Rates

When you buy automobile insurance, the rate you are charged is determined, in addition to your age and sex, by the following:

1. **The type of car you drive.** Insurance companies consider the safety record of a car and the costs to repair it if it is involved in an accident.

2. **Where you drive.** If the rate of thefts and accidents is high in an area, the risk to the insurance company is greater. A city, for example, would have more thefts and accidents than would a rural area. Therefore, the rate the insurance company charges in a city will be higher.

3. **What you use the car for.** If you drive your car for business on a daily basis, the rate will be higher than if you use it only for errands and occasional trips.

4. **Marital status.** In general, married men and women have lower accident rates than single men and women and, therefore, pay lower insurance rates.

5. **Safety record.** If you have a history of accidents and traffic tickets, then you will be charged a high rate. Whether a new driver has had driver education is often considered in determining a rate.

6. **Number of drivers.** The number of drivers using a car increases the insurance rate.

Insurance A major cost of owning an automobile, especially for someone under age 25, is insurance. Many states require that **liability insurance** be purchased before an automobile can be licensed. Insurance companies classify drivers in various ways, usually according to age, gender, and marital status. Rates depend on the category into which a person fits. These amounts are based on statistics that show that different types of drivers have different accident rates.

Young people almost always have to pay higher insurance rates. For example, single males in the 16–25 age group have the highest accident rate of all drivers. Not surprisingly, most insurance companies charge these drivers the highest insurance rates. Married women 25–45 have the fewest accidents and the lowest rates. Figure 6.13 shows factors in addition to age and sex that affect insurance rates. Rates cannot vary widely because states set limits on the rates companies can charge within their borders.

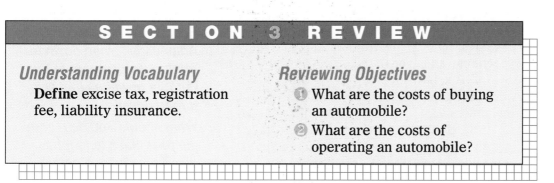

SECTION 3 REVIEW

Understanding Vocabulary
Define excise tax, registration fee, liability insurance.

Reviewing Objectives
1. What are the costs of buying an automobile?
2. What are the costs of operating an automobile?

Readings in Economics

KIPLINGER'S PERSONAL FINANCE MAGAZINE   **FEBRUARY, 1993**

FIGHTING RACIAL DISCRIMINATION IN HOME LENDING

by Elizabeth Razzi

Despite years of open-housing laws, African-American and Hispanic mortgage applicants are still much more likely to be turned down than whites, regardless of income, reports the Federal Reserve Board. Nationwide last year, the mortgage applications of 38% of African Americans, 27% of Hispanics, 17% of whites and 15% of Asians were rejected by lenders.

. . . Two years ago, Orlando and Gail Walton applied for a low-interest loan through an Ohio program for first-time buyers. . . . Gail's calls to the lender went unreturned.

Finally Gail arranged a meeting. She was told by the loan officer that there was "no way" she could get the loan because of her credit record. . . . Embarrassed and upset, she assumed that she and her husband didn't have a chance of getting the home they wanted.

"My husband got so discouraged," she says, "but I was determined that something was not right here.". . . The Waltons applied to another lender for the same loan in the same program. They got it, based on the same underwriting standards. Then, Gail's mother pointed her toward a Toledo fair-housing group.

The Waltons and the Toledo Fair Housing Center filed suit, charging that the first mortgage company had handled the Waltons' loan application differently from other borrowers' because of race. They settled with the mortgage company last fall for $20,000.

. . . If you are a member of a minority group and are turned down for a mortgage, describe your experience to a local fair-housing group. They can help confirm whether a denial was legitimate. Know your rights; if a lender denies you credit, the institution has 30 days from the day you applied to tell you why.

. . . If you believe you've been treated unfairly, . . . call the HUD Housing Discrimination Hotline . . . to file a complaint.

• THINK ABOUT IT •

1. **How do the figures for African Americans turned down for mortgages compare to the number of whites that are turned down?**

2. **What should you do if you suspect that a lender has discriminated against you?**

ECONOMICS IN ACTION

The Necessities: Housing and Transportation

Setting up the Video

With your classmates, view "The Necessities: Housing and Transportation" on the videodisc *Economics in Action*. The video focuses on factors to consider when buying a car or house, especially the trade-offs involved in each purchase. A news segment on the damage caused by Hurricane Hugo in Charleston, South Carolina, stresses the importance of insuring such major purchases.

Chapter 9
Disc 1, Side 2

View the video by scanning the bar code or by entering the chapter number on your keypad and pressing Search. *(Also available in VHS format.)*

Hands-On Activity

Select a car that interests you and estimate what buying it would cost. You should search for the best price in newspaper ads and find out how much you will need to pay for taxes, registration fees, tags, insurance, and annual maintenance. Finally, add up the total costs and estimate how much you would need to pay each month if you had a five-year loan at 9 percent interest. Share your findings with the rest of the class.

SURFING THE "NET"

Shopping for Cars

In this chapter you learned about buying automobiles. When it comes time to make that decision, you will probably want to look at several dealerships in your community to do comparison shopping before you buy. Whether you decide to purchase a new or a used automobile, you should follow the same principles to comparison shop. You can actually begin to comparison shop on the Internet.

Getting There

1. Use a search engine. Type in the word *automobile.*

2. After typing in *automobile,* enter a make of car that interests you to focus your search. For example, you might enter words like the following: *Ford, Chrysler, Buick, Chevrolet, Honda, Toyota.*
3. The search engine will provide you with a number of links to follow. Links are "pointers" to different sites on the Internet and often appear as blue, underlined words.

What to Do When You Are There

Click on the links to navigate through the pages of information. Gather your findings about the make and model of automobile that you would like to purchase. Using the findings, make an illustrated chart of the automobile and the list price.

6 Review

Identifying Key Terms

Write the letter of the definition in Column B below that correctly defines each term in Column A.

Column A
1. equity (p. 130)
2. depreciate (p. 126)
3. excise tax (p. 136)
4. liability insurance (p. 139)
5. closing costs (p. 129)
6. security deposit (p. 130)

Column B
a. pays for bodily injury or property damage
b. a tax on the manufacture, sale, or use within a country of specific products
c. to decline in value over time
d. usually one month's rent left on deposit with the landlord
e. fee charged by lender for paperwork, taxes, and other activities
f. market value of property minus debt owed on it

Use terms from the following list to fill in the blanks in the paragraph below.

lease (p. 126) real estate taxes (p. 125)
cooperative (p. 126) condominium (p. 126)
depreciate (p. 126)

Owners of (7) apartments do not own their apartments, but rather hold a (8) on their apartments so that they have a long-term agreement describing the terms under which the property is being rented. One of the things that such owners have to pay are (9), which are paid on the value of the land and buildings. The owner of a (10), in contrast, owns his or her unit separately. All types of housing tend to (11) and therefore must be maintained.

Recalling Facts and Ideas

Section 1
1. What is the type of ownership called if a person owns part of an apartment building and also owns in common the lobbies, recreational facilities, and so on?
2. What is one advantage and one disadvantage of living in each of the five types of housing?
3. What potential human and economic problems should friends seriously consider before sharing a rented house or apartment?

Section 2
4. What are some of the disadvantages of owning a house?
5. What are some of the disadvantages of renting a house or apartment?
6. What are some responsibilities of landlords?
7. How can you help make sure that you get your security deposit back if you rent?

Section 3
8. If you do not pay cash for a car, what expense must be included in the cost of buying the car?
9. What is included in the cost of operating an automobile?
10. A car's value tends to decrease over time. What do we call this process?
11. Virtually every state requires what type of insurance for owners of automobiles?

Critical Thinking

Section 1
Making Inferences Why do you think that in recent years condominiums have become increasingly popular among Americans?

Section 2

Making Comparisons The two basic types of mortgages used today are flexible rate and fixed rate. What are the advantages and disadvantages of each?

Section 3

Demonstrating Reasoned Judgment Why do you think that automobile insurance companies charge more for unmarried males between the ages of 16 and 25 than they do for married males between the ages of 16 and 25?

Applying Economic Concepts

Competition and Market Structure Examine your local newspaper carefully for at least one week. Cut out all of the ads that banks and mortgage companies present for mortgages. Write out a comparison table that shows the different mortgage rates.

Chapter Projects

1. **Individual Project** In the library or on the Internet, look up the section of the most recent Census of Housing entitled *Selected Housing Characteristics by States and Counties*. Make a table listing the following statistics for your county: (1) number of total housing units; (2) number of year-round housing units (those used throughout the year); (3) number of units occupied by owners; and (4) number occupied by renters.

2. **Cooperative Learning Project** Working in six groups, call separate automobile insurance agents and ask for a rate quote by giving the following facts:
   - Age: 21
   - Gender: Male or female (depending on who is calling)
   - Automobile type: 1998 Chevy Malibu
   - Use: Drive to college and part-time job—80 miles a week
   - Coverage desired: 100/300/50, which means up to $100,000 for one person injured in an accident, up to a total of $300,000 for all personal injuries suffered in the accident, and up to $50,000 for damages to private or public property caused by the accident
   - Collision and comprehensive deductible: $500; no medical or towing

After you receive the quotes, compare them.
   a. Which agent/insurance company gave the highest quote? The lowest?
   b. Was there a substantial difference between the insurance rates for females and males?
   c. What was the average percentage difference between the rates quoted for females and males?

Reviewing Skills

Using the Internet

Comparing Automobile Insurance Rates Go through the steps described on page 134 to search the Internet for information on automobile insurance in your community. Write an article detailing what companies sell insurance and how much they charge for basic coverage for drivers in your age group.

Technology Activity
Using a Word Processor

Refer to the record of the modes of transportation you used and the alternatives available in your community in Your Economics Journal on page 123. Use a word processor to write a paragraph in which you try to persuade someone to use public transportation rather than private automobiles. You may wish to emphasize the advantages of one type of transportation over another type.

7

SAVING AND INVESTING

Where can a person save besides banks and savings and loan associations?

Why are some investments risky?

How much should a person save?

What is the difference between savings and investments?

What are some reasons you might want to save?

What are some of the reasons people save money?

Who insures bank savings deposits?

Your Economics Journal

Keep a record of the names and types of the various institutions that offer to pay you interest for your savings. Next to each entry list the interest rate offered for different kinds of accounts.

time without paying a penalty—forfeiting any money—but there is a trade-off, as Figure 7.2 shows.

A **money market deposit account** (MMDA) is another type of account that pays relatively high rates of interest and allows immediate access to money. The trade-off is that these accounts also have a $1,000 to $2,500 minimum balance requirement. Customers can usually make withdrawals from a money market account in person at any time, but they are allowed to write only a few checks a month against the account.

Time Deposits

The term *time deposits* refers to a wide variety of savings plans that require a saver to leave his or her money on deposit for a certain period of time. The period of time is called the **maturity,** and may vary from seven days to eight years or more. Time deposits are often called **certificates of deposit** (CDs), or savings certificates as shown in Figure 7.3. They state the amount of the deposit, the maturity, and the rate of interest being paid. The amount of deposit and interest rates vary widely. Some CDs, particularly those paying higher interest, require a minimum deposit. The minimum may be as small as $250 or as large as $100,000. CDs at credit unions are called share certificates.

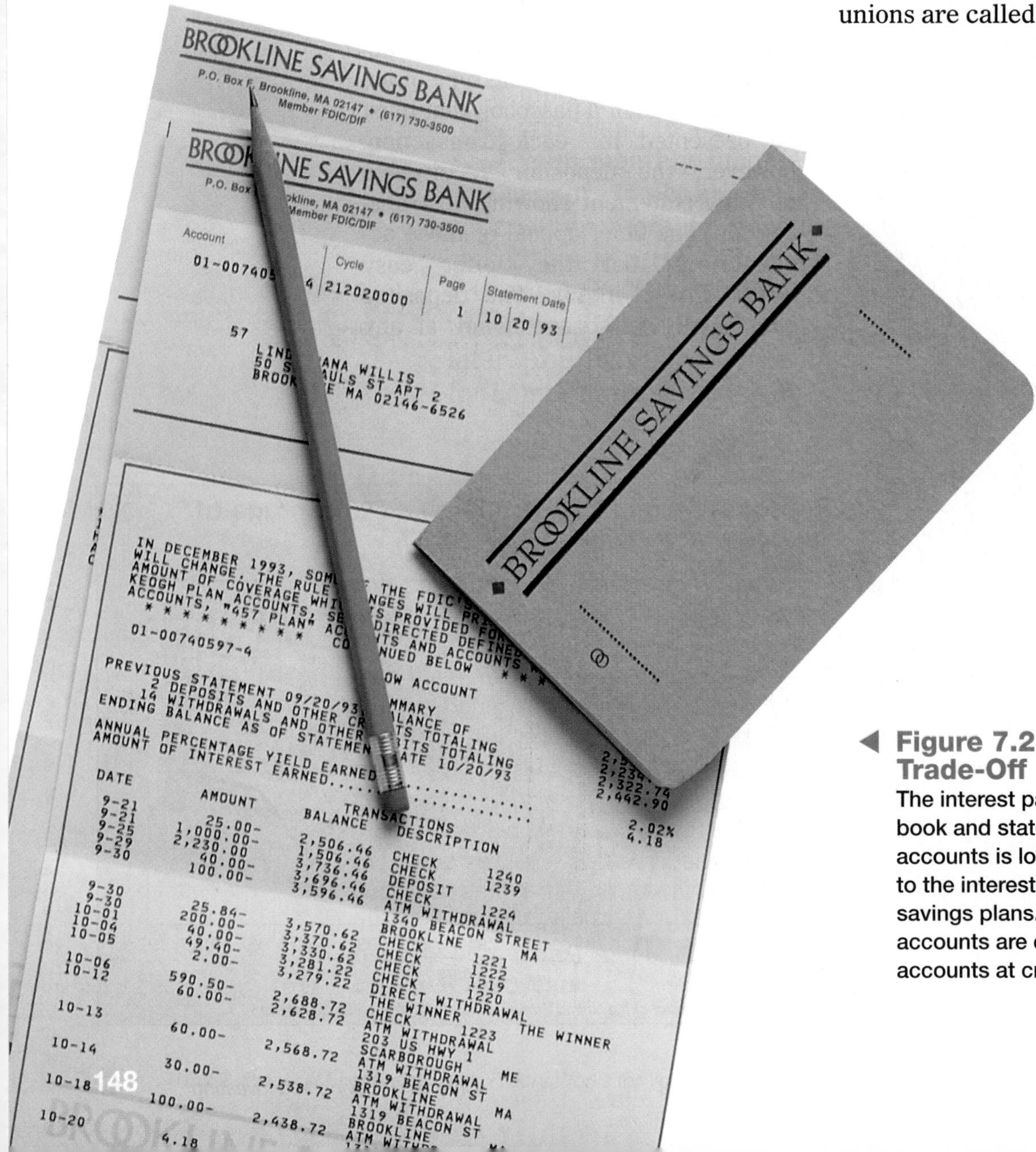

◀ **Figure 7.2 Savings Trade-Off**
The interest paid on passbook and statement accounts is low compared to the interest on other savings plans. Savings accounts are called share accounts at credit unions.

Insuring Deposits Before the 1930s, people who deposited money in banks risked losing their entire deposits if the bank failed. When the stock market collapsed in 1929, it caused a panic in the banking industry. The resulting crisis wiped out people's entire savings and destroyed investors' confidence in banks. Congress passed, and President Franklin Roosevelt signed, legislation to restore confidence in banks and to protect deposits. This legislation created the Federal Deposit Insurance Corporation (FDIC).

Today there are several federal agencies that insure most savings institutions in the United States. Each depositor's money is insured up to $100,000. If an insured institution fails, each depositor will be paid the full amount of his or her savings up to $100,000. **Figure 7.4** (page 150) lists the federal agencies that insure each type of institution and shows comparisons of the various places where you

◀ **Figure 7.3 Time Deposits**
Time deposits offer higher interest rates than passbook or statement savings accounts. The longer it is to the maturity date, the higher the interest rate that is paid. For example, a certificate of deposit (CD) with a short-term maturity of 90 days pays less interest than a CD with a two-year maturity. Savers who decide to cash a time deposit before maturity pay a penalty.

Financial institutions also offer a number of special CDs. One example is the small saver's certificates. Their rates are tied to the current interest rates the federal government pays on certain types of borrowing that it does.

Figure 7.4 Savings Institutions' Services and Insurers

Institution	Savings Services Offered	Insured by	Number of Institutions***
Commercial banks	Passbook and statement savings accounts, Certificates of deposit, Money market accounts	Federal Deposit Insurance Corporation (FDIC)	9,500
Savings and loan associations	Passbook and statement savings accounts, Certificates of deposit, Money market accounts	Savings Association Insurance Fund (SAIF)	750
Savings banks	Passbook and statement savings accounts, Certificates of deposit, Money market accounts	Federal Deposit Insurance Corporation* (FDIC)	650
Credit unions	Share drafts,** Share accounts, Share certificates	National Credit Union Share Insurance Fund	12,000

*Some insured by SAIF.

**Interest-earning account similar to checking account

***Number of saving institutions changes often.

can save your money. Keep in mind that different institutions may offer different rates on the same type of accounts. Different institutions may also use different methods for figuring interest. Some savings institutions are not insured, or they carry private insurance. Those who put their money in these institutions run a higher risk of losing funds if the institution fails.

SECTION 1 REVIEW

Understanding Vocabulary
Define saving, interest, passbook savings account, statement savings account, money market deposit account, time deposits, maturity, certificates of deposit.

Reviewing Objectives
1 What are three reasons that people save and invest?

2 Why is it more difficult for the beginning saver to open a money market deposit account than a passbook savings account?

3 What determines the rate of interest on a time deposit?

Alan Greenspan on the Importance of the Community Bank

Alan Greenspan, Chairman of the Federal Reserve Board spoke about the importance of the community bank in an address he delivered at the Annual Convention of the Independent Bankers Association of America in Phoenix, Arizona, on March 22, 1997. Mr. Greenspan noted:

Our banking system is the most innovative, responsive, and flexible in the world. At its core is a banking structure that is characterized by very large numbers of relatively small banks —more than 7000 separate banking organizations. This banking structure is very different from that of other industrialized nations— for example, there are less than 500 banks incorporated in England. Germany, and Canada combined. . . .

This highly decentralized, highly diverse banking structure is almost certainly the direct result of our market economy itself. Indeed, it is revealing that the first edition of Adam Smith's Wealth of Nations *was published in 1776, the year of the birth of our nation. Our market-driven economy, founded on Smith's principle of "natural liberty" in economic choice, and the banking structure that evolved within that economy, have proved to be re-markably resilient. . . .*

It is . . . freedom to take on risk that characterizes our economy and, by extension, our banking system. Legislation and regulation of banks, in turn, generally should not aim to curtail the predilection of businesses and their banks to take on risk—so long as the general safety and soundness of our banking system is maintained. As I have said many times, regulators and legislators should not act as if the optimal degree of bank failure were zero. . . . Indeed, even if a bank is well-managed, optimal risk-taking means that such a bank can simply get unlucky. Either through mistakes of management or through vagaries of economic luck, bank failure will occur, and such failure should be viewed as part of a natural process within our competitive system.

Checking for Understanding

1. What is at the core of the American banking system?
2. What does Greenspan believe is responsible for our decentralized banking system?
3. Why does Greenspan believe that some bank failures are unavoidable?

Motown Records

From Failure to Success In Detroit during the 1950s, Berry Gordy was a lover of music (especially jazz) and an aspiring songwriter. When he came out of the Army in 1953, he purchased the 3-D Record Mart, a store specializing in jazz records. In 1955, 3-D went under and Gordy went to work for Ford Motor Company. Working for Ford, however, did not satisfy Gordy. In 1957 he quit to concentrate on songwriting. He and Tyran Carlo co-wrote "Reet Petite," the song that launched pop singer Jackie Wilson's career. Gordy's own career, though, did not take off until 1959, when he borrowed $800 to found his first record label, Tamla Records. The first release on Tamla records was Marvin Gaye's "Come to Me."

From Tamla to Motown Gordy expanded his fledgling empire by establishing a second record label, Motown Records, in 1960. The first release under the Motown label was the Satintones' "My Beloved." Gordy established two separate record labels for a variety of reasons. At that time, his record labels were actually released by different record distributors. Gordy felt he could market the different labels to different distributors, thus getting more individual attention. The second label would also allow for more airplay, because many program directors would agree to play only one record per label at any given time. Finally, Gordy felt that having his employees compete against each other for competing labels would lead to greater productivity and creativity.

The Tamla and Motown record labels became successful very quickly. Tamla Records had its first million seller in 1961 (the Miracles' "Shop Around"). In 1962, yet a third record label, Gordy Records (originally Miracle Records) was established. Motown expanded still further when it went into the record pressing and distribution business. By the early 1960s, Gordy was running out of record companies to distribute his records, so he decided to press "Way Over There" by the Miracles himself, and ended up selling 60,000 copies.

Hitsville, U.S.A. From this beginning, Motown Records went on to be one of the most successful record labels of the 1960s and 1970s. Between 1960 and 1970, Motown released 535 singles, of which 357 were chart hits. In 1966 alone, 75 percent of the company's releases made the charts, in an industry where the average is about 10 percent. Part of the reason for this success came from Gordy's philosophy in choosing which songs to release. Unlike other record labels, Gordy did not release songs he did not believe were hit material. Overall, Gordy released less than 10 percent of the material that Motown recorded.

The $61 Million Sale By 1972 Gordy moved his company to Los Angeles and turned to film, producing such movies as "Lady Sings the Blues" and "The Wiz." During the 1980s, Motown's popularity declined. In 1984 Motown lost its ranking as the largest African American-owned company. In 1988 Gordy sold Motown Records to MCA and a private investment firm (Boston Ventures) for $61 million, but retained Motown's publishing division and film and television production company. It continues to publish sheet music and produce television shows today.

Free Enterprise in Action

1 What was Gordy's first record label called?
2 Why did Gordy choose to establish more than one record label?
3 Why do you think Motown was so successful in the 1960s and 1970s?

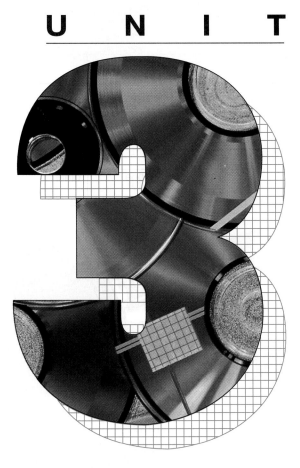

UNIT 3

MICROECONOMICS: MARKETS, PRICES, AND BUSINESS COMPETITION

Did You Know

- More than 10 million individuals own their own businesses.
- Corporations account for about 90 percent of all business revenues each year.
- About two out of three new businesses fail within the first few years after being started.
- Franchises like McDonald's and Hilton Hotels account for hundreds of billions of dollars of retail sales each year.
- The federal government often helps small businesses get started.

In this unit you will learn how supply and demand interact in our economy, and the different types of business organizations and how they affect the prices of the products you buy.

CHAPTER 8
SUPPLY AND DEMAND

What are these people doing?

Does anyone tell them how many CDs to purchase?

What determines how many CDs they want to purchase?

Will the price of CDs go up or down in the future?

Why are there sales for specific CDs at certain stores?

Does the government ever regulate the price of CDs?

Your Economics Journal

Keep a record of the things that you thought about buying, but did not buy during one week. After you list these items, indicate next to each one why you decided *not* to buy that item.

Demand Plays a Major Role in a Market Economy

When you buy something, do you ever wonder why it sells at that particular price? Few individual consumers feel they have any influence over the price of an item. In a market economy, however, all consumers collectively, or as a group, have a great influence on the price of all goods and services. Perhaps the best way to understand this is to look first at how people in the marketplace decide what to buy and at what price. This is demand. Then examine how the people who want to sell those things decide how much to sell and at what price. This is supply.

What is the marketplace? A market represents the freely chosen action between buyers and sellers of goods and services. A market for a particular item can be local, national, and international. In a market economy, individuals looking out for their own best interests decide for themselves the answers to the four basic economic questions you studied in Chapter 2.

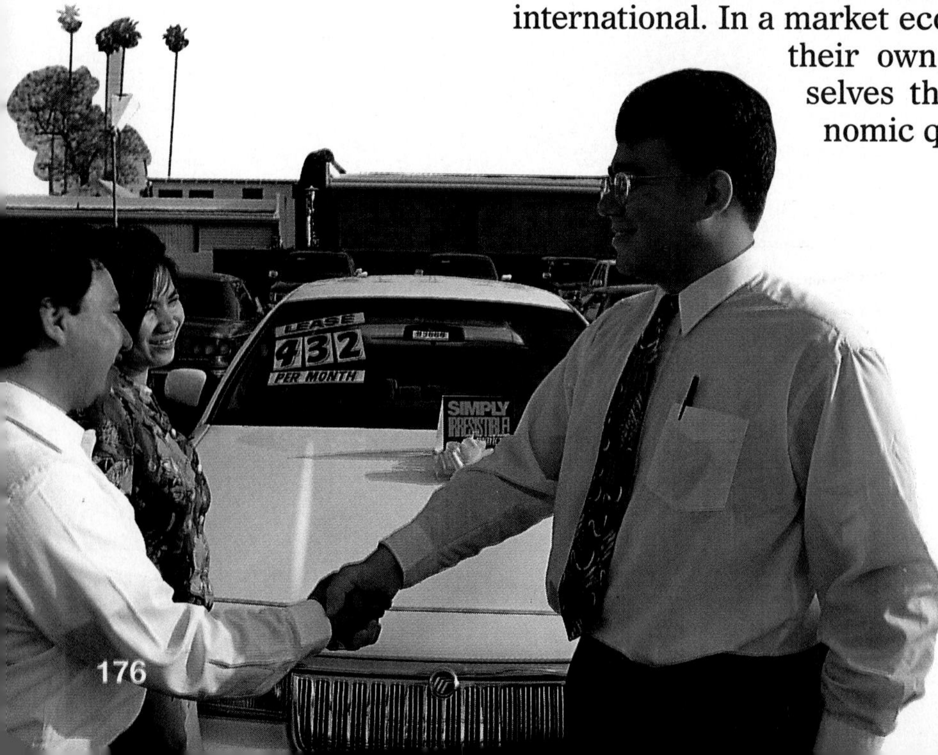

The Market and Voluntary Exchange

The basis of activity in a market economy is the principle of **voluntary exchange.** A buyer and a seller exercise their economic freedoms by working out on their own the terms of an exchange. For example in Figure 8.1, the seller of an automobile sets a price based on the market, and the buyer,

Figure 8.1 Voluntary Exchange
By definition, the two parties to a voluntary exchange are freely choosing to engage in that transaction, or business deal. In order to make the exchange, both must believe they will be better off—happier and richer.

through the act of buying, agrees to the product and the price.

Through the principle of voluntary exchange, supply and demand enter into the activity of a market economy. Remember, supply and demand analysis is a model of how buyers and sellers operate in the marketplace. Such analysis is a way of explaining cause and effect in relation to price.

The Law of Demand

The **law of demand** explains how people react to changing prices in terms of the quantities of a good or service that they purchase. Look at Figure 8.2 to see this relationship. The word *demand* has a special meaning in economics. It represents all of the different quantities of a good or service that consumers will purchase at various prices. It includes both the willingness and the ability to pay. A person may say he or she wants a new compact disc. Until that person is both willing and able to buy it, no demand for compact discs has been created by that individual.

Several factors affect how much people will buy of any item at a particular price. These factors include diminishing marginal utility, real income, and possible substitutes.

Diminishing Marginal Utility Almost everything that people like, desire, use, think they would like to use, and so on, gives satisfaction. The term economists use for satisfaction is *utility*. **Utility** is defined as the power that a good or service has to satisfy a want. People decide what to buy and how much they are willing and able to pay based on utility. In deciding to make a purchase, they decide the amount of satisfaction, or use, they think they will get from a good or service. Consider the utility that can be derived from a compact disc.

At $15.00 per compact disc, how many will you buy? Assuming that you have money, you will buy at least one. Will you buy a second? A third? A

fourth? That decision depends on the additional utility, or satisfaction, you expect to receive from buying and listening to another compact disc. You will have a higher level of total, or overall, satisfaction from owning more compact discs. Most likely, the satisfaction you receive from each additional one, however, will be less than for each previous one. This example explains the **law of diminishing marginal utility.** See Figure 8.3.

Your *total* satisfaction will rise with each unit bought. But the amount of *additional* satisfaction, or marginal

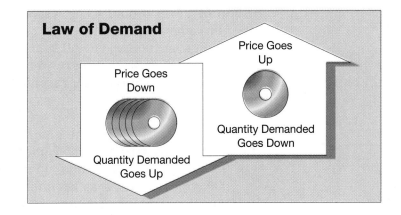

Law of Demand

Price Goes Down

Price Goes Up

Quantity Demanded Goes Up

Quantity Demanded Goes Down

▲ **Figure 8.2 The Law of Demand**
According to the law of demand, quantity demanded and price move in opposite directions.

As price goes up, quantity demanded goes down. As price goes down, quantity demanded goes up. There is an inverse, or opposite, relationship between quantity demanded and price.

Figure 8.3 Diminishing Satisfaction ▼
Regardless of how satisfying the first taste of an item is, satisfaction declines with additional consumption. Even at a zero price, eventually the consumer receives no additional satisfaction and stops eating.

177

utility, will diminish, or lessen, with each additional unit.

At some point, you will stop buying additional compact discs. At that point, the satisfaction that you receive from owning more compact discs is less than the value you place on the $15.00 that you must pay for the item. People stop buying an item when one event occurs—when the value that they place on additional satisfaction from the next unit of the same item becomes less than the price they must pay for it. Assume that at a price of $15.00 per disc, you have enough after buying three. Thus, the value you place on additional satisfaction from a fourth one would be less than $15.00. According to what will give you the most satisfaction, you will save or spend the $15.00 on something else.

What if the price drops? Suppose the owner of the music store decided to have a special and sell compact discs at $12.00 each. You might buy at least one additional one.

If you look at the law of diminishing marginal utility again, the reason becomes clear. People will buy an item to the point at which the value they place on the satisfaction from the last unit bought is equal to the price. At that point, people will stop buying. If the price falls again, the lower price will attract people to buy more. This principle is true even though the satisfaction from each additional unit is less. People will continue to buy to the point again at which the satisfaction they receive falls below the price they must pay. This concept explains part of the law of demand. As the price of an item that people want decreases, they will generally buy more.

Real Income Effect The basis for the law of demand, however, does not rest only on diminishing marginal utility. No one—not even the wealthiest person in the world—will ever be able to buy everything he or she wants to buy. People's incomes limit the amount of

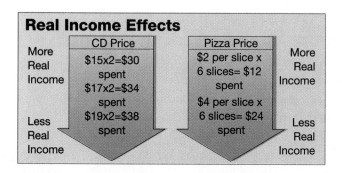

Real Income Effects

	CD Price	Pizza Price	
More Real Income	$15x2=$30 spent $17x2=$34 spent $19x2=$38 spent	$2 per slice x 6 slices= $12 spent $4 per slice x 6 slices= $24 spent	More Real Income
Less Real Income			Less Real Income

▲ **Figure 8.4**
Income Limits Spending

A Suppose that you normally buy two new compact discs (CDs) per month at $15 per disc. That means that you spend $30. If the price goes up to $17 per CD, you would have to spend $34 per month to buy two. If the price of CDs continues to rise while your income does not, eventually you would not be able to buy two CDs per month because your real income, or purchasing power, has been reduced.

money they are able to spend as shown in **Figure 8.4**.

Individuals cannot keep buying the same quantity of a good if its price rises while their income stays the same. This concept is known as the **real income effect** on demand. In order to keep buying the same number of compact discs per month, you would need to cut back on buying other things. The real income effect forces you to make a trade-off. The same is true for every item you buy, particularly those you buy on a regular basis.

The real income effect works in the opposite direction, too. If you are already buying two compact discs a month and the price drops in half, your real income increases. You will have more purchasing power and will probably increase the number of compact discs that you buy each month.

Substitution Effect Suppose two items that are not exactly the same satisfy basically the same need. Their cost is about the same. If the price of one falls, people will most likely substitute it in favor of the now higher-priced good. If the price of one of the items rises in relation to the price of the other, people will substitute the now lower-priced good. This principle is called the **substitution effect.** Suppose, for example, that you listen to both compact discs and audiocassettes. If the price of audiocassettes drops dramatically, you will probably buy more cassettes and fewer compact discs. In effect, you are substituting the lower-priced cassettes for the now relatively higher-priced compact discs. Alternatively, if the price of audiocassettes doubles, you probably will increase the number of compact discs you buy.

B Suppose you normally buy one medium cheese pizza every Saturday night. If the price of cheese pizzas doubles, you obviously cannot continue buying one every Saturday night and purchase everything else that you normally buy (with the same income, of course).

SECTION 1 REVIEW

Understanding Vocabulary

Define voluntary exchange, law of demand, utility, law of diminishing marginal utility, real income effect, substitution effect.

Reviewing Objectives

1. How does the principle of voluntary exchange operate in a market economy?

2. How do diminishing marginal utility, the real income effect, and the substitution effect influence the quantity demanded for a given product or service?

The Body Shop

Starting Out The Body Shop was founded by Anita Roddick, a 33-year-old English woman with two young daughters and a husband—Gordon. The original idea was to open a store that would feature lotions and cosmetics made from all-natural ingredients. Shortly after the first store was established, Gordon left on an extended trip to South America (a lifelong dream to ride from Buenos Aires to New York on horseback). Anita proceeded to open her second store (in Chichester, U.K.) using a small loan from a local gas station owner. By the time Gordon returned, the second store was successful. The Roddicks were ready to expand The Body Shop throughout England.

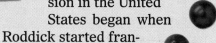

The company grew quickly, raising capital by a public stock offering in 1984. On the first day of its trading, the price of a share of The Body Shop stock rose dramatically. By 1988, Anita Roddick decided to expand to the United States. Originally, she planned to start slowly and forego franchising, but the slow expansion left The Body Shop lagging in the United States natural cosmetics market. Vigorous expansion in the United States began when Roddick started franchising The Body Shop in 1990.

180

By 1997 The Body Shop had more than 1,500 stores in 53 countries throughout the Americas, Europe, and Asia. The United States had Body Shops in 45 states and the District of Columbia.

Anita's Causes The success of The Body Shop is driven not only by its products, but by its "causes." Anita Roddick may be as well known for her environmentalism as  for her business sense. From the beginning, The Body Shop has been environmentally conscious, using, for example, biodegradable products and refillable containers. Roddick also uses her stores to promote such causes as saving the whales and saving rain forests. She has used her United States shops as voter registration centers, signing up thousands of new voters.

Information Please Part of The Body Shop's success stems from its unique marketing plan. The Body Shop has no official marketing department and does not advertise, but instead makes plenty of information available to clients inside the stores. Store shelves are packed with all sorts of information (labels, pamphlets, etc.) about its products. While most of the cosmetics industry promotes fantasy and glamour, The Body Shop promotes well-being. To reach the more socially conscious customer of the '90s, The Body Shop presents information that shows it really cares about its clients, as well as about environmental and social issues.

Free Enterprise in Action

1. What type of products does The Body Shop sell?
2. How does The Body Shop show concern for environmental and social issues?
3. Why would information replace advertising as a marketing tool?

SECTION 2 The Demand Curve and the Elasticity of Demand

Price and Quantity Demanded Are Directly Related

They say that a picture is worth a thousand words. For much of economic analysis the "picture" is a graph. The graph shows a picture of the relationship between two statistics or concepts that are related. Think about the relationship between height and weight. On average, people who are six feet tall weigh more than people who are five and one-half feet tall. If we wanted to graph this relationship it would look something like Figure 8.5.

**Figure 8.5
Height and Weight**
The graph shows a composite of heights and weights of men and women in the United States.

▼

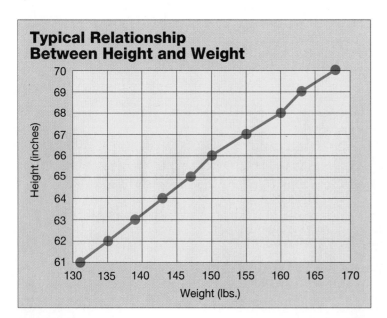

Typical Relationship Between Height and Weight

Graphing the Demand Curve

The law of demand can also be graphed. The relationship between the quantity demanded and price is one in which as the price goes up, the quantity demanded goes down. As the price goes down, the quantity demanded goes up. We should therefore be able to graph this relationship the same way we did the relationship between height and weight. We do so in Figure 8.6.

Let us use compact discs as an example. Figure 8.6A shows various prices and the quantity of compact discs demanded in a table. Figure 8.6B and Figure 8.6C show this same information as graphs.

Time and Quality Are Important Notice that on the bottom of the graphs in Figures 8.6B and 8.6C we refer to the quantity of compact discs demanded per year. The time period is one year. We could have said one day, one week, one month, or two years. Typically, economists talk about quantity demanded per year. It is important to know the

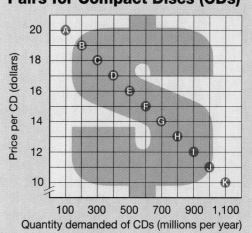

Plotting the Price-Quantity Pairs for Compact Discs (CDs)

▲ **B Plotting the Price-Quantity Pairs**
The bottom axis shows the quantity demanded. The side axis shows the price per compact disc.
Each pair of price and quantity demanded represents a point on the graph. We label these points A, B, C, D, E, F, G, H, I, J, K.

Various Prices and Quantity Demanded of Compact Discs

Price per compact disc	Quantity demanded (in millions)	Points in Figure 8.6B
$20	100	A
$19	200	B
$18	300	C
$17	400	D
$16	500	E
$15	600	F
$14	700	G
$13	800	H
$12	900	I
$11	1,000	J
$10	1,100	K

Figure 8.6 Relationship of Quantity Demanded to Price
The series of three graphs shows how the price of goods and services affects the quantity demanded.

▲ **A Table of Prices and Quantity Demanded**
The numbers in Figure 8.6A show that as the prices per CD decrease, the quantity of CDs demanded increases.

GO TO Lesson 3 of Interactive Economics! to learn more about "Demand Schedules and Curves."

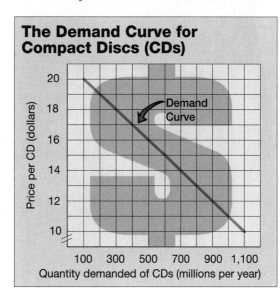

The Demand Curve for Compact Discs (CDs)

Demand Curve

C Demand Curve
When we connect the points from Figure 8.6B with a line, we end up with the **demand curve.**
A demand curve shows the quantity demanded of a good or service at each possible price. It slopes downward (falls from left to right). You can see the *inverse* relationship between price and quantity demanded here.

◄

time period during which you are measuring the quantity demanded. The longer the time period, the more the quantity demanded will be for any given price. Therefore, do not forget to indicate the time period in any discussion of the quantity demanded of anything.

Compact discs are not all of the same quality. Often in the "budget-lines" of CDs the sound quality is sort of tinny. When you talk about the demand curve for different items, you have to assume a *constant-quality unit*. You do not have to actually figure out what that standard quality unit is. Just be aware that when you draw a demand curve such as in **Figure 8.6C** (page 183) you are holding quality constant.

What if Demand Increases? Sometimes something happens that causes demand to increase for certain items. As **Figure 8.7** shows, demand increases can occur for many varied reasons. Using CDs as an example, **Figure 8.8**

shows what happens when demand increases.

Actually, the shift in the demand curve in **Figure 8.8** happens all the time to many goods and services simply because population increases. Even at the same price, more compact discs will be demanded 5 years from now because there will be more consumers.

The Price Elasticity of Demand

The law of demand is straightforward: The higher the price charged, the lower the quantity demanded, and vice versa. If you were the owner of a music store selling compact discs, how could you use this information? You know that if you lower prices, consumers will buy more compact discs. Imagine you have extra inventory, and you want to sell it quickly because you are expecting a new shipment of compact discs. You know that if you have a big sale and lower the price of compact discs, you are

**Figure 8.7
Increases in
Demand**

If suddenly fashion trends make everybody want to wear high-top tennis shoes, we say that the demand for high-top tennis shoes has increased. If latest medical research proves that taking vitamin E pills reduces the chance of heart attacks, the demand for vitamin E pills will increase. If scientists were to prove that listening to more music increases life span, then the demand for compact discs would increase.

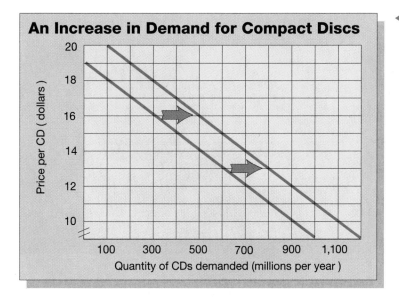

An Increase in Demand for Compact Discs

Price per CD (dollars)

Quantity of CDs demanded (millions per year)

GO TO

Lesson 3 of Interactive Economics! to learn more about "A Change in Quantity Demanded."

◀ **Figure 8.8**
An Increase in Demand for Compact Discs
An increase in demand for compact discs means that people will want, and be willing to buy, more compact discs per year at all prices. How do we show this with our demand curve? Here you see two demand curves. The first one is exactly the same as the one in Figure 8.6C. The second one has moved to the right. It has moved because of the increase in the demand for compact discs. Just take one price, for example, $15. Before the scientists proved that listening to more music increases life span, the quantity demanded was 600 million compact discs per year. Now that number has increased to 800 million compact discs per year. The quantity demanded at any price has gone up.

going to sell more. That is the law of demand. Should you lower your prices by 1 percent, 2 percent, or 30 percent in order to sell your excess stock? You cannot really answer this question unless you know how *responsive* consumers will be to a decrease in the price of compact discs. Economists call this price responsiveness **elasticity.** The measure of the **price elasticity of demand** is how much consumers respond to a given change in price.

A good way to think about elasticity is to use the example of two rubber dollar bills: one you can stretch very easily and the other you can hardly stretch at all, as Figure 8.9 (page 186) shows.

Elastic Demand For some goods a rise or fall in price greatly affects the amount people are willing to buy. The demand for these goods is considered elastic, as is the demand for the highly specific food products on the left side of Figure 8.10 (page 186). For example, one particular brand of coffee probably has a very **elastic demand.** Consumers consider the many competing brands to be almost the same. A small rise in the price of one brand will probably cause many consumers to purchase the cheaper substitute brands.

Inelastic Demand If a price change does not result in a substantial change in the quantity demanded, that demand is considered inelastic, as the general food categories on the right side of Figure 8.10 show. Electricity, salt, pepper, sugar, and certain types

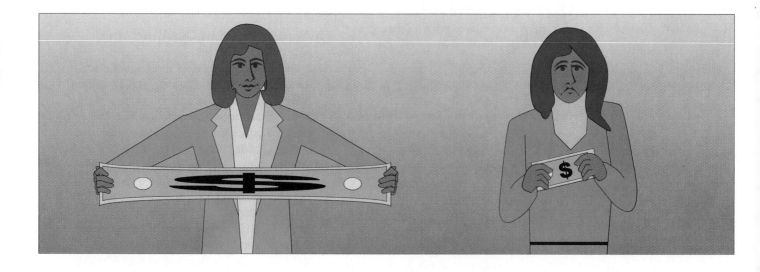

Figure 8.9 ▲ Elasticity
The economic concept of price elasticity deals with how much quantity demanded changes in reaction to a change in price.

of medicine normally have **inelastic demand.** We can compare a relatively inelastic demand with a relatively elastic demand at a particular price using two demand curves in one diagram. See Figure 8.11.

What Determines Price Elasticity of Demand? Why do some goods have elastic demand and others have inelastic demand? At least three factors determine the price elasticity of demand of a particular item: (1) the existence and similarity of substitutes, (2) the percentage of a person's total budget devoted to the purchases

of that good, and (3) how much time we allow for the consumer to adjust to the change in price.

Clearly, the more substitutes that exist for a good, the more responsive consumers will be to a change in the price of that good. A diabetic needs insulin, which has virtually no substitutes. The price elasticity of demand

Lesson 3 of Interactive Economics! to learn more about "Determinants of Demand Elasticity."

Figure 8.10 Elastic versus Inelastic Demand
If the prices of certain goods rise, consumers will buy more of other goods—an example of elastic demand. Inelastic demand means that price changes have little impact on quantity demanded.
▼

elastic demand

inelastic demand

for insulin, therefore, is very low—it is inelastic. The opposite is true for Diet Coke. If the price of Diet Coke goes up by very much, many consumers may switch to Diet Pepsi. Because of the many substitutes available, its demand is relatively elastic.

If you do not spend much of your total budget on a particular good, you probably will not often notice increases in the price of that good. The percentage of a family's budget devoted to pepper is very small. If the price of pepper goes up, most people will keep buying about the same amount. Their demand for pepper is relatively inelastic. People spend much of their budget, however, on housing. If the price of new housing increases rapidly, fewer new homes will be sold. Housing demand is relatively elastic because it represents such a large proportion of a household's total yearly budget.

Finally, people take time to adjust and adapt to all changes, even changes in prices. If the price of electricity goes up by 100 percent tomorrow, you will have a hard time adjusting your behavior immediately in the face of this higher price. The longer the time allowed for adjustment, however, the more you can figure out ways to reduce the amount of electricity you use—by putting in lower wattage light bulbs, learning to live with a warmer house in the summer and a colder house in the winter, adding insulation to your attic, and so on. Therefore, the longer the time allowed for adjustment to the changes, the greater the price elasticity of demand.

Determinants of Demand

Many factors help determine demand for a specific product. Among these factors are changes in population and income, and in people's tastes

GO TO

Lesson 3 of Interactive Economics! to learn more about "The Elasticity of Demand."

Figure 8.11

▼ **Graphing Elasticity of Demand**
The green line shows that with a very slight decrease in price around $5.00, the quantity demanded increases dramatically (elastic demand). The purple line shows that the quantity demanded is not as responsive to price around $5.00 (inelastic demand).

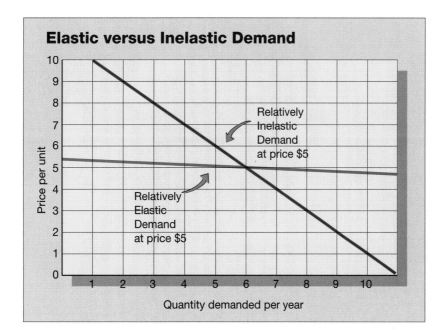

Elastic versus Inelastic Demand

Relatively Inelastic Demand at price $5

Relatively Elastic Demand at price $5

Price per unit

Quantity demanded per year

and preferences. Figure 8.13 shows some of the determinants of demand and the reasons for demand changes.

Substitutes The existence of substitutes also affects demand. People often think of butter and margarine as substitutes. Suppose that the price of butter remains the same and the price of margarine falls. People will buy more margarine and less butter at all prices of butter. The demand curve for butter will shift to the left. As the price of the substitute (margarine) decreases, the demand for the item under study (butter) also decreases. If the price of margarine rises, however, people will buy less margarine and more butter at all butter prices. The demand curve for butter will shift to the right. As the price of the substitute (margarine) increases, the demand for the item under study (butter) also increases. Figure 8.12

shows that not all substitutes are equal, however.

Complementary Goods Although bread and butter can be used separately, they are often used together. Suppose the price of butter remains the same. If the price of bread drops, people will probably buy more bread. They will also probably buy more butter to use on the bread. Therefore, a decrease in the price of bread leads to an increase in the demand for its **complementary good,** butter. As a result, the demand curve for butter will shift to the right. If the price of bread increases, however, consumers will buy less bread and, as a result, will need less butter. An increase in the price of bread leads to a decrease in the demand for butter. Consequently, the demand curve for butter will shift to the left.

**Figure 8.12
Substitutes**

Margarine is an obvious substitute for butter. The price of one directly affects the demand for the other. If, in contrast, the price of carrots increased, it would not affect the demand for broccoli as directly. People might substitute one of several other vegetables.

▼

What Determines Demand?

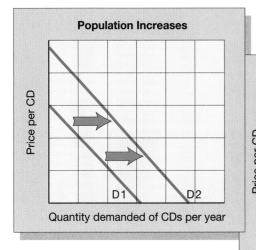

Population Increases

Price per CD

D1   D2

Quantity demanded of CDs per year

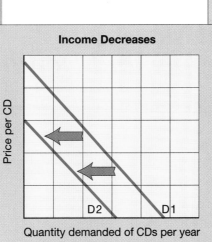

Income Decreases

Price per CD

D2   D1

Quantity demanded of CDs per year

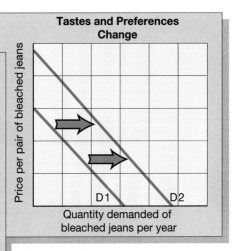

Tastes and Preferences Change

Price per pair of bleached jeans

D1   D2

Quantity demanded of bleached jeans per year

**Figure 8.13
What Determines Demand?**

A Population
When population increases, the market increases. Naturally, the demand for most products increases. This means that the demand curve for, say, CDs, shifts to the right. At each price, more CDs will be demanded as population increases. D1 represents CD demand before the population increased. D2 represents demand after the population increased. ▲

B Income
The demand for most goods and services depends on income. Your demand for compact discs would certainly decrease if your income dropped in half and you expected it to stay there. The demand curve for CDs for you would shift to the left as shown above. D1 represents CD demand before income decreased. D2 represents CD demand after income decreased. ▲

C Tastes and Preferences
One of the key factors that determines demand is people's tastes and preferences. If there were a sudden new fad at schools around the country in which everyone wants to wear bleached jeans, then the demand curve for bleached jeans will shift to the right as shown here. D1 represents demand for bleached jeans before they became a fad. D2 represents demand after they became a fad. ▲

SECTION 2 REVIEW

Understanding Vocabulary
Define demand curve, elasticity, price elasticity of demand, elastic demand, inelastic demand, complementary good.

Reviewing Objectives
❶ What does graphing the demand curve show you about the relationship between price and quantity demanded?
❷ What is the difference between a good that has elastic demand and one that has inelastic demand?
❸ What are the determinants of demand?

Personal Perspective

Alfred Marshall on Supply and Demand

Profile

■ 1842–1924

■ started career as a mathematician

■ chair of political economy at Cambridge University, England

■ developed supply and demand analysis as centerpiece of his work

■ published his *Principles of Economics* in 1890 and *Elements of Economics* in 1892

Alfred Marshall is known for introducing the concept of supply and demand analysis to economics. The following excerpt from *Elements of Economics* explains the equilibrium of supply and demand.

The simplest case of balance, or equilibrium, between desire and effort is found when a person satisfies one of his wants by his own direct work. When a boy picks blackberries for his own eating, the action of picking may itself be pleasurable for a while. . . .

Equilibrium is reached, when at last his eagerness to play and his disinclination for the work of picking counterbalance the desire for eating. The satisfaction which he can get from picking fruit has arrived at its maximum. . . .

Marshall explains how equilibrium is established in a local market. Buyers and sellers, having perfect knowledge of the market, freely negotiate for their own best interest. In so doing they arrive at a price that exactly equates supply and demand.

. . . [A price may be] called the true equilibrium price: because if it were fixed on at the beginning, and adhered to throughout, it would

exactly equate demand and supply. (i.e. the amount which buyers were willing to purchase at that price would be just equal to that for which sellers were willing to take that price). . . .

In our typical market then we assume that the forces of demand and supply have free play; that there is no combination among dealers on either side; but each acts for himself, and there is much free competition; that is, buyers generally compete freely with buyers, and sellers compete freely with sellers. But though everyone acts for himself, his knowledge of what others are doing is supposed to be generally sufficient to prevent him from taking a lower or paying a higher price than others are doing.

Checking for Understanding

❶ What does Marshall mean by "equilibrium between desire and effort"?

❷ What is an equilibrium price?

❸ What market conditions are necessary to establish an equilibrium price?

SECTION 3 FOCUS

Terms to Know law of supply, law of diminishing returns, supply curve

Objectives *After reading this section, you should be able to:*

1. Explain how the incentive of greater profit affects supply.
2. Describe the relationships that the supply curve shows.

In Addition to Demand, Supply is a Factor in Determining Price

The law of demand alone is not enough to explain what determines price. To understand how prices are set, you also have to look at supply—the willingness and ability of producers to provide goods and services at different prices in the marketplace. The **law of supply** states:

As the price rises for a good, the quantity supplied rises. As the price falls, the quantity supplied also falls.

Figure 8.14 shows this law. Unlike demand, a direct relationship between the price and quantity supplied exists. With demand, price and quantity demanded move in opposite directions.

Although producers may be willing, they may not be able. Increased costs and possibly a time lag affect a company's ability to respond to changes in price.

Figure 8.14 The Law of Supply
A larger quantity will generally be supplied at higher prices than at lower prices. A smaller quantity will generally be supplied at lower prices than at higher prices.
▼

The Incentive of Greater Profit

The higher the price of a good, the greater the incentive is for a producer to produce more. The producer will expect to make a higher profit because of the higher price. The profit incentive is one of the factors that motivates people in a market economy. Suppose you own a music company that produces and sells compact discs. Figure 8.15 (page 192) shows some of the costs involved in producing compact discs.

Figure 8.15 ▲
Some Costs of Producing CDs

The costs of producing CDs include: the price of the machines to make them; the price of the materials used in the compact disc itself; the price of the plastic "jewel box" in which they are sold; and even the price of paper and printing used to make the cover and booklet insert. You also have buildings in which to produce the compact discs, and you may have mortgage payments on those buildings and the land. You have employees to whom you must pay wages. You have taxes and insurance. These are all considered costs of production.

Suppose, for the moment, that the price you charge for your compact discs covers all of your costs and gives you a small profit. Under what circumstances would you be willing to produce more compact discs? Remember that increasing output means expanding production. Expanding production usually means higher costs because of the law of diminishing returns.

The Law of Diminishing Returns

Normally after some point, if you are expanding production, the additional workers that you hire do not add as much to total output as the previous workers that you hired. Assume you employ 10 workers. You hire an eleventh worker. Compact disc production increases by 1,000 per week. When you hire the twelfth worker, compact disc production might increase by only 900 per week. This example illustrates the **law of diminishing returns.** According to this law, after some point, adding units of a factor of production—such as labor—to all the other factors of production—such as equipment—increases total output for a time. After a certain point, however, the extra output for each additional unit hired will begin to decrease.

You Must Charge a Higher Price To

take on the expense of expanding production, you would have to be able to charge a higher price for your compact discs. If the price at which you could sell compact discs went up enough, you would probably be willing to hire more workers, buy more machines, and even build more factories.

At a higher price per compact disc, you would be willing to supply—

Figure 8.16 ▲
Higher Prices Attract New Suppliers
For many years, McDonald's restaurants had little competition because their prices were so low. When McDonald's prices reached the level at which competitors could make a profit, other fast-food restaurants such as Wendy's entered the market.

produce and sell—more than you would at the current lower price. Even though each compact disc might cost more to produce—because of overtime payments to workers, more repairs on machines, and so on—you could afford to pay the additional cost of increasing the quantity sold. This fact is the basis of the law of supply.

Many businesses produce compact discs in the United States. The law of supply works not only for each individual producer, but also for the industry as a whole. At a higher selling price of compact discs, it is even possible that new producers will enter the industry. They could be computer businesses that decide to branch out into the compact disc business because the profits seem so high. At a higher price, these potential compact disc producers see a possibility for a larger profit in that business than before the price of compact discs went up. This example, of course, assumes that no other prices in the economy increase.

An interesting question arises when new producers enter the industry simply because the price of the product went up. Why were they not producing before? The answer is that they were not as efficient as the other producers already in the industry. Their costs were too high. They had to wait until the price of the product went up in order to cover their higher costs. See Figure 8.16.

In any event, at higher prices, present suppliers will increase what they make or sell. And at higher prices *potential* suppliers will become *actual* suppliers because of the attraction of profits. Both add to the total output.

The Supply Curve

As with the law of demand, special tables and graphs can show the law of supply. Using the example of compact disc producers, how could we show a visual relationship between the price and the quantity supplied? Figure 8.17 (page 194) shows this process.

Figure 8.17 Relationship of Supply to Price

The series of three figures shows how the price of goods and services affects the quantity supplied.

GO TO Lesson 4 of *Interactive Economics!* to learn more about **"Supply Schedules and Curves."**

A **Table of Prices and Quantity Supplied** ▶
The numbers here show that as the price per CD increases, the quantity supplied increases.

Various Prices and Quantities Supplied Of Compact Discs

Price per compact disc	Quantity supplied (in millions)	Points in Figure 8.17B
$10	100	L
$11	200	M
$12	300	N
$13	400	O
$14	500	P
$15	600	Q
$16	700	R
$17	800	S
$18	900	T
$19	1,000	U
$20	1,100	V

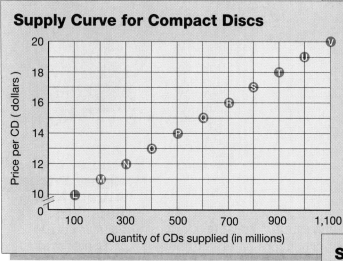

◀ B **Plotting the Price-Quantity Pairs**
The bottom axis shows the quantity supplied. The side axis shows the price per compact disc.

Each pair of price and quantity supplied represents a point on the graph. We label these points L, M, N, O, P, Q, R, S, T, U, V.

C **Supply Curve** ▶
When we connect the points from Figure 8.17B with a line, we end up with the **supply curve**.

A supply curve shows the quantities supplied at each possible price. It slopes upward from left to right. You can see that the relationship between price and quantity supplied is direct.

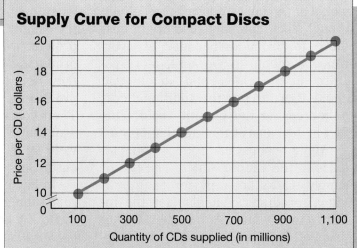

SECTION 3 REVIEW

Understanding Vocabulary
Define law of supply, law of diminishing returns, supply curve.

Reviewing Objectives
1. How does the incentive of greater profit affect the supply of a given good or service?
2. What does the supply curve show?

Critical Thinking Skills

Determining Cause and Effect

In order to understand economics, you have to know about cause and effect. Can you determine what is a cause and what is an effect?

Defining Cause and Effect

A cause is the action or situation that produces an event. An effect is the result or consequence of an action or situation. Often, the effect of one action or event causes yet another action or event. See Figure A.

Price and Quantity Demanded

The classic cause-and-effect relationship in economics is between price and quantity demanded. The law of demand is simply that: at higher prices, consumers purchase lower quantities. Look at the demand curve for home interactive entertainment systems in Figure B. If the price of interactive entertainment systems is $5,000, only 1 million will be demanded per year. If the price drops to $1,000, 5 million will be demanded per year. This cause-effect relationship is valid if other determinants of demand, such as population and income, do not change.

Figure A

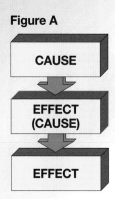

CAUSE

EFFECT (CAUSE)

EFFECT

Figure B

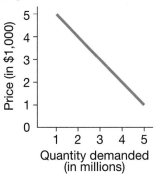

Price (in $1,000)

Quantity demanded (in millions)

Practicing the Skill

❶ Every time the moon is full, the price of a particular stock seems to go up. Can you therefore infer that the moon causes stock prices to change? Why or why not?

❷ Every President from William Henry Harrison to John F. Kennedy who was elected on the first year of a new decade died in office. What cause-and-effect conclusion, if any, can you draw from these data?

195

4 Putting Supply and Demand Together

SECTION 4 FOCUS

Terms to Know equilibrium price, technology, shortages, surplus

Objectives *After reading this section, you should be able to:*

1. List the four determinants of supply and describe how they change supply.
2. Explain how the equilibrium price is determined.
3. Explain how shortages and surpluses affect price.
4. Describe how shifts in equilibrium price occur.
5. Discuss how the forces underlying supply and demand affect prices.

The Interaction of Supply and Demand Determines Price

As with demand, several factors help determine supply. We know that when the price changes, the quantity supplied changes. What if factors other than price change? What would happen to the supply of compact discs if the cost of the machines used to produce them decreased? Producers would be able to supply more CDs at the same market price. See Figure 8.18. The price of inputs used to produce the product is, therefore, another factor that determines its supply.

◀ **Figure 8.18 Technology**
As the cost of technology decreases, the supply of CDs increases.

The Determinants of Supply

Look at Figure 8.19 and you will see an explanation of the price of inputs and some of the other determinants of supply. You see in Figure 8.19 that we show supply curves that shift in each of the explanations. A change in supply causes the entire supply curve to shift. See Figure 8.20 on page 198.

Equilibrium Price

In the real world, demand and supply operate together. As the price of a good goes down, the quantity demanded rises, and the quantity supplied falls. As the price goes up, the quantity demanded falls, and the quantity supplied rises.

Is there a price at which the quantity demanded and the quantity supplied meet? Yes. This level is called the **equilibrium price.** It means that the price of any good or service will find the level at which the quantity demanded and the quantity supplied are balanced. At this point, there is

Figure 8.19 The Determinants of Supply

Four of the major determinants of supply are explained here. These include the price of inputs, taxes, and the number of firms in the industry. They also include **technology**— the use of science to develop new products and new methods for producing and distributing goods and services.

GO TO Lesson 4 of Interactive Economics! to learn more about **"A Change in Supply"** and **"A Change in Quantity Supplied."**

The Determinants of Supply

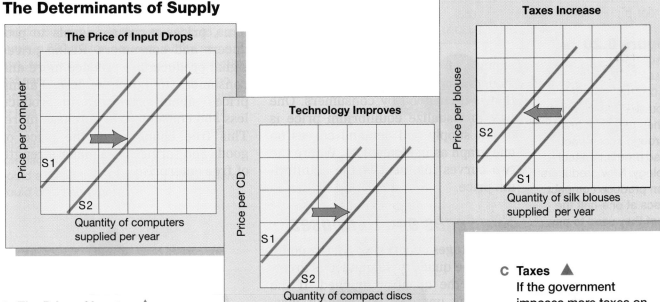

A The Price of Inputs ▲
If the price of inputs drops dramatically, the supply curve will shift to the right. This occurred, for example, when the price of computer processing and memory chips fell during the 1980s and 1990s. More computers were supplied at any given price than before. On the graph S1 equals the supply of computers before the price of memory chips fell. S2 equals the supply of computers after the price of processing and memory chips fell.

B Technology and Number of Firms ▲ **in the Industry**
Any improvement in technology will increase the supply curve to the right. The technology for making compact discs improved during the 1980s. The supply curve shifted to the right so that at each price a larger quantity was supplied. On the graph S1 equals the supply of CDs before the improvement in technology. S2 equals supply after the improvement.

Also, when more firms enter the industry, the supply curve shifts outward to the right from S1 to S2.

C Taxes ▲
If the government imposes more taxes on businesses, they will not be willing to supply as much as before. The supply curve for products will shift to the left. For example, if taxes increased on businesses supplying silk blouses, the supply curve would shift to the left. On the graph S1 equals the supply of silk blouses before the government raised taxes on this business. S2 equals the supply after the government raised taxes.

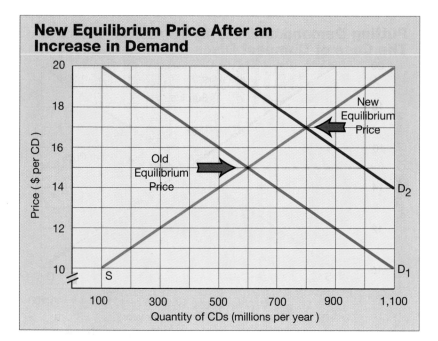

New Equilibrium Price After an Increase in Demand

Price ($ per CD)

Quantity of CDs (millions per year)

Old Equilibrium Price

New Equilibrium Price

S

D₁

D₂

Figure 8.23 ▲ Change in Equilibrium Price

The old equilibrium price was $15. But now the new demand curve intersects the supply curve at a higher price—$17. Price will go up at the same time that quantity supplied and demanded will increase. Can you show what would happen if, instead, scientists proved that listening to music decreases life span?

◄

music increases life span. This discovery will cause the demand curve to shift outward to the right, as shown in Figure 8.23.

What about changes in supply? You can show these in a similar fashion. Assume that there is a major breakthrough in the technology of producing compact discs. The supply curve shifts outward to the right. The new equilibrium price will fall, and the quantity both supplied and demanded will increase.

Forces Underlying Supply and Demand

Do supply and demand determine all prices? Yes and no. Supply and demand are important aspects of the economy, and they do affect prices. The *forces* that determine supply and demand, however, really determine prices. Many such forces operate in the economy. On the demand side are people's income and their tastes and preferences. On the supply side, among determining factors are the ability of suppliers to produce, the profit incentive, and costs of production. The forces underlying supply and demand really determine price. *Underlying* is the important word.

Difficult to Measure The forces underlying demand and supply are sometimes obscure and often hard to measure. This makes the task of determining the effect of demand and supply on price a difficult one. For example, in the 1950s and early 1960s, the supply of doctors in the United States grew at an annual rate of less than 2%. Medical costs meanwhile increased at about 8% per year. At this point it seemed easy to show that the forces of demand and supply were affecting health-care costs (prices). Demand for medical services was rising faster than the supply of doctors and accounted for much of the increase in prices. Doctors' incomes rose rapidly, attracting more people into the medical profession. By the 1980s there were many more doctors per capita than there were in the 1960s. One would have expected rising medical costs to slow down. They did not. Other underlying factors affected price. Increasing per capita use of medical services, rising costs of technology, the growth of the medical insurance industry, and aging of the population, among other things, affected medical care costs. See Figure 8.24.

Then, too, even these forces do not always determine price. Legislation or government regulations, for example, fix many prices in the United States. Some states set the rates public utilities may charge for natural gas and electricity. The forces of supply and demand set prices only in a market system. In a command economy, such as that of North Korea or parts of the People's Republic of China, government planners set many prices.

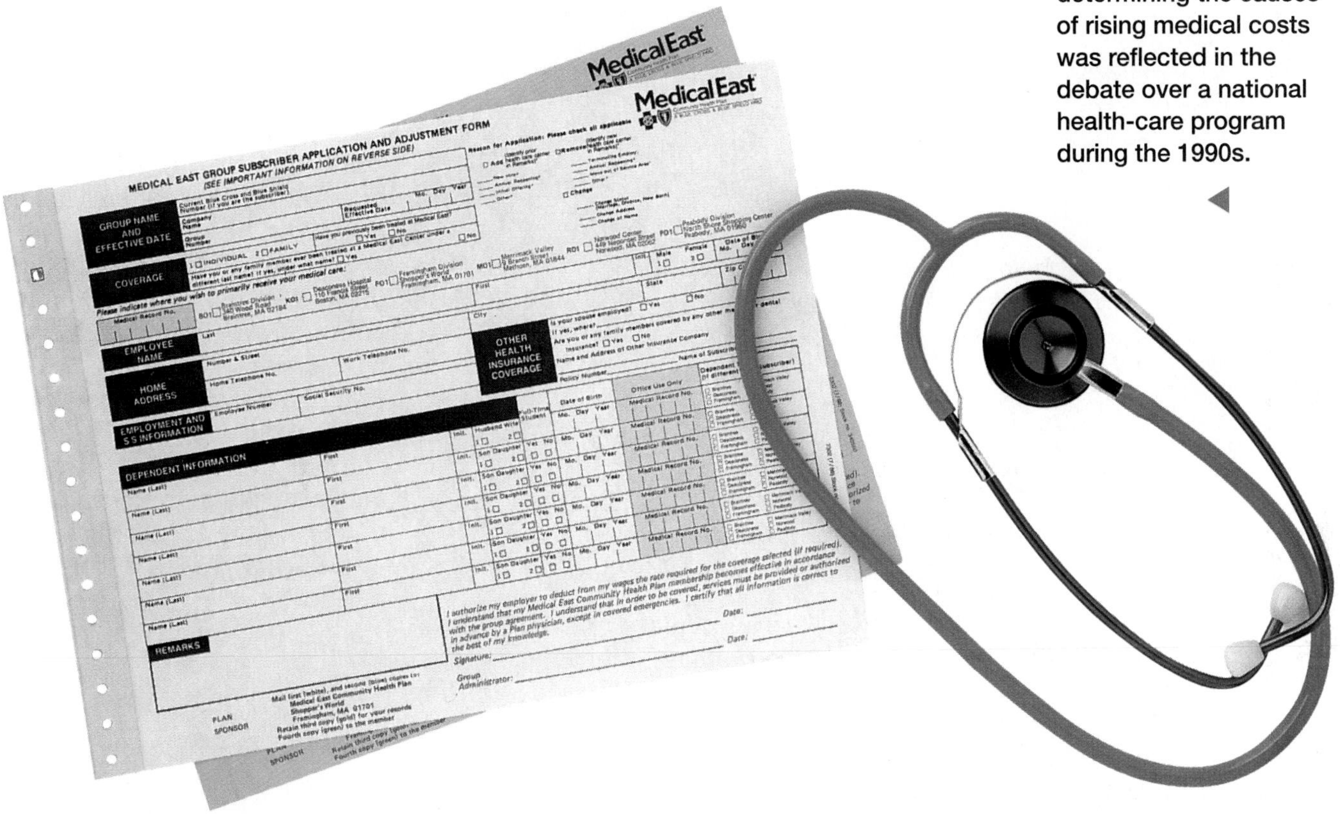

**Figure 8.24
Rising Medical Costs**
The difficulty in determining the causes of rising medical costs was reflected in the debate over a national health-care program during the 1990s.

SECTION 4 REVIEW

Understanding Vocabulary
Define equilibrium price, technology, shortages, surplus.

Reviewing Objectives
1. What are some of the determinants of supply?
2. When one of these determinants changes, what happens to the supply curve?
3. How do shortages and surpluses affect price?
4. In what ways do shifts in equilibrium price occur?
5. How do the forces underlying supply and demand affect prices?

Readings in Economics

KIPLINGER'S PERSONAL FINANCE MAGAZINE **AUGUST 1997**

LET'S GET DIGITAL

by Mark Henricks

You may be smart to wait awhile to buy a digital videodisc player—the latest and, if you believe the hype, greatest, technology to hit the home-entertainment market since the compact disc.

DVD—now correctly called digital *versatile* disc— is the new, megastorage format for prerecorded movies that, unlike VHS videotape, never wears out and offers picture and sound quality nearly equal to that in the-aters. . . .

But considering the spotty history of such revolutionary developments (remember digital audiotape and 12-inch video laser discs?), you could be purchasing a technology that's a nonstarter. . . .

Digital videodiscs closely resemble the familiar five-inch compact discs, and players and software use the same laser technology as CD players. But while compact discs strain to contain about an hour of high-fidelity music, a DVD holds 133 minutes of high-resolution video. . . .

One caveat is that the first players hitting the market are considerably more expensive than most CD players, which now sell for as little as $130. Also, they lack some of the features common to CD players. None of the first-generation machines, for example, has a carousel or other disc changer that would allow users to load several DVDs at a time.

DVD won't soon replace VHS, if for no other reason than the early machines' lack of recording capability. Nor are compact discs going to disappear immediately, because of the huge number of CD players that have been sold. Forecasts of first-year DVD sales range from 400,000 to 2.8 million units, and according to some estimates, by the year 2000 global sales may reach 25 million a year.

• THINK ABOUT IT •

1. *Why does the author believe that consumers should wait to buy DVD players?*
2. *Why does the author believe that DVD will not replace VHS?*

ECONOMICS IN ACTION

Supply and Demand

Setting up the Video

With your classmates, view "Supply and Demand" on the videodisc *Economics in Action*. The video focuses on the effect of supply and demand on prices of recycled products. It then explores inelastic demand in the case of medical services, for which price changes may not significantly affect quantity demanded.

‖‖‖‖‖‖‖‖‖‖‖‖‖‖‖‖ **Chapter 11**
               Disc 1, Side 2

View the video by scanning the bar code or by entering the chapter number on your keypad and pressing Search. *(Also available in VHS format.)*

Hands-On Activity

Imagine that a major storm (or heat wave) hit town next week. Such a major natural disaster would have a tremendous affect on the people of the community. What goods and services would people need after the storm, and how would you expect the cost of these items to compare to their cost before the storm? List the items as well as the factors that might account for the difference in their cost. Share your list with the class.

INTERACTIVE ECONOMICS!

Price Determination

Introduction

Lesson 5 of *Interactive Economics!* deals with prices. Because of the information they convey, prices are central to the way a market economy works. Prices serve as signals to both producers and consumers. High prices are signals for producers to supply more and for consumers to purchase less. Low prices do just the opposite.

In the American free enterprise system, the market itself determines prices. In most cases prices react quickly to changing market conditions.

Using the Software

1. Select "Price Determination" from the Main Menu.

2. Read the introduction to "Price Determination," then click on "Prices as Signals."
3. After reading the information, go back to the "Tutorial" menu and click on "How Prices Are Determined."
4. Finally, click on the "Advanced Topics Menu" and read about price adjustments and price elasticities.
5. Then click on "Economics Lab." Complete the lab by clicking and dragging the appropriate graphs to their cause identified in the illustration.
6. Print your completed lab.

8 Review

Identifying Key Terms

Write a short paragraph about demand using all of the following terms.

law of demand (p. 177)
law of diminishing
   marginal utility
   (p. 177)
real income effect
   (p. 179)
substitution effect
   (p. 179)
demand curve (p. 183)
price elasticity of
   demand (p. 185)

Use terms from the following list to fill in the blanks in the paragraph below.

law of supply (p. 191)
law of diminishing
   returns (p. 192)
supply curve (p. 194)
shortage (p. 198)
equilibrium price
   (p. 197)
surplus (p. 198)

The (1) indicates that at higher prices a larger quantity will generally be supplied than at lower prices. Therefore, the (2) slopes upward (rises from left to right). Suppliers face the (3) ; therefore when they add more workers, each worker contributes less and less to the increase in total output. When we put a supply curve and demand curve on the same graph, we come up with the (4) . Any price that is above the equilibrium price will create a (5) . Any price that is below the equilibrium price will create a (6) .

Recalling Facts and Ideas

Section 1
1. What is the basis of most activity in a market economy?

2. What generally happens to quantity demanded when the price of a good goes up (and other prices stay the same)?
3. Generally, the more you have of something, the less satisfaction you get from an additional unit. This principle is called what?
4. When the price of a good changes, what two effects tend to create the law of demand?

Section 2
5. What term identifies the graphic representation of the law of demand?
6. How do we show in a graph an increase in the demand for a good?
7. What is the distinction between elastic and inelastic demand?
8. How do the existence and similarity of substitutes affect the price elasticity of demand for a good?
9. If income and population increase, what tends to happen to demand curves?

Section 3
10. Do suppliers tend to produce more or less when the price goes up? Why?
11. What term identifies the graphic representation of the law of supply?

Section 4
12. What would an increase in taxes do to the position of the supply curve?
13. How do you find the equilibrium price on a graph of demand and supply?
14. If the price of a product is above its equilibrium price, what is the result?
15. If the price of a product is below its equilibrium price, what is the result?

Critical Thinking

Section 1

Making Generalizations To what extent do you think the law of demand is applicable in the world around you? Are there any goods or services that you think do not follow the law of demand?

Section 2

Making Comparisons If you had to guess the relative price elasticities of demand for compact discs compared to that of insulin needed by diabetics, what would you say?

Section 3

Making Predictions The price of computing power continues to fall, but some scientists believe that it cannot continue to fall as rapidly as it has in the last decade. What do you predict will happen to the change in the price of computers over the next 20 years?

Section 4

Drawing Conclusions You have been told that telecommunications depends on computers. Computers are getting cheaper. What conclusion can you draw about how much interchange will occur between nations in the future?

Applying Economic Concepts

The Interaction of Supply and Demand Some prices change in our economy very seldom and others change all the time, even daily. Make a list of products whose prices change slowly, if at all. Make another list of products whose prices you think change quickly. For example, the price of houses changes slowly. In contrast, the prices of other countries' currencies change every day and, in fact, change every second.

Chapter Projects

1. **Individual Project** Clip articles from newspapers or magazines that show the laws of supply and/or demand operating in the real-world. Possibilities would be weather damages to crops and economic conditions affecting housing starts, and so on.

2. **Cooperative Learning Project** Working in groups of four, each group will interview a local merchant. During the interview, ask the merchant at least the following questions:
   - What determines the prices that you charge?
   - What determines when you change prices?
   - Are there any costs to you of changing prices (such as reprinting price lists)?

   One person in each group should write a summary of the interview. Now compare these summaries.

Reviewing Skills

Determining Cause and Effect

The Supply of Beef Look at the table below. What do you infer as the cause-and-effect relationship here?

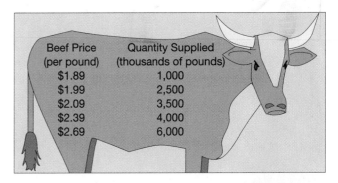

Beef Price (per pound)	Quantity Supplied (thousands of pounds)
$1.89	1,000
$1.99	2,500
$2.09	3,500
$2.39	4,000
$2.69	6,000

Technology Activity
Using a Word Processor

Refer to the list of goods that you did not buy in Your Economics Journal on page 175. Choose one of these goods. Then use a word processor to write a paragraph explaining your reasons for not making the purchase.

9 BUSINESS ORGANIZATIONS

BONANZA®
Steak • Chicken • Seafood • Salad

Who owns these businesses?

What are the costs of operating this kind of business?

FIVE LUNCH SPECIALS
WITH DRINK FOR 2.99
MON THRU FRI 11 TILL 4

TACO MAYO

THRU ➡

Why have they been successful?

Could you ever own a business such as this yourself?

What kinds of businesses are these?

Your Economics Journal

Keep track of all the goods that you and your family buy and the services that you purchase during one week. List these items with the name of the business that provided them. Indicate whether you think each business is small, medium, or large and whether it has one owner or several owners.

SECTION 1 Starting a Business

SECTION 1 FOCUS

Terms to Know entrepreneur, inventory

Objectives *After reading this section, you should be able to:*
1. List the **steps in starting a business.**
2. Explain the **four elements involved in every business.**

Starting a Business Involves Risks and Expectations

Suppose that you have been tinkering with electronic equipment since you were a child. By now you can take apart and reassemble cassette and CD players, VCRs, and televisions without difficulty. You are so good at repairing this kind of equipment that you have been doing it for your friends and relatives for some time. Then an idea occurs to you: Why not charge people for your services? Why not go into business for yourself? By starting your own business, you will become an entrepreneur.

The Steps in Starting a Business

Nearly every person who makes the decision to start a business is an **entrepreneur** because he or she is willing to take a risk. Usually people decide to start a business to gain profits and to "do something on their own" or to be their own boss.

Entrepreneurs then gather the factors of production and decide on the form of business organization that best suits their purposes. Anyone hoping to become an entrepreneur must also learn as much as possible about the business he or she plans to start. This process includes learning about the laws, regulations, and tax codes that will apply to the business.

Elements of Business Operation

Figure 9.1 shows four elements every business must consider.

To start a business, you must make potential customers aware that your services are available for a price. You could have one-page fliers printed to advertise your business and pass them out. You could also buy advertising space in the local newspaper.

Figure 9.1
Four Elements of Business

Every business, regardless of size, involves four elements: expenses, advertising, receipts and record keeping, and risk.

**We Paint:
Houses,
Fences,
Decks,
and Trim.**

Outdoor Work
Reasonable Rates

Pam Bowe and
ASSOCIATES

C Receipts and Record Keeping
No matter how small your business is, having a system to track your expenses and income is key to your success. All receipts should be safely filed and saved.

▼

B Advertising ▲
You will quickly find out that letting potential customers know that you are in business is costly. Once you have customers, however, information about your business will spread by word of mouth.

◄ **A Expenses**
If you own a painting business, you will need to purchase brushes and paint. As your business grows, you might invest in paint sprayers or electric sanders so that you can complete jobs faster. This new equipment would add to your income, but will probably take more money capital than you have on hand.

D Risk
Every business involves risks. You must balance the risks against the advantages of being in business for yourself—including profit versus loss.

◄

COLOR CREATIONS™
Interior-Exterior
HIGH GLOSS
Acrylic Latex
ENAMEL
Extra Durable
Quick Dry

209

Calculating Your Profit

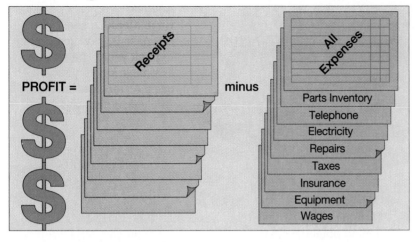

PROFIT = Receipts minus All Expenses

Parts Inventory
Telephone
Electricity
Repairs
Taxes
Insurance
Equipment
Wages

◄ Figure 9.2
Calculating Your Profit
By adding your wages to your other expenses, including taxes, and then subtracting the total from your receipts, you will have your profit. Keep records of how much you owe and to whom, and of how much your business is taking in. You will need this information to do your taxes.

Depending on the kinds of jobs you do, you will need equipment and replacement parts. At first, you might buy parts as you need them for a particular job. In time, you will find it easier to have an **inventory**. An inventory is a supply of whatever items are used in a business.

Will your business make a profit? Figure 9.2 shows how to determine your profit. Because you could be working for someone else and earning an income, you should pay yourself a wage equal to what you could earn elsewhere. It's important not to forget this opportunity cost when you figure out the profits and losses your new business is making.

Computers Probably one of the first things you want to do, if you have not already done so, is buy a computer. With the computer, you also should purchase the programs that will allow you to keep track of all your expenses and all your receipts. Many such programs exist and are relatively inexpensive. Programs write checks for you, calculate your monthly profit and loss, tell you the difference between

what you own and what you owe (called net worth), and so on. As an entrepreneur, you are taking many risks, but the profit you expect to make is your incentive for taking those risks. For example, if you spend part of your savings to pay for advertising and equipment, you are taking a risk. You may not get enough business to cover these costs. Whenever you buy a special part for a job, you are taking a risk. Suppose you do the work and your customer never pays you. The owner who started the small business shown in Figure 9.3 had to consider the risks.

The Time Factor You are even taking a risk with the time you spend. You are using time to think about what you will do, to write ads, to set up the bookkeeping, and so on. This time is an opportunity cost. You could have used it to do something else, including work for someone for a wage. If you work for someone else, you take only the risk of not being paid, which is usually small. As an entrepreneur your risks are great, but so are the potential rewards.

Figure 9.3
Owning a Business
What factors do you think the owner considered before he started his own business? What rewards do you think he might expect? ▼

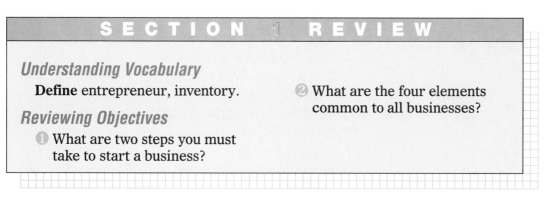

Personal Perspective

William Gates on the Future of Computing

Profile

- 1955–
- founder and chief executive officer of Microsoft, probably the most successful corporation of the 1980s and 1990s
- "the richest man in America," according to *Forbes* annual survey

The following excerpts are taken from an interview with William Gates by David Allison of the Division of Computers, Information, and Society of the National Museum of American History at the Smithsonian Institution in Washington, D.C. Mr. Gates was the recipient of the 1993 Price Waterhouse Leadership Award for Lifetime Achievement. The transcripts of this interview are now a permanent part of the Smithsonian's collections.

David Allison: *You mentioned your vision of where the PC will be on every desk and in every home. You clearly have had a vision about the kinds of products that would come out and yet you said a minute ago, "This is just the beginning." What do you see as lying ahead in terms of further unfolding of the vision that you have held onto so continuously over the last 20 years?*

William Gates: *Well, the PC will continue to evolve. In fact, you'll think of it simply as a flat screen that will range from a wallet size device to a notebook, to a desktop, to a wall. And besides the size of the screen, the only other characteristic will be whether it is wired to an optic fiber or operating over a wireless connection.*

And those computers will be everywhere. You can find other people who have things that are in common. You can post messages. You can watch shows. The flexibility that this will provide is really quite incredible. And already there is the mania in discussing this so called "Information Highway" which is the idea of connecting up these devices not only in business, but at home, and making sure that video feeds work very well across these new networks. So we've only come a small way. We haven't changed the way that markets are organized. We haven't changed the way people educate themselves, or socialize, or express their political opinions, in nearly the way that we will over the next ten years. And so the software is going to have to lead the way and provide the kind of ease of use, security, and richness that those applications demand.

Checking for Understanding

❶ What award did William Gates receive in 1993?

❷ What size will the PCs of the future be?

❸ What will software have to provide in the years ahead?

SECTION 2 Sole Proprietorships and Partnerships

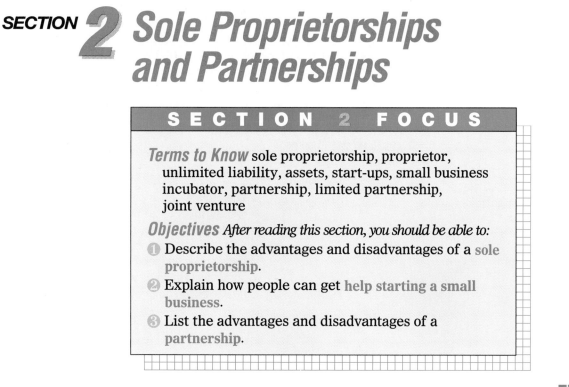

SECTION 2 FOCUS

Terms to Know sole proprietorship, proprietor, unlimited liability, assets, start-ups, small business incubator, partnership, limited partnership, joint venture

Objectives *After reading this section, you should be able to:*

1. Describe the advantages and disadvantages of a sole proprietorship.
2. Explain how people can get help starting a small business.
3. List the advantages and disadvantages of a partnership.

Sole Proprietorships and Partnerships Are Common in the United States Today

Business can be organized in the United States in a number of ways. The two most common are a sole proprietorship and a partnership.

Sole Proprietorship

The most basic type of business organization is the **sole proprietorship,** a business owned by one person. It is the oldest form of business organization and also the most common. The colonies of Maryland and Pennsylvania were founded as sole proprietorships. When we speak of a **proprietor,** we are always referring to the owner of a business as Figure 9.4 shows. The word *proprietor* comes from the Latin word *proprietas,* meaning "property." A business is a kind of property.

Today, the United States has about 11 million such businesses, and many of them are small. For that reason,

**Figure 9.4
One Owner**
This business has one owner as a sole proprietor who enjoys all the profits, but also must bear all the risks and losses.

▼

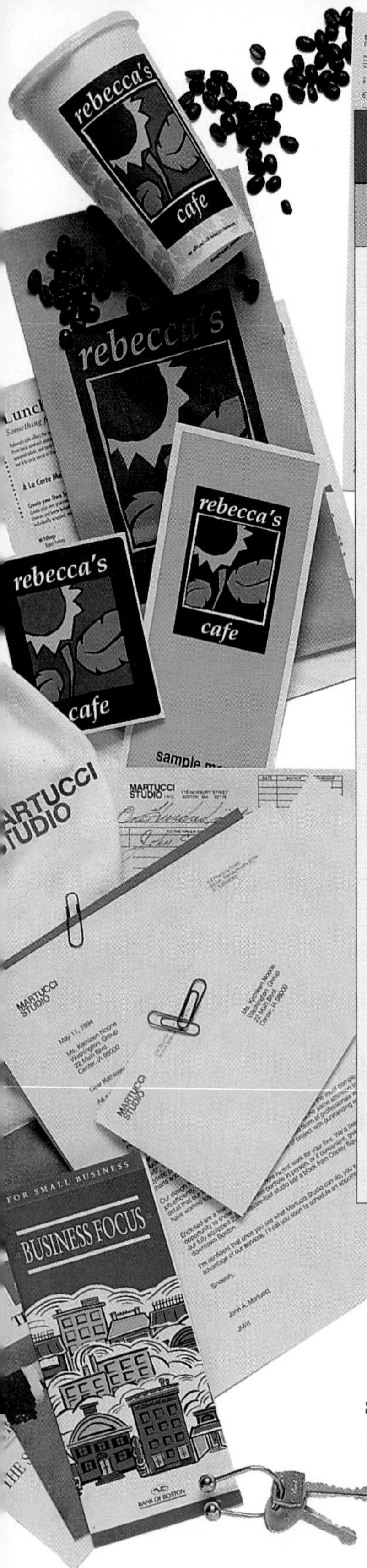

Figure 9.5 Advantages and Disadvantages of Sole Proprietorships

	Advantages	Disadvantages
Profits and losses	As sole owner, the proprietor receives all the profits because he or she takes all the risks.	Losses are not shared.
Liability		The proprietor has complete legal responsibility for all debts and damages brought upon oneself in doing business. This is known as **unlimited liability**. If the firm is unable to pay its bills or if someone is injured as a result of the business, the proprietor can be forced to sell his or her personal assets as well as the business to pay these debts. **Assets** are items of value such as houses, cars, jewelry, and so on.
Management	Decisions on starting and running the business can be made quickly because the owner does not have to consult with other people. Because a proprietorship is usually small, the operation of the business is less complicated than other types of business. There are generally fewer government regulations than with corporations.	A proprietor must handle all decision making, even for unfamiliar areas of the business. For example, the owner of a manufacturing firm may know a great deal about product design, but very little about selling. This is a severe problem for many sole proprietorships.

they usually are easier and less expensive to start and run. You probably have contact with many sole proprietorships every day without realizing it—owners of corner grocery stores, repair shops, dry cleaners, and so on. Many doctors, dentists, lawyers, and accountants are sole proprietors. In farming, construction, and contracting, sole proprietorships are the most numerous types of business organization. **Figure 9.5** lists the advantages and disadvantages of operating a sole proprietorship.

Help in Starting a Small Business

For a person who wants to start a sole proprietorship, help is available. The federal government's Small Business Administration often helps finance **start-ups**, which are new small businesses. State departments of commerce and community affairs also offer assistance. Many community college and university campuses have federally funded small business development centers that will help a small business get started.

Figure 9.5 Advantages and Disadvantages of Sole Proprietorships

	Advantages	Disadvantages
Taxes	A proprietor must pay personal income taxes on profits, but these taxes may be lower than taxes for a corporation.	
Personal satisfaction	The proprietor has full pride in owning the business. The person is his or her own boss and makes the business whatever it is.	Running a sole proprietorship is demanding and time-consuming. If the proprietor does not enjoy such responsibility, he or she will find ownership a burden.
Financing growth	Because the proprietor has liability for all debts, it is occasionally easier for a proprietorship to obtain credit than for a corporation of the same size. Lenders are more willing to extend credit knowing that they can take over not only the assets of the business, but also the assets of the proprietor if the loan is not paid back.	A sole proprietor must rely on his or her own funds plus money that can be borrowed from others. Borrowing small amounts may be easier for a sole proprietorship than for a corporation of similar size, but borrowing large amounts can be difficult.
Life of the business		A sole proprietorship depends on one individual. If that person dies, goes bankrupt, or is unwilling or unable to work, the business will probably close. This uncertainty about the future increases the risk to both employees and creditors.

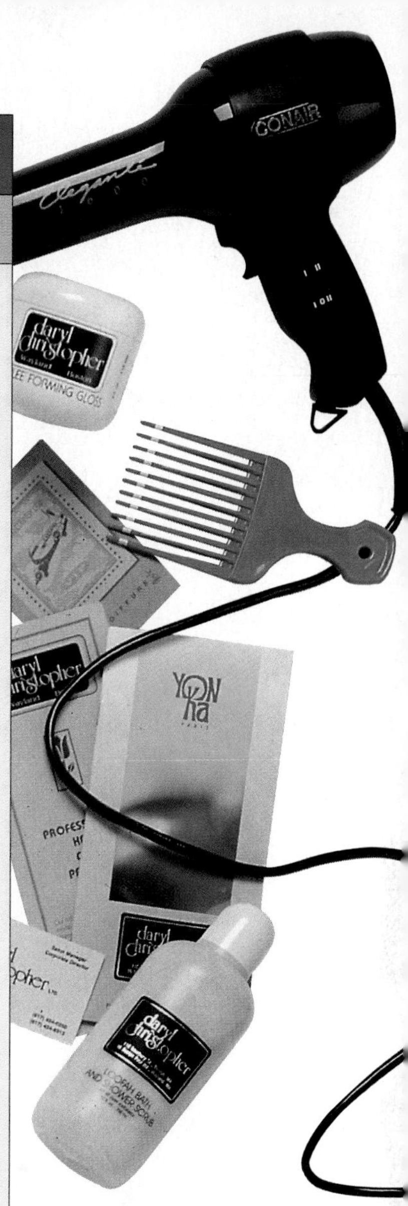

A **small business incubator** might also aid businesses. Just as incubators help hatch chickens, there are business incubators that help "hatch" small businesses. They are often operated with state and federal funds. A small business incubator might provide a low-rent building, management advice, and computers. The incubator's goal is to generate job creation and economic growth, particularly in depressed states.

Partnerships

To take the example of your repair business a little further, suppose that your business is doing so well that your workload has increased to the point at which you have little time for anything else. You could expand your business by hiring an employee. You also need financial capital, but would rather not take out a loan. You may look into taking on a partner.

Figure 9.6 Advantages and Disadvantages of Partnerships

	Advantages	Disadvantages
Profits and losses	Losses are shared. Several individuals can sometimes survive a loss that might bankrupt a sole proprietor.	Because partners share the risks of the business, they also share the profits.
Liability		Partners as a group have unlimited liability for all debts and damages incurred in business. If a partner is unable to pay his or her share of a debt, the others must make up for the difference.
Management	Partnerships are usually more efficient than proprietorships. They allow each partner to work in areas of the business that he or she knows most about or is best at doing.	Decision making is often slow because of the need to reach agreement among several people. Disagreements can lead to problems in running the business.
Taxes	Partners must pay personal income taxes on their share of profits. These taxes are sometimes lower than those for a corporation.	
Personal satisfaction	Partners, like sole proprietors, often feel pride in owning and operating their own company.	If partners do not get along with each other, trying to work together can result in constant arguments.
Financing growth	A partnership combines the capital of two or more people. It makes more money available to operate a larger and perhaps more profitable business. Because the risk is shared, creditors are often willing to lend more money to a partnership than to a sole proprietorship.	Like sole proprietorships, partnerships can have trouble obtaining large amounts of capital. The amount that partnerships can borrow is usually limited by the combined value of the assets of the business and of the partners.
Life of the business		If one partner dies or leaves, the partnership must be ended and reorganized. The others may be unable or unwilling to continue operating, and the business may close. This uncertainty is a risk to employees and creditors.

You decide that the best solution is to look for someone who can keep books, handle customers, and invest in the business. You offer to form a partnership. A **partnership** is a business that two or more individuals own and operate. You may sign a partnership agreement that is legally binding. It describes the duties of each partner, the division of profits, and the distribution of assets should the partners end the agreement.

Many doctors, dentists, architects, and lawyers work in partnerships. Two or more people often own small stores. Figure 9.6 lists some of the major advantages and disadvantages of partnerships.

Limited Partnerships A **limited partnership** is a special form of partnership in which the partners are not equal. One partner is called the general partner. This person (or persons) assumes all of the management duties and has full responsibilities for the debts of the limited partnership. The other partners are "limited" because all they do is contribute money or property. They have no voice in the partnership's management.

The advantage to the limited partners is that they have no liability for the losses beyond what they initially invest. The disadvantage, of course, is that they have no say in how the business is run. Limited partnerships must follow specific guidelines when they are formed. Two or more partners must sign a certificate of limited partnership in which they present, at a minimum, the following information:

- The company name
- The nature of the business
- The principal place of business
- The name and place of residence of each partner
- How long the partnership will last
- The amount of cash or other property contributed by each partner

Joint Ventures Sometimes individuals or companies want to do a special project together. They do not have any desire to work together after the project is done. What they might do is form a **joint venture.** A joint venture is a temporary partnership set up for a specific purpose and for a short period of time. Figure 9.7 shows one example.

Figure 9.7 A Typical Joint Venture

Suppose investors want to purchase real estate as a short-term investment. They may later plan to resell the property for profit. At that point, the joint venture ends—unlike a general partnership that is set up to be a continuing business.

▼

SECTION 2 REVIEW

Understanding Vocabulary

Define sole proprietorship, proprietor, unlimited liability, assets, start-ups, small business incubator, partnership, limited partnership, joint venture.

Reviewing Objectives

1. What are two advantages and two disadvantages of a sole proprietorship?

2. How can people starting a small business get help?

3. What are two advantages and two disadvantages of a partnership?

LEARNING ECONOMIC SKILLS

Reading the Financial Page

You can buy and sell shares of stock in corporations. The financial pages of newspapers provide information about the stocks.

Reading Stock Market Quotations

At the beginning of each trading day, stocks open at the same prices they closed at the day before. Prices will move up or down as shares are bought and sold. At the end of the day, each stock has a closing price. This and other information is provided in tables such as the one in **Figure A**.

Figure A Sample Stock Quotations

52-Week		Stock	Sales 100s	High	Low	Last	Change
High	Low						
$25\frac{1}{4}$	$20\frac{3}{4}$	TxEt pf	13	$24\frac{3}{4}$	$24\frac{1}{4}$	$24\frac{1}{4}$	$-\frac{3}{4}$
$37\frac{1}{4}$	$22\frac{1}{4}$	TexGT	77	$31\frac{5}{8}$	31	$31\frac{5}{8}$	$+\frac{5}{8}$
$32\frac{1}{8}$	18	TexInd	180	$31\frac{5}{8}$	$30\frac{5}{8}$	$31\frac{1}{2}$	$+1$
$111\frac{1}{2}$	$70\frac{1}{2}$	TexInst	1738	110	$105\frac{5}{8}$	110	$+4\frac{1}{8}$

Prices are listed in dollars and fractions of a dollar. $24\frac{1}{4}$, for example, means $24.25.

The name of each company is printed in an abbreviated form. In this listing, TexInst refers to Texas Instruments. The 52-Week High/Low columns show the highest and lowest price of the stock during the previous 52 weeks.

The number of shares bought and sold (in hundreds) is reported in the Sales column. The High column reports the highest price for that day, and the Low column reports the lowest. The closing price is shown in the Last column. The Change column shows the change in closing price from the previous day.

Figure B Stock Quotations

Stock	Sales 100s	High	Low	Last	Change
GlbPrt	347	$14\frac{7}{8}$	$14\frac{3}{4}$	$14\frac{3}{4}$	---
GlobYld	2175	$7\frac{7}{8}$	$7\frac{3}{4}$	$7\frac{3}{4}$	$-\frac{1}{8}$
GldWF	1278	$39\frac{5}{8}$	$39\frac{1}{4}$	$39\frac{1}{2}$	$+1$
Gdrich	621	$41\frac{7}{8}$	$41\frac{1}{2}$	$41\frac{5}{8}$	$-\frac{1}{2}$
Goodyr	4361	$44\frac{7}{8}$	44	44	$+\frac{5}{8}$
Grace	1513	$40\frac{3}{8}$	40	$40\frac{1}{8}$	$-\frac{1}{4}$
Graco	244	$34\frac{1}{2}$	33	$34\frac{1}{2}$	$+2$
GrhmFl	1242	$4\frac{7}{8}$	$4\frac{1}{4}$	$4\frac{1}{4}$	$+\frac{1}{2}$
Graingr	551	$58\frac{3}{8}$	$57\frac{1}{4}$	$57\frac{5}{8}$	---
Grndmet	2424	$27\frac{1}{4}$	$26\frac{3}{4}$	$27\frac{1}{4}$	$+\frac{3}{4}$

Practicing the Skill

❶ Find the listing for Goodyear Tire and Rubber Company (Goodyr) in **Figure B**. What was the closing price for this stock?

❷ How much of a change was this from the previous day?

SECTION 3 The Corporate World and Franchises

SECTION 3 FOCUS

Terms to Know corporation, limited liability, articles of incorporation, corporate charter, franchise

Objectives *After reading this section, you should be able to:*

1. Summarize the advantages and disadvantages of corporations.

2. Explain what types of businesses are involved in franchises.

Many People Share in the Ownership of a Corporation

Suppose your electronic repair business has grown. You now have several partners and have turned your garage into a shop. You would like to expand and rent a store so that your business would be more visible. See Figure 9.8. You would like to buy the latest equipment, charge a little less than your competitors, and capture a larger share of the market for electronic repair work. You need money capital, however.

You have decided that you do not want any more partners. You would have to consult with them about every detail of the business as you do now with your present partners. What you want is financial backers who will let you use their money while letting you run the business. What you are proposing is a corporation. Figure 9.9 (page 220) shows the advantages and disadvantages of corporations.

Corporations

A **corporation** is an organization owned by many people but treated by the law as though it were a person. It can own property, pay taxes, make contracts, sue and be sued, and so on. It has a separate and distinct existence from the stockholders who own

Figure 9.8 Business Location
When you select a location for your business, you must consider many factors including cost and parking areas for your customers.

◀

Figure 9.9 Advantages and Disadvantages of Corporations

	Advantages	Disadvantages
Profits and losses	Owners of the corporation—stockholders—do not have to devote time to the company to make money on their investment.	
Liability	The corporation, and not its stockholders, is responsible for its debts. If a corporation goes bankrupt or is sued, creditors cannot normally take personal property from stockholders to pay debts. This is known as **limited liability**, and may be the major advantage of the corporate form of business.	
Management	Responsibility for running a corporation is divided among many people. Decisions are made at many levels by individuals trained in specific areas, such as sales, production, and so on. This allows a corporation to handle large and complicated operations and to carry on many types of business activities at the same time.	Decision making can be slow and complicated because so many levels of management are involved. Also, the interests of those running the corporation, who may not be stockholders, are not always the same as those of the stockholders, who often seek an immediate return on investment.
Taxes		The federal government and some state and local governments tax corporate profits. The profits that are paid to stockholders as dividends are again taxed as income to those individuals. Some states also tax corporate property.
Personal satisfaction	An individual may feel satisfaction simply in owning a part of a corporation.	Individual stockholders have little or no say in how a corporation is run.
Financing growth	Corporations draw on resources of investors and may issue stock at any time to raise capital.	
Life of the business	The life of a corporation can continue indefinitely if it remains profitable. Its life is not affected by the death of stockholders.	

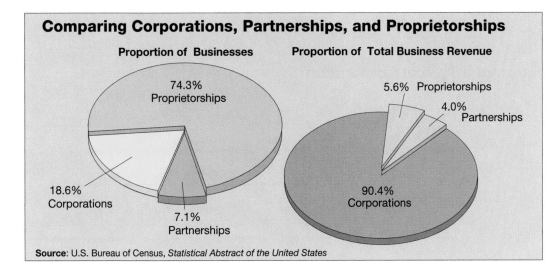

Comparing Corporations, Partnerships, and Proprietorships

Proportion of Businesses

74.3% Proprietorships

18.6% Corporations

7.1% Partnerships

Proportion of Total Business Revenue

5.6% Proprietorships

4.0% Partnerships

90.4% Corporations

Source: U.S. Bureau of Census, *Statistical Abstract of the United States*

Figure 9.10 Comparing Types of Business
Although only about 19 percent of American businesses are organized as corporations, they generate about 90 percent of total business revenue.

the corporation's stock. Stock represents ownership rights to a certain portion of the profits and assets of the company that issues the stock.

In terms of the amount of business done (measured in dollars), the corporation is the most important type of business organization in the United States today. Figure 9.10 compares corporations to other forms of business in terms of numbers and revenue.

In order to form a corporation, its founders must do three things. First, they must register their company with the government of the state in which it will be headquartered. Second, they must sell stock. Third, along with the other shareholders, they must elect a board of directors.

Registering the Corporation Every state has laws governing the formation of corporations, but most state laws are similar. Suppose that you and your partners decide to form a corporation. You will have to file an **articles of incorporation** application with the state in which you will run your corporation. In general, these articles include four items:

1. Name, address, and purpose of the corporation;
2. Names and addresses of the initial board of directors (these men and women will serve until the first stockholders' meeting, when a new board may be elected);
3. Number of shares of stock to be issued;
4. Amount of money capital to be raised through issuing stock.

If the articles are in agreement with state law, the state will grant you a **corporate charter**—a license to operate from that state.

Selling Stock To continue the example of your electronic repair business, you could sell shares of either common or preferred stock in your new corporation. Common stock gives the holder part ownership in the corporation and voting rights at the annual stockholders' meeting. It does not guarantee a dividend—money return on the money invested in a company's stock. Preferred stock does guarantee a certain amount of dividend each year. Preferred stock also guarantees to the stockholder first claim, after creditors have been paid, on whatever value is left in the corporation if it goes out of business. Holders of preferred stock usually do not have voting rights in the corporation, although they are part owners.

If your corporation were to become large, you might find its stock

Structure of a Typical Corporation

Figure 9.11 Typical Structure of a Corporation
Based on what you have read, how much power does the board of directors have over the way a corporation is run? ▶

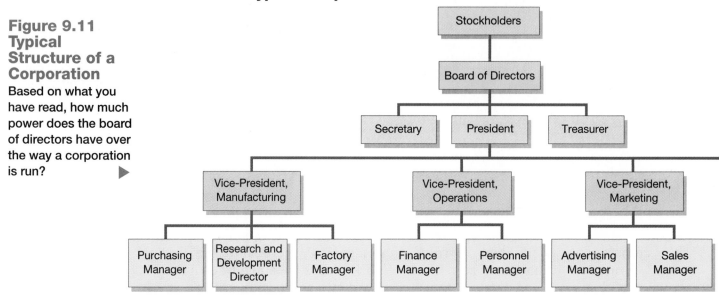

traded in the local stock market as over-the-counter stock. *Over-the-counter* means that individual brokerage firms hold quantities of shares of stocks that they buy and sell for investors. Should your corporation continue to grow, it would be traded on a regional stock exchange. It might be listed as an over-the-counter stock with the National Association of Securities Dealers Automated Quotation (NASDAQ) in one of their three lists. The largest corporations are usually listed on the New York Stock Exchange (NYSE).

Selling stock is not the only way a corporation can raise capital to develop or expand. It can also sell debt by issuing bonds. A bond promises to pay a stated rate of interest over a stated period of time; it also promises to repay the full amount borrowed at the end of that time.

Naming a Board of Directors To become incorporated, a company must have a board of directors. You and your partners, as founders of the corporation, would select the first board for your corporation. After that, stockholders at their annual stockholders' meetings would elect the board. The bylaws of the corporation govern this election. Bylaws are a set of rules describing how stock will be sold and dividends paid, with a list of the duties of the company's officers. They are written after the corporate charter has been granted.

The board is responsible for supervising and controlling the corporation. It does not run business operations on a day-to-day basis, however. Rather, it hires officers for the company—president, vice-president(s), secretary, and treasurer—to run the business and hire other employees. Figure 9.11 shows the typical structure of a corporation.

Franchises

Many hotel, motel, gas station, and fast-food chains are franchises. A **franchise** is a contract in which a franchisor (fran-chy-ZOR) sells to another business the right to use its name and sell its products. The person or business buying these rights,

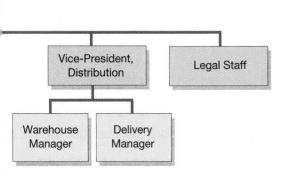

Figure 9.12 ▲
A Motel Franchise
One advantage of owning a motel franchise is that most people will decide to stay in a well-known motel chain in an unfamiliar city rather than spending the time looking for other lodging. They also want to be able to count on a certain quality of service.

called the franchisee (fran-chy-ZEE), pays a fee that may include a percentage of all money taken in. If a person buys a motel franchise like the one shown in Figure 9.12, that person agrees to pay the motel chain a certain fee plus a portion of the profits for as long as his or her motel stays in business. In return, the chain will help the franchisee set up the motel. Often, the chain will have a training program to teach the franchisee about the business and set the standards of business operations.

The chain will help in choosing a location for the building and in ar-

ranging credit. If necessary, it will train the new owner and his or her staff. Because the motel is part of the chain, the new owner benefits from the advertising campaigns that the chain runs. Travelers will identify his or her motel with the national chain.

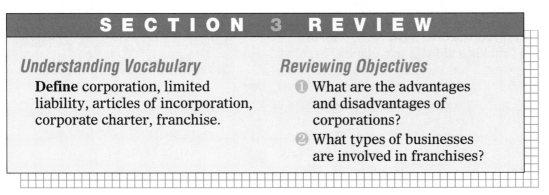

SECTION 3 REVIEW

Understanding Vocabulary
Define corporation, limited liability, articles of incorporation, corporate charter, franchise.

Reviewing Objectives
1 What are the advantages and disadvantages of corporations?
2 What types of businesses are involved in franchises?

Readings in Economics

YAHOO!

I n 1994, David Filo and Jerry Yang were in typical start-up mode—working 20 hours a day, sleeping in the office, juiced on the idea that people were discovering their concept and plugging in. There was only one difference between them and most new entrepreneurs: They weren't making any money. We're not talking about an absence of profitability. We're talking about an absence of revenue. There were no sales. None. And, the fact is, the Yahoo! founders didn't care. Filo and Yang were working like maniacs for the sheer joy of it.

Their mission? Bringing order to the terrible, tangled World Wide Web. Back then—in the prehistory of the Internet—plenty of interesting Web sites existed. But the forum wasn't organized; there was no system that enabled people to find the sites they wanted in an easy, orderly way.

Even Yang and Filo . . . found the Web cumbersome. . . . So the two created a list of their favorite Web sites, along with a framework for organizing the Web and a search engine that made finding the right site as simple as typing in the right keywords. They dubbed their service Yahoo!, an anagram for *Yet Another Hierarchical Officious Oracle*. And it took off. . . .

But can the momentum continue? Keeping the service fresh, fascinating and at the fore isn't easy. Every day, expectations rise, and new companies enter the fray. Then again, Yang and Filo have more than investment capital, a nifty computer program and 225 employees to help them stay online and on target. They've also got commitment. "We believe the Internet can change people's lives," says Yang. It certainly changed theirs.

• THINK ABOUT IT •

1. *What is Yahoo!?*
2. *Why are Filo and Yang optimistic about the future of Yahoo!?*

ECONOMICS IN ACTION

Business Organizations

Setting up the Video

With your classmates, view "Business Organizations" on the videodisc *Economics in Action.* The video focuses on factors to consider when starting a business. The video also explains how to read a daily stock listing.

**Chapter 12
Disc 1, Side 2**

View the video by scanning the bar code or by entering the chapter number on your keypad and pressing Search. *(Also available in VHS format.)*

Hands-On Activity

Create a database with examples of local, state, or national businesses for each type of business organization. Create fields such as Proprietorship, Partnership, and Corporation. You may find it useful to work with one of your classmates, particularly if you have never created a database before. Print your results and share your findings with the rest of the class.

SURFING THE "NET"

Forming a Business

In this chapter you learned that business organizations can be set up in one of three ways—as a sole proprietorship, as a partnership, or as a corporation. Sole proprietorships are small, easy-to-manage enterprises owned by one person. Partnerships are owned by two or more persons and are, for the most part, larger than sole proprietorships. Stockholders own corporations, which are run by professional management teams selected by a board of directors. You can learn more about business organizations on the Internet.

Getting There

1. Use a search engine. Type in the words *business organization.*
2. After typing in *business organization,* enter words like the following to focus your search: *sole proprietorship, partnership, corporation, franchise.*
3. The search engine will provide you with a number of links to follow. Links are "pointers" to different sites on the Internet and often appear as blue, underlined words.

What to Do When You Are There

Click on the links to navigate through the pages of information. Gather your findings. Using the findings, plan your own business. Will you be a sole proprietor, a partner, or will you incorporate and sell stock? What steps will you first take to start your business? You may want to interview local business owners to find out why their businesses are organized the way they are. Outline your product and your business decisions on poster board to display in the classroom.

Identifying Key Terms

Write the letter of the definition in Column B below that correctly defines each term in Column A.

Column A
1. inventory (p. 210)
2. corporate charter (p. 221)
3. assets (p. 214)
4. franchise (p. 222)
5. unlimited liability (p. 214)

Column B
a. items of value
b. supply of items that are used in a business
c. sale by a business of the right to use its name to another business or individual
d. right to operate
e. legal responsibility for all debts and damages incurred when doing business

Write a paragraph about the advantages and disadvantages of different types of business organizations using the following terms.

sole proprietorship (p. 213)
partnership (p. 217)
limited partnership (p. 217)
joint venture (p. 217)
corporation (p. 219)
franchise (p. 222)

Recalling Facts and Ideas

Section 1
1. Every business involves expenses and receipts and record keeping. What are two other elements?
2. When you calculate your profits, it is especially important for you to include the value of your time. What is this called?

Section 2
3. What is the most common form of business organization?
4. What are the advantages and disadvantages of a sole proprietorship?
5. If you need help in starting a small business, where can you look?
6. Often two or more individuals want to start a business. What is one form of business organization they can use?
7. What is the difference between a limited partnership and a joint venture?

Section 3
8. What are the elements of every corporation?
9. Who grants corporate charters?
10. Which group within a corporation chooses the board of directors?
11. How does a franchise operate?

Critical Thinking

Section 1
Demonstrating Reasoned Judgment Why do you have to include the opportunity cost of your time when you calculate your profits in your own business?

Section 2
Drawing Conclusions Why would a person decide in favor of a partnership rather than a sole proprietorship?

Section 3
Analyzing Information What kind of problems in a corporation might be due to its complex organizational structure?

Applying Economic Concepts

Comparing Business Organizations In this chapter you have seen numerous advantages and disadvantages of different types of business organizations. Make a list of the following: sole proprietorship, partnership, limited partnership, joint venture, corporation, and franchise. After each type, indicate the single most important advantage that you believe this form of business organization has.

Chapter Projects

1. **Individual Project** Three major business news magazines report the top several hundred corporations in America every year, usually in May or June. They are *Forbes, Fortune,* and *Business Week*. Find one or more of these magazines in a library. Make a list of the latest information on the top five industrial corporations, such as General Motors and Microsoft. Indicate for each the following information: (1) number of employees, (2) total sales in billions of dollars, (3) total market value as given by the stock market (if available), and (4) change in ranking from the previous year.

2. **Cooperative Learning Project** Work in groups of four. Each group should select a corporation listed in the financial pages of a newspaper. Then use business magazines and financial and annual reports, if possible, to determine the annual earnings, dividends, and stock prices of that corporation over the last year. Compare the corporation with those selected by other groups and discuss which stocks would have been the best investments during the past year.

Reviewing Skills

Reading the Financial Page

Review what you learned about reading the financial page in Learning Economic Skills on page 218. Apply what you have learned to answer the following questions about the stock listings reprinted below.

1. How many shares of Apple Computer (AppleCptr) were traded?
2. What was the net change in the price of the stock of Apple Computer on this day?
3. Compare this day's closing price for Apple Computer with its 52-week high. How much less is this day's closing price?

52 Weeks			Sales				
High	Low	Stock	100s	High	Low	Last	Change
19¼	14½	AMTROL	45	19½	18½	18½	-¾
16⅞	$5\frac{15}{16}$	AmvstrFnl	314	10⅜	10	10⅛	-¼
15½	5¾	AmylinPharm	96	9	8¾	8¾	-¼
16¾	10¼	Analogic	489	15½	15	15⅛	-⅜
14½	9¾	Anly&Tech	532	14½	13⅝	13⅝	-⅜
35¾	16¼	Anlyint	72	29	28	29	...
18	10⅞	Anangel	2	17⅛	17⅛	17⅛	...
15	5⅝	AnchrBcp	560	14¼	14	14¼	...
24¾	11⅞	AnchrBcpWis	117	22½	22	22½	+¼
14¾	5¾	AndovrBcp	193	14¼	13⅞	14⅛	...
4¾	2¼	AndovrTog	67	2½	2¼	2½	...
30¼	16	AndrewCp	1055	28¼	27¾	28	+¼
19¼	10⅞	Andros	44	14½	14	14⅜	-⅛
13½	5½	Anergen	8	7	6½	6½	-½
5⅝	$1\frac{7}{16}$	ApertusTech	341	3¼	3	3	-⅛
12½	8⅝	ApogeeEnt	82	12	11¾	12	+¼
65¼	26½	AppleCptr	72258	28¾	25½	25⅝	-1⅞
24¾	5⅝	AppleSouth	402	23	22¼	23	...
22¼	8¼	Applebee	323	20¼	19¼	19¾	-¼
20	8¾	ApplncRecyc	136	9¾	9	9¼	-¼
15¼	4½	AppldBiosci	254	6	5⅞	5⅞	...
2¼	⅞	AppliedCrbn	39	1½	1⅜	1⅜	-⅛
25¼	11	AppldImuSci	393	20¼	19½	19½	...
62½	18	AppldMati	2338	59¼	56½	58¼	+1

Technology Activity

Using the Internet

Refer to the list of goods and services that you recorded in Your Economics Journal on page 207. Choose one of these goods or services from a large business. Then use your favorite search engine to locate the company's home page on the World Wide Web. Most large businesses have these sites. Once you have located the site, access it and use the information to prepare an oral report on the company's products and businesses.

ISSUE: Role of the Government in the Economy: Should Industry be Deregulated?

Deregulation of industries gained popularity in the 1980s, especially during the Reagan years (1981-89). Airlines, banking, and trucking were three of the most important industries deregulated. Cable TV had also been deregulated, so consumers blamed rising cable charges on this action. In 1992 Congress reregulated the cable TV industry in the hope of promoting competition and lowering prices. Many now believe that the government should reregulate other industries although cable TV was again deregulated in 1996.

PRO Deregulation brought many changes to the airline industry. Economist Alfred E. Kahn, a former chairman of the Civil Aeronautics Board (disbanded with deregulation), writes that the two most important consequences of airline deregulation have been lower fares and higher productivity. He also asserts that safety has increased since deregulation. Accident rates dropped 20-45 percent from the regulated years.

Economist Thomas Gale Moore also argues that deregulation works. He writes that previous regulation of the trucking industry increased costs and rates significantly, as well as lowered quality of service. Rates for the industry fell after deregulation, and competition increased as well. Moore writes on this success of deregulation in stimulating competition:

The number of new firms has increased dramatically. By 1990 the total number of licensed carriers exceeded forty thousand, considerably more than double the number authorized in 1980. The ICC [Interstate Commerce Commission, eliminated in 1996] had also awarded nationwide authority to about five thousand freight carriers. The value of operating rights granted by the ICC, once worth hundreds of thousands of dollars when such authority was almost impossible to secure from the commission, has plummeted to close to zero now that operating rights are easy to obtain.

Finally, Alfred Kahn warns against the recent reregulation trend:

Airline deregulation has worked. It would be ironic if, by misdiagnosing our present discontents, we were to return to policies of protectionism and centralized planning at the very time when countries as dissimilar as China, . . . Chile, Australia, France, Spain, and Poland are all discovering the superiority of the free market.

Counterpoint

Those who oppose CON deregulation argue that it has a tendency to make markets less competitive. Since deregulation in 1986, monthly basic cable rates have increased sharply. Gene Kimmelman, legislative director of the Consumer Federation of America, states that the reregulating of the cable TV industry was "a first step in the right direction. It's the first real cost savings to consumers that's come out of the (FCC) in a decade."

Others worry that deregulating the airlines also may not have been such a good idea. Airline fares are lower, but those against deregulation see the price cutting as fare wars designed to drive weaker competitors out of business, thus leading to less competition and higher fares in the long run. John Greenwald explains this position in *TIME* :

But there is a darker side to the fare war: many experts see it as a thinly veiled declaration of war against low-cost rivals like TWA and Continental, which currently fly under the protective wing of the bankruptcy courts and thus pay no interest on part of their debt. Life will get rougher for them once they emerge from Chapter 11 protection and are forced to survive on their own resources—something many analysts fear these weaker carriers may be unable to do for long. Once rid of such pesky competitors and their cutthroat tactics, the major airlines could regain full control of airfares— and might then be free to raise them.

Exploring the Issue

Reviewing Facts

1 What kind of changes did deregulation bring to the airline industry?

2 What is one argument for deregulation? One against?

Critical Thinking

3 Why do you think deregulation brought higher cable rates but lower airline fares?

10 COMPETITION AND MONOPOLIES

Where can you obtain information on air fares?

How do airlines determine air fares?

How many airline companies can you name?

How do these companies compete for business?

Do you think all airline companies make profits?

American

Your Economics Journal

Keep track for one week of your use of the following items: soft drinks, breakfast cereals, toothpaste, and soap. List these items and the brand that you chose to use. Next to each item explain why you chose that brand over the many others that exist.

Perfect Competition—An Ideal Rarely Realized

Competition is one of the basic characteristics of our market economic system. Regardless of its legal form of organization, each business attempts to capture as large a share of its market as possible. Figure 10.1 shows the four basic market structures in the American economy.

Conditions of Perfect Competition

All businesses must engage in some form of competition as long as other businesses produce similar goods or services. When a market includes so many sellers of a particular good or service that each seller accounts for a small part of the total market, a special situation exists. Economists term it **perfect competition.** Perfect competition has five conditions as shown in Figure 10.2.

On the supply side, perfect competition requires a large number of suppliers of a similar product. On the demand side, perfect competition requires a large number of informed buyers who know exactly what the market price is for the good or service. The market price is the equilibrium price. In a perfectly competitive market, total supply and total demand are allowed to interact to reach the equilibrium price. That is the only

Comparing Four Market Structures

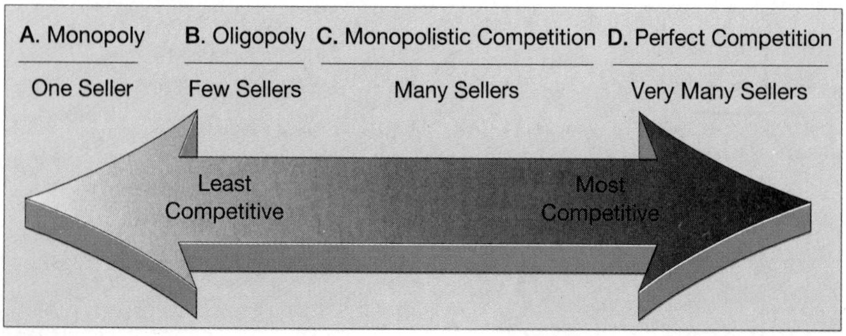

A. Monopoly	B. Oligopoly	C. Monopolistic Competition	D. Perfect Competition
One Seller	Few Sellers	Many Sellers	Very Many Sellers

Least Competitive ← → Most Competitive

**Figure 10.1
Comparing Market Structures**
Markets that are either perfectly competitive or pure monopolies are rare. Most industries in the United States fit one of the two other forms.

◄

price at which quantity demanded equals quantity supplied. In a world of perfect competition, each individual seller would accept that price. Because so many buyers and sellers exist, one person charging a higher or lower price would not affect the market price.

Perfect competition is rarely seen in the real world. For one thing, information is not often easily obtainable. In order for the price of a good or service to be the same for all sellers at every moment, all buyers and sellers would have to know what is happening to prices for that good or service everywhere at every moment. Obviously, business information is never that complete.

Agriculture as an Example

Few perfectly competitive industries exist in the United States. The one that perhaps comes closest is agriculture before the 1930s, when the federal government started to protect and regulate it. Since that time the government has sought to protect farmers by keeping the prices of some

▼ **Figure 10.2**
The Five Conditions of Perfect Competition
Perfect competition is rare, as these five conditions are difficult to attain all at once.

1 **A Large Market**   Numerous sellers and buyers.
2 **Similar Product**   A nearly identical good or service is sold.
3 **Easy Entry and Exit**   Sellers already in the market cannot prevent competition, or entrance into the market. In addition, the initial costs of investment are small, and the good or service is easy to learn to produce.
4 **Easily Obtainable Information**
Information about prices, quality, and sources of supply is easy for both buyers and sellers to obtain.
As a result, there is:
5 **No Control Over Price**
The workings of supply and demand control the market, not a single seller or buyer.

Figure 10.3 ▶
Five Factors that Make Wheat Farming Competitive

Consider the wheat market.

1 Thousands of wheat farmers and thousands of wholesalers buy wheat.
2 All wheat is fairly similar.
3 The costs of buying or renting farmland are low compared to starting a corporation, and farming methods can be learned.
4 Because wheat is sold to wholesalers, information about prices is fairly easy to obtain.
5 No one farmer has any great influence on price.

agricultural products high and by restricting the production of some products. Nonetheless, the agricultural market is often used as an example of perfect competition, because individual farmers have almost no control over the market price of their goods. The wheat farm illustrated in Figure 10.3 provides one example.

The interaction of supply and demand determines the price of wheat. The supply is the total supply all wheat farmers produce. The demand is the total demand for all uses of wheat. The equilibrium price is the price where supply and demand meet.

Individual wheat farmers have to accept the market price. If the price is $5 per bushel, that is the price every farmer must accept. Farmers who attempt to raise their price above $5 will find that no one will buy their wheat. Neither will a farmer sell his or her crop for less than $5 per bushel. The market price is the only price that both buyers and sellers will accept.

The demand for wheat—and food in general—is somewhat different from the demand for many other products. People's demand for food is, for the most part, inelastic. People can use wheat in only so many ways, and people can eat only so many wheat products. The supply side of most agricultural markets is also unique. It is highly dependent on conditions over which farmers have little control such as those shown in Figure 10.4.

The Desirability of Perfect Competition

While we know that perfect competition is possible only in theory, any industry that tends toward it does have special characteristics. The intense competition in a perfectly competitive industry forces the price down to one that just covers the costs of production plus a normal profit. This price is beneficial to society because it means that consumers of products from perfectly competitive industries are paying only what society has to put in to make those products—the opportunity cost of the use

of land, labor, capital, and entrepreneurship. The price that consumers pay for such products is a correct signal about the value of that product in society. Perfectly competitive industries yield economic efficiency. No rearrangement of the land, labor, capital, and entrepreneurship would generate a higher valued output. In an efficient situation such as this, it is impossible to make one person better off without making some other individual worse off. All inputs are used in the most advantageous way possible, and society therefore enjoys an efficient allocation of productive resources. All goods and services are sold at their opportunity cost.

**Figure 10.4 ▲
Disasters for Farmers**
Variations in weather, a crop disease, or a crop-destroying insect can wipe out entire harvests. This means that farmers may have a good harvest one year and a poor one the next. As a result, there are widely fluctuating, or changing, supplies of goods in the agricultural market.

SECTION 1 REVIEW

Understanding Vocabulary
Define perfect competition.

Reviewing Objectives
1. What five requirements are needed to have perfect competition?

2. What elements of agriculture make it almost perfectly competitive?

3. Why is perfect competition good for consumers?

Using a Computerized Card Catalog

Using a computerized card catalog makes it easy to find any information you need for a term paper or research project. The following guidelines will help you get started in your search for information.

Using the Catalog

Type in the subject you want to research or the name of an author whose work might be helpful to you.

Suppose you want to find information about government monopolies in the United States. You could search by entering **s** (for **subject**)/government monopolies, United States.

First, you will see a list of titles. Select one of these, and a "card" will appear on the screen. This shows important information about the book.

Searching the Catalog

Use the following steps in a search for information about American Airlines:

❶ Type s/American Airlines. Choose a title from the list that appears. You might see a screen similar to the one shown here.

❷ From the description on the screen, determine whether the book will give you the information you need, and then determine the book's availability.

❸ Remember to follow the directions at the bottom of the screen. These enable you to change screens or find additional information about the book.

Practicing the Skill

Using a computerized card catalog, compile a list of 10 sources you might use to write an essay about monopolistic competition in the United States.

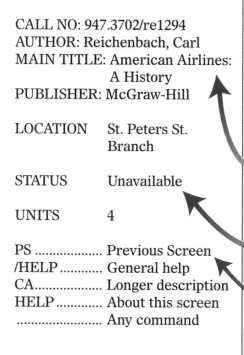

CALL NO: 947.3702/re1294
AUTHOR: Reichenbach, Carl
MAIN TITLE: American Airlines:
　　　　　　　A History
PUBLISHER: McGraw-Hill

LOCATION　　St. Peters St.
　　　　　　　Branch

STATUS　　　Unavailable

UNITS　　　　4

PS .... Previous Screen
/HELP .... General help
CA.................... Longer description
HELP .... About this screen
.... Any command

SECTION 2

Monopoly, Oligopoly, and Monopolistic Competition

SECTION 2 FOCUS

Terms to Know imperfect competition, pure monopoly, barriers to entry, cartel, natural monopolies, geographic monopolies, technological monopoly, patent, government monopolies, product differentiation, oligopoly, monopolistic competition

Objectives *After reading this section, you should be able to:*

1. List the four characteristics of a pure **monopoly**.
2. Describe the five characteristics of an **oligopoly**.
3. Explain the five characteristics of **monopolistic competition**.

From One Seller to Many Sellers—Different Market Structures

Most industries in the American economy are not perfectly competitive. Most represent some form of imperfect competition. **Imperfect competition** exists when any individual or group buys or sells a good or service in amounts large enough to affect price. Many market structures are imperfectly competitive, including monopoly, oligopoly, and monopolistic competition.

Monopoly

The most extreme form of imperfect competition is a **pure monopoly** whereby a single seller controls the supply of the good or service and thus determines the price. A few such markets do exist in the real world. Some local electric utilities like the one in Figure 10.5 are monopolies. The United States Postal Service's delivery of first-class mail is another example of a pure monopoly. Figure 10.6 (page 238) shows four characteristics of a pure monopoly.

Figure 10.5
Local Electric Companies
Because some local electric utilities are the sole providers and the consumer has no other option, they are monopolies.

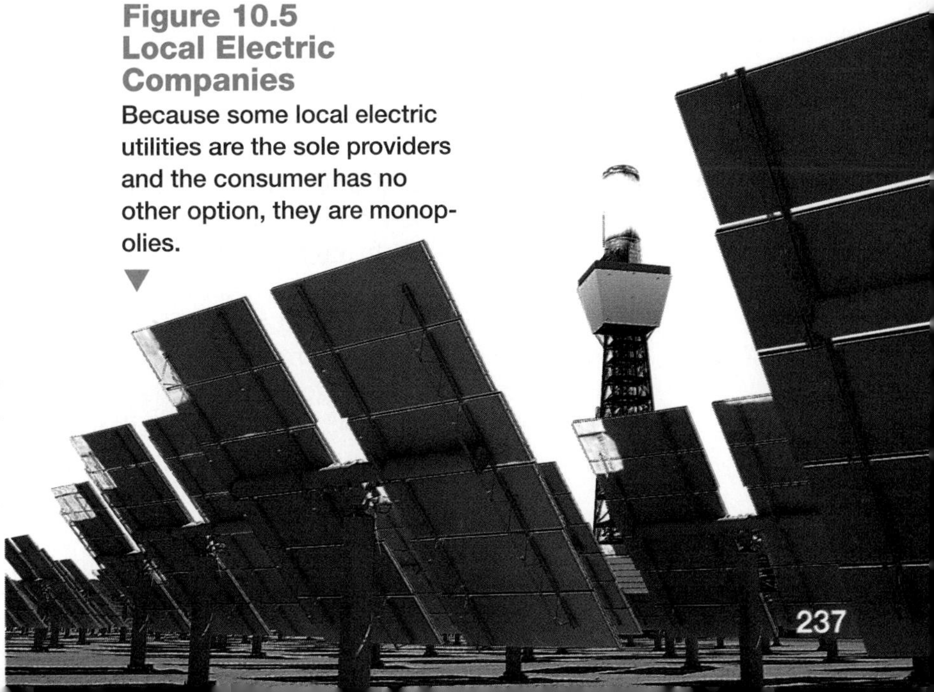

Figure 10.6 ▶
What Makes a Pure Monopoly?
Four specific characteristics must exist:
1 A Single Seller
2 No Substitutes
3 No Entry
4 Almost Complete Control of Market Price

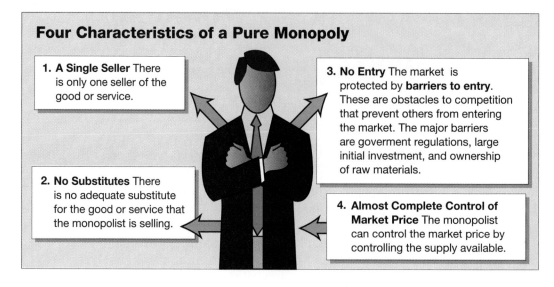

Four Characteristics of a Pure Monopoly

1. **A Single Seller** There is only one seller of the good or service.

2. **No Substitutes** There is no adequate substitute for the good or service that the monopolist is selling.

3. **No Entry** The market is protected by **barriers to entry**. These are obstacles to competition that prevent others from entering the market. The major barriers are goverment regulations, large initial investment, and ownership of raw materials.

4. **Almost Complete Control of Market Price** The monopolist can control the market price by controlling the supply available.

In a pure monopoly, the supplier can raise prices without fear of losing business to competitors. Unless buyers choose to pay the new price, they have nowhere else to buy the good or service. A monopolist, however, cannot charge outrageous prices. In a monopoly market, the law of demand is still operating. As the price of a good or service rises, consumers buy less. Profits, as a result, may decrease. In other cases buyers may turn to an alternative good or service.

For example, some people believe that for years the United States Postal Service has provided poor service for the delivery of first-class mail, at steadily rising prices. Customers have increasingly turned to alternatives, such as telephone calls, fax transmissions, and overnight delivery service provided by such competitors as Federal Express, Airborne, United Parcel Service, and DHL. Also, it is now possible to easily send documents around the world through computers via E-mail and the Internet. Hence, the United States Postal Service's monopoly on first-class mail has not meant that it can charge any price and provide any level of service and still keep customers using it at the same level as before.

Barriers to Entry The most obvious barriers to entry into a monopolistic market are legal ones. For example, some state laws prevent a competing electric, gas, or water company from operating in an area where there already is a public utility company. The reasoning against competition in public utility industries is that too much competition may lead to wasteful duplication. For example, if your town had two electric companies, they might both have electric lines strung around the city. They might be duplicating efforts, which might result in a wasteful use of resources. It might also result in higher rates to customers because of the lack of efficiency in operation.

Another barrier to entry is the cost of getting started. This barrier to entry is called excessive money capital costs. It is found in industries, such as cars and steel, in which initial investment is high because of the amount and cost of the equipment. The first company to make the investment will clearly have an advantage over later companies that want to enter the market.

Ownership of essential raw materials can also provide a barrier to entry. A good example is the diamond industry. The DeBeers Company of the Republic of South Africa controls the marketing of nearly all the world's diamonds. An example from American history is the Aluminum Company of America (ALCOA). At the turn of the twentieth century, it controlled almost all sources of bauxite (BAHK-syt), the major ore used in aluminum. For many years, ALCOA was able to keep its near-monopoly in aluminum because it would not sell bauxite to potential competitors.

Types of Monopolies Pure monopolies can be separated into four categories depending on why the mono-

poly exists. **Figure 10.7** explains these categories.

An international form of monopoly is the cartel. A **cartel** is an arrangement among groups of industrial businesses, often in different countries, to reduce international competition by controlling price, production, and the distribution of goods. Among the best-known cartels is the Organization of Petroleum Exporting Countries (OPEC), which was formed in 1960. Today OPEC includes several nations in the Middle East and North Africa,

B Geographic Monopolies
- Best location
- But less important now; customers can buy from catalogs, etc.

Example: A small-town auto repair shop ▼

C Technological Monopoly
- Seller has a government **patent,** the right to exclusively manufacture an invention for a specified number of years

Example: Polaroid film ▼

Figure 10.7 Types of Monopolies

Monopolies can be separated into four categories:

A Natural Monopolies
- Produce products for lowest cost and force competitors out of business
- Need large investment
- More efficient to have one company

Example: Some electric companies ▼

D Government ▶ Monopolies
- Created by legal barriers to entry

Example: Tennessee Valley Authority (TVA)

Figure 10.8 Characteristics of an Oligopoly

The domestic airline industry illustrates the characteristics of an oligopoly.

1 **Domination by a Few Sellers**
Several large firms dominate the entire industry.

2 **Barriers to Entry**
Capital costs of airlines are high, and it may be difficult for new companies to enter major markets.

3 **Identical or Slightly Different Products**
Most airlines offer essentially the same service.

4 **Nonprice Competition**
While most airline services are about the same, some competition takes the form of **product differentiation.** Advertising emphasizes minor differences and attempts to build customer loyalty.

5 **Limited Control Over Price**
The airline industry has frequent price wars. If one airline lowers its fares, other airlines lower theirs even more.

▼

as well as Nigeria, Gabon, Venezuela, Ecuador, and Indonesia.

How Important Are Monopolies?
Monopolies today are far less important than they once were. Geographic monopolies probably have little effect because of potential competition from mail-order businesses. You can also be fairly certain that a technological monopoly will not last much longer than the life of a patent. Because of modern technology, competitors can make and patent slight variations in new products quickly. The microcomputer revolution in the early 1980s followed such a pattern. One company copied another's product, making changes and adding features to obtain a patent of its own.

International Business Machines (IBM) had at one time controlled a "lock" on the computer business. It sold mainframes—the biggest kind of computer—and made huge profits. In the early 1990s, IBM faced decline because of the technological revolution in microcomputers. IBM had failed to adapt quickly enough to the changing market and lost its near monopoly.

Oligopoly

An **oligopoly** (AHL-uh-GAHP-uh-lee) is an industry in which a few suppliers that exercise some control over price dominate. Some economists argue that the airline industry, as **Figure 10.8** suggests, is an example of an oligopoly. They point out that until very recently, it was almost impossible for foreign airlines to compete in domestic markets.

Figure 10.9 shows a number of industries in which the four largest firms produce more than 80 percent of the total industry output. All these industries are oligopolies. Saying that an industry is an oligopoly does not necessarily mean that the situation should be changed.

Stable Prices A surprising feature of the general criticism of oligopolies is that little proof exists that they are harmful. It is true that consumers may be paying more than if they were buying in a perfectly competitive market in which supply and demand would set the price. Oligopolistic markets, however, tend to have generally stable prices. They also offer consumers a wider variety of different products than would a perfectly competitive industry.

Monopolistic Competition

In **monopolistic competition,** a large number of sellers offer similar but slightly different products. Obvious examples are such brand-name items as toothpaste, cosmetics, and designer clothes.

Monopolistic competition characterizes many industries in the United States. Qualities of this type of industry are shown in Figure 10.10 (page 242).

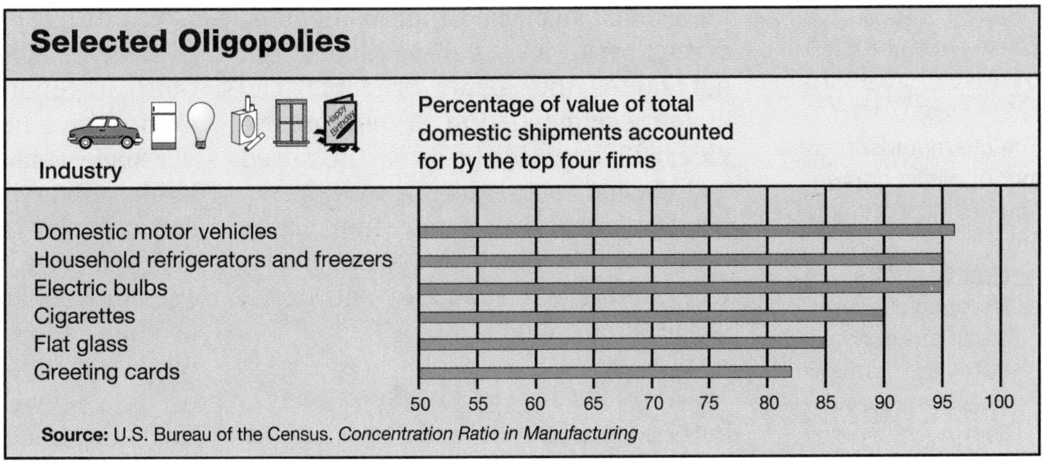

Comparisons of Oligopolies and Pure Monopolies

Many of the characteristics of monopolistic competition are the same as those of an oligopoly. The major differences, however, are in the number of sellers of a product and in the product. In an oligopoly, a few companies dominate an industry, and control over price is interdependent. The products may or may not be similar. Monopolistic competition has many firms, no real interdependence, and some slight difference among products.

Perfect competition has so many buyers and sellers that no one has any control over price. Everyone must take the price the interaction of total demand and total supply determines. In monopolistic competition each competitor has some control over the price of its product. A monopolistic competitor, however, does not have as much control over price as a pure

Selected Oligopolies

Industry	Percentage of value of total domestic shipments accounted for by the top four firms
Domestic motor vehicles	
Household refrigerators and freezers	
Electric bulbs	
Cigarettes	
Flat glass	
Greeting cards	

50 55 60 65 70 75 80 85 90 95 100

Source: U.S. Bureau of the Census. *Concentration Ratio in Manufacturing*

▲

**Figure 10.9
Oligopolies**

Oligopolies exist in a number of industries throughout the United States. Here, a wide range of industries are highlighted.

Figure 10.10 Characteristics of Monopolistic Competition

The characteristics of monopolistic competition within an industry are:

1 **Numerous Sellers** No one seller or small group dominates the market.

2 **Relatively Easy Entry** Entry is easier than in other types of imperfectly competitive markets. One drawback is the high cost of advertising.

3 **Differentiated Products** Each seller sells a slightly different product to attract customers.

4 **Nonprice Competition** Businesses compete by product differentiation and by advertising. These result in:

5 **Some Control Over Price** Each firm has some control over the price it charges due to customer loyalty and product differentiation. ▶

monopolist because other monopolistic competitors are selling almost, but not quite, the same product. The quantity demanded of a good or service will drop if the price is raised and cheaper substitutes are available. If one monopolistic competitor raises the price too much, most customers will buy another brand, or substitute, of the same good.

Neighborhood Businesses Neighborhood businesses such as cleaners and drugstores are involved in monopolistic competition. Each business within the neighborhood has an identity of its own even though the differences between its good or service and those of its competitors may be small.

Competitive Advertising Competitive advertising is especially important in monopolistic competition. Competitive advertising attempts to persuade consumers that the product being advertised is different from, and superior to, any other. Businesses also compete for shelf space—space on store shelves for displaying their products and attracting buyers. A cosmetics company, for example, may produce several lines of cosmetics. Each is aimed at a different market segment, or section. By having three lines, the company competes in three areas with competitors. The differences in products attract different customers and add to the profits of the company.

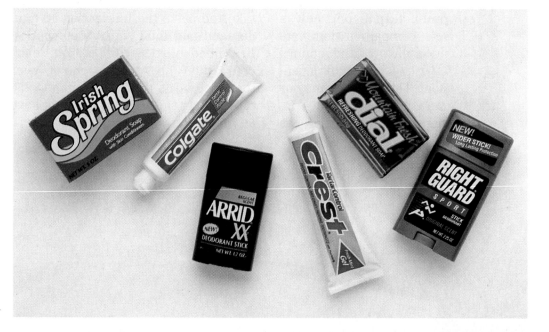

SECTION 2 REVIEW

Understanding Vocabulary

Define imperfect competition, pure monopoly, barriers to entry, cartel, natural monopolies, geographic monopolies, technological monopoly, patent, government monopolies, product differentiation, oligopoly, monopolistic competition.

Reviewing Objectives

1 What are the four characteristics of a pure monopoly?

2 What characteristics of an oligopoly allow it to have a limited control over price?

3 What are the five characteristics of monopolistic competition?

Personal Perspective

Joan Robinson on Imperfect Competition

Profile

- 1903–1983
- was Professor of Economics at Cambridge University in England
- best known for developing theory of monopolistic competition
- authored many books, including *The Economics of Imperfect Competition* (1933) and *Economic Heresies: Some Old-Fashioned Questions in Economic Theory* (1971)

Joan Robinson, who produced her first major work in economics during the Great Depression, believed that there was something wrong with the theory of competition. Adam Smith had said competition would benefit society as individuals maximized their own best interests. Robinson disagreed. She criticized economists who ignored social and moral issues. In *The Economics of Imperfect Competition*, Robinson said the model of competition Smith used does not exist in the real world.

The traditional assumption of perfect competition is an exceedingly convenient one for simplifying the analysis of price, but there is no reason to expect it to be fulfilled in the real world. It depends, in the first place, upon the existence of such a large number of producers that a change in the output of any one of them has a negligible effect upon the output of the commodity as a whole, and it depends, in the second place, upon the existence of a perfect market. The first condition may often be approximately fulfilled, but the existence of a perfect market is likely to be extremely rare in the real world.

Robinson believed that price is only one of the factors that consumers consider. Convenience, quality, speed of service, or even the manners of salespeople influence consumers.

. . . Rival producers compete against each other in quality, in facilities, and in advertisement, as well as in price, and the very intensity of competition, by forcing them to attract customers in every possible way, itself breaks up the market and ensures that not all the customers, who are attached in varying degrees to a particular firm by the advantages which it offers them, will immediately forsake it for a rival who offers similar goods at an infinitesimally smaller price.

Checking for Understanding

1. What two conditions are necessary to have perfect competition?
2. Which condition of perfect competition is extremely rare?
3. Besides price, what do producers use to attract customers?

The Government Regulates Business in an Attempt to Protect Consumers

Historically, one of the goals of government in the United States has been to encourage competition in the economy. Through the years, federal and state governments have passed laws and established regulatory agencies in an attempt to force monopolies to act more competitively. Known as **antitrust legislation,** these laws act to prevent new monopolies, or trusts, from forming and to break up those that already exist. See Figures 10.11 and 10.12.

Figure 10.11 Antitrust History
President Theodore Roosevelt, portrayed here breaking up trusts in the early 1900s, believed monopolies were "the tyranny of mere wealth."

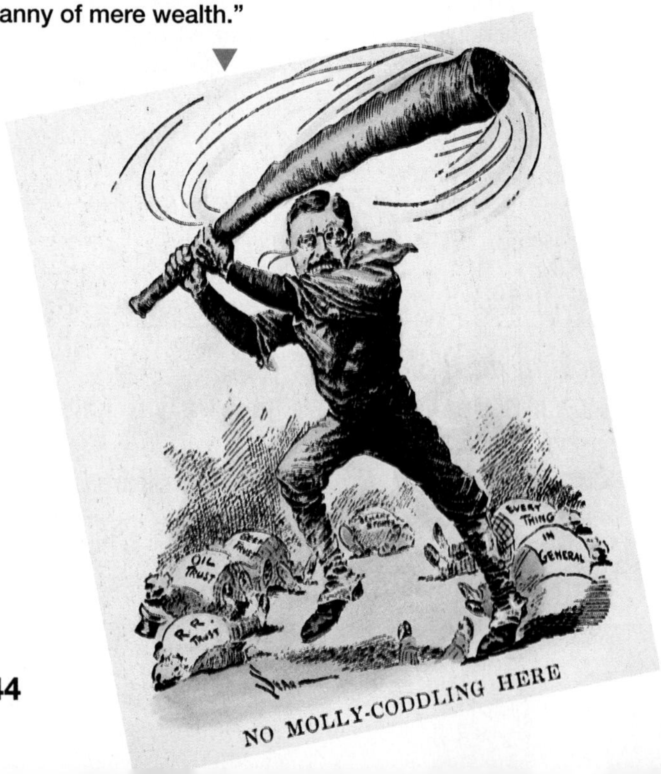

NO MOLLY-CODDLING HERE

Interlocking Directorates and Mergers

You should be familiar with two terms from the table: *interlocking directorate* and *merger*. An **interlocking directorate** occurs when some members of the boards of directors of competing corporations are the same. In effect, only one group of people manages both companies. Because the same people control both companies, it is easy for them to make sure that the two companies do not compete with one another.

The last point in the table under the Clayton Act refers to corporate mergers. A **merger** occurs when one

Figure 10.12 Antitrust Legislation

Federal Law	Function
Sherman Act (1890)	Outlawed agreements and conspiracies that restrain interstate trade. Made it illegal to monopolize or even attempt to monopolize any part of interstate commerce.
Clayton Act (1914)	Restricted the practice of selling the same good to different buyers at different prices. Prohibited sellers from requiring that a buyer not deal with a competitor. Outlawed interlocking directorates between competitors. Outlawed mergers that substantially lessen competition.
Federal Trade Commission Act (1914)	Established the Federal Trade Commission (FTC) as an independent antitrust agency. Gave the FTC power to bring court cases against private businesses engaging in unfair trade practices.
Robinson-Patman Act (1936)	Strengthened the law against charging different prices for the same product to different buyers. An amendment to the Clayton Act of 1914.
Celler-Kefauver Antimerger Act (1950)	Strengthened the law against firms joining together to control too large a part of the market. An amendment to the Clayton Act of 1914.
Hart-Scott-Rodino Antitrust Improvements Act (1976)	Restricted mergers that would lessen competition. It required big corporations planning to merge to notify the Federal Trade Commission (FTC) and the Department of Justice. They would then decide whether to challenge the merger under the terms of the Clayton Act of 1914.

corporation joins with another corporation.

Three kinds of mergers exist. When the two corporations are in the same business, it is called a **horizontal merger.** When a business that is buying from or selling to another business merges with that business, a **vertical merger** takes place. Some corporations have become big by buying out other corporations dealing in totally unrelated activities. These expanded corporations are called **conglomerates.** The buying out of an unrelated business is termed **conglomerate merger.**

The Clayton Act forbids mergers when they tend to lessen competition substantially. The Clayton Act, however, does not state what the term *substantially* means. As a result, it is up to the federal government to make a subjective decision as to whether the merging of two corporations would substantially lessen competition.

Regulatory Agencies

Besides using antitrust laws to foster a competitive atmosphere, the government uses direct regulation of business pricing and product quality.

Government regulatory agencies oversee these regulations. See Figure 10.14. These agencies exist not only at the federal level, but at the state level and even at local levels.

Although the aim of most government regulations is to promote efficiency and competition, recent evidence indicates something quite different. Many regulations, as a byproduct of their goals to protect consumers and companies within industries from unfair practices, have actually decreased the amount of competition in the economy.

The Interstate Commerce Commission (ICC) raised the prices that consumers paid to ship goods by preventing entry into the trucking industry and restricting price competition.

For many years the Federal Communications Commission (FCC), in an effort to help UHF stations, in effect prevented the entry of competitive pay-TV, cable, and satellite systems into the television market.

While the Civil Aeronautics Board (CAB) regulated air fares, these fares were 20 to 30 percent higher than they were after deregulation when competition was allowed to set prices.

Because of findings such as these, the 1980s were called the years of **deregulation** as government gradually reduced regulations and control over business activity. For example, the

CAB no longer controlled air fares or route selection by the nation's airlines. The cable television industry provides another example, as Figure 10.13 shows. The many regulations in the banking industry were slowly decreased, allowing consumers to obtain competitive interest rates on savings for the first time in years.

Should There Be Reregulation?

Congress has considered **reregulation** of a number of formerly heavily regulated industries. Many heads of airlines have asked for reregulation of the airline industry. Many people criticized the deregulation of the cable TV industry. Consequently, Congress began reregulation with the 1992 Cable Reregulation Act. Then, in 1996 it loosened cable regulation again.

Figure 10.13 ▶
Cable Deregulation
The Federal Communications Commission (FCC), which had prevented the entry of pay-TV, cable, and satellite systems into the TV market, now allows almost open competition in the direct-satellite television transmission fields.

Figure 10.14 Federal Regulatory Agencies

Agency	Function
Federal Trade Commission (FTC) (1914)	Regulates product warranties, unfair methods of competition in interstate commerce, and fraud in advertising.
Food and Drug Administration (FDA) (1927)	Regulates purity and safety of foods, drugs, and cosmetics.
Federal Communications Commission (FCC) (1934)	Regulates television, radio, telegraph, and telephone; grants licenses, creates and enforces rules of behavior for broadcasting; most recently, partly regulates satellite transmissions and cable TV.
Securities and Exchange Commission (SEC) (1934)	Regulates the sale of stocks, bonds, and other investments.
Equal Employment Opportunity Commission (EEOC) (1964)	Responsible for working to reduce discrimination based on religion, gender, race, national origin, or age.
Occupational Safety and Health Administration (OSHA) (1970)	Regulates the workplace environment; makes sure that businesses provide workers with safe and healthful working conditions.
Environmental Protection Agency (EPA) (1970)	Develops and enforces environmental standards for air, water, and toxic waste.
Nuclear Regulatory Commission (NRC) (1974)	Regulates the nuclear power industry; licenses and oversees the design, construction, and operation of nuclear power plants.

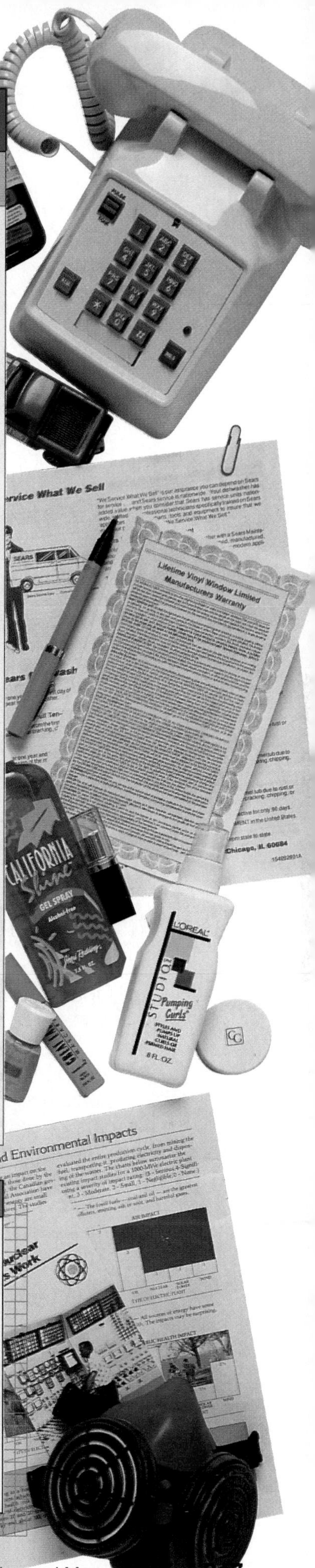

SECTION 3 REVIEW

Understanding Vocabulary

Define antitrust legislation, interlocking directorate, merger, horizontal merger, vertical merger, conglomerates, conglomerate merger, deregulation, reregulation.

Reviewing Objectives

1. How do interlocking directorates differ from mergers?
2. What are some major federal regulatory agencies in the United States?
3. Why do some Americans favor reregulation?

Readings in Economics

THE NEW YORK TIMES   JUNE 7, 1997

NIKE—IN A LEAGUE OF ITS OWN

by Jennifer Steinhauer

Slouched in their chairs, eyes fixed on a table littered with shoes, they give their grim assessments. A sneaker by Fila? Overpriced. A pair of new Reeboks? The group is more charitable, though one person says the bubbled soles look like "something for NASA." . . .

Finally, out comes **Nike** Inc.'s new shoe, named for Anfernee (Penny) Hardaway, the star guard for the Orlando Magic. The room, filled with high school students, breaks into applause, undeterred by the Penny's $180 price tag.

If Nike is the Chicago Bulls of the athletic shoe market, retailers are holding their breath for a strong underdog player to emerge. There is no question that shoe merchants have raked in profits right along with Nike during its near decade of dominance. And if the applause from the students . . . is any indication, they will continue to do so. . . .

"No retailer wants its fortunes to rise and fall with one vendor. So the shoe merchants are crossing their fingers, hoping that one or more companies with significantly less than Nike's 43 percent market share will pump out a product that makes them a contender. . . .

Still, Nike, based in Beaverton, Ore., is simply too far ahead—with plenty of kick left in its legs, not to mention cash in its advertising and research budgets—to be overtaken any time soon, many in the industry say. . . .

But many retailers are rankled, analysts say. "Because Nike has been so big, they have been able to dictate a lot of things to retailers, and retailers are not too comfortable with the situation," said Faye Landes, an analyst at Smith Barney. . . .

There isn't a retailer who has been born that wouldn't like three or four vendors to play off each other," he said, "But there is no one in the second tier that can really challenge Nike in a significant way right now. But remember, never is a long time."

• THINK ABOUT IT •

1. *Who is Nike's new shoe named for?*

2. *Why would retailers welcome successful competitors into the athletic shoe business?*

ECONOMICS IN ACTION

Competition and Monopolies

Setting up the Video

With your classmates, view "Competition and Monopolies" on the videodisc *Economics in Action.* The video focuses on competition in a free enterprise system, using the airline industry as an example. It demonstrates that in cities where a monopoly or oligopoly exists (where only one or just a few airlines serve a city) ticket prices are high. The video goes on to examine a proposed merger in the toy industry that would have virtually eliminated competition in that industry.

Chapter 14
Disc 1, Side 2

View the video by scanning the bar code or by entering the chapter number on your keypad and pressing Search. *(Also available in VHS format.)*

Hands-On Activity

With two of your classmates, choose a major industry such as banking, automobile, telephone and communications, steel, or food processing. In making your choice, consider industries that have a major impact on your community's economy. Research the level of competition in the industry you have chosen and predict whether the number of competitors in the industry is likely to increase or decrease. Be certain to explain why you believe competition will increase or decrease. Share your findings with the class during a class discussion focusing on competition in your community.

SURFING THE "NET"

Government Regulation

Today, government has the power to maintain competition and to regulate certain monopolies that exist for the public welfare. In some cases government has taken over certain economic activities and runs them as government-owned monopolies. Since the late 1800s, the United States has passed laws to restrict monopolies, combinations, and trusts—legally formed combinations of corporations or companies. You can learn more about government regulation of business on the Internet.

Getting There

1. Use a search engine. Type in the words *government regulation.*

2. After typing in *government regulation,* enter words like the following to focus your search: *mergers, antitrust, monopoly, oligopoly,* and *price-fixing.*
3. The search engine will provide you with a number of links to follow. Links are "pointers" to different sites on the Internet and often appear as blue, underlined words.

What to Do When You Are There

Click on the links to navigate through the pages of information. Gather your findings. Using the findings, write several paragraphs describing recent governmental antitrust regulations. Take a position for or against these antitrust regulations and support your position with examples from your research.

Identifying Key Terms

Write the letter of the definition in Column B below that correctly defines each term in Column A.

Column A
1. barriers to entry (p. 238)
2. deregulation (p. 246)
3. conglomerate (p. 245)
4. interlocking directorate (p. 244)
5. natural monopoly (p. 239)
6. merger (p. 244)

Column B
a. large corporation made up of smaller companies dealing in unrelated activities
b. the joining together of two corporations
c. obstacles to competition that prevent new companies from being formed
d. process of removing goverment restrictions of business
e. production by one company rather than several, due to efficient operation
f. situation in which some of the board of directors for competing companies are the same

Use terms from the list below to fill in the blanks in the paragraph that follows.

monopolistic competition (p. 240)
oligopoly (p. 240)
government monopoly (p. 239)
geographic monopoly (p. 239)
antitrust legislation (p. 244)

One form of imperfect competition in which a few firms compete is __(7)__. Another form of imperfect competition in which many firms compete, but each has a differentiated product is __(8)__. Monopolies have great control over price. Even a small mom and pop store in an isolated town has a __(9)__. Many times the federal government creates legal barriers to entry and thereby forms a __(10)__, such as the United States Postal Service. In order to prevent monopolies, there are federal laws called __(11)__.

Recalling Facts and Ideas

Section 1
1. In a perfectly competitive market structure, how much control does a single seller have over market price?
2. What is the relationship between the types of products that sellers sell in a perfectly competitive market?
3. What is one example of an almost perfectly competitive market?

Section 2
4. What are the three types of imperfectly competitive market structures?
5. What is the difference between a geographic monopoly and a technological monopoly?
6. How much control does an oligopoly have over price?
7. In monopolistic competition, how many sellers are there?

Section 3
8. What is the difference between a horizontal merger and a vertical merger?
9. What two methods does the federal government use to keep business competitive?

Critical Thinking

Section 1

Identifying Central Issues Explain in a paragraph how supply and demand work in the agricultural market when government controls are not operating.

Section 2

Making Generalizations Explain how the free enterprise system works to break the power of monopolies.

Section 3

Making Comparisons What are the fundamental differences between the goals of antitrust legislation and the goals of federal government regulations enforced through regulatory agencies?

Applying Economic Concepts

Competition and Market Structure Make a list of the different types of monopolies that can exist. Under each type, make a list of examples. Under government monopolies, for example, you have already learned about the United States Postal Service and the Tennessee Valley Authority. Others exist at the state and local levels.

Chapter Projects

1. **Individual Project** Choose one of the regulatory agencies mentioned in this chapter and write to the agency for information about its functions. Use the information you receive to write a report summarizing the main functions of that agency.
2. **Cooperative Learning Project** Numerous firms operate in imperfectly competitive market structures. Work in three groups— one representing monopolies, one oligopolies, and one monopolistic competition. Each member of each group should clip out ads and articles that give examples of firms that have the characteristics of the type of mar-

ket structure her or his group represents.

Compare the sets of ads for each of the three groups. There undoubtedly will be some overlap. One group might claim that a particular company is an oligopoly, whereas another group might claim that it is a monopoly. Your group should be able to defend the reason it places a particular company in its particular grouping.

Reviewing Skills

Using a Computerized Card Catalog Use the card catalog computer in your school or local library to find out more about oligopolies in the United States.
- Type "s/oligopolies."
- From the list of subjects that appears on the screen, determine which might apply to the United States.
- Follow the instructions on the computer screen to display all the titles under each subject you selected.
- Record the titles and call numbers of four works that might be useful for your research.

Technology Activity
Using E-Mail

Refer to the list of goods that you recorded in Your Economics Journal on page 231. Choose one of these goods from a large business. Then use your favorite search engine to locate the home page of the product's manufacturer on the World Wide Web. Most large businesses have these sites. Once you have located the site, access it and find the E-mail address for the customer service department. Compose an E-mail in which you ask for more information on the product. Share the E-mail response you receive with the class.

Running a Business

From the classroom of Judy B. Smitherman, Thompson High School, Alabaster, Alabama

In Unit 3 you read about markets, prices, and business competition. In this lab, you will make decisions as the sole proprietor of a business called Sidewalk Tees that sells screen printed T-shirts. (You may want to reread the material on pages 208–211 of the text.)

Tools

1. Ruler, pencils, writing paper, graph paper
2. Calculator

Procedures

Step A Read the following description of your production requirements and costs:

The screen printing equipment and display hangers cost $4,800. For this you need a bank loan. The monthly payment on this loan is $220. One month's supply of ink and screens costs $240. The best wholesale price for good T-shirts is $3.25. You should order an equal number of large and extra-large shirts in assorted colors. Gas for your car for business purposes costs $15 each week. Utilities and miscellaneous costs will be an additional $40 per month. Bank checking charges total $8 monthly. A yearly business license costs $52, and you can rent a booth from the Beachfront Flea Market for $26 per day. You plan to rent a booth Friday, Saturday, and Sunday each week. Operating alone, you can produce 80 shirts in a 20-hour week (4 per hour). By adding a part-time worker for 20 hours, you can produce 200 shirts (10 per hour). Expenses for a part-time worker total $7 per hour.

Step B Using a table like the one below, draw up a weekly financial plan for Sidewalk Tees.

Example

TOTAL WEEKLY COSTS

Item	Cost per week
Booth rental	
Utilities, gasoline, and miscellaneous costs	
Bank loan	
Bank checking	
Ink and screens	
T-shirts	
License	
Wages	
Total weekly costs	

Step C Pricing your product is important because your prices will help determine how well the product sells and how much profit you make. After studying the market for T-shirts, you project the effect of price changes on quantities demanded in a table like this one:

Price per shirt	Quantity demanded per week
$ 8.00	200
$ 9.00	170
$10.00	140
$11.00	110
$12.00	90

Determine your costs for each shirt, and find your profits. Remember that labor and other variable costs will change depending on the quantity of goods you produce. Copy the following table and complete different pricing plans:

Example

PRODUCT PRICING AND PROFIT

Item	Amount	
	Plan A	Plan B
Price per unit		
Estimated units sold per weekend		
Net revenues per weekend		
Less expenses per week		
Weekly gross profits		
Less 8% taxes		
Weekly net profits		

Step D Review your decisions. What are your variable costs? Could you have earned more profit by increasing or reducing your part-time worker's hours? What would result if you increased or reduced prices for the T-shirts?

Lab Report

Step E Use your projected weekly costs and product pricing and profits to answer the questions below.

1. How did you arrive at a unit price for the T-shirts?
2. What options do you have regarding employing your part-time helper?
3. What would you do if a stormy weekend reduced your sales by half?
4. What would you do if a nearby competitor began to sell T-shirts for less?
5. What decision could be made if your inventory of yellow T-shirts was three times larger than any other color?

Step F Use the following question for class discussion.

If profits remain high each week, how might you plan to expand your T-shirt business?

U N I T 4

MICROECONOMICS: AMERICAN BUSINESS IN ACTION

11 FINANCING AND PRODUCING GOODS

How much do you think it cost to build and equip this plant?

What is being produced here?

Would the product being produced cost more or less if everything were done by hand?

Do you think this physical work would be interesting or boring?

Why is the production process set up in this way?

Your Economics Journal

Keep track of the consumer products that you use in your house during a one-week period, excluding food, cosmetics, and the like. List these items as simple or complex and explain whether you think the production process used for each was highly automated.

Readings in Economics

JUICE UP YOUR IMAGE

It's not the lively purple and green graphics, nor the quaint sight of wheat grass growing in the display case that gets you first. It's the scent of oranges, so piquant and insistent that your mouth puckers and your stomach starts grumbling in sync with the blenders. You are in smoothie heaven, swirling in a vortex of delicious dilemmas. Do your taste buds demand raspberries or strawberries, bananas or oranges? . . . Whichever way you go, you'll leave Jamba Juice positively vibrating with health and vitality—even if some of that buzz exists only in your mind.

Welcome to Kirk Perron's vision of 21st century marketing, where advertising isn't king. Though the San Francisco-based Jamba Juice Co. does have a marketing program—and a fine one at that—founder and CEO Perron knows that no direct-mail, coupon-driven, broadcast-based, image-enhancing stunt is going to outperform the real hook at his outrageous fruit juice and smoothie stores. His secret: *It's the experience, stupid. . . .*

The Jamba Juice story begins in 1990, when a health-crazed Perron decided to turn his "juicing" habit into a business. His particular brand of high-quality, high-energy Juice Club smoothies and juices became so popular, expansion was inevitable. . . .

Though the Juice Club formula had been an unqualified success, Perron felt it could use a little tweaking to compete. . . .

So Juice Club got itself some *jamba*, a West African word for "celebration," and gave itself a hipper, more global feeling. What was once a sterile, health-food-store atmosphere has been replaced by vibrant purple, green, orange and hot pink colors and natural wood.

"This business may look like one where you can buy a few blenders and make a fortune, but it's more than that," Perron says. "Our company exists not simply to make money. We're providing enrichment to our customers' lives. People aren't stupid."

• THINK ABOUT IT •

1. Why did Juice Club change its name to Jamba Juice?

2. What does Perron mean when he states: "Our company exists not simply to make money."?

ECONOMICS IN ACTION

Financing and Producing Goods

Setting up the Video

With your classmates, view "Financing and Producing Goods" on the videodisc *Economics in Action.* The video focuses on factors affecting business efficiency and profitability. Reports on the steel and textile industries show how small, efficient competitors have caused problems for large, established manufacturing operations.

Chapter 16
Disc 2, Side 1

View the video by scanning the bar code or by entering the chapter number on your keypad and pressing Search. *(Also available in VHS format.)*

Hands-On Activity

Work with six of your classmates to set up an assembly line producing sample flash cards for the alphabet. Begin with a sheet of notebook paper. You should make four cards out of each sheet of paper. First set up an assembly line with two workers. Time the number of cards they make in five minutes. Then add one worker. How many cards can the three workers make in five minutes? Add another worker. How many cards can the four make in five minutes? Continue adding workers until you reach the point of diminishing returns. Report your findings to the class.

SURFING THE "NET"

Investing Globally

In this chapter you learned about types of corporate financing, including stocks and bonds. Companies around the world rely on stocks and bonds for long-term financing. These investments are available to investors throughout the world through stock exchanges. Although you have learned about stock exchanges in the United States, did you know that stock exchanges exist around the world? You can learn more about stock exchanges in other nations on the Internet.

Getting There

1. Use a search engine. Type in the words *stock exchange.*

2. After typing in *stock exchange,* enter words like the following to focus your search: *Africa, Asia, North America, Latin America, Australia, South America.*
3. The search engine will provide you with a number of links to follow. Links are "pointers" to different sites on the Internet and often appear as blue, underlined words.

What to Do When You Are There

Click on the links to navigate through the pages of information. Gather your findings. Using the findings, prepare an oral presentation on a stock exchange in the country of your choice.

Identifying Key Terms

Write a short paragraph about alternative types of short-term and intermediate-term financing using all of the following terms.

trade credit (p. 266)   line of credit (p. 266)
promissory note (p. 266)   leasing (p. 266)
accounts receivable (p. 266)

Use terms from the following list to fill in the blanks in the paragraph below.

trade credit (p. 266)   producer goods
consumer goods (p. 271)   (p. 271)
long-term   cost-benefit analysis
   financing (p. 265)   (p. 258)
assembly line (p. 275)   division of labor
                            (p. 275)

   As with any activity, the decision to obtain financing for an investment expansion requires using a (1) . Besides short-term and intermediate-term financing, there is (2) . Sometimes businesses finance purchases by taking posession now but paying for them in the future. This is called (3) . The goods that businesses make are either (4) or (5) . Sometimes they are produced on a highly automated (6) . This leads to an extreme form of (7) .

Recalling Facts and Ideas

Section 1
1. How do individuals turn savings into investments?
2. Outline the steps you would use in reaching a necessary financial decision.
3. Which types of businesses will most often pursue financing?

Section 2
4. What are two reasons a business may need short-term financing?
5. Leasing is a form of what type of financing?
6. Do holders of common stock have any rights in a corporation? Explain.

Section 3
7. Besides quality and inventory control, what other steps are involved in the production process?
8. When did assembly-line production first develop in the United States?
9. What does assembly-line production require?

Critical Thinking

Section 1
Understanding Cause and Effect How does the free enterprise system cause financing to be used for projects that have the most profit potential?

Section 2
Identifying Alternatives Assume that you have to buy new inventory that you sell off completely by the end of each month. Determine the most appropriate type of financing to use when you buy this inventory.

Section 3
Evaluating Information "Because full automation eliminates workers from the assembly line, soon there will be no need for any workers." What is wrong with the line of reasoning in this statement?

Applying Economic Concepts

Making Financing Decisions In your lifetime, you will make a large number of financing decisions to purchase things that will last, such as expensive stereos, major appliances, cars, and houses. Imagine you are a businessperson who has to make decisions about financing. Make a list of the kind of business expansions that might require financing. Note after each type of business expansion, such as buying a low-powered desk computer, what the appropriate type of business financing might be.

Chapter Projects

1. **Individual Project** The federal government's Small Business Administration (SBA) was designed to help small businesses with short-term financing. You can obtain information about this federal government agency by calling or writing the SBA in Washington, D.C. Research and write a three-paragraph report describing the functions of the SBA.
2. **Cooperative Learning Project** Work in three groups. As a group, work on one of the following topics:

   A. Division of Labor The most famous example of the division of labor focuses on a pin factory. Adam Smith discussed it in his book *The Wealth of Nations*. The group studying this example should do the following:
   - find the passage in the book about the pin factory
   - develop a chart showing the elements of Adam Smith's arithmetic example
   - calculate the percentage increase in productivity due to the division of labor

   B. Assembly-Line Techniques This group can divide into two smaller groups. One will develop a report on how Henry Ford developed the assembly-line process. The second group will look at what Eli Whitney developed with the use of interchangeable parts. This second group will write a report explaining the importance of interchangeable parts in the manufacturing process.

   C. Robotics This group will research how robotics developed and how much of American manufacturing uses robotics. One part of this group can look at the future of robotics.

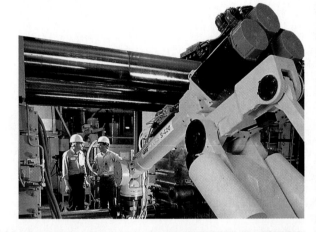

Reviewing Skills

Building Graphs
Making a Circle Graph Here is some sample information about the ownership of Texas farms. Make a circle graph showing this information.

> sole proprietorships = 167,602
> partnerships = 15,947
> family held corporations = 3,414
> other = 1,826

Technology Activity
Using E-Mail

Refer to the list of products you made in Your Economics Journal on page 257. Choose one of these products and find out more about how it was produced. First, find the name of the manufacturer. Then use the Internet to find the Web Site and the E-mail address of the manufacturer. E-mail the manufacturer, explaining that you want to know more about the production process used to manufacture the product. Share the response to your E-mail with your classmates.

Is listening to music a need or a want?

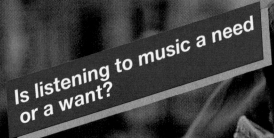

What influenced the type of portable cassette player each person decided to buy?

Where can you buy these products?

Could these students have bought such small cassette players 30 years ago?

Are there alternatives to portable cassette players today?

Your Economics Journal

During a one-week period, keep track of the products that you see offered for sale directly to consumers, either through the mail or over the phone, whether they are advertised on TV, in magazines, or in the newspaper. Make a list, noting after each item how it was advertised and why you think it was advertised for sale directly to you.

Marketing Helps Determine the Economic Value of Goods and Services

In addition to financing and producing a product, businesses must promote and eventually sell the products and services they produce. **Marketing** involves all of the activities needed to move goods and services from the producer to the consumer. These activities include market research, advertising and promotion, and the actual distribution of goods and services from the producer to the consumer. Some economists estimate that about 50 percent of the price people pay for an item is for the cost of marketing.

The Development of Marketing

The idea and importance of marketing in the United States has changed considerably since 1900. Historically, marketing has developed through four stages: production, sales, marketing, and consumer sovereignty. Figure 12.1 shows this development.

The 1950s saw the rise of marketing as a combining of the production and sales functions. At the same time, a greater variety of goods became available to satisfy consumer needs.

By the late 1950s and early 1960s, marketing had changed. Instead of just attempting to create demand, businesses found they could take a larger share of the consumer dollar by designing products that matched what consumers wanted.

Today, marketing involves many activities, all of which add to the utility that marketing creates. **Utility** is the ability of any good or service to satisfy consumer wants. Utility can be divided into four major types: form utility, place utility, time utility, and ownership utility. Figure 12.2 (page 284) illustrates the differences among these types of utility.

Figure 12.1 Four Stages of Marketing

A The Early 1900s
Marketing at this time dealt with getting goods to the consumers who wanted them. Supply was often unable to satisfy demand. Companies emphasized the production of goods.

B The 1920s and 1930s
Many consumers had most of the necessities and some of the luxuries of American life by this time. Technology was increasing productivity. Companies found that to increase sales they had to stimulate demand by actively selling their products. They began to use advertising to promote their goods.

C The 1950s
Businesses were able to produce more than consumers normally would use, actively created demand for the goods and services that they sold, and faced increased competition.

D The Late 1950s and Early 1960s
Producers began researching and meeting consumer tastes and preferences. The consumer became the most important element in product development. Consumer sovereignty had arrived.

Figure 12.2
Types of Utility

Utility can be divided into four major types.

A **Form utility**, created by production, is the conversion of raw materials to finished goods. An example is refining crude oil into gasoline. ◀

B **Place utility** is created ▼ by having a good available where a consumer wants to buy it. Locating a gas station on a busy corner is an example.

▲

C **Time utility** is created by having a good available when a consumer wants to buy it. This 24-hour coffee shop is one example.

D **Ownership utility** is created by assuring orderly transfer of ownership of desired goods. Catalog selling is one example. ◀

Market Research

Finding out what consumers want can be difficult. It is crucial, however, because so many markets are nationwide. An increase in sales of a few percentage points can result in millions of dollars in profits. Therefore, before a product is produced or a service is offered, businesses research their market. Market in this sense means the people who are potential buyers of the good or service. Through **market research** a company gathers, records, and analyzes data about the types of goods and services that people want. From cosmetics companies to automakers to frozen food processors, all major companies and many smaller ones do market research.

During the **market survey**, researchers gather information about who might be possible users of the product. Such characteristics as age, sex, income, education, and location—urban, suburban, rural—are important to a producer in deciding the market at which to aim a product. For example, in the 1980s and 1990s the concern of Americans with physical fitness and good health led many cereal companies to test and then market bran, oat, and granola cereals. Though there had been some "adult" cereals before this, most cereals had been presweetened and aimed at children.

A market survey typically involves a series of carefully worded questions. The questions may be administered in the form of a written questionnaire, which is mailed to consumers. Market researchers might also conduct personal interviews. Manufacturers of such small appliances as hair dryers and microwave ovens often put a questionnaire on the back of the warranty card that purchasers are to return.

When Should Market Research Be Done?

Market research may be done at several stages of product development. It can be done at the very beginning when the first ideas about a new product are being developed. It can be conducted again to test sample products and alternative packaging designs.

Early market research has several purposes. It helps producers determine whether there is a market for their good or service and what that market is. It can also indicate any changes in quality, features, or design that should be made before a product is offered for sale.

To investigate initial consumer response, market research is often done immediately after a product is released for sale. Some companies even test their advertising to make sure it is attracting the market for which the product was designed. Information can also be gathered about a product that has been on the market for a while. Market researchers then attempt to discover what should be done to maintain or increase sales.

Testing New Products As a final step before offering a product for national distribution, market researchers will often test market a product such as a detergent or a toothpaste. **Test marketing** means offering a product for sale in a small area, perhaps several cities, for two months to two years to see how well it sells before offering it nationally. For example, before attempting to market a new granola cereal, a company might sell it in several selected areas where the product is most likely to attract the market that the company is seeking.

Researchers keep track of the units sold and test different prices and ad campaigns within the test markets. If the cereal is successful, the company will offer it nationally. If sales are disappointing, the company has two choices. It can make changes based on the data collected in the test market. Or, rather than spend more money redesigning the product, the company can abandon the idea.

Most new products introduced every year in the United States are not profitable and do not survive in the marketplace. It is the constant lure of developing a high-profit item, however, that motivates companies to continue developing new products.

SECTION 1 REVIEW

Understanding Vocabulary

Define marketing, utility, form utility, place utility, time utility, ownership utility, market research, market survey, test marketing.

Reviewing Objectives

1. What are the four stages of the development of marketing in the United States?
2. If you want to do market research, what do you have to do?

Harley-Davidson

The Early Years When you think about motorcycles, there is a very good chance you will think of Harley-Davidsons. In 1901, William S. Harley and Arthur Davidson of Milwaukee strapped a gasoline engine to a bicycle, and started production shortly thereafter. Harley-Davidson has been building motorcycles since 1903. For years motorcycles were a small but profitable segment of the motor vehicle industry. Harley-Davidson motorcycles became a symbol of defiance and the "age-old hobo-rebel."

Prince Axel of Denmark and his H.-D.

Bad Times In 1969 Harley-Davidson was bought by sporting goods manufacturer AMF. AMF immediately modernized production facilities and increased production from 15,000 units annually to more than 50,000 units. Most business analysts agreed that the heavy investment in equipment was necessary for the firm, but it was also accompanied by a decline in quality. The quick rise in production led to lower-quality motorcycles. Harley-Davidsons slowly lost their image.

In the 1970s the public perception of motorcycles changed. The oil crisis and resulting high gasoline prices left the average driver searching for alternatives. Experts predicted that gasoline prices would continue to rise to astronomical levels. Motorcycles suddenly seemed to be a fuel-saving alternative to traditional automobiles. People started buying more motorcycles, and forecasters predicted that demand would continue to increase. What happened, instead, was that the experts significantly overestimated demand. Japanese manufacturers flooded the American market with motorcycles and then were left with large inventories. Motorcycle prices collapsed.

Emphasis on Quality Against this backdrop, a group of AMF executives led a management buyout and took Harley-Davidson private. The new owners revived the company by completely changing the way Harley-Davidson did business. They changed the production process, management philosophy, and marketing strategy.

Harley-Davidson started to use some Japanese production techniques, reducing inventory and freeing up capital and labor. By reducing inventory, any defects and quality problems became easier to spot, while at the same time inventory costs were reduced. Workers were encouraged to make suggestions and were given more authority to make quality checks.

Harley-Davidson devised a new marketing technique, encouraging the formation of the Harley Owners Group (HOG), a social club for Harley owners operating out of local dealerships. These clubs became a means of getting Harley owners together. This made Harley-Davidsons more visible to the general public.

The owners took Harley-Davidson public again in 1986, and the company has been highly successful in the 1990s. In 1995 the company had record sales of 105,104 motorcycles—more than a 100 percent increase since the 1981 buyout. Harley-Davidson once again is a symbol for quality.

Free Enterprise in Action

1. Who bought Harley-Davidson in 1969?
2. Why did the oil crisis of the 1970s stimulate demand for Harley-Davidsons?
3. How did the new management and production techniques employed by Harley-Davidson after its buyout in 1981 lead to a higher-quality product?

SECTION 2 The Marketing Mix

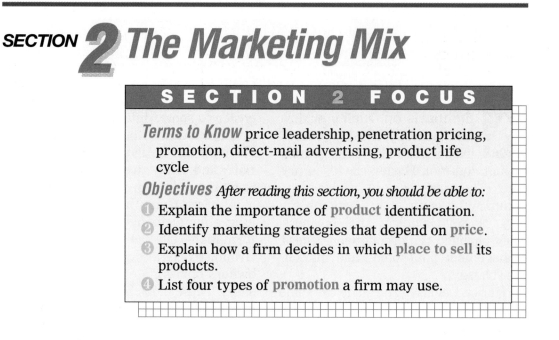

SECTION 2 FOCUS

Terms to Know price leadership, penetration pricing, promotion, direct-mail advertising, product life cycle

Objectives *After reading this section, you should be able to:*

1. Explain the importance of product identification.
2. Identify marketing strategies that depend on price.
3. Explain how a firm decides in which place to sell its products.
4. List four types of promotion a firm may use.

The Four "Ps" of Marketing

In today's highly competitive world, simply producing a product and offering it for sale is not enough. Companies, through their marketing departments, plan a marketing strategy, which details how the company will sell the product effectively. The marketing strategy, or plan, combines the "four *Ps*" of marketing: product, price, place, and promotion. Decisions about each topic are based on the data collected through the company's market research.

Product

Besides deciding on the actual product, market research helps a company determine what services to offer with the product, how to package it, and what kind of product identification to use.

Warranties are customary with many manufactured products, but some manufacturers offer special services free or for a small charge. For example, if you buy a camera, you may be able to purchase from the manufacturer a 2-year extended warranty in addition to the 1-year warranty given by the company. Automakers used to offer 1-year or 12,000-mile warranties on new cars. Today a 5-year or 50,000-mile warranty is a common offer.

Packaging is also an important factor in selling a product. The "right" packaging combines size, design, and color to attract potential consumers. Compact discs, books, and food are especially dependent on packaging. Such words as *New and Improved* or *Economy Size* are used to attract customers. For economy-minded shoppers, manufacturers add cents-off coupons and rebate offers to their packages. Cents-off coupons are used to persuade consumers to make a repeat purchase and develop the habit of buying the product.

Once a product is offered for sale, product identification becomes important. Product identification can involve the use of a logo or of certain colors on a package. It can also involve a certain type of packaging, a particular slogan, or anything that can be associated with and identify a product.

As **Figure 12.3** shows, product identification is meant to attract consumers to look at, buy, and remember a particular product.

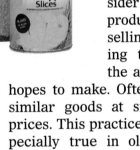

Price

Supply and demand help determine the price of a good or service. According to the law of supply, at higher prices, a larger quantity of a product will generally be supplied than at lower prices. The law of demand states that as the price of a good or service falls, a larger quantity will be bought. Conversely, as the price rises, a smaller quantity will be bought.

Because of the laws of supply and demand, the price at which a product sells may help determine whether it is successful in attracting buyers, while being profitable to its maker. In setting a price, a company has to consider the costs of producing, advertising, selling, and distributing the product, and the amount of profit it hopes to make. Often companies sell similar goods at similar prices. This practice is especially true in oligopolies and is known as **price leadership.** For example, one major airline may lower its price and then all of the other major airlines will follow.

Figure 12.3
Product Identification
From the Pillsbury Dough Boy to the colorful Pepsi logo, all of these items are good examples of packaging to achieve product identification.

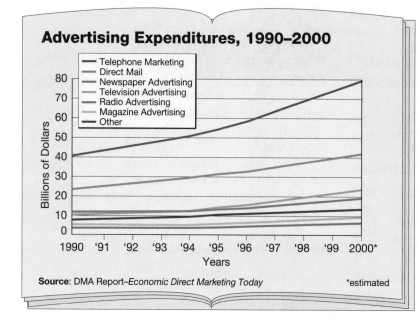

Advertising Expenditures, 1990–2000

Telephone Marketing
Direct Mail
Newspaper Advertising
Television Advertising
Radio Advertising
Magazine Advertising
Other

Billions of Dollars

80
70
60
50
40
30
20
10
0

1990 '91 '92 '93 '94 '95 '96 '97 '98 '99 2000*

Years

Source: DMA Report–*Economic Direct Marketing Today*   *estimated

Figure 12.4 Advertising Expenditures
American corporations nearly doubled their advertising expenditures from $101.3 billion in 1990 to an estimated $191.7 billion in 2000.
◄

Selling a new product at a low price is another marketing strategy. This strategy is called **penetration pricing.** The low price is meant to attract customers away from an established product.

Place to Sell

Where the product should be sold is another decision of the marketing department. Should it be sold through the mail, by telephone, in department stores, in specialty shops, in supermarkets, in discount stores, or door-to-door? Usually, the answer is obvious because of past experience with similar products. A cereal company, for example, would most likely market a new cereal in supermarkets. Another company might decide that its goods would appeal to only a limit-

ed market and therefore choose to sell its goods in specialty shops.

Promotion

Promotion is the use of advertising and other methods to inform consumers that a new or improved product or service is available and to convince them to purchase it. As **Figure 12.4** indicates, businesses spend billions of dollars each year to advertise through direct-mail pieces and in newspapers, magazines, radio, and television. Other promotional efforts include free samples, cents-off coupons, gifts, and rebates. Where and how a product is displayed are important as well. For example, paperbacks and magazines are often placed on racks next to checkout lines where people wait.

Figure 12.5 ►
A Typical Product Life Cycle
A product life cycle has no fixed number of months or years. A fad item has a much shorter product life cycle than established items such as typewriters.

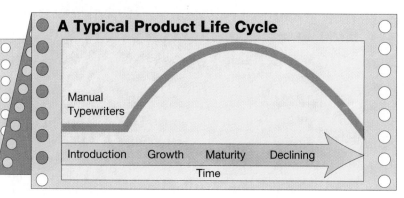

A Typical Product Life Cycle

Manual Typewriters

Introduction   Growth   Maturity   Declining

Time

Types of Promotion The particular types of promotion that a producer uses depend on three factors: (1) the product, (2) the type of consumer that the company wants to attract, and (3) the amount of money it plans to spend. Magazines, credit card companies, and insurance companies often use **direct-mail advertising.** The mailer usually includes a letter describing the product or service and an order blank or application form.

Product Life Cycle If you were to look in a Sears & Roebuck catalog from the early 1900s, it would seem strange. Many of the products advertised no longer exist. The cruel fact of marketing is that most products go through what is known as a **product life cycle.** This cycle is a series of stages from first introduction to complete withdrawal from the market. Figure 12.5 shows the four stages of a typical product life cycle.

People involved in marketing products need to understand the stages of each product's life cycle because marketing programs are different for each stage. A product in its introductory stage has to be explained and promoted much differently from one in its maturity stage. Also, pricing can be different depending on the stage. Prices of products tend to be relatively high during the growth stage.

Many marketers attempt to extend the life of old products by using a number of techniques. Figure 12.6 illustrates how this can be accomplished.

◀ **Figure 12.6**
Three Ways to Extend the Life of an Old Product

1 **Find New Uses for the Product**
Arm & Hammer Baking Soda is now advertised as a cleaning agent, toothpaste, first aid remedy, and refrigerator deodorizer.

2 **Change How the Product Looks**
Packaging, labeling, and size can all be changed.

3 **Change Advertising Focus**
Persuade consumers they need the product and its new uses.

SECTION 2 REVIEW

Understanding Vocabulary
Define price leadership, penetration pricing, promotion, direct-mail advertising, product life cycle.

Reviewing Objectives
① How does packaging contribute to product identification?

② What two marketing strategies depend on price?

③ How does a firm decide where to sell its products?

④ What are four ways a firm may promote a product?

Personal Perspective

Charles Wang on Challenges in the Computer Industry

Charles Wang built a successful software firm through technological innovation and acquisition. Wang, a college math and physics major, is not a typical business manager. His unconventional style is evident in the following excerpts from interviews in the *New York Post*, February 17, 1992; *Newsday*, April 16, 1989; and *Mass High Tech*, July 13, 1992.

... We developed more products than we acquired. People don't realize this.... You've got to make sure what comes in exceeds what goes out. If you can count, you can do that. It's not that complicated. That's it! And the difference is called profit.

Charles Wang trains his own executives, moves managers often, and reorganizes the entire company every April based on what he calls zero-based thinking.

You ever hear of the government saying we need less people anywhere? No. That's incremental thinking. So what I try to do is force my people to look at it fresh. Justify it to me again. [For example, suppose] we went and bought a new computer. It's supposed to save something, so why are you asking for more people again?

Another unique approach Wang takes is that he does not adopt every new system that comes along, just because it is new.

... The common characteristic of the mythmakers is that they must destroy the old in order for the new to succeed. Old technologies must be proven to be useless to create a market for the new. ...

Wang explains his evolutionary approach.

... One, you do not throw your legacy systems away. Imagine leveling a building every time you wanted to add a new door or central air-conditioning. It's the same thing with implementing new technology.

Checking for Understanding

1. What is Wang's definition of "profit"?
2. What does Wang mean by zero-based thinking?
3. According to Wang, how should old technology be treated when new technology is developed?

SECTION 3 FOCUS

Terms to Know channels of distribution, wholesalers, retailers

Objectives *After reading this section, you should be able to:*
1. Explain the difference between wholesale and retail distribution.
2. List two new types of distribution channels.

Moving Goods to Market

Distribution, moving goods from where they are produced to the people who will buy them, is another function of marketing. The routes by which goods are moved are called **channels of distribution.** Figure 12.8 (page 294) Shows the various distribution channels for different kinds of goods.

Wholesalers and Retailers

Some consumer goods, such as clothing and farm products, are usually sold by a producer to a wholesaler and then to a retailer, who sells them to consumers. See Figure 12.7. Other consumer goods, such as automobiles, are normally sold by the producer directly to a retailer and then to consumers. With each transaction, or business deal, the price increases. Some goods, such as vegetables sold at a farmer's roadside stand, go directly from producer to consumer.

Wholesalers **Wholesalers** are businesses that purchase large quantities of goods from producers for resale to other businesses. They may buy goods from manufacturers and sell them to retail stores that then deal directly with consumers. They may also buy and sell raw materials or producer goods to manufacturers. Various types of wholesalers exist.

Full-service wholesalers warehouse goods and deliver them once retailers buy them. They may also extend trade

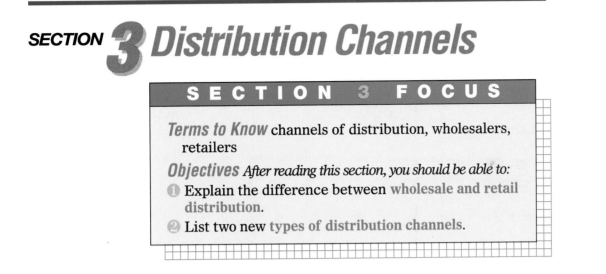

Figure 12.7 Distributing Goods
Orchard owners have sold these limes to wholesalers who will package them and transport them to grocery stores to be sold to consumers.

293

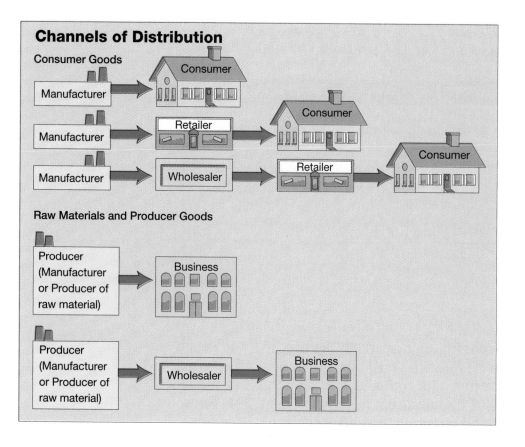

Channels of Distribution

Consumer Goods

Manufacturer → Consumer

Manufacturer → Retailer → Consumer

Manufacturer → Wholesaler → Retailer → Consumer

Raw Materials and Producer Goods

Producer (Manufacturer or Producer of raw material) → Business

Producer (Manufacturer or Producer of raw material) → Wholesaler → Business

Figure 12.8 Channels of Distribution

The routes by which goods are moved depend upon the type of good being sold.

credit. Wholesalers known as drop shippers, in contrast, never take possession of goods. They buy merchandise with the agreement that the producer will store it. After the drop shipper sells the goods, the producer must deliver them. A cash-and-carry wholesaler has inventory and sells merchandise, but the buyer must ship it. A truck wholesaler sells and delivers at the same time.

Retailers Retailers sell consumer goods directly to the public. Hundreds of thousands of retailers sell all types of goods. You are probably familiar with many of them: department stores, specialty stores such as bookshops, discount stores, supermarkets, mail-order houses, and so on.

Storage and Transportation Part of the distribution process is warehousing goods for future sales. The producer, wholesaler, or retailer may perform this function. Most retailers keep some inventory on hand for immediate sale. Many have a two- to three-month supply, depending on the type of merchandise.

Transportation involves the physical movement of goods from producers and/or sellers to buyers. Various means of transportation, such as airlines, railroads, trucks, and automobiles, can be used. Pipelines transport some goods such as petroleum and natural gas. In deciding the method of transportation, businesspeople must consider the type of good, such as perishable food. The size and weight of the good are also important. Airfreighting tons of wheat is impractical, but airfreighting small machine parts is not. Speed may be necessary to fulfill a sale or to get fresh fruit to a food plant. The cost of the different types of transportation is a factor.

Expanding Types of Distribution Channels

In the last 10 to 15 years, distribution channels have expanded rapidly due to the growth of club warehouses and direct marketing. Some of the biggest club warehouses are Price/ Costco and Sam's (a division of Wal-Mart). Figure 12.9 shows some of the characteristics of warehouse club shopping.

Direct marketing is done mainly through catalogs as illustrated in Figure 12.10 (page 296). Advertising called space ads in newspapers and magazines is also direct marketing.

One reason that catalog shopping has become a popular distribution channel is to avoid state sales taxes. As state sales taxes have increased in most states, consumers have purchased more goods through catalogs from out-of-state companies. The purchaser of catalog goods normally does not pay sales tax if the catalog company is located in another state. The same holds true for goods purchased through the Internet.

Figure 12.9
Differences in Warehouse Club Shopping

A typical club warehouse requires membership. Memberships usually cost $25 a year for individuals and more for businesses. Individual club members usually have to be part of a larger group such as a teacher's union or a credit union. A typical club warehouse, unlike other stores, is an extremely large building, where the choices of merchandise and food are often limited, but the prices are usually lower than most others available in the immediate geographical area. The club warehouse formula is to buy a limited number of models and brands of each product in such huge quantities that the club warehouse gets very favorable prices from the manufacturers. Typically, the listed price in the club warehouse is what the individual member pays. Businesses get a 5 percent discount off that price.

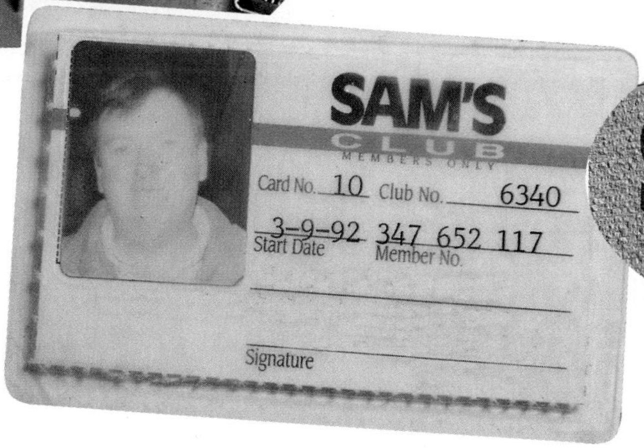

▼

SAM'S
CLUB
MEMBERS ONLY
Card No. 10 Club No. 6340
3-9-92 347 652 117
Start Date Member No.

Signature

SAM'S
CLUB
MEMBERS ONLY
A DIVISION OF WAL-MART STORES INC.

Figure 12.10
Catalog Boom
Catalog shopping has increased dramatically in the United States in the last 20 years. Virtually everything is available by catalog overnight. As an expanding distribution channel, this form of direct marketing has yet to reach its full potential. It also must compete with Internet shopping, a rapidly expanding distribution channel.

▼

SECTION 3 REVIEW

Understanding Vocabulary
Define channels of distribution, wholesalers, retailers.

Reviewing Objectives
① How would you describe the difference between a wholesaler and a retailer?

② What are two relatively new distribution channels for goods?

Critical Thinking Skills

Distinguishing Fact From Opinion

Whenever you are listening to someone talk, reading a newspaper, or watching a news program on TV, you are bombarded with facts. Many times, however, you are being given personal opinions. Do you know how to distinguish between fact and opinion?

What is a Fact?

A *fact* is a statement that can be proven by such evidence as records, documents, government statistics, and unbiased historical sources. Figure A lists some facts that few people would dispute.

Discovering Opinions

An *opinion* is a statement that may contain some truth, but it also contains a personal view or judgment, sometimes called a value-based statement. Consider the following statement: "The state fund for the arts does not have enough money." Whether this agency has enough money is a matter of opinion, based on personal values. Consider the statements of opinion in Figure B.

Use the following guidelines when distinguishing between fact and opinion.

❶ For each statement ask yourself what idea the writer or speaker wants you to accept.
❷ Ask yourself if and how these statements can be verified or proven.

Practicing the Skill

Read several paragraphs of a politician's speech from a newspaper or magazine. Make a list of statements of fact and statements of opinion. Tell why you classify each statement as you do.

Figure A
Facts

- The population of the United States exceeds 250 million people.
- There is normally less sun on rainy days than on other days.
- President Bill Clinton took office in 1993.
- During the majority of years since World War II, average prices have increased in the United States.

Figure B
Opinions

- The crime rate is too high.
- We should eliminate poverty in the United States.
- We are not spending enough money on public education.
- Young people today do not take school seriously enough.

Readings in Economics

| TIME | APRIL 26, 1993 |

TESTING THE WATERS
by Thomas McCarroll

The label on Crystal Geyser Natural Alpine spring water boasts that it is nothing less than "nature's perfect beverage." The drink, reads the label, "begins as the pure snow and rain that falls on 12,000-ft. Olancha peak in the towering Sierra. This pristine water is naturally filtered through the mountain's bedrock."

The language is evocative and the imagery idyllic. Unfortunately Crystal Geyser's claims are something of an exaggeration. Or so says the North Carolina agriculture department, which recently ordered Crystal Geyser and seven other bottled waters, including the popular Naya and Poland Spring brands, removed from store shelves in that state because of "false and deceptive labeling."

... That is bad news for producers of the nation's 700 brands of bottled water, many of which convey the impression in their advertising that they have tapped an unspoiled river.... Regulators and consumer groups are starting to question whether bottled waters are worth the $2.7 billion a year that customers spend on them....

In an effort to clean up the industry, the FDA is proposing the most sweeping new regulations in two decades. The most controversial would set uniform definitions for types of bottled waters, such as "artesian," "mineral," "distilled," and "natural spring." These terms are now generally ill-defined. Some names, such as Grayson's "mountain water" and Music's "glacier water," defy definition since no such categories exist.

• THINK ABOUT IT •

1. Why did the North Carolina agriculture department pull certain brands of water from store shelves?

2. What is the FDA currently proposing?

ECONOMICS IN ACTION

Marketing and Distribution

Setting up the Video

With your classmates, view "Marketing and Distribution" on the videodisc *Economics in Action.* The video focuses on how products are marketed. It explains that companies conduct market research to find out if their product will appeal to consumers. In a news segment on Spanish-language radio, the video describes the challenges of marketing.

Chapter 17
Disc 2, Side 1

View the video by scanning the bar code or by entering the chapter number on your keypad and pressing Search. *(Also available in VHS format.)*

Hands-On Activity

Work with several of your classmates to think of a new product to introduce in your school. The product should help to make life more convenient for students and teachers alike. The product should be relatively easy to manufacture and should be relatively inexpensive. You should develop a marketing plan that includes test marketing, a method for obtaining consumer reactions, and one advertisement. Share your plans with the class.

SURFING THE "NET"

Catalog Shopping

In this chapter you learned about the routes by which goods are moved from producers to consumers. One of the fastest markets for distributing goods in the United States is through direct-mail catalogs. Virtually everything is available by catalog overnight. You can learn more about catalog shopping on the Internet.

Getting There

1. Use a search engine. Type in the words *catalog shopping.*
2. After typing in *catalog shopping,* enter words like the following to focus your search: *clothing, apparel, athletic wear, business clothing, designer clothing, discount clothing.*

3. The search engine will provide you with a number of links to follow. Links are "pointers" to different sites on the Internet and often appear as blue, underlined words.

What to Do When You Are There

Click on the links to navigate through the pages of information. Gather your findings. Using the findings, create a shopping list of four items that you would like to purchase. Include the price and description of each item, the company you are ordering from, and the shipping charges. Total your shopping list. Then find comparable items in stores in your community and create another shopping list. Which method of shopping was less expensive? Share your findings with the class.

CHAPTER 12 Review

Identifying Key Terms

Write the letter of the definition in Column B below that correctly defines each term in Column A.

Column A
1. test marketing (p. 285)
2. penetration pricing (p. 290)
3. price leadership (p. 289)
4. retailer (p. 294)
5. promotion (p. 290)

Column B
a. use of advertising to inform consumers about a product and to persuade them to purchase it
b. business that sells goods directly to the consumer
c. selling a new product at a low price to attract new customers away from an established product
d. offering a product in a small area for a limited time to see how well it sells
e. setting prices close to those of competing companies

Recalling Facts and Ideas

Section 1
1. What is the relationship between marketing and utility?
2. How is market research conducted?
3. What are the historic stages of development of marketing in the United States?

Section 2
4. What are the "four *P*s" of planning a marketing strategy?

5. How are goods and services promoted?
6. In the marketing mix, to what does *place* refer?
7. What are the last two stages of a typical product life cycle?

Section 3
8. What are distribution channels?
9. How does a club warehouse differ from a standard retail outlet?
10. Who may perform the storage function of distribution?
11. What are the factors that a business must consider in choosing a method of transporting goods?

Critical Thinking

Section 1
Formulating Questions Suppose you were put in charge of doing a market survey for a new type of running shoe. What questions should you ask? Where would you conduct the survey?

Section 2
Identifying Alternatives What are alternative ways to extend the life of an old product that is in its declining stage?

Section 3
Making Generalizations Write a summary of the information on channels of distribution found in **Figure 12.8.**

Applying Economic Concepts

The Rising Opportunity Cost of Time When individuals earn higher incomes, by definition the opportunity cost of their time increases. Economic theory says that they will react in a predictable way—reducing the amount of time they spend shopping. Make a list of the various methods that people can use to reduce the time they spend when they shop for (1) presents for various holidays, Mother's Day, birthdays, etc., (2) food, and (3) photographic and stereo equipment.

Chapter Projects

1. **Individual Project** Suppose you are about to try a new product on the market such as cereal or soap. **(a)** In making your decision to try the new product, how important is each of the "four *P*s"? **(b)** Rank them in their order of importance to you, and write a paragraph explaining why you chose this ranking related to trying the new product.

2. **Cooperative Learning Project** Work in three or more groups. Each group will choose a particular product from the following categories of consumer goods:
   - Home electronics
   - Food
   - Clothing
   - Electric steam generators
   - Automobiles
   - Computers

   After each group has chosen one product or brand within one of the above categories, research, as a team or alone, depending on the number in your group, the following:
   - Product packaging
   - Pricing strategies
   - The place where the product is sold
   - How the product is promoted
   - The product life cycle

   Each person or team within each group should write a summary of the research results, preferably in graphic form. When the results of each group are finished, contrast and compare the differences in the five categories across the various products.

Reviewing Skills

Distinguishing Fact From Opinion

1. **When the Distinction is Clear** Which of the following statements are fact and which are opinion?
   a. Unemployment in the early 1990s exceeded 6 percent.
   b. Millions of Americans did not have jobs.
   c. During the early 1990s, the inflation rate was less than 6 percent per year.
   d. This was a good rate of inflation.
2. **When the Distinction is Not Clear** Try to pick out the statements in the following paragraph that are not necessarily facts or at least that you would want to confirm.

   The club warehouse phenomenon has been around the United States since the 1970s. The people who shop at club warehouses swear by them. They know that they are a good deal for everybody because prices are so low. Because club warehouses price their products so low, though, they force many small retailers out of business. This is bad. Nonetheless, club warehouses are here to stay because they offer such a great deal.

Technology Activity
Developing a Multimedia Presentation

Refer to the list of advertisements that you compiled in Your Economics Journal on page 281. Group the advertisements into four categories: mail order, telephone solicitation, radio or television ads, and print ads. Develop a videotaped guide to compare the ads of each group. Differentiate the points that the advertisers claim in each type of ad. Combine music, still and moving images, and text within your video production. Share your production with the members of the class.

ISSUE: Is Affirmative Action Necessary to End Discriminatory Hiring Practices?

Affirmative action means that employers and other institutions must take steps to remedy the effects of past discrimination against women and minorities. Does it work? Or does it harm the economy by giving special status to certain groups? Affirmative action began in 1965 with the monitoring of the hiring and promotion practices of federal contractors. By the 1990s, many Americans believed that affirmative action did more harm than good and should be ended.

PRO Those who favor government-sponsored affirmative action programs feel that, even though affirmative action has not worked perfectly, things are better today than they would have been without it. David J. Shaffer, staff writer for the *Indianapolis Star*, tells about some of the positive aspects of affirmative action. He presents the following view:

"While it has helped, it hasn't been completely successful," said Suzanne Steinmetz, sociology department chairwoman of the IU School of Liberal Arts at Indiana University-Purdue University at Indianapolis.

"It's going to take many generations until our visions of what kinds of people are appropriate for certain jobs are no longer tied to race and gender," Steinmetz said. "However," she added, "as bad as things are, we don't know what things would have been like without affirmative action."

Many executives feel that affirmative action is still needed to correct past hiring injustices. There are a number of women and minority executives who are upset because affirmative action stirs up such negative connotations to many people in recent years. Some individuals, especially white males, talk about "reverse discrimination." In a *Washington Post* article, staff writer Lynne Duke quotes investment banker Crystal Jones on the way some people have misinterpreted the goals and effects of affirmative action:

While I believe that the concept of affirmative action needs to stay in place in order to preserve access, people twist it around to make us feel we don't deserve to be where we are.

Counterpoint

CON Those who argue against affirmative action say that it is nothing but a system of quotas that has devastating effects on the American economy. According to Peter Brimelaw and Leslie Spencer, writing for *Forbes* magazine, the two major arguments—that quotas are necessary to force companies to tap new labor pools and that companies need a diverse work force to service a diverse population—are simply wrong. The markets should take care of these things.

Economist and Nobel Laureate Gary Becker also argues that free markets and competition should eventually tend to eliminate discrimination. The process is hampered by government intervention and monopoly; in competitive situations, discrimination should decline itself with no need for quotas.

Finally, those against affirmative action claim it is very expensive. Economist Peter Griffin estimates that affirmative action programs have increased federal contractors' labor and capital costs by about 6.5 percent. Brimelaw and Spencer write in *Forbes* about these costs:

> *What does the replacement of merit with quotas cost the American people? The answer is: plenty. The impact may easily have already depressed GNP [now GDP] by a staggering four percentage points—about as much as we spend on the entire public school system. . . .*
>
> *Corporate America seems to have resigned it-self to quotas as yet another tax. But they are a peculiarly debilitating sort of tax, levied not on the bottom line but on every phase of the corporation's activities, increasing inefficiency throughout. . . .*
>
> *That affirmative action quotas lead to lowered standards is all but guaranteed by the fact that all standards are suspect to Equal Employment enforcers. "Many of these people believe there really is no such thing as job performance or productivity objectively defined . . . ," says Frank Schmidt, a University of Iowa industrial psychologist.*

Exploring the Issue

Reviewing Facts

1. What is affirmative action?
2. Who benefits from affirmative action? Who loses?

Critical Thinking

3. Do you think the benefits of affirmative action outweigh the costs? Why or why not?

CHAPTER

13

THE AMERICAN LABOR FORCE

What skills are required for this job?

Who is likely to seek this kind of employment?

For how many years will these individuals probably do this activity?

SUPER SIZE FRIES   145

Do any government regulations restrict how little these individuals can be paid?

Do any government regulations restrict how long they can work each day or each week?

Who determines how much they are paid?

Your Economics Journal

Keep track of the employed individuals with whom you come in contact over a one-week period. Write down the types of jobs that they do. Next to each type, indicate whether you think their work would be considered low skilled, semiskilled, or highly skilled.

Figure 13.8 Time Line of American Unionism

1790s	Skilled workers in a particular craft join to fight division of labor and unfair hiring practices. To save money, employers are organizing workers into teams to do only parts of jobs and hiring women and children at low wages for some jobs. Most associations disband after demands are met.
1820s-1850s	Skilled workers such as carpenters and printers form citywide craft unions. Some local unions form nationwide associations. Because of poor economic conditions, many unions disappear in the late 1830s, but reappear in the 1840s and 1850s as the economy improves. African Americans and women are not included in these craft unions.
1866	National Labor Union (NLU) becomes first nationwide federation of craft unions, but disbands in 1872 after it fails to improve conditions.
1869	National Colored Labor Union formed to avoid hostility of white members of NLU. Knights of Labor set up by group of Philadelphia clothing workers as an industrial union. Members include skilled and unskilled workers as well as farmers and merchants—black and white.
1877	Baltimore & Ohio Railroad Workers strike after wages are cut during economic depression. Federal troops break up strike after rails are torn up, stations burned, and freight cars smashed.
mid-1880s	Knights of Labor claim 700,000 members. Series of violent strikes results in decline in membership and end of group by early 1900s.
1886	American Federation of Labor (AFL) is formed to bring independent craft unions together into a national federation. Membership is limited to white male skilled workers. Haymarket Riots in Chicago protest police action against strikers at a local factory. Seven police are killed. Eight labor leaders are sentenced to death and four are hanged although no evidence is found.
1892	Amalgamated Association of Iron, Steel and Tin Workers strikes the Homestead plant of Carnegie Steel after management demands a wage cut and a 70-hour work week. Armed guards are called in and several strikers as well as guards are killed. The state militia breaks up the strike.
1894	Pullman factory workers and American Railway Unions strike the Pullman Company after a wage cut, and after a union leader is fired. The strike halts rail traffic in and out of Chicago and interrupts rail service in many states. Federal troops and local militia are called. Some strikers and several other people are killed.
early 1900s	AFL concentrates on improving wages and working conditions and claims over 2 million members by 1914 and over 4 million by 1920.
1911	Triangle Shirtwaist Factory fire claims 143 lives, mostly young women clothing workers, trapped on the top floors of a tenement factory.

Figure 13.8 Time Line of American Unionism

1920s	Opposition by business, unfavorable court rulings, and rising anti-labor and anti-immigration feelings cause decline in union membership.
1929	The Great Depression begins. Sympathy grows among the general public for concerns of organized labor.
1932	Congress passes Norris-LaGuardia Act, the first major pro-labor legislation. Act limits power of the courts to stop picketing and boycotts and makes yellow-dog contracts illegal. This is the practice whereby employers require that employees pledge not to join a union.
1935	National Labor Relations Act (Wagner Act) guarantees labor's right to organize and bargain collectively. Act sets up National Labor Relations Board (NLRB) to oversee the establishment and operation of unions.
1938	To organize unskilled workers in such industries as automobiles and steel, some leaders of the AFL form the Congress of Industrial Organizations (CIO). CIO encourages membership of African Americans and women.
1945-47	Wave of strikes to improve wages and working conditions follows end of World War II and contributes to growing anti-union feelings.
1947	Congress passes Labor-Management Act (Taft-Hartley Act) over strong objections of labor. Act outlaws certain strike tactics, permits states to pass laws making union shops illegal, and allows the President to delay a strike if it will threaten the nation's health and safety.
1955	AFL and CIO unite into a single union, AFL-CIO.
1959	Congress passes Labor Management Reporting and Disclosure Act (Landrum-Griffin Act). Act increases government control over unions and guarantees union members certain rights, such as freedom of speech in union activities and control over union dues.
1962	President Kennedy signs into law an order giving federal employees the right to organize into unions, but not to strike. Union membership among government workers grows during the 1960s and 1970s.
mid-1960s-1970s	Union membership among African Americans, women, Hispanics, and agricultural workers increases.
1981	President Reagan fires 11,400 air traffic controllers for striking illegally. AFL-CIO warns of growing anti-union feelings as economy worsens. Some large unions such as the United Auto Workers negotiate contracts that give back some of their earlier gains.
1982-1998	Union membership decreases to about 15 percent of wage and salary workers.

UNIT 5

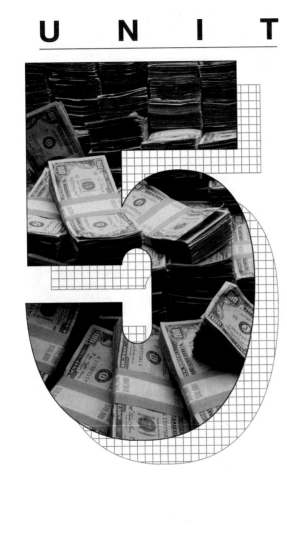

MACROECONOMICS: MANAGING THE NATION'S ECONOMY

Did You Know

- ◆ Nothing "backs" the $1, $5, and other bills that you carry around in your wallet or purse.
- ◆ The average American works until about the first week in May to pay for all local, state, and federal taxes.
- ◆ Prices rise much less rapidly in the United States than in many countries of the world.
- ◆ During national business slowdowns, unemployment among teenagers increases more rapidly than among older people.

In this unit you will be looking at the interrelationships of all sectors of the economy—consumers, businesses, and government. This overall picture is the study of macro-economics, or the economy as a whole.

CHAPTER 14
MEASURING THE ECONOMY'S PERFORMANCE

How does the free enterprise system depend on scenes such as these?

What motivates businesses to operate here?

Who provides the income these people might spend here?

What are these people doing?

What choices do these people have as they shop?

Your Economics Journal

For one week, keep track of references in the media to the following: unemployment, consumer spending, manufacturing trends, recession, and prices. After each entry, indicate whether the information was, in your view, positive or negative to the overall economy.

National Income Accounting

SECTION 1 FOCUS

Terms to Know national income accounting, gross domestic product (GDP), net exports, depreciation, net domestic product (NDP), national income (NI), personal income (PI), transfer payments, disposable personal income (DI)

Objectives After reading this section, you should be able to:

❶ List the four categories of GDP in terms of types of goods produced.

❷ Compare the three measurements of income—national, personal, and disposable.

A Healthy GDP Equals a Healthy Economy

People can measure how successful they are economically by the size of their incomes and by their overall standard of living, including how much their spendable income will buy. Figure 14.1 shows one example.

The well-being of the overall economy is measured in a similar way. Economists constantly measure and record such factors as the amount of goods and services produced yearly by the nation and the amount of income individuals have to spend.

The measurement of the national economy's performance is called **national income accounting.** This area of economics deals with the overall economy's income and output. It also measures the interaction of consumers, businesses, and governments. The major measurements used for the nation's income and production are gross domestic product, net domestic product, national income, personal income, and disposable personal income. Figure 14.2 shows gross domestic product and its components in descending order of value.

Measuring Gross Domestic Product

The broadest measure of the economy's health is **gross domestic product (GDP).** This is the total dollar value of all *final* goods and services produced in the nation during a single

**Figure 14.1 ▶
Vacations**
People who can afford luxuries such as cruises have a relatively high standard of living.

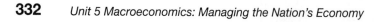

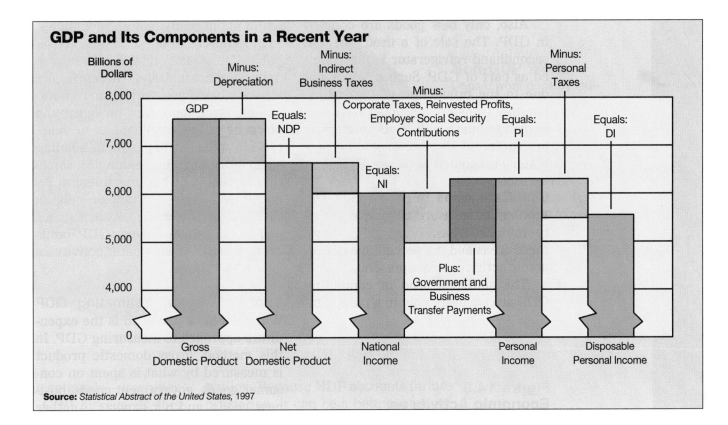

GDP and Its Components in a Recent Year

Billions of Dollars

Minus: Depreciation

Minus: Indirect Business Taxes

Minus: Personal Taxes

GDP

Equals: NDP

Minus: Corporate Taxes, Reinvested Profits, Employer Social Security Contributions

Equals: PI

Equals: DI

Equals: NI

Plus: Government and Business Transfer Payments

Gross Domestic Product	Net Domestic Product	National Income	Personal Income	Disposable Personal Income

Source: *Statistical Abstract of the United States*, 1997

applies t
and equ
factor. I
that son
keep m
working
when the

Net
counts f
sures G
value of
preciatio
amount
for depr
than 10
example
Subtract
preciatio

year. This figure tells how much goods and services Americans have produced in that year that is available for people to purchase. GDP is one way to measure the nation's material standard of living. It also provides a way of comparing what has been produced in one year with what was produced in another year.

Mea

Wa

Wages,
all form
income

Note the word *value* in the definition. Simply adding up the *quantities* of millions of different items produced, such as shoes and cars, would not mean much. How can we measure the strength of the economy, for example, if we know that 3 billion safety pins and 2 space shuttles were produced? What needs to be totaled is the value of the items, using some common measure. Economists use the dollar as this common measure of value. As a result, GDP is always expressed in dollar terms. For example, in 1997, GDP totalled about $8 trillion.

The word *final* is also important. To measure the economy's performance accurately, economists add up only the value of final goods and services to avoid *double counting*. To add the price of memory chips to the price of a computer is not realistic. The final price to the buyer already includes the price of the memory chips.

**Figure 14.2 ▲
GDP and Its
Components**
What is the difference in dollars between gross domestic product and disposable personal income?

ownership of the other factors of production. National income is equal to NDP minus indirect business taxes, including items such as sales and property taxes, and license fees.

As GDP is divided into four areas of economic activity, similarly, NI is divided into five types of income. Figure 14.6 shows all of these divisions. NI is equal to the sum of all income resulting from these five different areas of the economy.

Figure 14.6 National Income
National Income (NI) is the total of income from all sources shown here. Wages and salaries, however, make up three-fourths of NI.

▼

Personal Income The total income individuals receive before personal taxes are paid is called **personal income (PI).** PI can be derived from NI through a two-step process. First, corporate income taxes, profits that businesses put back into their businesses to expand, and Social Security contributions employers make are subtracted from NI. These are subtracted because they represent income that is not available for individuals to spend.

Then, transfer payments are added to NI. **Transfer payments** are welfare payments and other supplementary payments, such as unemployment compensation, Social Security, and Medicaid, that a state or the federal government makes to individuals. These transfer payments add to an individual's income even though they are not in exchange for any current productive activity.

Disposable Personal Income The income that people have left after taxes, including Social Security contributions, is called **disposable personal income (DI).** It is the income available to an individual for the immediate purchase of goods and services and for savings. DI equals PI minus personal taxes. DI is an important indicator of the economy's health because it measures the actual amount of money income people have available to spend.

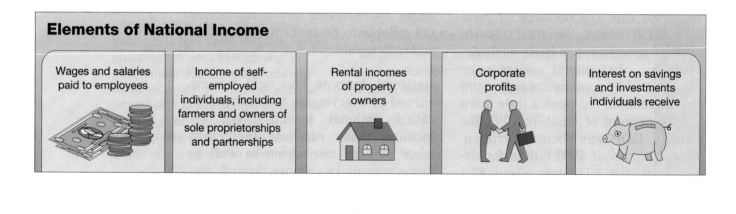

Elements of National Income

| Wages and salaries paid to employees | Income of self-employed individuals, including farmers and owners of sole proprietorships and partnerships | Rental incomes of property owners | Corporate profits | Interest on savings and investments individuals receive |

SECTION 1 REVIEW

Understanding Vocabulary

Define national income accounting, gross domestic product (GDP), net exports, depreciation, net domestic product (NDP), national income (NI), personal income (PI), transfer payments, disposable personal income (DI).

Reviewing Objectives

1. What four categories of economic activity are used to measure GDP?
2. What must be subtracted from national income to determine personal income? What must be added?

Using Index Numbers: Price Indexes

Most statistics on prices are expressed in terms of price indexes. Do you know what the concept of a price index is and how to use it?

Measuring Inflation

If last year a light bulb cost 50¢ and this year it costs 75¢, there has been a 50 percent price increase. The price is 1.5 times as high. An index number of this price rise is simply 1.5 multiplied by 100; that is, the index number would be 150.

To compare prices, you must decide the base year. A **base year** is the year to which all other years' prices will be compared.

Computing a Price Index

When we deal with many goods, we must pick a representative sample, called the market basket. We compare the cost of the market basket of goods over time. When we do this, we obtain a price index, which is defined as the cost of a market basket of goods today expressed as a percentage of the cost of the market basket of goods in some base year. In the base year, the price index will always be 100.

Calculating a Price Index

Figure A shows two goods in our market basket—corn and computers. The *quantities* in the basket remain the same between the base year, 1983, and the year 1999. Only the price changes.

Figure A

Market Basket Quantity

Corn	100 bushels
Computers	2

1983 Unit Price

Corn	$4
Computers	$500

1983 Market Basket Cost

Corn	$400
Computers	$1,000
Total	$1,400

1999 Unit Price

Corn	$8
Computers	$450

1999 Market Basket Cost

Corn	$800
Computers	$900
Total	$1,700

$$\text{Index} = \frac{1999 \text{ cost}}{1983 \text{ cost}} \times 100$$

$$\frac{\$1,700}{\$1,400} \times 100 = \$121.43$$

Practicing the Skill

In the example in Figure A, assume that the price of computers in 1999 was $400. Recompute the price index.

Readings in Economics

FORBES   **JULY 28, 1997**

FRUGAL MOGUL
by Carrie Shook

To make some extra dough, Harvard juniors John Chuang, Steven Kapner and Mia Wenjen started a desktop publishing business in 1986, using their school's Macintosh computers and laser printers to turn out résumés for classmates.

The little business quickly outgrew Chuang's dorm room, so the partners convinced their parents to cosign a $5,000 loan. . . .

The trio . . . managed to gross $147,000 the first full year. It was too good to abandon on graduation but not big enough to support all three. In June 1987 Chuang, a lanky economics major and the only child of Taiwanese immigrant parents, volunteered to run the company in return for an 82% stake; his ex-partners would get 9% each and go their own ways. . . .

With the résumé business as a base, Chuang started a temp agency providing Macintosh-literate students from nearby MIT, Harvard and Tufts. He renamed the firm MacTemps, Inc., and placed a small ad in a trade publication. "You didn't buy just any computer, don't hire just any temp to use it," the ad read. . . .

When you start a business without much capital, you have to count on reinvested profits. Chuang knew every penny he held on to was that much more money to reinvest. No frills? What about asking workers to bring their own pens to work. . . .

Last year MacTemps earned $6 million on revenues of $77 million. It has 220 employees, 7,000 temps and offices in 30 cities in 7 countries. . . .

Chuang still pours back into the business every penny he can. Continuing to live in a working-class neighborhood of Boston, he drives the same Toyota Corolla he had while an undergraduate. . . .

Employees are still asked to bring their own pens to work.

• THINK ABOUT IT •

1. What service does MacTemps provide?

2. In what way does Chuang's image not fit that of the principal owner of a successful business?

ECONOMICS IN ACTION

Measuring the Economy's Performance

Setting up the Video

With your classmates, view "Measuring the Economy's Performance" on the videodisc *Economics in Action*. The video focuses on the statistical measurements used to monitor the economy's performance. A news report examines how the CPI is compiled and stresses its importance in monitoring inflation.

||||| (barcode) |||||

**Chapter 19
Disc 2, Side 1**

View the video by scanning the bar code or by entering the chapter number on your keypad and pressing Search. *(Also available in VHS format.)*

Hands-On Activity

The absence of inflation in recent years has alarmed many economists who fear that the nation will lapse into a period of deflation, or falling prices. During deflation, consumers postpone purchases because they think that prices will continue to fall. As consumer demand slows, industries often lay off workers.

Work with a group of your classmates to learn more about current economic conditions. Is inflation again a threat? Or has deflation become an even greater concern? Use resources in your school or public library or on the Internet to answer these questions. Share your findings with the class.

INTERACTIVE ECONOMICS!

Macroeconomic Equilibrium

Introduction

Lesson 6 of *Interactive Economics!* deals with macroeconomic equilibrium. When economists analyze the economy at the macroeconomic level, they have to account for all producers and all consumers. Accordingly, their models make use of aggregate supply and aggregate demand curves. Because these curves are the summation of behaviors at the individual level, economists need to understand how their tools are constructed from the beginning—and then they can put them to work.

Using the Software

1. Select "Macroeconomic Equilibrium" from the Main Menu.

2. Read the introduction to "Macroeconomic Equilibrium," then click on "The Aggregate Demand Curve."

3. After reading the information, go back to the "Tutorial" menu and click on "The Aggregate Supply Curve."

4. Finally, click on the "Advanced Topics Menu" and read about adjustments to macroeconomic equilibrium and how fiscal policy and monetary policy affect macroeconomic equilibrium.

5. Then click on "Economics Lab." Complete the lab by clicking and dragging the appropriate captions to their proper locations.

6. Print your completed lab.

14 Review

Identifying Key Terms

Write the letter of the definition in Column B below that correctly defines each term in Column A.

Column A
1. base year (p. 340)
2. trough (p. 348)
3. economic indicators (p. 355)
4. expansion (p. 348)
5. real GDP (p. 341)
6. business cycle (p. 347)

Column B
a. economic activity is at its lowest point
b. figures for the nation's total income that have been corrected for inflation
c. measurement of specific aspects of the economy such as stock prices
d. used as a point of comparison for other years in a series of statistics
e. periodic ups and downs in the nation's economic activity
f. business recovery period, when economic activity increases

Recalling Facts and Ideas

Section 1
1. Net exports and government goods are two components of gross domestic product. What are the other two components?
2. Besides profit and rents, what two other categories of income are added in the income approach to estimating GDP?
3. If you were given the statistic on disposable personal income, what other information would you need to derive personal income?

Section 2
4. What are the most commonly used price indexes?
5. What is the difference between inflation and deflation?
6. How would you determine *real* GDP if you knew only GDP?

Section 3
7. Why does the aggregate demand curve slope down?
8. Why does the aggregate supply curve slope up?
9. What is determined at the intersection of the aggregate supply and aggregate demand curves?

Section 4
10. What are the main phases of a business cycle?
11. When the economy enters a recession, what normally happens?
12. When was the most serious downturn in economic activity in the twentieth century in the United States?

Section 5
13. What are two theories of the causes of the ups and downs in overall business activity?
14. How might psychological factors affect the business cycle?
15. What two aspects of government activity affect business cycles?

Critical Thinking

Section 1
Evaluating Information How might knowledge of nationwide economic statistics help you?

Section 2

Determining Cause and Effect "Inflation just keeps getting worse because the purchasing power of money is going down." Why is this statement meaningless?

Section 3

Making Comparisons What is the difference between the aggregate demand curve and the demand curve in Chapter 8 that discussed the demand for individual goods and services?

Section 4

Analyzing Information Why is it probably better to talk about business fluctuations rather than business cycles?

Section 5

Making Inferences Many theories try to explain why business cycles occur. None of them can be considered "the truth." Why not?

following:

- Lagging indicators
- Coincident indicators
- Leading indicators

Each group will do library or Internet research to determine the following:

- For each type of indicator, what are the various subgroups?
- How long has the indicator been reported in the United States?
- Can you find instances when the indicator was wildly inaccurate? For example, what if the leading indicator was still indicating that times were good when, in fact, the economy was already in a serious recession?

Have a class discussion about how useful any of these indicators might be in accurately predicting changes in overall national economic activity.

Applying Economic Concepts

Understanding the Business Cycle Try to analyze what you think occurs throughout the economy during a recession. Make a list of some of the things that business owners may do to react to a recession, such as reduce employees' overtime hours.

Chapter Projects

1. **Individual Project** Go to the library or use the Internet and find the latest edition of the *Statistical Abstract of the United States*. Locate the tables in the "Prices" section that give price indexes for consumer goods for selected cities and metropolitan areas. Make a line graph showing the rise in the index for "all items" over the last six years. Draw on the same graph a line indicating the "city average" index for "all items" in a city or area near you during the same period of time.
2. **Cooperative Learning Project** Work in three groups. Each group will choose one of the

Reviewing Skills

Using Index Numbers: Price Indexes

Constructing a Price Index Assume the following data on the price of comparable personal computers: 1993 $1,000; 1994 $800; 1995 $700; 1996 $600; 1997 $500; 1998 $250; 1999 $200. Construct a price index for computers using 1993 as the base year.

Technology Activity

Using E-Mail

Refer to the statistics about unemployment, consumer spending, manufacturing trends, recession, and prices that you recorded in Your Economics Journal on page 331. Choose one of these statistics. Then E-mail your United States representative or senator about the statistic. Ask your elected official to explain what he or she thinks about the statistic as a measure of the overall health of the economy. Share the E-mail response you receive.

15

MONEY AND BANKING

Why are these people waiting in line?

How do you operate an automated teller machine (ATM)?

Why do people need cash?

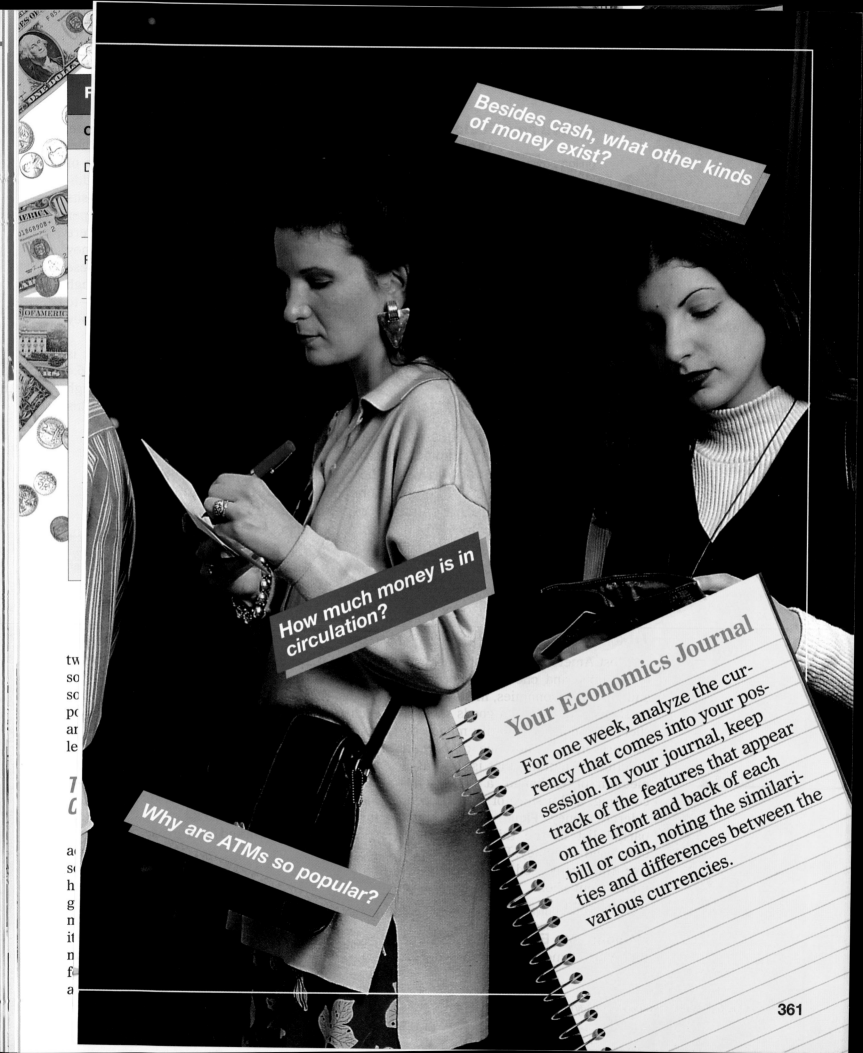

Besides cash, what other kinds of money exist?

How much money is in circulation?

Why are ATMs so popular?

Your Economics Journal

For one week, analyze the currency that comes into your possession. In your journal, keep track of the features that appear on the front and back of each bill or coin, noting the similarities and differences between the various currencies.

Point

ISSUE: Can the Economy Be Fine-Tuned Using Fiscal and Monetary Policies?

For years, economists have debated the question of whether the government should enact activist fiscal and monetary policies to fix economic problems. Not only do economists debate whether these policies should be used, but they also debate whether the policies even work. Traditional Keynesian economics tells us that government should spend more and tax less during bad economic times. Some economists argue that this type of fiscal policy is irresponsible, enlarging the deficit while helping the economy very little.

 PRO In an article in *The New York Times,* Peter Passell presents the traditional Keynesian view. He refers to the Keynesian economists as "they":

As recently as the early 1970s most economists thought they knew how to take the sting out of recessions. A decline in the inclination of businesses and consumers to spend, they said, could leave a gap between the total demand for goods and the economy's capacity to provide them. And while the gap would eventually close without government intervention, eventually could be a very long time indeed. What was needed to offset swings in private demand, they argued, was some combination of tax cuts and government spending, plus an increase in funds available for bank loans.

In the early 1980s, economist and Nobel Laureate James Tobin offered his view of activist policies to smooth out business cycles:

. . . I don't believe stable government policies necessarily mean the economy will be stabilized. History doesn't suggest the economy will stay on even keel if the government just keeps its hands off or runs things according to some well understood rules. Shocks of nongovernmental origin—from overseas, and in our technology and the tastes of consumers—have created business fluctuations throughout the history of capitalism. What governments have tried to do since 1945 is to offset these shocks.

Sometimes, it is true, government has been the source of shocks. But if you compare pre-World War II history with the recent era, in which governments . . . have pursued activist economic policies, the results of activism have been very good.

Counterpoint

Milton Friedman has been one of the major critics of activist fiscal and monetary policies. He writes that, because of time lags involved in fiscal policy, any government action may make the problem even worse. He claims that government intervention policies have intensified business cycles. He also blames the monetary policy of the Federal Reserve for contributing to economic instability, leading to more inflations and contractions than in the pre-Fed years. Friedman has often written in favor of a "monetary rule," whereby the money supply would increase at a fixed rate that does not change to counter business cycles.

In his article in *The New York Times*, Peter Passell writes that today the economics establishment has lost faith in the ability of the government to fine-tune the economy. He quotes economist Gregory Mankiw of Harvard on some of the problems of fiscal policies:

Once the need for fiscal stimulus is recognized, he notes, it may take months to pass the necessary legislation. Hence the full impact may only hit the economy after the recovery is under way and the stimulus is no longer welcome. Even if the stimulus does hit in timely fashion, public fears that it will ignite inflation may push up interest rates and slow business investments.

That should not be a significant problem if the public is convinced that the spending of

tax stimulus is indeed temporary and will evaporate by the time offices and factories are running full tilt. But such convictions do not come easily to a public grown cynical about Washington: "Whenever I hear a politician say 'never again' I don't believe it," Mr. Mankiw, the Harvard economist, said.

Exploring the Issue

Reviewing Facts

1. What does Tobin view as the purpose of fiscal policy?
2. According to Milton Friedman why does fiscal policy harm the economy?

Critical Thinking

3. What do you think a "traditional Keynesian" economist would think of Friedman's idea of a monetary rule?

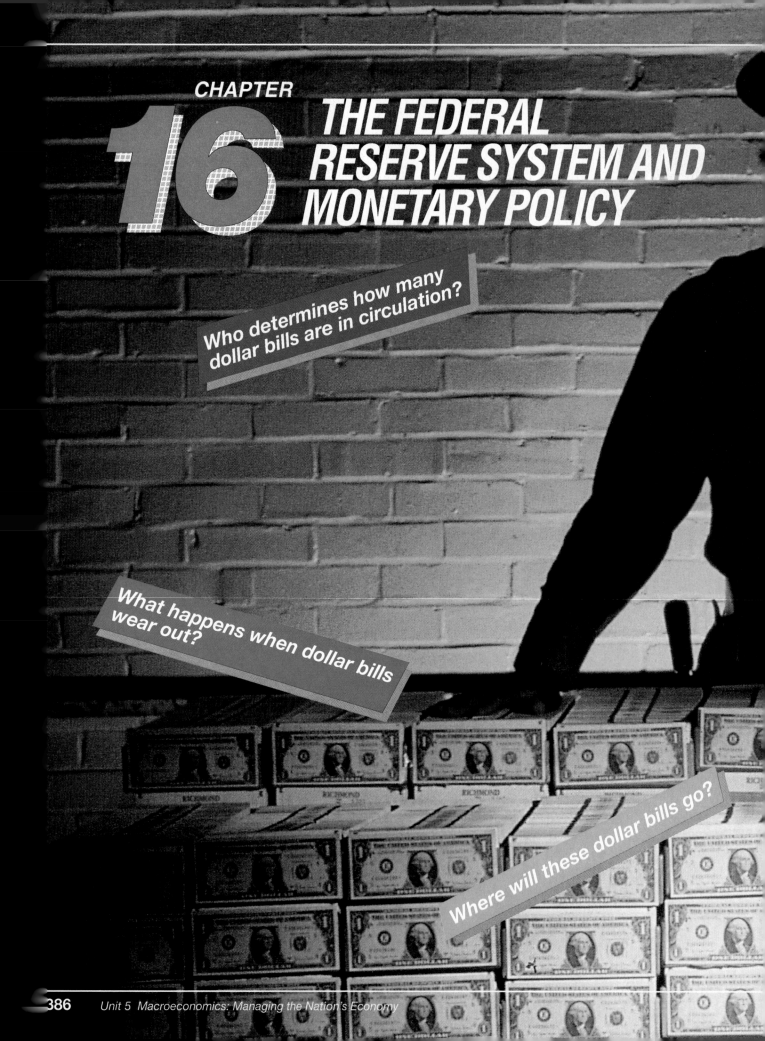

CHAPTER

16

THE FEDERAL RESERVE SYSTEM AND MONETARY POLICY

Who determines how many dollar bills are in circulation?

What happens when dollar bills wear out?

Where will these dollar bills go?

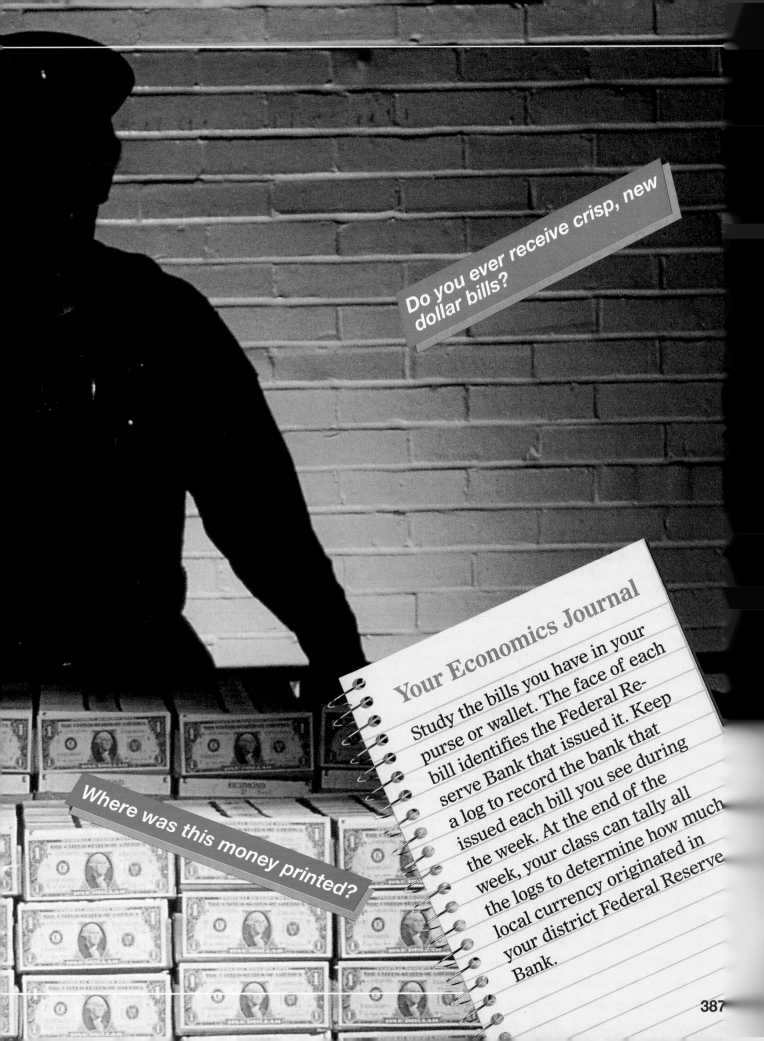

Do you ever receive crisp, new dollar bills?

Where was this money printed?

Your Economics Journal

Study the bills you have in your purse or wallet. The face of each bill identifies the Federal Reserve Bank that issued it. Keep a log to record the bank that issued each bill you see during the week. At the end of the week, your class can tally all the logs to determine how much local currency originated in your district Federal Reserve Bank.

1 *Money Supply and the Economy*

Terms to Know the Fed, monetary policy, loose money policy, tight money policy, fractional reserve banking, reserve requirements

Objectives *After reading this section, you should be able to:*

① Contrast **loose money and tight money policies.**

② Describe **fractional reserve banking.**

③ Explain **money expansion** in the banking system.

The Federal Reserve and the Money Supply

Congress created the Federal Reserve System in 1913 as the central banking organization in the United States. Its major purpose was to end the periodic financial panics that had occurred during the 1800s and into the early 1900s. Over the years, many other responsibilities have been added to the Federal Reserve System, or **the Fed**, as it is called. See Figure 16.1. The jobs of the Fed today range from processing checks to serving as the government's banker. Its most important function, however, involves control over the rate of growth of the money supply.

**Figure 16.1
The Fed**

The 12 Federal Reserve banks that serve the nation's banks are distributed throughout the country. Trillions of dollars a year pass through the Fed.

Loose and Tight Money Policies

You may have read a news report in which a business executive or public official complained that money is "too tight." You may have run across a story about an economist warning that money is "too loose." In these cases the terms *tight* and *loose* are referring to the monetary policy of the nation's Federal Reserve System. **Monetary policy** involves changing the rate of growth of the supply of money in circulation to affect the amount of credit and, therefore, business activity in the economy.

Credit, like any good or service,

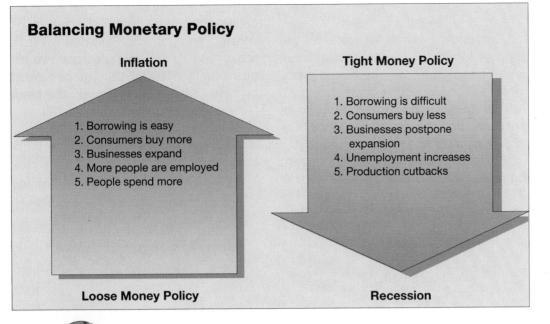

Balancing Monetary Policy

Inflation

1. Borrowing is easy
2. Consumers buy more
3. Businesses expand
4. More people are employed
5. People spend more

Loose Money Policy

Tight Money Policy

1. Borrowing is difficult
2. Consumers buy less
3. Businesses postpone expansion
4. Unemployment increases
5. Production cutbacks

Recession

Figure 16.2 Loose Money Versus Tight Money
Look at the chart and determine the differences between loose money policy and tight money policy. Which of these can lead to a recession? Why is this possible?

GO TO

Lesson 8 of Interactive Economics! to learn more about "An Introduction to Monetary Policy."

is subject to the laws of supply and demand. Also, like any good or service, credit has a cost. The cost of credit is the interest that must be paid to obtain it. As the cost of credit increases, the quantity demanded decreases. In contrast, if the cost of borrowing drops, the quantity of credit demanded rises.

Figure 16.2 shows the results of monetary policy decisions. If a country has a **loose money policy,** credit is inexpensive to borrow and abundant. If a country has a **tight money policy,** credit is expensive to borrow and in short supply.

If this is the case, why would any nation want a tight money policy? The answer is to control inflation. See Figure 16.2. If money becomes too plentiful too quickly, prices increase and the purchasing power of the dollar decreases dramatically. This situation occurred during the Revolutionary War. The supply of Continental currency grew so rapidly that notes became almost worthless.

The goal of monetary policy is to strike a balance between tight and loose money. It is the Fed's responsi-

bility to ensure that money and credit are plentiful enough to allow expansion of the economy. The Fed cannot, however, let the money supply become so plentiful that rapid inflation results.

Fractional Reserve Banking

Before you are able to understand how the Fed regulates the nation's money supply, you need to understand the basis of the United States banking system and the way money is created. The banking system is based on what is called **fractional reserve banking.**

Since 1913 the Fed has set specific **reserve requirements** for many banks. They must hold a certain percentage of their total deposits either as cash in their own vaults or as deposits in their district Federal Reserve bank. Currently most financial institutions must keep 10 percent of their checkable deposits in reserves with the Federal Reserve. They do not have to keep any reserves on so-called nonpersonal time deposits.

Money Expansion

Figure 16.3
Expanding the Money Supply
The chart shows how $1,000 expands to $5,000 by simple loans. How does this happen?
▼

Currency is a small part of the money supply. A larger portion consists of bank deposits the public owns. Because banks are not required to keep 100 percent of their deposits in reserve, they can use their deposits to create what is, in effect, new money.

Suppose you sell a government bond to the Fed and receive $1,000. This is $1,000 in "new" money be-

cause the Fed simply creates it by writing you a check. You deposit it in a bank. With a 10 percent reserve requirement, $100 of that money must be held in reserve. However, the bank is free to lend the remaining $900.

Suppose another customer asks the same bank for a $900 loan. The bank creates $900 simply by transferring $900 to the customer's checking account. The bank must keep in reserve

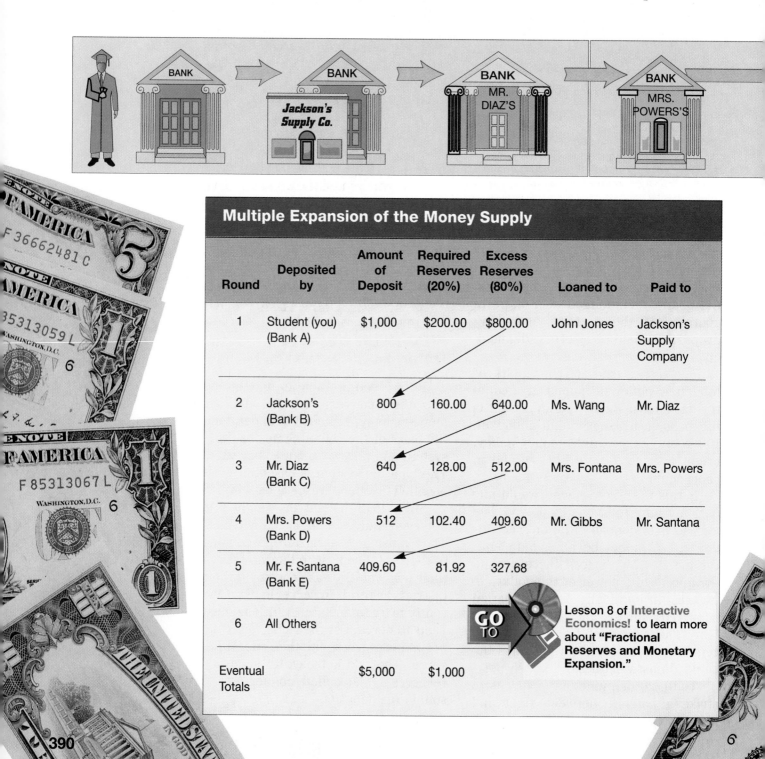

Multiple Expansion of the Money Supply

Round	Deposited by	Amount of Deposit	Required Reserves (20%)	Excess Reserves (80%)	Loaned to	Paid to
1	Student (you) (Bank A)	$1,000	$200.00	$800.00	John Jones	Jackson's Supply Company
2	Jackson's (Bank B)	800	160.00	640.00	Ms. Wang	Mr. Diaz
3	Mr. Diaz (Bank C)	640	128.00	512.00	Mrs. Fontana	Mrs. Powers
4	Mrs. Powers (Bank D)	512	102.40	409.60	Mr. Gibbs	Mr. Santana
5	Mr. F. Santana (Bank E)	409.60	81.92	327.68		
6	All Others					
Eventual Totals		$5,000	$1,000			

GO TO Lesson 8 of Interactive Economics! to learn more about "Fractional Reserves and Monetary Expansion."

10 percent of this new deposit—$90, but now it can lend the remaining $810. This $810 is in turn treated as a new deposit. Ninety percent of it—$729—can again be lent. The original $1,000 has become $3,439. So it goes; each new deposit gives the bank new funds to continue lending.

Of course, a bank is not likely to continue lending and receiving back the same money. Its customers will most likely withdraw money and spend it or deposit it in another bank; however, this does not stop the creation of money. As the money finds its way into a second and third bank, and so on, each bank can use the nonrequired reserve portion of the money to make more loans.

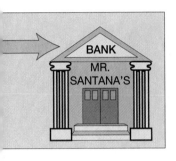

How the Money Supply Increases
Money expansion may seem confusing. Let's examine step by step the example shown in Figure 16.3. **Round 1:** Suppose you have $1,000 that you take to your bank (Bank A) and deposit in your checking account. Assume that the Fed requires your bank to keep 20 percent of its total deposits on re-serve. Your bank must hold $200 of your deposit on reserve. This leaves the bank with $800 of excess reserves, which is not earning interest.

Round 2: Bank A decides to loan out $800 to earn interest. John Jones applies to the bank for an $800 loan. Bank A finds him creditworthy and credits his account with $800. Mr. Jones borrowed the money to buy a machine for his business from Jackson's Supply Company. He writes a check to Jackson's, and the company deposits it at Bank B, which credits $800 to Jackson's account balance. Bank B's reserves increase by $800. Of this amount, $160 (20 percent of $800) are required reserves, and the remaining $640 are excess reserves.

Round 3: To earn profits, Bank B loans its excess reserves to Ms. Wang, who wants to borrow $640. She, in turn, buys something from Mr. Diaz, who does his banking at Bank C. He deposits the money from Ms. Wang. Bank C now has $640 in new deposits, of which $128 are required reserves. Bank C now loans $512 of excess reserves to Mrs. Fontana, who buys something from Mrs. Powers, and so on. The result is that a deposit of $1,000 in new money that was outside of the banking system has caused the money supply to increase to $5,000. This process is called the multiple expansion of the money supply.

SECTION 1 REVIEW

Understanding Vocabulary
Define the Fed, monetary policy, loose money policy, tight money policy, fractional reserve banking, reserve requirements.

Reviewing Objectives
1. What is the difference between loose money and tight money policies?
2. What is the purpose of fractional reserve banking?
3. If there is a 10 percent reserve requirement, how much does the money supply expand if the Fed injects $100 of new money?

Personal Perspective

Milton Friedman on the Federal Reserve

Profile

- 1912–
- won Nobel Prize for Economics in 1976
- leading supporter of monetarism
- among his many publications are *The Monetary History of the U.S. 1867–1960* with Anna J. Schwartz (1963), *Capitalism and Freedom* (1962), and *Free to Choose* with Rose Friedman (1980)

Milton Friedman has written extensively on the monetary history of the United States. He is often critical of the actions of the Federal Reserve System. In the following excerpt from *Capitalism and Freedom*, Friedman explains why he does not approve of the Federal Reserve and gives a possible replacement solution to regulating the money supply.

The establishment of the Federal Reserve System ... established a separate official body charged with explicit responsibility for monetary conditions, and supposedly clothed with adequate power to achieve monetary stability or, at least, to prevent pronounced instability. It is therefore instructive to compare experience as a whole before and after its establishment—say, from just after the Civil War to 1914 and from 1914 to date.

... The stock of money, prices, and output was decidedly more unstable after the establishment of the Reserve System than before. ...

The Great Depression in the United States, far from being a sign of the inherent instability of the private enterprise system, is a testament to how much harm can be done by mistakes on the part of a few men when they wield vast power over the monetary system of a country.

... Any system which gives so much power and so much discretion to a few men that mistakes—excusable or not—can have such far-reaching effects is a bad system. It is a bad system to believers in freedom just because it gives a few men such power without any effective check by the body politic—this is the key political argument against an "independent" central bank.

... My choice at the moment would be ... instructing the monetary authority to achieve a specified rate of growth in the stock of money. ... I would specify that the Reserve System shall see to it that the total stock of money so defined rises ... at an annual rate of X per cent, where X is a number between 3 and 5.

Checking for Understanding

1. What does Friedman's study reveal about the stability of monetary conditions in the United States after the establishment of the Fed?
2. What is Friedman's argument against an "independent" central bank?
3. What rule does Friedman propose to govern decisions of the Federal Reserve System?

2 *Organization and Functions of the Federal Reserve System*

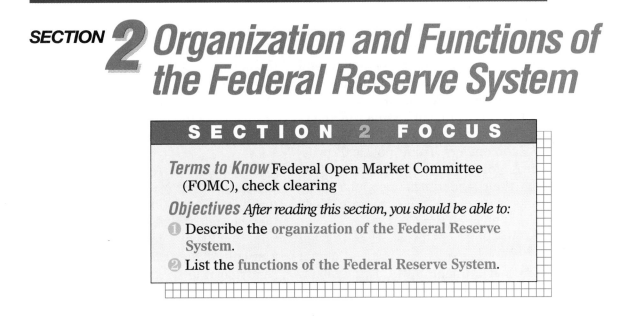

SECTION 2 FOCUS

Terms to Know Federal Open Market Committee (FOMC), check clearing

Objectives *After reading this section, you should be able to:*

❶ Describe the organization of the Federal Reserve System.

❷ List the functions of the Federal Reserve System.

The Federal Reserve Serves Many Functions

The organization of the Federal Reserve System is shown in Figure 16.5 on page 394. As its name states, the Fed is a system, or network, of banks. Power is not concentrated in a single central bank but is shared by a governing board and 12 district banks.

Organization of the Federal Reserve System

The Federal Reserve System is made up of the Board of Governors assisted by the Federal Advisory Council, the Federal Open Market Committee, 12 Federal Reserve banks, and about 5,000 member banks. This system is responsible for monetary policy in the free enterprise system of the United States.

Board of Governors The Board of Governors directs the operations of the Fed. It establishes policies regarding such things as reserve requirements and discount rates. The board also supervises the 12 district Federal Reserve banks and regulates certain activities of member banks and all other depository institutions.

The seven full-time members of the Board of Governors are appointed

by the President of the United States with the approval of the Senate. See Figure 16.4. The President chooses one member as a chairperson. Each member of the board serves for 14 years.

**Figure 16.4
The Board**
The Board of Governors can raise or lower the discount rate in relation to prevailing market rates.

The terms are arranged so that an opening occurs every two years. Members cannot be reappointed, and their decisions are not subject to the approval of the President or Congress. Their length of term, manner of selection, and independence in working frees members from political pressures. Members do not have to fear that their sometimes-unpopular decisions will cause them to lose their jobs at election time.

The Board of Governors is assisted by the Federal Advisory Council (FAC). It is made up of 12 members elected by the directors of each Federal Reserve bank. The Federal Advisory Council meets at least 4 times each year and reports to the Board of Governors on general business conditions in the nation.

Federal Open Market Committee

The **Federal Open Market Committee (FOMC)** meets 8 to 10 times a year to decide the course of action that the Fed should take to control the money supply.

Federal Reserve Banks

Each of the 12 Federal Reserve district banks is set up as a corporation owned by its member banks. A 9-person board of directors made up of bankers and businesspeople supervises each Federal Reserve district bank. The system includes 25 Federal Reserve branch banks as shown on the map in Figure 16.6. These smaller banks act as branch offices and aid the district banks in carrying out their duties.

Member Banks

All national banks—those chartered by the federal government—are required to become members of the Federal Reserve System. Banks chartered by the states may join if they choose to do so. Currently, member banks include all of the national banks and some of the state banks. To become a member bank, a national or state bank buys stock in its district's Federal Reserve bank.

Figure 16.5
Organization of the Federal Reserve System
Since the change in banking regulations in the early 1980s, nonmember banks are also subject to some control by the Federal Reserve System.

▼

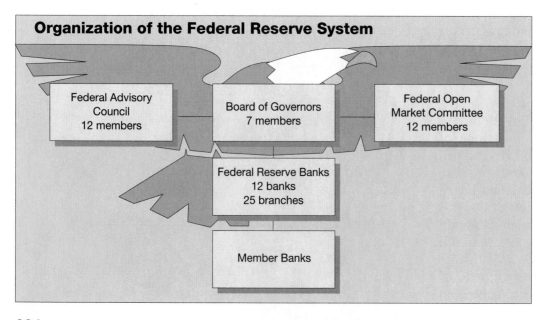

Organization of the Federal Reserve System

Federal Advisory Council
12 members

Board of Governors
7 members

Federal Open Market Committee
12 members

Federal Reserve Banks
12 banks
25 branches

Member Banks

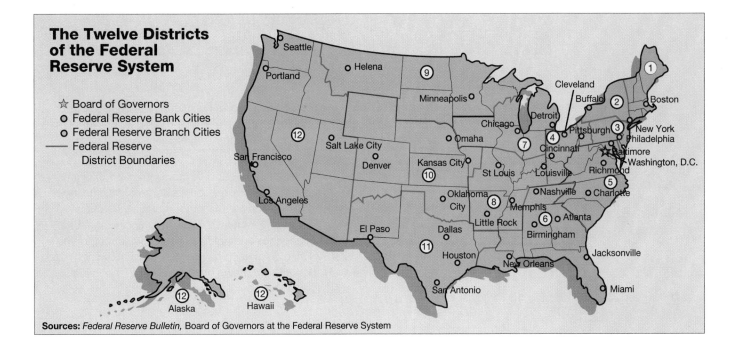

The Twelve Districts of the Federal Reserve System

☆ Board of Governors
○ Federal Reserve Bank Cities
○ Federal Reserve Branch Cities
— Federal Reserve District Boundaries

Seattle
Portland
Helena
Minneapolis ⑨
Cleveland
Buffalo ②
Boston ①
Chicago
Detroit
Pittsburgh
③ New York
④ Philadelphia
⑫ San Francisco
Salt Lake City
Denver
Omaha
⑦
Cincinnati
☆ Baltimore
Washington, D.C.
Kansas City
⑩
St Louis
Louisville
Richmond ⑤
Los Angeles
Oklahoma City
⑧
Nashville
Charlotte
Memphis
Little Rock
⑥ Atlanta
Birmingham
El Paso
Dallas
⑪
Houston
New Orleans
San Antonio
Jacksonville
Miami
⑫ Alaska
⑫ Hawaii

Sources: *Federal Reserve Bulletin,* Board of Governors at the Federal Reserve System

In the past, only member banks were required to meet regulations, such as those setting specific reserve requirements. Now all institutions that accept deposits must keep reserves in their district Federal Reserve bank. Federal Reserve services are also available to all depository institutions—member or nonmember—for a fee.

Figure 16.6 ▲
The Federal Reserve System
Look at the map of the Federal Reserve System above. Note that the Fed is headquartered in Washington, D.C. The United States Treasury appears on the back of the $10 Federal Reserve Note. Find and list the 12 Federal Reserve district bank cities.
▼

IN GOD WE TRUST

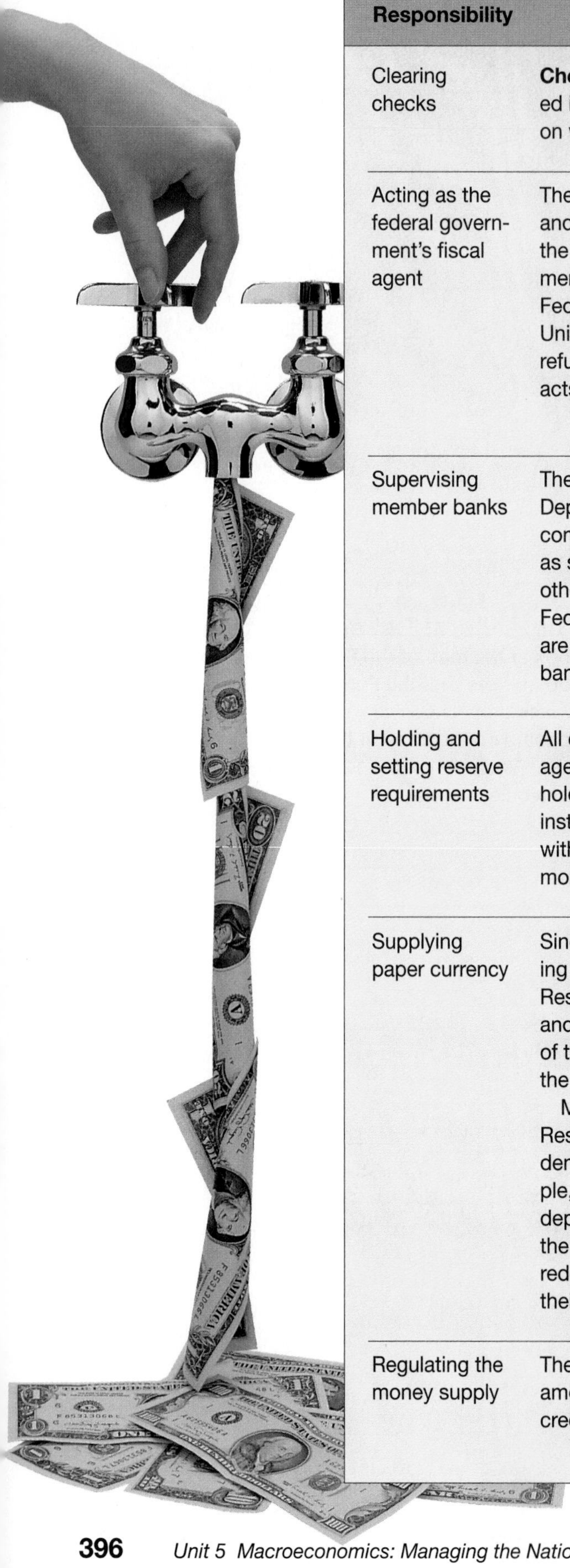

Figure 16.7 Functions of the Federal Reserve

Responsibility	Description
Clearing checks	**Check clearing** is the method by which a check that has been deposited in one depository institution is transferred to the depository institution on which it was written. Figure 16.9 (page 398) explains this process.
Acting as the federal government's fiscal agent	The federal government collects large sums of money through taxation and spends and distributes even more. It deposits some of this money in the Federal Reserve and distributes the rest among thousands of commercial banks. As the federal government's fiscal, or financial, agent the Fed keeps track of these deposits and holds a checking account for the United States Treasury. Checks for such payments as Social Security, tax refunds, and veterans' benefits are drawn on this account. The Fed also acts as a financial adviser to the federal government.
Supervising member banks	The Fed along with the Comptroller of the Currency and the Federal Deposit Insurance Corporation (FDIC) supervises and regulates member commercial banks. Nonmember commercial and savings banks as well as savings and loan associations and credit unions are regulated by other agencies. Because the comptroller supervises national banks, the Fed oversees state-chartered member banks. Among the Fed's duties are setting limits for loans and investments by member banks, approving bank mergers, and examining the books of member banks.
Holding and setting reserve requirements	All depository institutions are required by law to keep a certain percentage of their deposits in reserve. Each of the 12 Federal Reserve banks holds the reserve requirements of member and nonmember depository institutions in its district. By raising or lowering the percentage required, within the limits set by Congress, the Fed can change the amount of money in circulation.
Supplying paper currency	Since 1914 the Federal Reserve System has been responsible for printing and maintaining much of the nation's paper money. All Federal Reserve notes are printed in Washington, D.C., at the Bureau of Printing and Engraving. Each note, however, has a code number indicating which of the 12 Federal Reserve banks issued it. The money is shipped from the bureau to the appropriate bank to be put into circulation. Much of this money simply replaces old bills; however, each Federal Reserve bank must have on hand a sufficient amount of cash to meet the demands for paper currency during different times of the year. For example, during the Christmas season, commercial banks find that their depositors withdraw large amounts of cash. The banks then must turn to the Federal Reserve banks to replace it. After Christmas, depositors redeposit their money. The banks can then return what they borrowed to their district Federal Reserve bank.
Regulating the money supply	The primary responsibility of the Federal Reserve is determining the amount of money in circulation, which, in turn, affects the amount of credit and business activity in the economy.

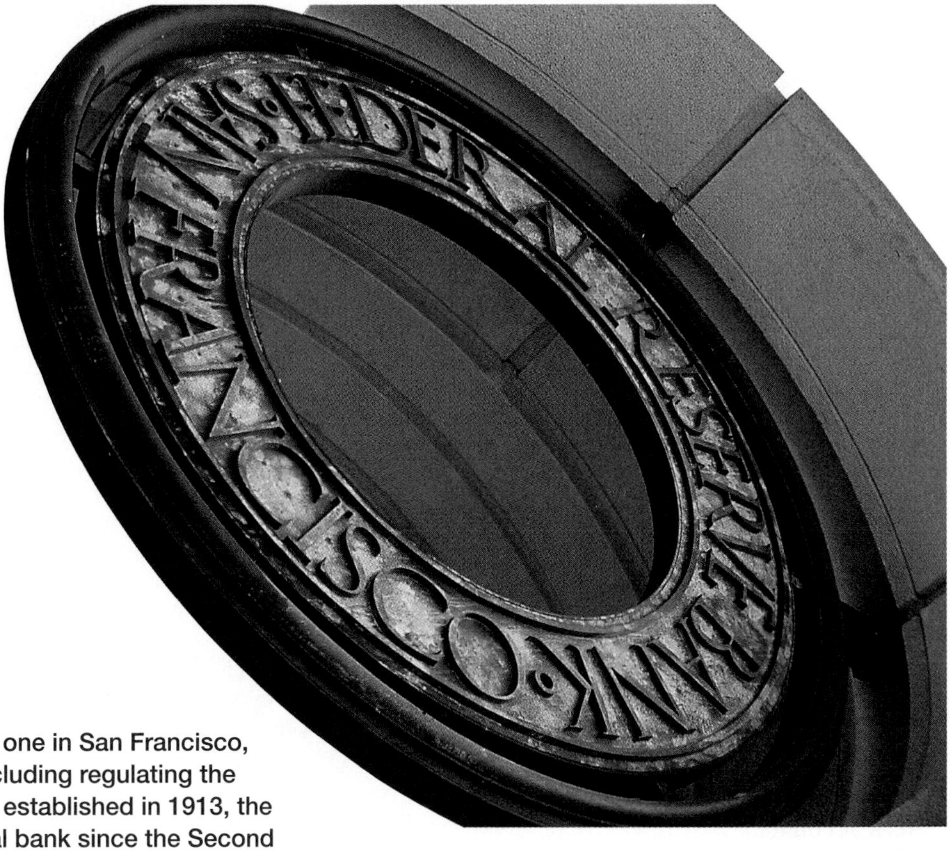

Figure 16.8 ▶
Federal Reserve Banks
All Federal Reserve banks, like the one in San Francisco, help formulate monetary policy, including regulating the money supply. Before the Fed was established in 1913, the United States had not had a central bank since the Second Bank of the United States in the mid-1800s, and individual banks often printed money.

Today the major advantage of membership is that member banks, as stockholders in their district bank, are able to vote for six of its nine board members. Member banks also receive dividends on their stock in the district bank.

The Functions of the Federal Reserve System

The Federal Reserve has a number of functions as shown in Figure 16.7. Among them are check clearing, acting as the federal government's fiscal agent, supervising member banks, holding reserves, setting reserve requirements, supplying paper currency, and regulating the money supply.

The most important function of the Fed is regulating the money supply. See Figure 16.8. Check clearing is also an important and complex function. See Figure 16.9 (page 398).

Consumer Protection The Federal Reserve also sets standards for certain types of consumer legislation, mainly truth-in-lending legislation. By law, sellers of goods and services must make some kinds of information available to people who buy on credit. This information includes the amount of interest and size of the monthly payment to be paid. The Federal Reserve System decides what type of credit information must be supplied to consumers.

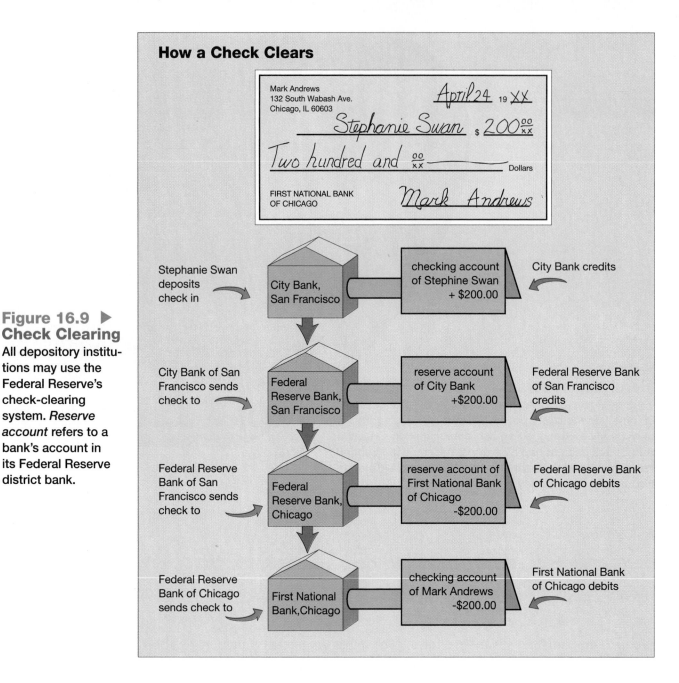

How a Check Clears

Mark Andrews
132 South Wabash Ave.
Chicago, IL 60603

April 24 19 XX

Stephanie Swan $ _200.⁰⁰/ₓₓ_

Two hundred and ⁰⁰/ₓₓ ——————— Dollars

FIRST NATIONAL BANK
OF CHICAGO

Mark Andrews

Stephanie Swan deposits check in → City Bank, San Francisco → checking account of Stephine Swan + $200.00 ← City Bank credits

City Bank of San Francisco sends check to → Federal Reserve Bank, San Francisco → reserve account of City Bank +$200.00 ← Federal Reserve Bank of San Francisco credits

Federal Reserve Bank of San Francisco sends check to → Federal Reserve Bank, Chicago → reserve account of First National Bank of Chicago -$200.00 ← Federal Reserve Bank of Chicago debits

Federal Reserve Bank of Chicago sends check to → First National Bank, Chicago → checking account of Mark Andrews -$200.00 ← First National Bank of Chicago debits

Figure 16.9 ▶
Check Clearing
All depository institutions may use the Federal Reserve's check-clearing system. _Reserve account_ refers to a bank's account in its Federal Reserve district bank.

SECTION 2 REVIEW

Understanding Vocabulary

Define Federal Open Market Committee (FOMC), check clearing.

Reviewing Objectives

❶ How is the Federal Reserve System in the United States organized?

❷ The Federal Reserve clears checks and acts as the government's fiscal agent. What are three other functions of the Federal Reserve?

LEARNING ECONOMIC SKILLS

Understanding Real and Nominal Values

Inflation has been a problem since World War II. This means that to make comparisons between the prices of things in the past and those of today, you have to make the distinction between *nominal*, or current, and *real*, or constant, values.

The Price of Houses

If a couple told you that they bought their house for $50,000 10 years ago and sold it for $100,000 today, would they have made a "profit" of $50,000? The answer is no, because of inflation. If, for example, the consumer price index (CPI) was 100 when they bought the house and had risen to 200 when they sold their house, the *real* price of their house would not have changed at all, as Figure A shows.

Determining What Happens to Your Income

Sometimes much of the raise a worker receives is eaten away by inflation. To determine the real value of a raise, subtract the rate of inflation. For example, assume you are making $10 an hour (after taxes) this year and next year your boss gives you a 5 percent raise. Are you 5 percent better off? The answer depends on the rate of inflation during that year. If the increase in the CPI was 3 percent, your real salary increase was only 2 percent as Figure B shows.

The government uses an implicit price deflator to compare GDP year by year. See Figure C

Practicing the Skill

Real GDP in 1992 was $6,244.4 billion. In 1996, nominal GDP was $7,579.9 billion. The implicit GDP price deflator was 109.7. What was real GDP in 1996 expressed in 1992 dollars?

Figure A
Determine Percentage Increase in Nominal Price

Divide amount of increase by original price. Multiply result by 100 to get percent.

$$\frac{50,000}{50,000} = 1 \times 100 = 100\%$$

Determine Percentage Increase in Consumer Price Index

Divide amount of increase in CPI by original index. Multiply result by 100 to get percent.

$$\frac{100}{100} = 1 \times 100 = 100\%$$

Determine Percentage Increase in Real Price

Subtract percentage increase in CPI from percentage increase in nominal price.

100%	increase in nominal price
−100%	increase in CPI
0%	increase in real price

Figure B

Real salary increase equals increase in nominal salary minus rate of inflation.

5%	nominal raise
− 3%	inflation rate
2%	real raise

Figure C

The real GDP is found by dividing the nominal GDP by the implicit price deflator and multiplying the result by 100.

$$\frac{\text{nominal GDP}}{\text{implicit price deflator}} \times 100 = \text{real GDP}$$

3 Regulating the Money Supply

SECTION 3 FOCUS

Terms to Know discount rate, prime rate, open-market operations

Objectives *After reading this section, you should be able to:*
1. Describe the way the Federal Reserve changes the money supply by **changing reserve requirements**.
2. Describe the way the Federal Reserve changes the money supply by **changing the discount rate**.
3. Identify how the Fed uses **open-market operations**.
4. List the **difficulties of monetary policy**.

**Figure 16.10
The Economy**
When a nation's economy is running smoothly with low inflation, people are more inclined to spend income on nonessentials or luxuries. Restaurants enjoy more business during economic booms.

▶

The Fed's Difficult Job

The Federal Reserve has as its goal maintaining enough money to keep the money supply growing steadily and the economy running smoothly without inflation. See Figure 16.10. To accomplish this, it has three major tools: reserve requirements, the discount rate, and open-market operations.

Changing Reserve Requirements

The Federal Reserve can choose to control the money supply by changing the reserve requirements of financial institutions. The lower the percentage of deposits that must be kept in reserve, the more dollars are available to loan. The reverse is also true. Figure 16.11 explains how changes in the reserve requirement affect the nation's money supply.

As Figure 16.11C shows, the Fed may raise reserve requirements. To build up its reserves to meet the new requirement, a bank has several possibilities. It can call in some loans, sell off securities or other investments, or borrow from another bank or the Fed-

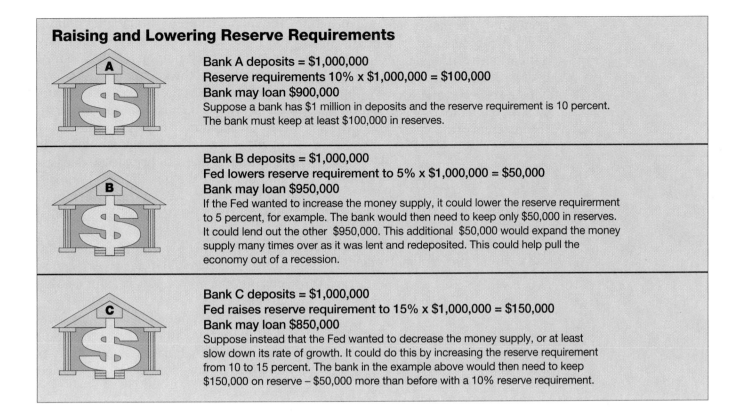

Raising and Lowering Reserve Requirements

Bank A deposits = $1,000,000
Reserve requirements 10% x $1,000,000 = $100,000
Bank may loan $900,000
Suppose a bank has $1 million in deposits and the reserve requirement is 10 percent. The bank must keep at least $100,000 in reserves.

Bank B deposits = $1,000,000
Fed lowers reserve requirement to 5% x $1,000,000 = $50,000
Bank may loan $950,000
If the Fed wanted to increase the money supply, it could lower the reserve requirement to 5 percent, for example. The bank would then need to keep only $50,000 in reserves. It could lend out the other $950,000. This additional $50,000 would expand the money supply many times over as it was lent and redeposited. This could help pull the economy out of a recession.

Bank C deposits = $1,000,000
Fed raises reserve requirement to 15% x $1,000,000 = $150,000
Bank may loan $850,000
Suppose instead that the Fed wanted to decrease the money supply, or at least slow down its rate of growth. It could do this by increasing the reserve requirement from 10 to 15 percent. The bank in the example above would then need to keep $150,000 on reserve – $50,000 more than before with a 10% reserve requirement.

eral Reserve. Obviously, because all banks would have to increase their reserves, this action would greatly decrease the amount of money in the economy. This could be used to help slow down the economy if it were expanding too rapidly.

Even small changes in the reserve requirement can have major effects on the money supply. As a result, some believe that this tool is not precise enough to make frequent small adjustments to the money supply. In recent years, changing the reserve requirement has not been used often to regulate the money supply.

Changing the Discount Rate

Sometimes a depository institution will find itself without enough reserves to meet its reserve requirement. This situation may occur if customers unexpectedly borrow a great deal of money or if depositors suddenly withdraw large amounts.

The bank must then borrow to meet its reserve requirement, at least temporarily. One of the ways it can do this is to ask its district Federal Reserve bank for a loan. The district bank, like any other bank, will charge interest. The rate of interest the Fed charges is called the **discount rate.**

A bank, like a consumer, follows the law of demand. At higher discount rates, a bank may decide to borrow fewer reserves from the Fed or none at all. It could meet its reserve requirement by borrowing from another bank. This money would then be taken out of circulation and would not be available for lending to individuals or businesses.

If a bank does decide to borrow at a high discount rate, it will need to pass its increased costs on to customers in the form of higher interest rates on loans. For example, it might raise its **prime rate**—the rate it charges its best business customers. High discount rates, by discouraging borrowing, will also keep down the

▲
Figure 16.11 Reserve Requirements
Look at the chart above to see how depository institutions are affected if the Federal Reserve decides to raise or lower the reserve requirement.

growth of the money supply. In contrast, if the discount rate is low, even a bank with sufficient reserves might borrow money. The loan will raise the bank's reserves and increase its ability to make loans. Thus, a reduction in the discount rate increases the total money supply.

Open-Market Operations

Buying and selling United States securities, called **open-market operations,** is the tool the Fed most often uses. Open-market operations affect the money supply by changing depository institution reserves, thereby putting money into or taking it out of circulation in the economy.

The term *open market* is used because these securities are traded in the open market through regular securities dealers. An open market is one that is open to private businesses and one that the government does not own or control. When the government buys securities such as Treasury bills, it pumps new reserves into the economy. When the government sells Treasury bills, it takes reserves out of circulation. Figure 16.12 examines this process.

Of course, individuals using cash do not carry out most open-market transactions. Financial institutions and large investors such as mutual

Figure 16.12
Buying and Selling Treasury Bills
Look at this diagram that examines the process of buying and selling Treasury bills. Explain how the government is able to affect the money supply through this process. ▼

Lesson 8 of Interactive Economics! to learn more about "Open-Market Operations," "The Reserve Requirement," and "The Federal Discount Rate."

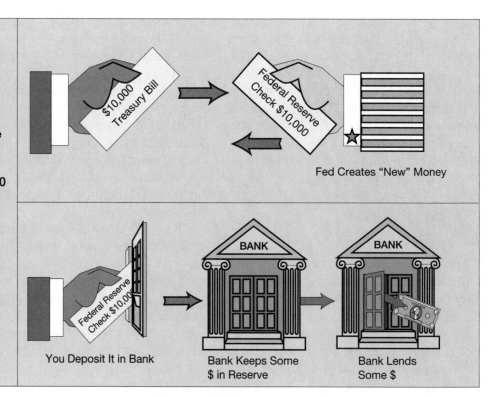

A. Suppose you sell a $10,000 Treasury bill to the Federal Reserve and receive that amount of money in the form of a Federal Reserve check. This is "new" money because the Fed created it simply by writing the check on itself. When you deposit the $10,000 in a bank, that bank will keep part in reserve and lend the rest. *The process of money creation has begun.*

Fed Creates "New" Money

You Deposit It in Bank

Bank Keeps Some $ in Reserve

Bank Lends Some $

funds make most transactions. If a bank purchases Treasury securities from the Fed, the purchase amount will be deducted from the bank's reserve account. The bank then has less money to lend, and the money supply eventually will be smaller. If a bank sells its government securities, the Fed will credit the money to the bank's reserve account. The bank can then make additional loans, and the money supply will grow. In each case, however, the Fed must decide which course is best for the economy in the long-run.

Monetary Policy Decision Making

The Federal Open Market Committee (FOMC) meets periodically to decide how best to control the money supply through open-market operations. At the beginning of each meeting, staff economists present data about what has happened to the money supply in the past, what current credit conditions are like, and what is likely to happen to the economy in the future. Statistics on unemployment, retail sales, gross domestic product, and so on, are presented. The information is discussed, and at the end of the meeting the committee votes on a course of action. The FOMC's decision summarizes current economic conditions and outlines the Fed's long-term goals for its monetary policy. To help meet these goals, the FOMC also sets objectives for the rate of growth of the money supply or the cost of credit for the next month or so.

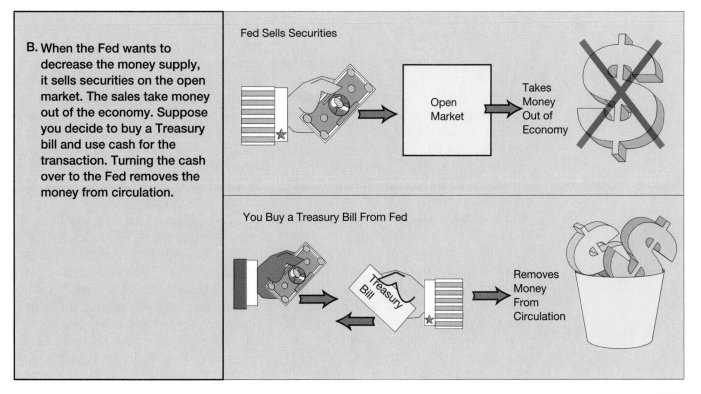

B. When the Fed wants to decrease the money supply, it sells securities on the open market. The sales take money out of the economy. Suppose you decide to buy a Treasury bill and use cash for the transaction. Turning the cash over to the Fed removes the money from circulation.

Fed Sells Securities

Open Market

Takes Money Out of Economy

You Buy a Treasury Bill From Fed

Treasury Bill

Removes Money From Circulation

Figure 16.13 ▶
Changing the
Money Supply
The brake/accelera-
tor model is one way
to remember how
the Fed can regulate
the money supply.
Explain how the
model works.

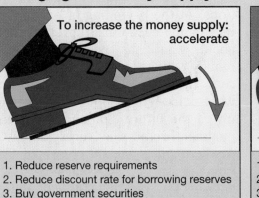
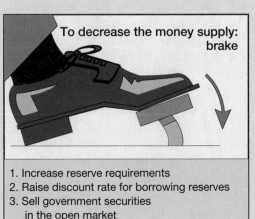

Changing the Money Supply

To increase the money supply: accelerate
1. Reduce reserve requirements
2. Reduce discount rate for borrowing reserves
3. Buy government securities in the open market

To decrease the money supply: brake
1. Increase reserve requirements
2. Raise discount rate for borrowing reserves
3. Sell government securities in the open market

**Figure 16.14
Independence of the Fed**
The Fed is free of executive branch control. For example, when President Clinton, a Democrat, took office, Alan Greenspan, whom President Reagan, a Republican, had appointed to chair the Fed, continued his term.

The Difficulties of Monetary Policy

Economists sometimes describe the Fed's control over the money supply as similar to a driver's control over a car. Like a driver, the Fed can accelerate or brake, depending on what phase of the business cycle the economy is in. See **Figure 16.13**. Remember, though, that this is only a model and, therefore, simplified. In reality, the Fed cannot control the money supply as quickly and as surely as a driver can control a car.

One problem is the difficulty in gathering and evaluating information about M1 and M2. As you know, the money supply is measured in terms of M1—currency, traveler's checks, and checkable accounts—and M2—M1 plus certain near moneys. In recent years, new savings and investment opportunities have appeared. Keeping track of the growth of M1 and M2 becomes more difficult as money is shifted from savings accounts into interest-paying checkable accounts or from checkable accounts into money market deposit accounts (MMDAs). The increased use of credit cards and electronic funds transfer has also changed the way money circulates through the economy.

Throughout its history, the Federal Reserve's monetary policies have been criticized. In instances of rising inflation, the Federal Reserve increased the amount of money in circulation, thereby worsening inflation. During other periods when the economy was slowing down and going into recession, the Federal Reserve decreased the money supply. This action made the recession worse. To prevent such misjudgments, some critics of the Federal Reserve have requested that the money supply simply be increased at the same rate every year. They recommend that the Fed *not* engage in monetary policy.

The Fed's Board of Governors is protected from direct political pressure. See Figure 16.14. It nonetheless still receives conflicting advice from many directions as shown in Figure 16.15. The President could suggest one course of action—lower interest rates, for example—while members of Congress may be urging a different course. Private business may call for one policy, while organized labor asks for the opposite. Finally, the Fed is not the only force working to affect the economy. The spending and taxing policies of the federal government are also at work. The Federal Reserve's task is to consider all these factors as it plots a course for the growth of the economy.

Pressures on the Fed

PRESIDENT — Lower the Discount Rate

CONGRESS — Raise the Discount Rate

BOARD OF GOVERNORS

BUSINESS — Reduce Reserve Requirements

LABOR — Buy Treasury Bills

Figure 16.15 Pressures
Examine the chart and explain how the Federal Reserve could be influenced by outside pressures.

SECTION 3 REVIEW

Understanding Vocabulary
Define discount rate, prime rate, open-market operations.

Reviewing Objectives
1. How can the Federal Reserve System use reserve requirements to alter the money supply?
2. How does the discount rate affect the money supply?
3. How does the Fed use open-market operations?
4. What are some of the difficulties of carrying out monetary policy?

News Clip

Readings in Economics

THE NEW YORK TIMES ON THE WEB   MAY 9, 1997

CHANGING THE NATURE OF MONEY

by Jason Chervokas & Tom Watson

Forget reaching into your pocket for coins and crumpled bills. In the near future, . . . consumers will be reaching into their wallets for special cards to pay for everything. . . .

The international leader in this technology is a British company called Mondex International Limited. . . .

The new card is just the latest kind of "smart card" to creep into the market. There are smart cards with medical information encoded on them and pre-paid telephone cards. . . .

But the substitution of Mondex-type cards—called "stored-value cards"—for money could have the most immediate impact. . . .

Big deal, you say, I already pay for gas and groceries with my debit card. What's the difference? In the case of "stored-value cards" the difference is considerable. A debit card or credit card requires that the seller clear the transaction with a central *system* that checks the price of the transaction against your bank account or credit line. With a stored-value card the bank downloads digits to your card that actually represent cash. The value of the money resides not in some central *system* but on the card.

Big deal, you say, there's no practical difference. Merchants can check my debit and credit cards in a matter of seconds.

But there are three very big differences. First, because of the high price of maintaining the central database's *system*, credit card and debit card transactions cost too much money for them to be used in small payments. . . .

Second, the most robust stored-value cards, like Mondex's, are based around semi-conductors mounted on a credit card-sized piece of plastic—not magnetic strips or visible embossed account numbers. This allows the digits encoded on stored-value devices to be heavily encrypted, which means that the hustler who is able to bootleg your credit card with a copy of a discarded credit card slip will need an electron microscope, some serious computing devices, and a lot of free time to bootleg your stored-value card. . . .

Finally, the digits encoded on a stored-value card represent the actual value. . . . That means the digits are virtual money. . . .

• THINK ABOUT IT •

1. **What company is the major producer of stored-value cards?**

2. **What are the three differences between debit cards and stored-value cards?**

ECONOMICS IN ACTION

Federal Reserve and Monetary Policy

Setting up the Video

With your classmates, view "Federal Reserve and Monetary Policy" on the videodisc *Economics in Action.* The video focuses on how the Federal Reserve System (the Fed) controls the money supply. It shows that when the economy is sluggish, the Fed can encourage loans by making money inexpensive to borrow. When inflation is high, the Fed can make money expensive to borrow.

**Chapter 21
Disc 2, Side 1**

View the video by scanning the bar code or by entering the chapter number on your keypad and pressing Search. *(Also available in VHS format.)*

Hands-On Activity

A key interest rate is the prime rate—the rate banks charge to their best customers. Because most credit card interest rates are tied to the prime rate, consumers feel the effects of a rate hike almost immediately. Assume that you have credit-card debt of $12,700. Your current interest rate, tied to the prime, is 16.9 percent. What is your annual interest payment? If the prime rate rose 1 percent, what would your new interest payment be? How much more per year does your credit card now cost? Prepare a table showing the increasing payments that a 2 percent and a 4 percent hike would cost.

INTERACTIVE ECONOMICS!

Monetary Policy

Introduction

Lesson 8 of *Interactive Economics!* deals with monetary policy. Monetary policy is one of the most powerful ways to affect the health of the economy today. It is normally conducted by the Federal Reserve System, or Fed, and it affects both the cost and availability of credit. Monetary policy is possible because of the fractional reserve system in use today, and because of the ability of the Fed to expand and contract the money supply.

Using the Software

1. Select "Monetary Policy" from the Main Menu.
2. Read the introduction to "Monetary Policy," then click on "An Introduction to Monetary Policy."
3. After reading the information, go back to the "Tutorial" menu and click on "Fractional Reserves and Monetary Expansion."
4. Finally, click on the "Advanced Topics Menu" and read about open-market operations, the reserve requirement, and the federal discount rate.
5. Then click on "Economic Lab." Complete the lab by clicking and dragging the appropriate glossary terms to the location that best completes the sentences.
6. Print your completed lab.

16 Review

Identifying Key Terms

Write the letter of the definition in Column B below that correctly defines each term in Column A.

Column A
1. the Fed (p. 388)
2. prime rate (p. 401)
3. tight money policy (p. 389)
4. reserve requirements (p. 389)
5. monetary policy (p. 388)
6. open-market operations (p. 402)

Column B
a. the central banking system in the United States
b. means of changing the growth rate of supply of money in the economy
c. purchases and sales of United States securities by the Federal Reserve System
d. situation in which credit is expensive to borrow and in short supply
e. interest rate that the Federal Reserve charges banks for loans
f. require banks to keep a certain percentage of their deposits as cash on account with the Federal Reserve

Use terms from the following list to fill in the blanks in the paragraph below.

fractional reserve banking (p. 389)
check clearing (p. 396)
discount rate (p. 401)
loose money policy (p. 389)

When credit is inexpensive to borrow, we can be pretty sure that the Fed has engaged in (7) . Because banks do not have to keep 100 percent of their deposits on reserve, we have a (8) system. One of the functions in the Federal Reserve is to handle (9) , which is the method by which a check deposited in one bank is transferred to another bank. Sometimes banks need to borrow from a Federal Reserve district bank. The rate that they pay is called the (10) .

Recalling Facts and Ideas

Section 1
1. What are the two basic types of monetary policies?
2. In a fractional reserve banking system, what happens to the money supply when the Fed injects $100 of new money into the American economy?
3. Why do banks have to keep money in reserve accounts?

Section 2
4. What does the Board of Governors do within the Federal Reserve System?
5. How many Federal Reserve banks and branches are there?
6. Which agency of the federal government supplies paper currency to the economy?

Section 3
7. The Fed can change the money supply in circulation by changing reserve requirements. What are two other methods that it can use to do this?
8. If the Fed wants to decrease the money supply, what can it do?
9. Why is it difficult for the Fed to gather and evaluate information about M1 and M2?
10. Why do some of the Fed's critics think the Fed should not engage in monetary policy?

Critical Thinking

Section 1
Expressing Problems Clearly Draw a flowchart to show how the banking system creates money.

Section 2
Making Comparisons What is the advantage to Federal Reserve membership today? How does this differ from the past?

Section 3
Analyzing Information How do you think the Fed would operate differently if it were under the control of the executive branch?

Applying Economic Concepts

Monetary Policy Imagine that you are a member of the Federal Open Market Committee. Eight to ten times a year, you meet with the other members of the FOMC. The research staff presents information on the state of the economy. Write a list of the different types of information you think the members of the FOMC receive during their meetings.

Chapter Projects

1. **Individual Project** In a library or on the Internet, check the most recent issue of the *Federal Reserve Bulletin* for the current reserve requirements and discount rate. Check the same month's issue for the last four years to see how often they have changed and how much. Track these data on a chart.
2. **Cooperative Learning Project** Work in three groups. Each group will study one potential tool of monetary policy:

   - changing reserve requirements
   - changing the discount rate
   - changing the money supply via open-market operations

The task of each group is to develop a convincing argument in favor of its monetary tool over the use of the other two monetary tools. Members of each group can contribute separate arguments. Appoint one member to summarize the arguments and present that summary in a short speech to the class using an outline.

Reviewing Skills

Understanding Real and Nominal Values
The Real Cost of College Below are some hypothetical numbers that show a price index each year and the nominal dollar price of attending one academic year in a private university.

Private University

Year	Price Index	Tuition/Room and Board
1980	68.4	$10,040
1985	96.0	$12,343
1990	104.0	$16,420
1995	119.0	$21,200
2000	125.0	$26,000

What was the real cost for each academic year in a private university?

Technology Activity
Using the Internet

Refer to the list of Federal Reserve Banks that you kept in Your Economics Journal on page 387. Choose one of these banks. Then, using a search engine, type in *Federal Reserve Banks* to locate the home page of the bank you have chosen. Visit the Web site to learn about the operations of that particular bank. Write a one-page summary of your findings to share with your classmates.

17
GOVERNMENT SPENDS, COLLECTS, AND OWES

Who decides what paintings and sculptures to put in museums?

Who usually owns big museums?

Why are there not more museums?

How expensive is it to operate a museum?

Why do people go to museums?

Your Economics Journal

Keep track of what you do during a one-day period. List each activity. Indicate what role the government might have in that activity. For example, when you drive, it is usually on a government-provided public road

SECTION 1 Growth in the Size of Government

SECTION 1 FOCUS

Terms to Know public-works projects, Medicare

Objectives *After reading this section, you should be able to:*
① Describe two measurements of government growth.
② Explain why government has grown rapidly.

Is More Government Better Government?

In the United States, the forces of supply and demand operating in the marketplace affect many of the decisions that answer the basic economic questions you learned about in Chapter 2. The United States is not a pure market economy, however. In addition to market forces, other forces affect the distribution of resources throughout the economy. One of the most important of these forces is government on all levels—local, state, and federal. Government at every level is involved in almost every aspect of the United States economy.

Government Growth

Government has grown considerably in the last 50 or so years. In 1929, just before the Great Depression began, government at all levels employed slightly more than 3 million civilian workers. During the Depression, however, there was a need for more government services, as **Figure 17.1** illustrates. Today about 2.7 million people work for the federal government alone. If you add local and state employees, the government employs about 19.6 million civilian workers. This figure represents more than a sixfold increase during a period in which the population only doubled.

As the functions of government have grown, so has government spending. **Figure 17.2** shows one way of looking at government activities.

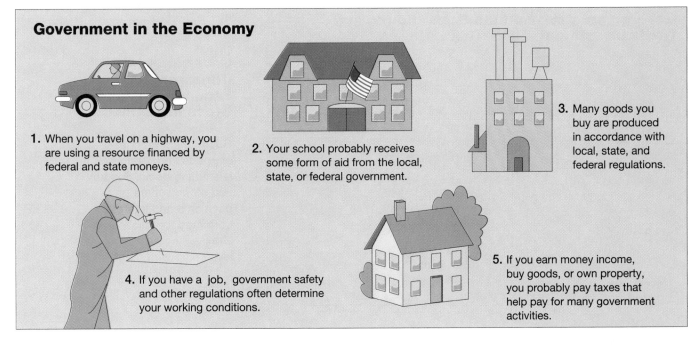

Government in the Economy

1. When you travel on a highway, you are using a resource financed by federal and state moneys.

2. Your school probably receives some form of aid from the local, state, or federal government.

3. Many goods you buy are produced in accordance with local, state, and federal regulations.

4. If you have a job, government safety and other regulations often determine your working conditions.

5. If you earn money income, buy goods, or own property, you probably pay taxes that help pay for many government activities.

Figure 17.1
Government Growth
As more people lost their jobs during the Great Depression, local government services, such as soup kitchens, proved inadequate. New government services and a larger government labor force resulted.

▼

Figure 17.3 (page 414) shows another.

As you can see from Figure 17.3, the different levels of government have grown at different rates. During the late 1960s, state and local governments spent less than the federal government. The federal government paid for national defense, **public-works projects,** and the salaries of members of Congress, federal judges, and the employees of executive departments such as the State Department. This situation continued until about 1970. Then, state and local government spending for such items as sewers, roads, and schools increased rapidly.

Why Has Government Grown?

Economists have often tried to explain the huge growth in government spending since the Great Depression. One theory is that as the nation became richer, especially in the late 1960s and early 1970s, people demanded more government services to even out certain income inequities. This goal relates to the economic

Figure 17.2 ▲
Government in the Economy
Government plays a major role in most aspects of our lives. Some individuals argue that government should be even larger. Others believe that government has grown too large and that the private sector should provide goods and services without government intervention.

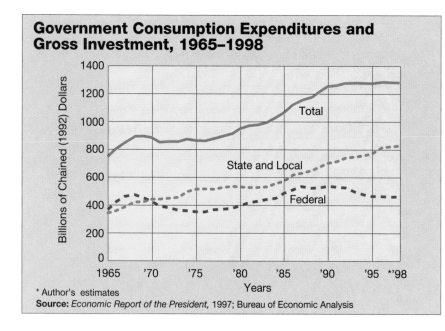

Government Consumption Expenditures and Gross Investment, 1965–1998

Billions of Chained (1992) Dollars

Total

State and Local

Federal

1965   '70   '75   '80   '85   '90   '95   *'98

Years

* Author's estimates

Source: *Economic Report of the President,* 1997; Bureau of Economic Analysis

◀ **Figure 17.3 Government Consumption Expenditures and Gross Investment, 1965–1998**

Government purchases of goods and services (excluding Social Security and other welfare payments and interest) corrected for inflation show an increase in all levels of government.

▼ **Figure 17.4 Government Spending as a Percentage of Gross Domestic Product, 1965–1998**

Total government expenditures, including Social Security and other welfare payments, as well as interest payments, expressed as a percentage of GDP have grown from 1965 to the present.

question of who should share in what is produced.

In the late 1970s and early 1980s, however, the economy suffered a series of recessions. Americans began to feel that maintaining all the programs they wanted was too costly. At some point, Americans—voters and politicians alike—had lost sight of the economic principle of scarcity. To remedy the situation, politicians began to think of ways to cut government spending. In doing so, they had to decide on the trade-offs Americans

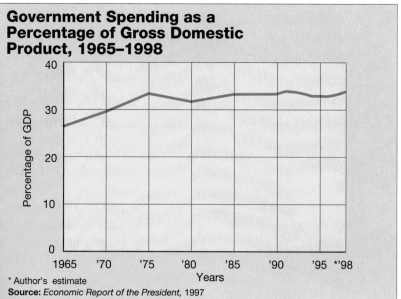

Government Spending as a Percentage of Gross Domestic Product, 1965–1998

Percentage of GDP

1965   '70   '75   '80   '85   '90   '95   *'98

Years

* Author's estimate

Source: *Economic Report of the President,* 1997

would be willing to accept: fewer services and less money for research, education, public assistance, and health care, for example.

Today total government *purchases* represent about 18 percent of GDP. This figure, however, does not include such items as interest payments on the national debt and transfer payments such as welfare programs. Total government *outlays* exceed one-third of GDP. See Figure 17.4. Moreover, the size of government cannot be measured only by the cost of government spending. Any discussion of government's size must include where government spends this money.

The True Size of Government
When the government taxes you to provide you with a particular service, such as **Medicare** (health care for the aged), this cost of government is included in government spending. What if the government legislates a requirement that your employer provide that same service? Is there any difference? State governments are doing just that. In Massachusetts, for example, employers with five or more employees must provide medical insurance for each employee. The federal government taxes employees to pay for government-provided health insurance and, a state government requires that employers provide health insurance directly. The true size of government may be even greater than government estimates show.

Can We Say That the Growth of Government Is Good or Bad?
Everyone knows that government in the United States has grown in the 1900s—particularly during the Depression and during the 1960s and 1970s. See Figure 17.5. Can we say whether this is good or bad for society?

Is there an answer to such a debate? Not really, because the side that one takes depends on one's values. No right or wrong answer exists when values are at stake.

Figure 17.5 ▶
1960s and 1970s Government Growth
More aid was demanded for education, medical care, welfare, and so on. The economy was booming, and many believed that taxpayers could afford higher government spending.

SECTION 1 REVIEW

Understanding Vocabulary
Define public-works projects, Medicare.

Reviewing Objectives
❶ How rapidly has government grown since 1929?
❷ What do some economists believe caused the rapid growth of government?

SECTION *2* The Functions of Government

Lesson 7 of **Interactive Economics!** to learn more about **"The Role of Government."**

What Government Does for You

Government in the United States serves four important functions: (1) providing public goods, (2) redistributing income and providing for the public well-being, (3) regulating economic activity, and (4) ensuring economic stability. Federal, state, and local governments share responsibilities for the first three functions. The fourth responsibility, ensuring economic stability, is handled almost entirely by the federal government.

Providing Public Goods

Public goods are a special type of goods or services that government sometimes supplies to its citizens. Many individuals can use these goods at the same time, without reducing the benefit each person receives. Public goods include national defense.

National defense is one of the few public goods only the federal government provides. Usually different levels of government share responsibilities. For example, the legal system, which is a type of public good, involves all three levels. Federal, state, and local governments maintain separate systems of courts, correctional institutions, and law-enforcement agencies.

Merit Goods In any society, certain goods and services are considered to have special merit. A **merit good** is defined as any good that the government has deemed socially desirable. Examples of merit goods in our society are museums, ballets, and virtually all plays and classical music concerts. The

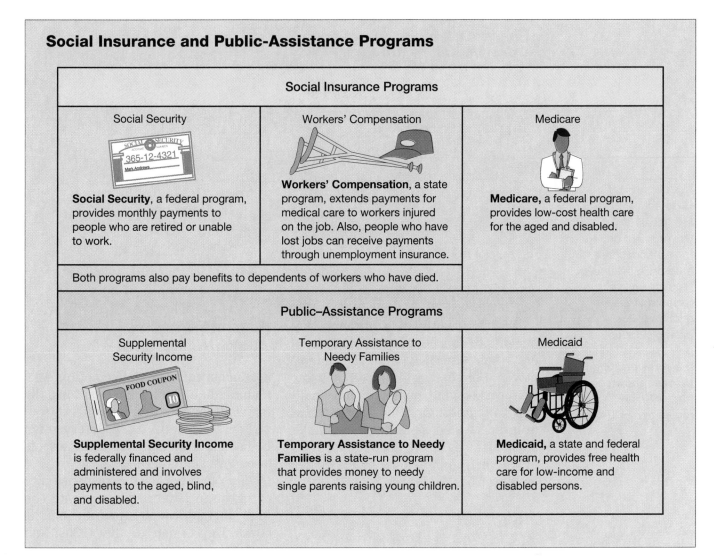

Social Insurance and Public-Assistance Programs

Social Insurance Programs

Social Security

Social Security, a federal program, provides monthly payments to people who are retired or unable to work.

Workers' Compensation

Workers' Compensation, a state program, extends payments for medical care to workers injured on the job. Also, people who have lost jobs can receive payments through unemployment insurance.

Medicare

Medicare, a federal program, provides low-cost health care for the aged and disabled.

Both programs also pay benefits to dependents of workers who have died.

Public–Assistance Programs

Supplemental Security Income

Supplemental Security Income is federally financed and administered and involves payments to the aged, blind, and disabled.

Temporary Assistance to Needy Families

Temporary Assistance to Needy Families is a state-run program that provides money to needy single parents raising young children.

Medicaid

Medicaid, a state and federal program, provides free health care for low-income and disabled persons.

---

government may wish to provide these merit goods to the people in society who would not otherwise purchase them at a full market price. Governments, therefore, often subsidize classical music concerts, ballets, museums, and plays.

Demerit Goods At the opposite end of the socially desirable spectrum are **demerit goods,** goods that the government has deemed socially undesirable. Gambling and injurious drugs such as heroin are examples. The government exercises its role in the area of demerit goods by taxing, regulating, or prohibiting the manufacture, sale, and use of such goods. For example, governments justify very high taxes on alcohol and tobacco products

by declaring them demerit goods. The government prohibits many other drugs and strictly regulates prescription medicines.

Redistributing Income

Another function of government is to provide for the public well-being by assisting specific groups such as the aged, the ill, and the poor. Through their elected representatives, Americans have chosen to see that almost everyone in the nation is provided with a certain minimum level of income. See Figure 17.6. This task is accomplished primarily through **income redistribution,** using tax receipts to help citizens in need.

Figure 17.6 ▲
Social Insurance and Public Assistance
Government programs that redistribute income taken from some people through taxation and given to others fall into two areas: social insurance and public assistance.

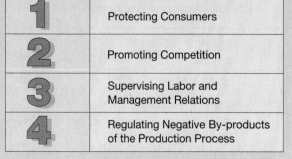

Figure 17.7 Major Functions of Government Regulations

1	Protecting Consumers
2	Promoting Competition
3	Supervising Labor and Management Relations
4	Regulating Negative By-products of the Production Process

Figure 17.7 ▶ Government Regulations
Government under the American free enterprise system regulates certain aspects of the economy. For example, industrial processes, such as the spray painting process shown on page 419, are regulated.

Social insurance programs pay benefits to retired and disabled workers, their families, and the unemployed. Benefits are financed by taxes that workers and employers have paid into the programs. **Public-assistance programs,** often called **welfare,** make payments based on need, regardless of whether an individual or his or her employer has paid taxes.

Regulating Economic Activity

Figure 17.7 illustrates the four major ways in which the government regulates economic activity. One of the most important regulatory functions concerns the production process and emitting pollutants into the atmosphere as **Figure 17.8** shows. When a steel mill produces steel, for example, the resulting pollution from the smokestacks may cause health problems in the surrounding area. The steel mill does not have to correct these negative by-products in the absence of a law. Therefore, the federal government has often stepped in to require plants to install equipment that will reduce pollution. Local and state governments also have pollution laws. These include everything from city laws against littering to state laws regulating the dumping of toxic wastes in rivers.

Promoting Economic Stability

Encouraging and promoting economic stability means smoothing the ups and downs in the nation's overall business activity. Such intervention helps shield citizens from the effects of business fluctuations.

This function is the responsibility of only the federal government. The high unemployment rates during the Great Depression of the 1930s, and new theories about possible ways in which government could reduce unemployment, led to a landmark piece of legislation at the end of World War II. The Employment Act of 1946 specifies clearly the federal government's responsibility for economy-wide stabilization:

The Congress hereby declares that it is the continuing policy and responsibility of the Federal Government to use all practicable means consistent with its needs and obligations and other essential considerations of national policy, with assistance and cooperation of industry, agriculture, labor and State and local governments, to coordinate and utilize all its plans, functions, and resources for the purpose of creating and maintaining, in a manner calculated to foster and promote free

◀
**Figure 17.8
Protecting Citizens**
Government, through the Environmental Protection Agency, regulates industrial emissions of pollutants. For example, industrial processes, such as high-pressure spray painting, must comply with emissions regulations.

competitive enterprise and the general welfare, conditions under which there will be afforded useful employment opportunities, including self-employment, for those able, willing, and seeking to work and to promote maximum employment, production, and purchasing power.

One way that the federal government attempts to stabilize the overall national economy is through monetary policy. The federal government also can use fiscal policy, which is the government's set of financial policies on taxation and spending, to even out the business cycle.

SECTION 2 REVIEW

Understanding Vocabulary

Define public goods, merit good, Social Security, workers' compensation, Supplemental Security Income, Temporary Assistance to Needy Families, Medicaid, demerit goods, income redistribution, social insurance programs, public-assistance programs, welfare.

Reviewing Objectives

1. What are public goods?
2. How does government redistribute income?
3. How does government regulate economic activity?
4. What two tools does the government use to promote economic stability?

Personal Perspective

Alexis Herman on the Department of Labor

Profile

- born July 16, 1947
- graduate of Xavier University
- founder and president of A.M. Herman & Associates in the 1980s
- director of the Women's Bureau of the Department of Labor during the Carter Administration
- appointed secretary of labor in 1997

Alexis M. Herman became the first African American Secretary of Labor in 1997. Ms. Herman brought more than two decades of leadership to her cabinet position. In the excerpt below, Ms. Herman shares her visions for the Department of Labor with members of a House subcommittee.

I want to work with every one of you—and in partnership with the business community, the labor community, and civic, charitable, and professional organizations, to make sure that all Americans have the education, the training, and the skills they need to succeed in the new economy. . . .

Together, we have made great progress in helping America's working families build a better future for themselves. The economy is growing steadily. More than 12 million new jobs have been created since January, 1993. Unemployment is at its lowest rate in 23 years. . . .

Yet, we still face the challenge of helping every working American to participate and prosper in the new economy. The new economy harnesses high technology—and requires highly skilled workers—to make the highest-quality products and offer the highest-quality services for markets at home and abroad. . . . It is our responsibility to make sure that all workers—

regardless of how they earn their living today—have the opportunity to find and hold secure jobs, with good wages, reliable pensions, health benefits and opportunities to improve their skills.

The goals I have set for the Labor Department answer these challenges and build on the successes of the past four years. My goals are:

- *First, to equip every working American with the skills to find and hold good jobs, with rising incomes throughout their lives;*
- *Second, to help people move from welfare to work;*
- *Third, to assure that working Americans enjoy secure pensions when they retire;*
- *Fourth, to guarantee every American a safe and healthy workplace;*
- *And fifth, to help working people balance work and family.*

Checking for Understanding

1. What economic progress does Ms. Herman note?
2. What does the new economy require of American workers?
3. What are Ms. Herman's five goals for the Department of Labor?

The Federal Budget and the National Debt

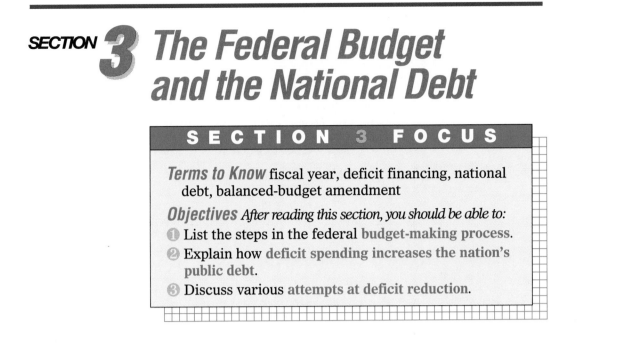

S E C T I O N 3 F O C U S

Terms to Know fiscal year, deficit financing, national debt, balanced-budget amendment

Objectives After reading this section, you should be able to:

❶ List the steps in the federal **budget-making process.**

❷ Explain how **deficit spending increases the nation's public debt.**

❸ Discuss various **attempts at deficit reduction.**

Budget Deficits Add to the National Debt

To carry out all of its functions, government must spend large sums of money. As a result, the federal budget is huge and has numerous categories. Figure 17.9 shows the major areas of spending.

Considerable debate and compromise are necessary in preparing an annual budget. Because all resources are scarce, an increase in spending in one area will cause a decrease in spending in some other area. Every spending action by the government has its own opportunity cost, and trade-offs between types of spending, even for the government, always exist. This fact was overlooked in some years when the economy was booming and government was collecting large revenues. In the 1990s all levels of government became more aware of the dangers of overspending because of the massive federal debt.

The Budget-Making Process

A complicated budget-making process goes on throughout every year, not only in Washington, D.C., but in every state and local government unit.

Figure 17.9 Federal Spending

The federal budget is based on a fiscal, rather than a calendar, year. Spending is calculated from the beginning of the budget year on October 1 of one year to September 30 of the next year, which is the federal government's **fiscal year.** ▼

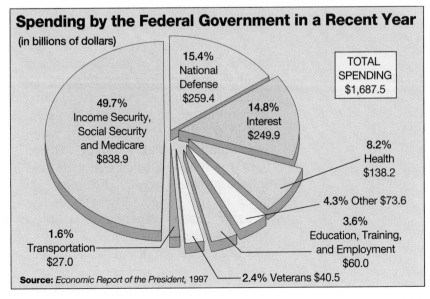

Spending by the Federal Government in a Recent Year
(in billions of dollars)

TOTAL SPENDING $1,687.5

49.7% Income Security, Social Security and Medicare $838.9

15.4% National Defense $259.4

14.8% Interest $249.9

8.2% Health $138.2

4.3% Other $73.6

3.6% Education, Training, and Employment $60.0

2.4% Veterans $40.5

1.6% Transportation $27.0

Source: *Economic Report of the President, 1997*

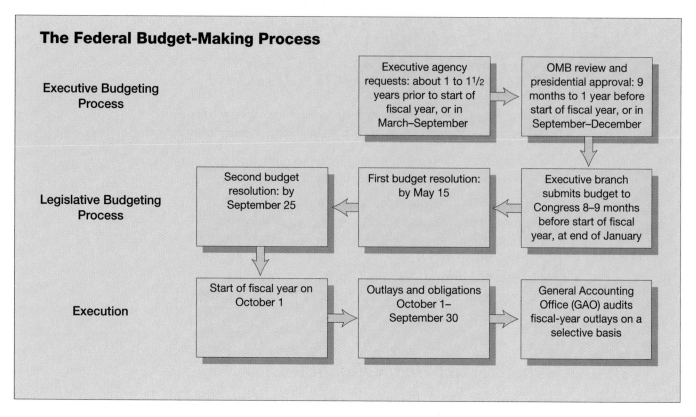

The Federal Budget-Making Process

Executive Budgeting Process

| Executive agency requests: about 1 to 1½ years prior to start of fiscal year, or in March–September | → | OMB review and presidential approval: 9 months to 1 year before start of fiscal year, or in September–December |

Legislative Budgeting Process

Second budget resolution: by September 25 ← First budget resolution: by May 15 ← Executive branch submits budget to Congress 8–9 months before start of fiscal year, at end of January

Execution

Start of fiscal year on October 1 → Outlays and obligations October 1–September 30 → General Accounting Office (GAO) audits fiscal-year outlays on a selective basis

**Figure 17.10 ▲
The Federal Budget-Making Process**
The Office of Management and Budget (OMB) starts the budget process, with the advice of the Council of Economic Advisers (CEA) and the Treasury Department.

The Federal Budget About eighteen months before the fiscal year begins on October 1, the executive branch of the government begins to prepare a budget as Figure 17.10 shows. Working with the President, the Office of Management and Budget (OMB) makes an outline of a tentative budget for the next fiscal year. The various departments and agencies receive this outline and usually start bargaining with the OMB for a larger allocation of federal funds. See Figure 17.11.

The President reviews and approves the budget plan. The budget is printed, and the President submits the budget to Congress by January. Then its committees and subcommittees examine the budget's proposals, while the Congressional Budget Office (CBO) advises the committees and subcommittees about different aspects of the budget. Throughout the summer each subcommittee then holds a series of discussions.

Congress is supposed to pass a sec-ond budget resolution setting binding limits on spending and taxes for the upcoming fiscal year. In practice, however, the required budget resolutions often do not get passed on time. Moreover, when they are passed, the resolutions are not always treated as binding. As a result, the fiscal year sometimes starts without a budget, and the agencies must operate on the basis of a continuing congressional resolution. They can continue spending as they spent the year before until the new resolution is passed.

State and Local Budgets Figure 17.12 shows how state and local governments spend the revenues they collect. By far the largest single category in state and local expenditures is education because state and local funds provide most elementary and secondary education, as well as a considerable portion of higher education. Other large expenses are for public assistance (welfare), hospitals, health

GO TO

Lesson 7 of Interactive Economics! to learn more about "The Federal Budget."

Figure 17.11
The Budget Challenge

In 1997 Congress and the President unveiled plans to balance the budget by 2002. According to the cartoonist, why will the budget be balanced by 2002?

maintenance, and highways. The "other" general expenditure also is large. It includes expenditures for state parks. See Figure 17.13 (page 424).

Deficit Spending and the Nation's Public Debt

In spite of the budget process outlined above, federal government revenues have not been equal to government expenditures. For years, the federal government has spent more than it has received. When government spends more than it collects through taxation, it must raise the extra money through borrowing. This borrowing is similar to an individual overspending his or her income and using credit. The government's spending more money than it takes in is called **deficit financing**. From 1940 through 1999, the federal government

**Figure 17.12
Government Spending**

State and local government expenditures increased in recent years, as these governments shouldered the rising costs of social welfare programs.

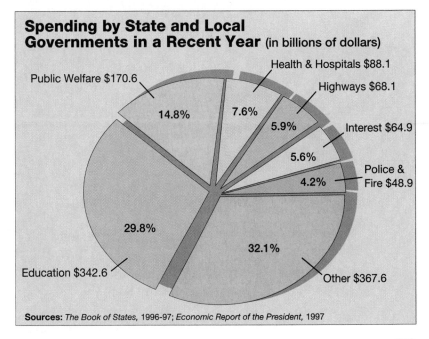

Spending by State and Local Governments in a Recent Year (in billions of dollars)

Public Welfare $170.6 — 14.8%
Health & Hospitals $88.1 — 7.6%
Highways $68.1 — 5.9%
Interest $64.9 — 5.6%
Police & Fire $48.9 — 4.2%
Other $367.6 — 32.1%
Education $342.6 — 29.8%

Sources: *The Book of States*, 1996-97; *Economic Report of the President*, 1997

had a deficit in 53 out of the 60 years. Federal government spending averaged 23 percent of GDP through the early 1990s. Federal government revenues, however, were roughly 19 percent of GDP. The difference had to be made up by borrowing.

Government Borrowing Government borrows by selling securities to individuals and businesses. Federal securities include Treasury bonds, notes, and bills. When you buy United States savings bonds, you are also lending money to the federal government. In

**Figure 17.13
State Preservation**
Sometimes states need local pressure to preserve landmarks. In 1903, for example, Adina Emilia De Zavala was one of the first Texans to try to preserve sites important in Texas history. She barricaded herself inside the Alamo to prevent it from being torn down. Today the Alamo is a state park and the state's number one tourist attraction.

▼

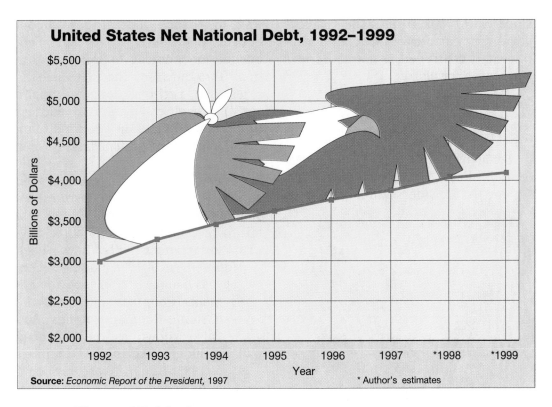

United States Net National Debt, 1992–1999

Billions of Dollars

$5,500
$5,000
$4,500
$4,000
$3,500
$3,000
$2,500
$2,000

1992   1993   1994   1995   1996   1997   *1998   *1999

Year

Source: *Economic Report of the President,* 1997   * Author's estimates

Figure 17.14 ▲
Net National Debt
The national debt of the
United States increased 37
percent between 1992 and
1999. Many feared that such
a rise would mortgage
young Americans' futures.

addition, individual agencies of the federal government, such as the Tennessee Valley Authority, are authorized to sell bonds. State and local governments can borrow by selling municipal bonds to finance some of their activities.

Each year the federal government creates new debt by issuing new securities. At the same time, it retires old debt by paying off bonds, notes, and bills as they come due. The total amount of debt outstanding for the federal government is called the **national debt** or public debt. As you can see from Figure 17.14, in recent years the dollar amount of the national debt has been growing at a steep rate. This increase concerns many public officials and private citizens who think the government is living too far beyond its means. Others, however, have pointed out that the national debt expressed as a percentage of GDP has actually decreased steadily

**Figure 17.15
Cutting
Government
Programs
to Reduce
the Deficit**
The Budget Reconciliation Act of 1997 proposed spending cuts in many programs. Among the programs slated for reduced funding were student loans.

▶

since World War II until the last few years. They believe that federal borrowing, if controlled, is not necessarily a reason for alarm.

Attempts at Deficit Reduction

Some argue that congressional legislation should limit the deficit. See Figure 17.15. Others think the only way to reduce federal government budget deficits is by a **balanced-budget amendment** to the Constitution. Two-thirds of the state legislatures can petition Congress for a constitutional convention to address this issue. To date, the required number of legislative petitions has not been filed.

As an alternative, Congress has the option of passing such a constitutional amendment, which it would then submit to the states for ratification. Several amendment bills have been proposed. As of 1998, however, Congress had passed no such amendment. Congress did pass the Gramm-Rudman-Hollings Act, also known as the Balanced Budget Act, in December 1985. Its goal was to reach a balanced budget by fiscal year 1991. After Congress failed for two years to comply with the act's target deficit reductions, Congress revised it. Congress again failed to meet the required deficit reductions for the first four years of the revised act. Yet another revision was passed in 1990, only to be virtually eliminated by the Budget Enforcement Act of 1990. As the deficit fell during the robust economy of the Clinton administration, the issue became less pressing.

SECTION 3 REVIEW

Understanding Vocabulary
Define fiscal year, deficit financing, national debt, balanced-budget amendment.

Reviewing Objectives
❶ What are the steps in the federal budget-making process?

❷ In what type of activity does the federal government engage when it spends more than it receives?

❸ What attempts have been made to reduce the federal deficit?

Using E-Mail

Telecommunication refers to communicating at a distance through the use of a telephone, video, or computer. How can you get your own computer to "talk" with other computers?

What You Will Need to Begin

A computer is ready for telecommunication after two parts are added to it. The first is a piece of hardware called a *modem*. A modem is a device that enables computers to communicate with each other through telephone lines.

The second part is *communications software,* which lets your computer prepare and send information to the modem. It also lets your computer receive and understand the information it receives from the modem.

E-Mail

Electronic mail, or "E-mail" for short, is one way of sending and receiving messages electronically. Anyone who has E-mail can send and receive private messages.

If you have E-mail, you have a specific address such as the ones shown in **Figure A**. This address identifies the location of your electronic "mailbox"—the place where you receive your E-mail. To send an E-mail message to another person you must include that person's E-mail address.

Many corporations and government agencies are using E-mail communications. For example, if you want to write to the President, you would simply address your letter to the location in **Figure B**.

Practicing the Skill

To E-mail a friend, complete the following steps.
❶ Select the "message" function and type a message.
❷ Type the E-mail address and click on "send."

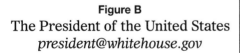

Figure A
fhernadez@aol.com
gjohansen@webtv.net
wgaul@scsn.net
mmartinson@usuc.net
sq496tg@ibmmail.com

Figure B
The President of the United States
president@whitehouse.gov

Taxation

Taxes Distribute the Cost of Government Among Taxpayers

You, the American taxpayer, are the source of most of the money the government spends. Almost all federal, state, and local government revenue comes from taxation. Figure 17.16 lists the major taxes that the various levels of government use to raise revenue.

Principles of Taxation

Taxes can be justified according to one of two major principles. Under the **benefits-received principle,** those who use a particular government service support it with taxes in proportion to the benefit they receive. Those who do not use a service do not pay taxes for it. For example, a gasoline tax to pay for highway construction and repair is based on the benefits-received principle. Those who use the highways often buy more gasoline and, therefore, pay more in gasoline taxes.

A tax based on the benefits-received principle is useful in raising money to pay for a service only certain individuals use. Many government services, however—national defense, for example—benefit everyone equally. Also, those who most need services, such as the aged and poor, are the individuals least able to pay taxes.

Under the **ability-to-pay principle,** those with higher incomes pay more taxes than those with lower incomes, regardless of the number of government services they use. For example, in most cities all property owners, even those without school-aged children, must pay property taxes to support the local school system.

Forms of Taxation

Actual taxes are classified according to the effect they have on those who are taxed as shown in Figure 17.17 (page 430). In the United States today, these classifications include progressive taxes, regressive taxes, and proportional taxes. Congress

Figure 17.16 Major Taxes

Tax	Description	Type
Personal income	Tax is a percentage of income and a major source of federal revenue; many states and local governments also levy	Progressive at the federal level, but is sometimes proportional at the state level
Social insurance	Taxes covered by the Federal Insurance Contributions Act (FICA); second largest source of federal revenue	Proportional up to $72,900 in 2000, regressive above that (as estimated by the Social Security Administration)
Corporate income	Federal tax as a percentage of corporate profits; some states also levy	At the federal level, progressive up to $10,000,000, proportional above that
Excise	Tax paid by the consumer on the manufacture, use, and consumption of certain goods; major federal taxes are on alcohol, tobacco, and gasoline; some states also levy	Regressive if people with higher incomes spend a lower proportion of income on taxed items
Estate	Federal tax on the property of someone who has died; some states also levy	Progressive; percentage increases with the value of the estate
Inheritance	Tax paid by those who inherit property; state tax only	Varies by state
Gift	Tax paid by the person who gives a gift; federal tax only	Progressive; percentage increases with the value of the gift
Sales	Tax paid on purchases; almost all states as well as many local governments levy; rate varies from state to state and within states; items taxed also vary	Regressive if people with higher incomes spend a lower proportion of income on taxed items
Property	State and local taxation of the value of property; both real property, such as buildings and land, and personal property, such as stocks, bonds, and home furnishings, may be taxed	Proportional; percentage is set by state and local governments
Customs duties	Tax on imports; paid by the importer	Proportional

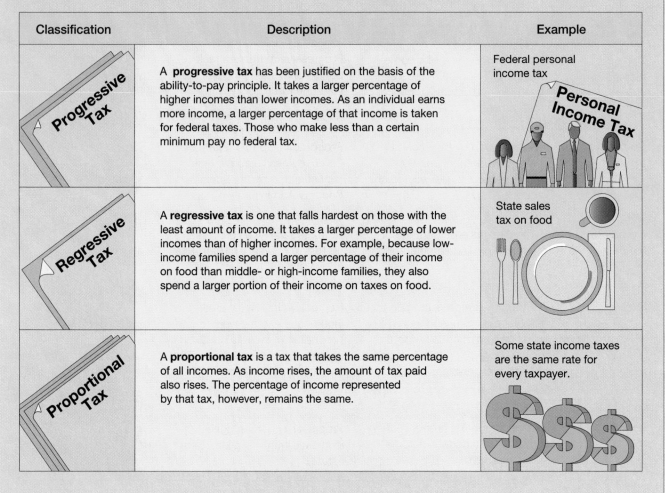

Taxes Classified by Their Effects

Classification	Description	Example
Progressive Tax	A **progressive tax** has been justified on the basis of the ability-to-pay principle. It takes a larger percentage of higher incomes than lower incomes. As an individual earns more income, a larger percentage of that income is taken for federal taxes. Those who make less than a certain minimum pay no federal tax.	Federal personal income tax
Regressive Tax	A **regressive tax** is one that falls hardest on those with the least amount of income. It takes a larger percentage of lower incomes than of higher incomes. For example, because low-income families spend a larger percentage of their income on food than middle- or high-income families, they also spend a larger portion of their income on taxes on food.	State sales tax on food
Proportional Tax	A **proportional tax** is a tax that takes the same percentage of all incomes. As income rises, the amount of tax paid also rises. The percentage of income represented by that tax, however, remains the same.	Some state income taxes are the same rate for every taxpayer.

Figure 17.17 ▲ Taxes Classified by Their Effects
Do you think that higher taxes for the wealthy are fair? Why or why not?

passed a tax law in 1986 to make the tax code more fair. It eliminated many of the deductions and tax shelters that had seemed to favor the wealthy. The new tax code lowered the top tax rates for individuals gradually from 50 percent to 28 percent. It also shifted some of the tax burden from individuals by raising corporate taxes. Tax legislation in 1993 increased the top tax rates for high-income earning individuals to 39.6 percent. Corporate taxes were also increased.

Taxes as a Way of Directing Economic Activity

Taxation is more than a way for government to raise money. It is also a way in which government can direct the use of resources by businesses and individuals and a way to regulate economic activity.

Encouraging Business Taxes are commonly used to encourage certain activities by businesses and individuals. Often cities and states will temporarily reduce or exempt taxes for a company as a way of persuading it to locate in a particular area. Governments at all levels encourage investment in their bonds by offering tax-free interest. Taxes are also used to direct resources toward investments that are desirable but costly. See Figure 17.18.

Discouraging Activities Taxes can also be used to discourage certain activities. Excise taxes that are supposed to discourage the use of such items as cigarettes and alcohol are sometimes known as sin taxes. Customs duties are supposed to reduce sales of imported goods. Other taxes are used as penalties for certain actions. For example, a person withdrawing money from an Individual Retirement Account (IRA) before age 59½ must pay 10 percent of it as a federal tax penalty.

Controlling Economic Activity
Taxes also can be used to control the nature and growth of economic activity. Government does this by adjusting tax rates and the distribution of taxes—who pays which taxes. Government officials, however, must keep in mind that individuals and businesses may react to these changes. For example, raising taxes for a state or city can actually decrease revenues if businesses and homeowners move away to escape high taxes. A city can also find itself short of funds if it grants too many tax reductions to try to attract business.

Figure 17.18 ▲
Tax Deductions
Many states encourage homeowners to insulate their homes by allowing the cost to be deducted from their income before computing their state income taxes.

SECTION 4 REVIEW

Understanding Vocabulary
Define benefits-received principle, ability-to-pay principle, progressive tax, regressive tax, proportional tax.

Reviewing Objectives
1. Gasoline taxes and property taxes are examples of what principles of taxation?
2. What are the three forms of taxation, according to their effect on taxpayers?
3. How does government use taxes to encourage or discourage certain activities?

News Clip

Readings in Economics

THE NEW YORK TIMES   OCTOBER 4, 1997

FOLKS SAY NO TO CABLE COMPANIES

by Barnaby J. Feder

In a country where free-enterprise advocates have routed their critics, few people would expect local *governments* to plunge into competition with the private sector in the fast-evolving information industries. Yet that is what is happening in a growing number of communities across the United States.

From old mill towns like Holyoke, Mass., to port cities like Tacoma, Wash., to suburbs like Newman, Ga., south of Atlanta, voters and local officials are telling their municipal utilities to go ahead and invade private-business turf, starting with the cable-television industry....

Cable companies have responded to the consumer revolt by cutting rates and improving local service. In Harlan [Iowa], a quiet town of 5,000 surrounded by cornfields, that makes for some lively competition. Harlan spent $3.8 million to build a fiber-optic and cable network that passes every home and business. It has signed up more than 1,000 cable customers in its first year, despite TCI's [the cable company] opposition....

Indeed, TCI chose Harlan as one of the first 30 Iowa towns to get digital service that will provide a clearer picture and raise the number of channels from 35 to 77. More dramatically, it cut the price for its extended basic service in Harlan by nearly 40 percent this summer. And it also rolled out marketing offers like three free months for returning subscribers.

"We had three TCI salesmen come to our door, each one adding another month of free service," said Cleo Anderson, who switched back to TCI in August after calculating he would save $100 this year. "But I told them I'm going back to the town if they raise their rates a dollar. I won't send a check out of town to save a few cents."

COMPARE CABLE LINEUPS

The **Harlan Municipal Utilities** has the cable lineup to please every Harlanite with 53 channels available (46 expanded & 11 premium). Look over our lineup against the competition and you'll choose Harlan's only locally owned cable system.

Expanded TV Lineup

HMU	TCI
46 channels	30 channels

• THINK ABOUT IT •

1. **How have cable companies responded to the consumer revolt?**

2. **What did TCI do in Harlan to counter the municipal cable company's offers?**

ECONOMICS IN ACTION

How Government Spends, Collects, and Owes

Setting up the Video

With your classmates, view "How Government Spends, Collects, and Owes" on the videodisc *Economics in Action.* The video focuses on the federal budget deficit. It describes the deficit and explains that the federal government covers the deficit by selling bonds. The video closes by showing how a healthy economy helps reduce the deficit.

**Chapter 23
Disc 2, Side 1**

View the video by scanning the bar code or by entering the chapter number on your keypad and pressing Search. *(Also available in VHS format.)*

Hands-On Activity

Study the graph of the National Debt on page 425, Figure 17.14. Note that the deficit has been growing at a slower rate during the late 1990s than it did at the beginning of the decade. Locate the latest *Statistical Abstract of the United States* or the *Economic Report of the President* or use the Internet to update the deficit figures. Draw your own graph with the updated figures and share it with the rest of the class.

SURFING THE "NET"

Tax Reform

In this chapter you learned about tax revision laws that have gone into effect since 1980. In 1981 the government reduced individual and corporate tax rates. The 1986 tax reform law closed some loopholes opened in 1981 and made the individual tax code more proportional. The Omnibus Budget Reconciliation of 1993 added marginal tax brackets to the individual tax code. You can learn more about tax reform on the Internet.

Getting There

1. Use a search engine. Type in the words *tax reform.*

2. After typing in *tax reform,* enter words like the following to focus your search: *individual tax code, capital gains, inheritance tax,* and *sales tax.*
3. The search engine will provide you with a number of links to follow. Links are "pointers" to different sites on the Internet and often appear as blue, underlined words.

What to Do When You Are There

Click on the links to navigate through the pages of information. Gather your findings. Using the findings, create a brochure describing recent tax reforms. Include information from your research, sources for further readings, and graphics to illustrate the brochure.

Identifying Key Terms

Write the letter of the definition in Column B below that correctly defines each term in Column A.

Column A
1. benefits-received principle (p. 428)
2. public goods (p. 416)
3. ability-to-pay principle (p. 428)
4. income redistribution (p. 417)
5. national debt (p. 425)

Column B
a. the taking of money from some to give to others
b. system by which those with higher incomes pay higher taxes
c. payment for a particular government service by those who use the services
d. goods and services whose use by one person does not reduce use by another
e. amount of money the government owes

Use terms from the following list to fill in the blanks in the paragraph below.

Medicare (p. 415)
Supplemental Security Income (p. 417)
workers' compensation (p. 417)
Social Security (p. 417)
Medicaid (p. 417)
welfare (p. 418)

Major income redistribution programs are in place in the United States. Social insurance programs pay benefits to people in the form of __(6)__, __(7)__, and __(8)__. Many public assistance programs are often called __(9)__. They include Temporary Assistance to Needy Families as well as __(10)__ and __(11)__.

Recalling Facts and Ideas

Section 1
1. In what ways has the government grown since the Great Depression?
2. What percent of GDP is accounted for by total government purchases of goods and services?

Section 2
3. What are the main functions of government?
4. Give some examples of public goods (but do not confuse them with all government-provided goods).
5. If the government designates a particular good or service as a merit good, what does the government normally do?

Section 3
6. What are the main steps in the federal government budget-making process?
7. How frequently has the federal government used deficit financing since World War II?
8. What causes the nation's public debt?

Section 4
9. What are the principal taxes that exist in the United States today?
10. If all income were taxed at exactly the same rate, what type of tax would be in existence?
11. Besides raising revenue, what other uses does government have for taxes?

Critical Thinking

Section 1
Synthesizing Information Look at **Figure 17.3** on page 414. When did federal government purchases drop below state and local purchases?

Section 2

Making Comparisons What is the difference between Medicare and Medicaid?

Section 3

Determining Cause and Effect Why is it impossible for the government to spend more than it receives without increasing the national debt?

Section 4

Drawing Conclusions What is the process by which taxes can direct economic activity?

Applying Economic Concepts

Theories of Taxation You learned about two theories of taxation, one of which was the benefits-received theory. Assume that you want to use this theory to justify a progressive income tax system. Write a list of the reasons explaining why, as a person's income goes up, that person receives more benefits from the government and therefore should be taxed progressively.

Chapter Projects

1. **Individual Project** A number of states have laws that require a balanced state budget. Check your state constitution to see if your state has such a requirement. Research and write a brief report explaining why and when the amendment was passed, and whether it makes the budget process more difficult.

2. **Cooperative Learning Project** Work in groups representing each of at least three regions of the United States. Each member of each group should pick one or more states to research. The information needed will be:

   - Highest tax rate applied to personal income
   - Highest tax rate applied to corporate income
   - Sales tax rate

   Each group should determine which states have the highest tax rate.

Reviewing Skills

Using E-Mail

Using your communications software, type a message asking 10 registered voters for their opinions of the federal budget deficit. Then ask the recipients for suggestions on decreasing the deficit. Be certain that your message includes the following questions:

1. How serious is the federal deficit for the future of the United States?
2. Why do you think that the government constantly runs deficits?
3. What measures should the federal government take to reduce the deficit as quickly as possible?
4. If we do not eliminate the deficit, what consequences do you foresee, particularly for the generation currently attending high school?
5. What sacrifices would you be willing to make to help reduce the deficit? Would you be willing to pay sharply higher taxes?

Share your responses with the class.

Technology Activity
Developing a Multimedia Presentation

Refer to the list of your daily activities and the role of government in your life that you kept in Your Economics Journal on page 411. Then develop a video tracing your daily routine and examining each part of your life where the government is involved. For example, if you take a bus to school, videotape the bus and explain that this is an example of property taxes being used to fund school transportation. Continue filming throughout the day as you come in contact with government services. Show your completed video to the class.

CHAPTER 18
CONTROLLING UNEMPLOYMENT AND INFLATION

How might this project benefit the economy?

Who will benefit from this project?

If these people were not working on this project, what might they be doing?

Who pays for federally funded projects?

How does federal spending affect employment?

Your Economics Journal

Keep track of the number of times that you read about or hear about the topics of unemployment and inflation. Write down the source from which you heard or read this information. After each entry, indicate whether the economic news was good.

19 TRADING WITH OTHER NATIONS

How many Americans will travel abroad this year?

What happens to the dollars they spend outside the United States?

How much will they spend in other countries?

What percent of goods in American stores are foreign-made?

Do any government restrictions affect what Americans can buy from abroad?

Are there any restrictions on who may buy and sell real estate in the United States?

Why are these properties being sold?

Who determines the prices for each property?

Who owns these houses?

Who has put these houses up for sale?

Who is permitted to buy these houses?

Your Economics Journal

Keep track of the products and services you buy during the week. For each, try to find out whether the price was determined by supply and demand or by an agency of government. For example, cable TV rates are regulated by the federal government.

Point

Issue: Does Free Trade Help or Hurt Americans?

Although most economists favor free trade, some people believe that free trade steals American jobs and helps other countries at the expense of the United States. In particular, many people feel that we import too much from Japan, while Japan restricts American imports. They feel that only through protectionism (more tariffs and quotas) or managed trade (asking that a minimum percentage of Japans's industrial needs will be purchased from American suppliers) can the United States lower its trade deficit and Japanese trade surplus. Those in favor of free trade feel just as firmly that more protectionism or managed trade will hurt the United States as much as any other country.

PRO

Marc Levinson writes in *Newsweek* that, even though some jobs disappear as a result of free trade, this is simply a result of economic change. More new jobs will be created to replace the old ones, and imports from free trade lead to greater efficiency and actually keep down the inflation rate. He says industries sheltered from foreign competition have the greatest price rises.

Economist Alan Binder agrees that protectionism only leads to "job swapping" — protecting jobs in some industries while destroying jobs in others. He argues that the cost of saving jobs is extremely high and that it is doubtful that any jobs are actually saved in the long run. Finally, Martin B. Zuckerman writes in *U.S. News and World Report* that protecting American jobs is actually putting the United States last, not first:

America-first protectionists never work through to the logical end of their policies; if they did, America would come last. Yes, some jobs may be saved by keeping out a cheaper foreign product. But it does not end there. Take steel. Some 17,000 jobs have been saved through restrictions on imports. But stop cheering. According to the Center for the Study of American Business, the more expensive domestic steel has cost an extra $150,000 for every single job saved. That higher cost has been paid by steel users not simply in cash but also in work lost. In fact, 54,200 jobs were lost in other industries to save the 17,000 in steel. Another example is textiles and apparel. Tariffs are adding about $20 billion annually to consumer bills, leaving less to spend on the output of other workers.

Counterpoint

CON A poll by *Newsweek* magazine showed that nearly 4 out of 5 respondents felt that imports are at least partly to blame for slow economic growth. Business executives, farmers, and labor unions want the United States to enact more import restrictions. They believe imports and foreign competition have wiped out American jobs in some sectors of the economy.

A survey by the *Los Angeles Times* found that 70 percent of respondents would support protectionist measures against Japan, and 41 percent selected "tightening restrictions on trade with Japan" as the best way to stimulate the U.S. economy. In presenting the results of this poll, staff writer Karl Schoenberger presents a typical view of those against free trade:

Another respondent . . . said it's not the fault of the Japanese that they have prospered while America's economy declined. The blame, he said, should be placed on the U.S. Government, which "is responsible for the trade agreements we make with foreign governments and should make sure we get treated fairly.

"I don't believe we have a fair deal in our trade with Japan, because we're open to their products and they're closed to ours." . . . "I believe in an eye for an eye, and it's not Japan's fault that the American government doesn't protect our interests."

Katherine Newman writes in *Newsweek* about the future and places the blame on United States trade policies:

The international economy is less an opportunity than a threat. It's not just that imports have put their jobs at risk. Their unhappiness is broader . . . and the blame is pinned squarely on what is perceived to be America's diminished position in the world economy.

. . . Here, voices rise in criticism of our international competitors, and our politicians. . . . International competition means endless worries about future living standards.

Exploring the Issue

Reviewing Facts

❶ Why does it seem that economists and non-economists disagree over the free trade issue?

Critical Thinking

Analyzing Information

❷ If free trade means that some jobs are lost, while others are created, why should anyone be unhappy?

CHAPTER

21 ECONOMIC GROWTH IN DEVELOPING NATIONS

What will be the benefits of building this dam in Brazil?

How much does a project like this cost?

Who is paying for this construction project?

Should the United States increase foreign aid for projects like this?

Who is employed on this project?

Your Economics Journal

Keep track of all the foreign countries that you read about or hear mentioned on the radio or on TV. Collect clippings and make a list of these countries. After the name of each country, indicate whether you think it is a developing country.

SECTION 1 Characteristics of Developing Nations

SECTION 1 FOCUS

Terms to Know developed nations, developing nations, subsistence agriculture, infant mortality

Objectives *After reading this section, you should be able to:*

1. Indicate about how many developed and developing nations exist in the world.
2. List five characteristics of developing nations.
3. List the Four Tigers.

How the Other Three-Fourths of the World Lives

Many Americans may not realize it, but even the poorest families in the United States usually have an income far above the average income in much of the rest of the world. About one-half of the world's population lives at or close to subsistence, with just enough to survive.

Developed and Developing Nations

Of the more than 180 nations in the world, only about 35 are considered **developed nations**. See Figure 21.1. These nations include the United States, Canada, most European countries, plus Japan, Australia, and New Zealand.

The remaining parts of the world's population live in **developing nations.** These are nations with less industrial development and a relatively low standard of living. Within this general definition, however, nations differ in many ways. Figure 21.2 compares two developing nations, Madagascar and Mexico. The average income per person in Mexico is only one-fifth that of the United States. In contrast, Mexico is much more developed and prosperous than almost all other developing na-

Figure 21.1
Life in Developed Nations
Many people in developed nations with industrial economies live comfortably. These nations with about 25 percent of the world's population account for almost 80 percent of world GDP. ▼

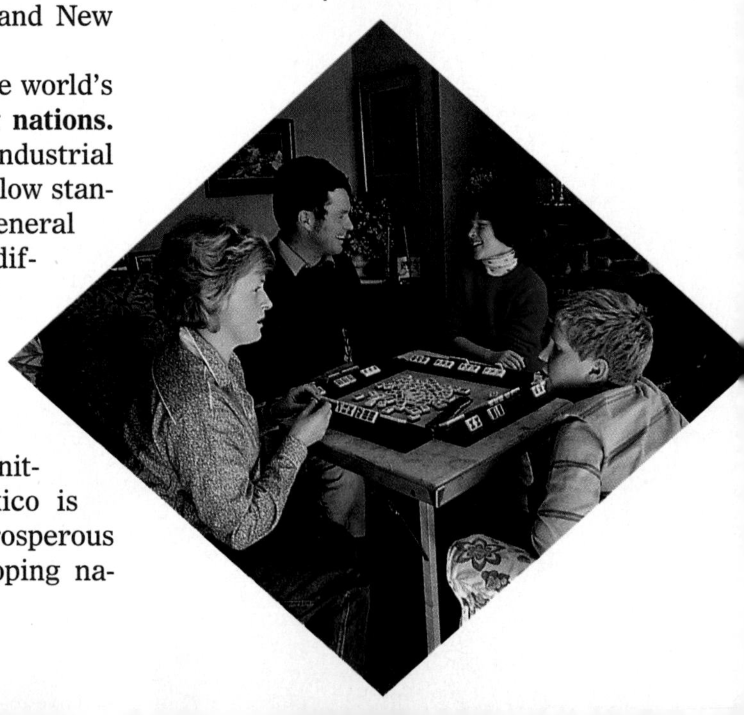

tions. In Madagascar, average per capita income is very much less than average per capita income in Mexico.

Besides differences in the standard of living among developing nations, great differences often exist within a nation. For example, about 26 percent of India's population lives and works in urban areas, many of which are like those in developed nations. In rural India, however, some of the population may not have enough to eat. Many families live three to a room, often in mud houses. Only a fraction of these homes have running water and electricity.

Economic Characteristics

Economists often use per-person GDP as a rough measure of a nation's prosperity. While source estimates of world economic data vary, the United States and other developed nations have per capita GDP that ranges between $12,000 per year and about $27,000 per year.

Low GDP Per capita GDP in developing nations, in contrast, is considerably less, and in the world's poorest nations it is extremely low. Look at Figure 21.3 (page 506), which shows per capita GDP for a number of developing countries and for a number of developed countries. While developing nations may have many natural and human resources, they lack the equipment, financing, and knowledge necessary to put those resources to use.

An Agricultural Economy Agriculture is central to developing nations' economies. Much of the population exists through **subsistence agriculture.**

Figure 21.2 ▶
Two Developing Nations
Among developing nations there is a wide variance in standards of living. How does the per capita GDP of Madagascar compare to that of Mexico?

▼

Two Developing Nations*	Madagascar	Mexico
Percent employed in agriculture	90	25
Average per capita GDP	$230	$7,050
Telephones per 100 population	0.4	14.1
Life expectancy at birth	53.5 years	72.6 years
*Figures representative of period 1991–1995.		

Sources: *Statistical Abstract of The United States,* 1997: *World Tables,* 1997

505

Review

Identifying Key Terms

Write the letter of the definition in Column B below that correctly defines each term in Column A.

Column A
1. foreign aid (p. 512)
2. subsistence agriculture (p. 505)
3. developing nations (p. 504)
4. technical assistance (p. 513)

Column B
a. raising food sufficient for one's own or one's family's needs only
b. nonindustrialized countries
c. money, goods, and services given by one nation to another nation
d. aid in the form of professional expertise from engineers, doctors, teachers, and other specialists

Write a paragraph on different types of development problems, using the following words.

developed nations (p. 504)
bureaucracies (p. 517)
nationalization (p. 519)
property rights (p. 523)
vicious cycle of poverty (p. 524)

Recalling Facts and Ideas

Section 1
1. The per capita income in countries such as the United States, Japan, and Germany is approximately how many thousands of dollars?
2. What characteristics identify most developing nations?
3. What area of the world has seen rapid economic growth in recent years?

Section 2
4. List two affiliates of the World Bank.
5. What is the difference between military assistance and technical assistance?
6. In what stage of development are most developing nations?
7. What are some reasons for giving foreign aid?

Section 3
8. How does defense spending expressed as a percentage of GDP compare in many developing countries with the same variable in the United States?
9. How is rapid population growth an obstacle to economic development?
10. How do international trade restrictions hinder economic growth of developing nations?

Section 4
11. What is true about the early history of every developed country in the world today?
12. Why are property rights a factor in economic development?
13. How can a developing nation's government influence foreign investment?

Critical Thinking

Section 1
Making Inferences Some developed countries in the world today, such as the United States, have large natural resource bases. Does this necessarily mean that many natural resources are required in order for a country to have economic growth and development?

Section 2

Making Comparisons What is the difference between the level of development and education that existed in Europe's war-torn economy at the end of World War II and the level of development and education that exists in today's developing nations? How does your answer impact on the potential use of foreign aid in today's developing nations?

Section 3

Drawing Conclusions Why do restrictions on international trade represent an obstacle to economic growth for a developing nation?

Section 4

Determining Cause and Effect What is the relationship between well-defined and government-enforced private property rights and the incentive structure for investment in a nation?

Applying Economic Concepts

Foreign Aid Many republics of the former Soviet Union are extremely poor. Even the largest and one of the richest republics, Russia, has a per capita income that is a small percentage of that in the United States. The developed countries have been giving foreign aid to Russia during the 1990s. Use the information you have obtained in this chapter about the problems facing developing countries and the difficulty of using foreign aid correctly. Make a list of the obstacles that Russia faces in properly putting to good use the foreign aid that it is receiving.

Chapter Projects

1. **Individual Project** Select a developing nation and write a research report about the economic and social conditions of that nation by collecting facts on housing, food production, transportation, medical care, and the role of the government. The most reliable sources are the International Monetary Fund Reports, United Nations reports, and government statistical bulletins.

2. **Cooperative Learning Project** Organize into at least five groups. Each group will study one part of the world, such as: northern Africa, Central Africa, Southeast Asia, Central America, or western Europe.

   The goal of each group is to determine the percentage of the economy devoted to agriculture and the percentage devoted to industry. Each member of each group will obtain the relevant information for one or more countries in his or her chosen region. Compare the information obtained, selecting one person to prepare summary statistics for your group's region.

Reviewing Skills

Using a Spreadsheet

Tracking Stocks Use a spreadsheet to enter the daily high, low, and closing prices of a selected international stock for four weeks. At the end of this period, calculate the average price. Then use the spreadsheet to make line graphs showing the monthly high, low, and closing prices for your stock.

Technology Activity
Using E-Mail

Refer to the list of countries that you compiled in Your Economics Journal on page 503. Choose one of these countries to investigate further. One way to do so would be to E-mail the embassy of that country in Washington, D.C. To do so, you will first need to use the Internet to locate the embassy's E-mail address. Using your favorite search engine, type the name of the country. Then explore the sites listed until you find the E-mail address. Finally, write an E-mail asking for information on the country's history as well as current statistics on the country's economic development. Share your responses with the class.

How does the state of Japan's economy affect our economy?

How would a person in Tokyo find out a day's closing figures on the New York Stock Exchange?

How have improved methods of worldwide communications impacted economic fluctuations?

Does the United States have many investments in foreign markets?

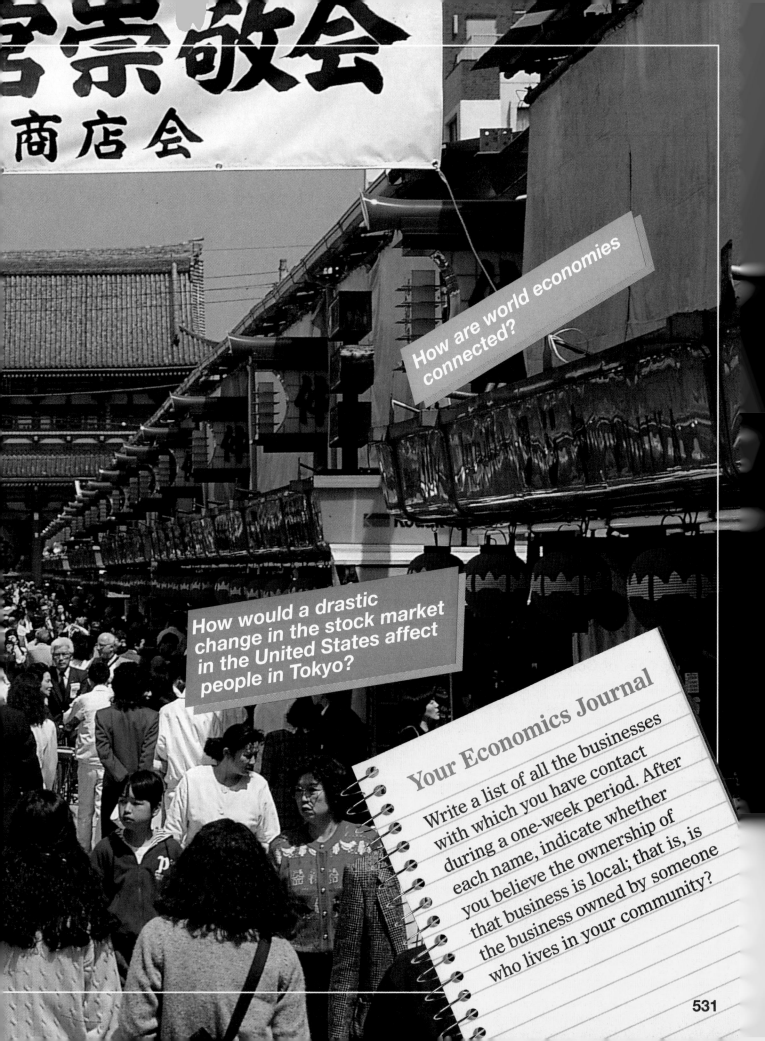

How are world economies connected?

How would a drastic change in the stock market in the United States affect people in Tokyo?

Your Economics Journal

Write a list of all the businesses with which you have contact during a one-week period. After each name, indicate whether you believe the ownership of that business is local; that is, is the business owned by someone who lives in your community?

SECTION 1 FOCUS

Terms to Know global integration, telecommunications

Objectives *After reading this section, you should be able to:*

❶ Explain how **improved telecommunications** have caused increased global integration.

❷ Name three kinds of financial instruments now traded in **global markets**.

❸ Identify a major **problem with the worldwide stock market**.

Global Trade Affects All of Us

In the United States it would not be unusual to ride on a bus that was made in Germany or in a Japanese-made car. Suppose you eat lunch at a local restaurant. You may not know it, but a Canadian owns the restaurant. Some of the restaurant's food has been imported from Mexico, France, and Spain. While reading the newspaper at lunch, you read about interest rates falling because political upheavals in other countries have caused businesses there to invest their money capital in politically stable America.

We now live not just as Americans, but as part of the global economy. **Global integration** has increased dramatically over the past several decades. Many reasons explain this increase. One has to do with improved **telecommunications,** or long-distance electronic communications.

Improved Telecommunications

The first transatlantic telegraph cable was completed in 1866. Before then it took two weeks to find out the price of the dollar in London. The telegraph cable reduced that time to two minutes. With the invention of the semiconductor—the computer chip—

Figure 22.1 Decreasing Costs

The price per million units of computing power (expressed in millions of instructions per second) from 1978 to 1997 fell dramatically. ▼

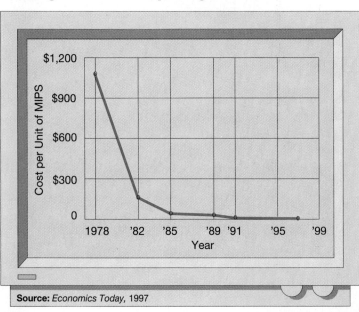

Falling Cost of Computing Power

Source: Economics Today, 1997

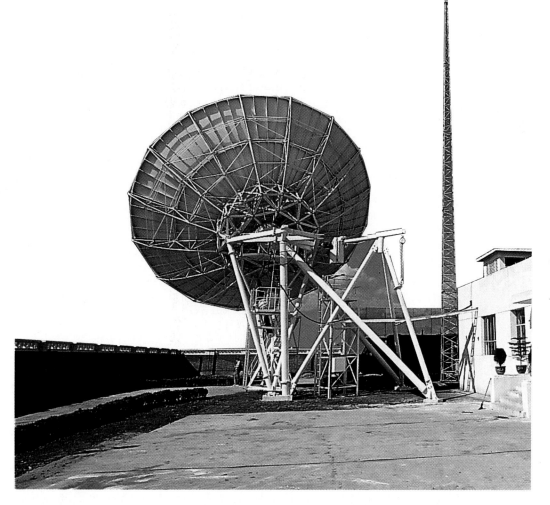

**Figure 22.2
Satellite
Communications**
Even in the People's
Republic of China—
where the government
has much control—
satellite dishes
(although often illegal)
are a growth industry.
More Chinese are see-
ing how the rest of the
world looks, thinks, and
operates.

◀

telecommunications really took off. Look at how much the price of computing power has fallen just in the last few years in Figure 22.1.

Several other inventions and factors have influenced the rapid improvement in worldwide telecommunications. Communications satellites circle the earth day and night. Radio and television waves, beamed up to them, are reflected down to other parts of the earth. On the earth itself, fiber-optic cables are being placed throughout much of North America and already exist in parts of Europe. The rapid expansion of the Internet has also been an important aspect of the worldwide communications system.

Consider some of the ways cheap and readily available satellite television has transformed the information received in the Eastern Hemisphere.

Before the 1990s virtually all of the television (and radio) available in the Eastern Hemisphere was state-run and state-controlled. Viewers saw few programs and advertisements from other parts of the world. Today, people in Asia receive sports, music, soap operas, news, and advertisements free of government control via satellite. See Figure 22.2.

How does this increase in communications affect the rest of the world, particularly Asia? Viewers in other parts of the world are changing their habits. In India they go so far as to buy copies of outfits worn by popular music television personalities. In addition, because most popular programs are transmitted in English throughout the world, more of the world's people want to learn English as a second language.

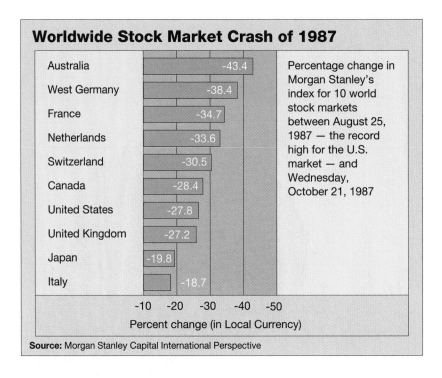

Figure 22.3
Global Crash
Examine the graph to see how the stock market crash of 1987 affected certain nations of the world. Which nation shown experienced the greatest change as a result of the 1987 stock market crash? Which nation shown was least affected? ▶

Worldwide Stock Market Crash of 1987

Nation	Percent change
Australia	-43.4
West Germany	-38.4
France	-34.7
Netherlands	-33.6
Switzerland	-30.5
Canada	-28.4
United States	-27.8
United Kingdom	-27.2
Japan	-19.8
Italy	-18.7

Percent change (in Local Currency)

Percentage change in Morgan Stanley's index for 10 world stock markets between August 25, 1987 — the record high for the U.S. market — and Wednesday, October 21, 1987

Source: Morgan Stanley Capital International Perspective

The Globalization of Financial Markets

Because of the speed and power of computers and the affordability of telecommunications, the world has become one financial market. This globalization started in the 1960s and 1970s, when United States banks developed worldwide branch networks for loans and foreign exchange trading. Today money and financial capital markets are truly global, and many instruments are traded on them.

Markets for United States government securities (bonds the United States government sells), foreign exchange, and shares of stocks are now trading continuously, in vast quantities, around the world. For example, trading in United States government securities is the world's fastest growing 24-hour market. Foreign exchange—the buying and selling of foreign currencies—became a 24-hour worldwide market in the 1970s. Worldwide markets exist in commodities such as grains, gold and silver, and stocks. The worldwide stock market, started in about the mid-1970s, however, has some problems.

Problems With the Worldwide Stock Market

When each country's stock market is linked worldwide, problems can arise. One such problem occurred during the biggest one-day stock market crash that the United States has ever faced. Historians emphasize the Great Depression that started when the stock market crashed on October 28, 1929. Another huge stock market crash occurred on October 19, 1987, almost 60 years later. The Dow Jones Industrial Average fell 508 points, the largest one-day loss in United States history. In less than seven hours, more than $500 billion of corporate value disappeared. The stock markets in Sydney, London, and Hong Kong soon followed. Two years later the United States stock market finally regained its previous level, but several other world markets took even longer to recover.

The important lesson of the crash of 1987 was that a globalized financial market, through its electronic information system, now causes everybody everywhere to feel the effects of a financial panic. In **Figure 22.3** you see

that many other countries experienced even more severe drops in their stock market index than the United States did in the crash of 1987.

Many managers of investment companies looked worldwide to sell their shares on October 19, 1987. They did not think they could sell their shares in the United States at very attractive prices because of the declining stock market. Investment managers in other countries did the same thing. The United States crash led to stock sales in foreign markets, which caused their stock markets to crash, too. Foreigners sold in the United States market in response. This vicious cycle continued for several days. Figure 22.4 gives some idea of the worldwide impact.

Figure 22.4 ▲
Impact of the '87 Crash
The collapse of the stock market affects most of the world's people in one way or another. It is, therefore, major news. The newspapers shown here devoted their front pages to the story and news magazines ran feature stories in their next issues.

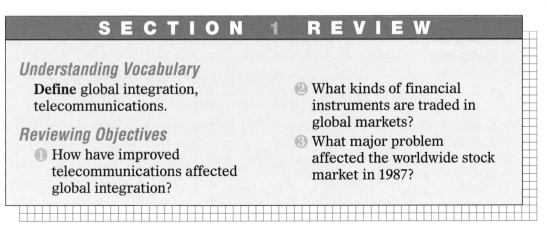

SECTION 1 REVIEW

Understanding Vocabulary
Define global integration, telecommunications.

Reviewing Objectives
❶ How have improved telecommunications affected global integration?

❷ What kinds of financial instruments are traded in global markets?

❸ What major problem affected the worldwide stock market in 1987?

Critical Thinking Skills

Making Inferences From Statistics

To infer means to evaluate information and arrive at a conclusion. For example, a person may infer that an item is not selling well because prices for that item are declining. To imply is to express or to suggest something indirectly. Generally, a speaker or writer implies, and a reader infers. Making inferences is an important study skill and a vital economics skill.

Analyzing Statistics

Often a graph or a table contains more information than a reader may see at first glance. For example, Figure A shows changes in United States military aid by region between 1990 and 1993. To make inferences from this, follow these steps:

❶ Read the labels on the table to understand exactly what is being reported.

❷ Compare the statistical information to determine trends or changes.

❸ Ask yourself why the changes may have occurred.

❹ Apply related information that you may already know to make inferences from the table.

For example, based on decreased military aid to Latin America, you might infer that the region had fewer conflicts in 1993 than it did in 1990.

Figure A

United States Military Aid by Region, 1990 and 1993 (in millions of dollars)

Region	1990	1993
Europe	$ 939	$863
Near East and South Asia	3,236	3,158
Africa	39	24
Latin America	234	74

Figure B

Direct Foreign Investment (millions of dollars)

Region	1990	1993
New England	$ 19,402	$ 25,212
Middle Atlantic	71,136	93,388
West South Central	82,951	95,663
Mountain	33,077	36,921
Pacific	120,164	142,151

Practicing the Skill

Study the statistics in Figure B about direct foreign investment in various regions of the country. From the data, what can you infer about the relationship between geography and foreign investment? Why does this relationship exist?

Direct Foreign Investment—Should We Be Worried?

SECTION 2 FOCUS

Terms to Know direct foreign investment (DFI)

Objectives *After reading this section, you should be able to:*

1. Explain the history of foreign investment in the United States.
2. Indicate how important Japanese foreign investment is in the United States.
3. Describe concerns that nations may have about direct foreign investment.

Who Owns Whom?

Nothing seems more American than Burger King or the Pillsbury Dough Boy, right? Not quite, for those companies are now owned by the British. In addition, the Japanese own about 30 percent of the office space in downtown Los Angeles. An Indonesian firm owns Chicken of the Sea Tuna, and a German company owns A&P Supermarkets. A group from East Asia owns the Algonquin Hotel in New York— a famous gathering place of American writers and artists. Mitsubishi, a Japanese company, at one time owned half of Rockefeller Center in the middle of Manhattan. Foreign investment in the United States, however, is not new. See Figure 22.5.

Figure 22.5 Foreign Investment
Foreign investment in the United States is not new. In the late 1800s, for example, the British helped finance the expansion of the railroads. ▼

Foreign Investment, Then and Now

Direct foreign investment (DFI) in the United States has increased to the point where some Americans want to restrict it. Direct foreign investment is evidence of the global integration of the American economy. In any one year, foreigners purchase billions of dollars of American real estate and businesses. Any time political upheaval strikes any other part of the world, foreign investment in the United

Figure 22.6 Foreign Investment in the United States

Foreigners own much of downtown Los Angeles as well as many formerly American-owned companies. S.A.Q. of Switzerland now owns the Carnation Company. The Japanese company Bridgestone owns Firestone Tire and Rubber. Carnation and Firestone were both formerly American owned.

▶

States increases because we remain a politically stable country.

Foreigners Have Always Invested in the United States The United States has a long history of foreign investment. For example, Great Britain was the biggest foreign investor in American railroads in the late 1800s and early 1900s. At the beginning of World War I, the United States owed more money to foreign lenders than any other country in the world.

Foreign Control of American Companies Many people argue against foreign ownership of American companies because they are worried about foreign control. Is foreign control important? See Figure 22.6. Presumably, foreign investors purchase American assets in order to maximize profits. Foreigners' interest in running a corporation would seem to be identical to the interest of any domestic investor who owned the same corporation. The profit-making behavior of a corporation presumably does not depend on the nationality of that corporation. If the British took over a hotel on Miami

Beach, would the service necessarily be any different in the long run? Economists do not think so.

What about the foreign investors' influence over the United States government? Foreigners own about 27 percent of all United States government securities that now exist. Can they use this to control United States foreign policy? Probably not. Foreigners purchase United States government securities when they think the rate of return is higher than they can get elsewhere. Remember that whenever foreigners buy United States government securities or private corporate securities, they free up United States financial capital for other productive uses.

It is actually the United States government that has more control over foreigners. Because they own about 27 percent of the United States public debt, as you can see in Figure 22.7, foreign investors are subject to United States government policy. For example, the federal government could, through its Federal Reserve System, create tremendous inflation. In so doing, it would wipe out the real value of the United States government debt that foreigners own.

Finally, in a larger sense, because foreign corporations do invest in the United States, they may indirectly influence our government. Our government cannot make the business climate in America too difficult for these corporations or they will take their investments elsewhere.

Japanese Investment

In recent years the Japanese have invested heavily in the United States, as Figure 22.8 (page 540) shows. Some social, political, and economic commentators have raised the question of whether they are "buying up America." A few years ago an American historian, Theodore White, wrote, "The Japanese are on the move again in one of history's most brilliant commercial offenses as they go about dismantling American industry." Mr. White suggested that the Japanese economic invasion of the United States during the 1980s was equivalent to its military attack on Pearl Harbor in 1941. Is this true?

Europe's Share of the United States Today, western European investors own about 50 percent of all foreign-owned assets in the United States.

Japan's share of total foreign holdings in the United States is less than 15 percent. Japan owns a little more than 1 percent of an estimated $16 trillion in American capital. Compared to western European ownership of American assets, Japan's does not look so imposing.

Why does Japanese investment in the United States seem like such a threat today? The answer probably lies with the more visible direct investments that Japan has made. Conspicuous Japanese investment in the United States also reminds Americans of the special relationship that exists between Japan and the United States: Japan relies almost exclusively on the United States for its national defense. In effect, the American taxpayer provides Japan's national defense system. This special relationship has allowed Japan to concentrate on economic growth while the United States has presumably borne a disproportionate share of defense costs.

Direct Foreign Investment

Despite the concern some have about foreigners owning the United States, the total share of foreign ownership of American industries is about 6 percent.

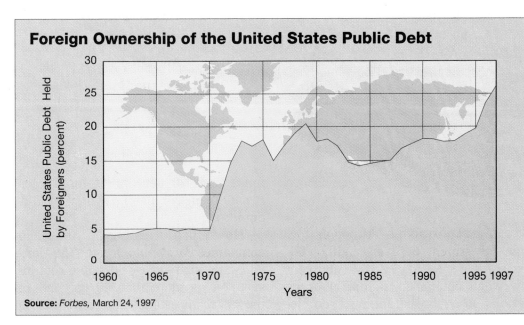

Foreign Ownership of the United States Public Debt

United States Public Debt Held by Foreigners (percent)

Years

Source: *Forbes*, March 24, 1997

Figure 22.7 Foreign Ownership

Examine this graph carefully to see how foreign ownership of the United States public debt has changed. When did foreigners own their largest percentage? What has been the most recent trend? How do you explain this?

Figure 22.8 ▶
Direct Investment Positions, United States and Japan
Clearly, Japan has invested much more heavily in the United States than this country has in Japan. When the Japanese purchased 51 percent of an American landmark—Rockefeller Center in New York City —it generated a great deal of publicity, although it was sold back to Americans in 1996. ▼

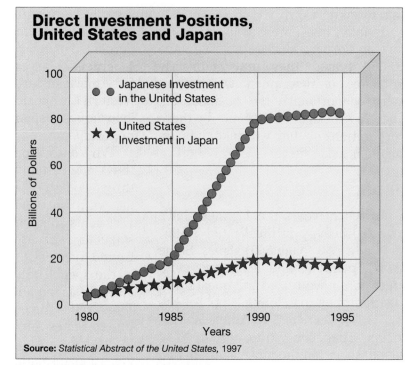

Direct Investment Positions, United States and Japan

- ● ● Japanese Investment in the United States
- ★ ★ United States Investment in Japan

Billions of Dollars (y-axis: 0, 20, 40, 60, 80, 100)
Years (x-axis: 1980, 1985, 1990, 1995)

Source: *Statistical Abstract of the United States, 1997*

The Final Analysis Although foreign investment here is readily visible, as Figure 22.9 shows, it is relatively low when compared to that of other nations. In Great Britain, for example, more than 20 percent of total sales comes from companies owned by foreigners.

How much investing do American companies carry out abroad? The United States' share of worldwide direct investment is more than 40 percent. In the 1970s, for example, there were cries

in Europe, especially France, that the United States was going to dominate its society. Indeed, throughout the world many people fear that United States culture has taken over everybody else's culture. Some people have called this *economic imperialism.*

Here is another way to view investment: If a Texas company purchases a business in Omaha, Nebraska, not many people worry. Nebraska will not likely try to pass legislation to prevent Texans—or other Americans, for that matter—from owning any kinds of businesses there. No one doubts that the reason the Texas firm purchased the Nebraska firm was to make a profit.

Most purchasers of goods and services anywhere in the world have little knowledge about who ultimately owns the company that provided the good or service—and they do not really care.

Some even argue that we should *encourage* direct investment and debt purchases by foreigners. Why? Foreigners then would have an increased incentive for the American economy to remain strong, for real estate prices *not* to collapse, for the legal structure to stay on a stable course, and for United States businesses to compete effectively by providing goods and services that consumers want.

Figure 22.9 ▲
Visible Foreign Investment
Unlike Burger King or Firestone or some other companies that are not obviously owned by foreigners, there are some companies that are clearly visible as being foreign-owned. Mazda and Toyota are only two of these.

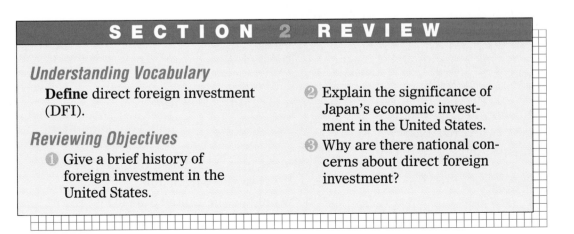

SECTION 2 REVIEW

Understanding Vocabulary
Define direct foreign investment (DFI).

Reviewing Objectives
1. Give a brief history of foreign investment in the United States.

2. Explain the significance of Japan's economic investment in the United States.

3. Why are there national concerns about direct foreign investment?

Laura Tyson on the Global Economy

Profile

- 1948–
- Ph.D. from Massachusetts Institute of Technology
- Chairperson of President Clinton's Council of Economic Advisers, 1993–1995
- professor at the University of California at Berkeley
- advocate of economic and trade policies to spur United States competitiveness abroad

In this article from *Fortune* magazine, Laura Tyson talks about free trade in the real world. She believes free trade may not be a real choice for policy-makers in a world where protectionist policies create unfair advantages for foreign competitors.

Trade isn't always free. And the choice of policy-makers is often not between free trade and protectionism. It is somewhere in the middle, between one kind of manipulated trade and another.

In an ideal world, our competitive industries would not be meeting subsidized or protected industries abroad. But that is not the world we face.... Do we want to be in the business of influencing market outcomes? It's a very hard call, and it is not one that I think any of us take lightly. We would much rather start with an effort to try to reduce the subsidy or protectionist activity abroad.

...There is no social or global justification for certain types of subsidies. Production subsidies... are simply market grabbing. But research and development subsidies may have the defense of at least possibly creating innovations.

Laura Tyson describes how the United States can improve its trade balance with Japan. She hints that the United States might limit imports through "quantitative market-share indicators."

The trade imbalance between the U.S. and Japan is primarily a macroeconomic phenomenon, the result of big U.S. budget deficits and big Japanese surpluses. The U.S. is now on an appropriate course, and it's time for the Japanese to get on one as well, by stimulating their economy.

When you have negotiated and been unable to address the problem of structural barriers, and there is evidence that competitive opportunities in an industry are not being accorded to competitive producers, then moving to a set of quantitative market-share indicators for foreign imports may be defensible. This should be a last step.

Checking for Understanding

❶ What is the choice that policy-makers often face?

❷ What measures would be the United States' first effort to make trade fair?

❸ What would be the United States' last resort?

3 Multinationals and Economic Competition

SECTION 3 FOCUS

Terms to Know multinationals, allegiances, foreign affiliates, alliances, tolerance

Objectives *After reading this section, you should be able to:*

1. Indicate the number of multinationals in the world today.
2. Identify important cross-border investments.
3. Describe the advantages of corporate alliances.
4. Explain why South Korea has lost foreign investment dollars.
5. Discuss how recent immigration patterns have increased the need for tolerance in the United States.

Figure 22.10 Multinationals
A multinational firm is simply one that does business in many countries and has offices and factories in many countries around the world. In a sense, a multinational firm has many national **allegiances,** or loyalties, not necessarily just to the country in which it has its main or principal office. ▼

Cross-Border Investing by Multinationals

For the last few years, international investing has grown faster than world output and faster than world trade. Much cross-border investing is undertaken by **multinationals.** See Figure 22.10. In the past, critics argued that because these firms are so large, they may dominate the world economy. Such firms were seen as ruthless companies that would exploit the poor and manipulate governments. Few people agree with such sentiments today. Multinationals bring modern technology and management skills to developing countries.

The Size and Number of Multinationals

In the 1970s, many people predicted that a few hundred multinationals would control 80 percent of the world's production by the mid-1980s. By the late 1990s, there were an estimated 37,000 multinationals with about 200,000 **foreign affiliates,** or branches of their firms. The largest 100 multinationals (excluding those in banking and finance) account for more than $3 trillion of worldwide assets. Figure 22.11 (page 544) lists the top 25 American-owned multinationals.

Figure 22.11 The Largest American Multinationals

Largest American Multinationals, 1997, Ranked by Foreign Revenues

Rank	Corporation	Foreign Revenue*	Total Revenue*	Foreign Revenue as % of Total	Foreign Assets*	Total Assets*	Foreign Assets as % of Total
1	Exxon	89,608	116,728	76.8	55,589	95,527	58.2
2	General Motors	51,000	164,069	31.1	58,735	222,142	26.4
3	Mobil	48,533	72,267	67.2	31,330	46,408	67.5
4	Ford Motor	48,104	146,991	32.7	79,106	262,867	30.1
5	IBM	46,552	75,947	61.3	42,007	81,132	51.8
6	Texaco	31,385	59,205	53.0	14,312	31,443	45.5
7	General Electric	23,361	79,179	29.5	82,976	272,402	30.5
8	Chevron	22,220	47,798	46.5	17,420	38,378	45.4
9	Hewlett-Packard	21,379	38,420	55.6	15,191	27,699	54.8
10	Citicorp	19,772	32,605	60.6	161,000	270,000	59.6
11	Philip Morris	19,628	54,553	36.0	20,558	54,871	37.5
12	Procter & Gamble	17,682	35,284	50.1	11,222	27,730	40.5
13	El du Pont de Nemours	16,525	38,349	43.1	15,435	37,987	40.6
14	American Internal Group	14,991	28,205	53.2	56,343	148,431	38.0
15	Motorola	12,600	27,973	45.0	8,604	24,076	35.7
16	Coca-Cola	12,449	18,546	67.1	6,090	16,161	37.7
17	Intel	12,179	20,847	58.4	4,784	23,735	20.2
18	Xerox	12,038	20,621	58.4	14,541	28,120	51.7
19	Dow Chemical	11,264	20,053	56.2	14,047	24,673	56.9
20	Johnson & Johnson	10,721	21,620	49.6	9,147	20,010	45.7
21	United Technologies	10,080	23,512	42.9	6,374	16,745	38.1
22	Digital Equipment	9,436	14,563	64.8	5,178	10,075	51.4
23	PepsiCo	9,197	31,645	29.1	7,802	24,512	31.8
24	Eastman Kodak	8,515	15,968	53.3	5,740	14,438	39.8
25	Compaq Computer	8,428	18,109	46.5	3,306	10,526	31.4

Source: *Forbes,* July 28, 1997   *in millions of dollars

Figure 22.11 ▲
The Largest American Multinationals
Examine the chart above. Notice that the largest four corporations deal in transportation and oil. Why do you think this is the case?

Worldwide Ownership The top 100 multinationals are very important, accounting for probably about 45 percent of all cross-border assets. This means nothing, however, without comparing these assets to the worldwide total. No one knows the value of the world's assets today, but a best guess is about $20 to $25 trillion. If this is true, the top 100 multinationals account for only about 15 percent of the world's productive assets—hardly a dominant share.

It is also true today that the United States and Great Britain no longer dominate multinationals. In 1970, for example, of the 7,000 multinationals identified by the United Nations, the Americans and the British owned more than 50 percent. Today, Americans, Japanese, Germans, and the Swiss own about half of the 37,000 multinationals. Numerous multinationals are based in the industrializing Asian countries such as Taiwan and South Korea.

The Regional Flavor of Cross-Border Investments

While it may be true that many of the biggest multinationals invest everywhere in the world, most do not. Most invest in regions that are closest to home. For example, the European Union (EU) plus Switzerland engage in more foreign direct investment in western Europe itself than anywhere else.

In a world in which borders matter less, the line separating sales at home and those abroad becomes less important. The most appropriate way to look at patterns of direct investment is to include direct domestic sales as a part of regional sales. European firms principally invest in western Europe. American firms principally invest in the United States, Canada, Mexico, and South America. Japanese firms principally invest in Japan, South Korea, Greater China, and Southeast

Asia. Figure 22.12, for example, shows Japanese investment in Tokyo. Some obvious exceptions to this rule of regional investing by multinationals do exist. For historical reasons, the British as part of the EU invest heavily in India, once a colony of Great Britain.

Beyond Multinationals—Alliances

In addition to multinational direct investments in other countries, firms in different countries are forming **alliances.** These may be joint ventures. Indeed, many foreign governments have insisted that multinationals enter their markets through joint ventures with local firms in the hope that locals will capture some of the profits. Companies also make licensing deals. For example, an American jogging shoe company licensed its design to a company in South Korea.

Most alliances have been between firms from industrialized countries. Alliances are even popular within nations like the United States. For example, International Business Machines (IBM) developed its personal computer in alliance with Microsoft (for the software), Intel (for the central processing unit), and Lotus. In the late 1980s, IBM entered into an alliance with Siemens of Germany to work on memory chips. In the 1990s, IBM

Figure 22.12 Japan's Major Investment
Japan, like most countries, invests most heavily in its own nation. Downtown Tokyo shows evidence of how heavily Japanese companies dominate the nation's capital. ▼

Figure 22.13 Investing in South Korea
Many multinationals pulled out of South Korea in the early 1990s. How might this affect other potential foreign investors' decisions? ▶

entered into an alliance with Apple Computers, once its archrival.

Alliances can be seen as each firm's acceptance of its own limitations, whether they be financial, technological, or geographical. Alliances can be used to help a firm leapfrog its competitors or catch up with them. Such a strategy is particularly effective in an industry that has seen rapid changes such as computer memory chips and software.

A Case Study in South Korea

Multinationals, by their very nature, can move money capital from one part of the world to another. One reason they move money capital is if they think they can make a higher long-run average rate of return on their investment elsewhere. When one country starts offering better "deals" to multinational firms, they will take them. When one country makes life difficult for multinationals or foreign investors in general, money capital will flow out of that country.

This capital flow is exactly what has happened to South Korea. See **Figure 22.13**. In the early 1990s, foreign investors withdrew large amounts of money capital from South Korea. As reasons they cited complex govern-

ment regulations and a lack of incentive to remain in the country. In 1992 new foreign investment dropped more than 35 percent from the previous year. The value of the joint ventures South Korea lost in 1992 was more than five times the value of the previous year's losses. In the early 1990s, General Motors Corporation, Goodyear Tire and Rubber Company, and DuPont Company abandoned their plans to build sophisticated production facilities in South Korea.

ALCOA Consider one specific example. The Aluminum Company of America (ALCOA) created a joint venture with South Korea's Samsun Industrial Company. The American company wanted skilled labor to manufacture aircraft parts for export to Asia. The South Korean company wanted technology that it did not yet have. The plan was for ALCOA to take over and retool one of Samsun's aluminum plants. The total investment by both companies was to be about $40 million, but the deal went sour. ALCOA wanted to build defense-related component parts as well as commercial ones. South Korea's military establishment was worried. The government therefore issued guidelines to give other companies a better chance at obtaining defense industry business. ALCOA pulled out.

Other companies have found that it takes years before their request to build factories is approved. Cargill Corporation had to wait four years after its application to build a $21 million soybean processing plant.

Investing in the People's Republic Where are many foreign investors taking their money? Increasingly, many of them are going to the People's Republic of China. See **Figure 22.14**. Much of the money being invested in China is being taken out of South Korea. In a world of mobile financial capital, governments cannot treat foreign businesses poorly and expect them to continue investing.

The Global Village and Tolerance

One of the results of the globalization of our world is increased immigration. America has become a truly multicultural society because of such immigration. In many cities the combined numbers of African Americans, Hispanics, Asians, and other minorities now constitute a majority of the population. In the 1980s, for example, the Asian population in America increased more than 100 percent and the Hispanic population more than 50 percent. Public schools are more diverse than ever. This diversity means that the need for

tolerance and open-mindedness is more important today than it ever has been. **Tolerance** can be defined as a fair, objective, and permissive attitude toward the opinions, practices, religions, races, and nationalities of others that differ from one's own. It also includes an interest in and concern for the ideas, opinions, and practices that are foreign to one's own. For Americans this includes learning one or more foreign languages and maintaining friendships with those of different ethnic/cultural/national/religious backgrounds.

Nothing in our Constitution or in our laws requires us to be open-minded and tolerant. These qualities are part of our heritage. Those who acquire and use them will benefit, as will the nation as a whole.

Figure 22.14 The China Business Boom
China used to be known as an impossible place to do business. It was not attractive to foreign investors. Today foreign investors are investing at the rate of $50 to $75 million a day in the People's Republic of China. ▼

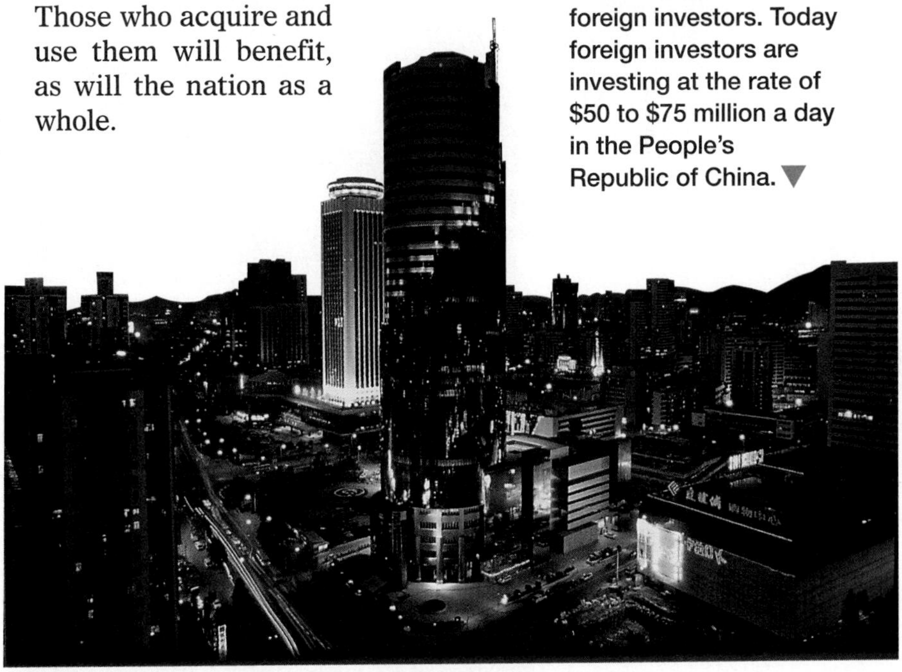

SECTION 3 REVIEW

Understanding Vocabulary
Define multinationals, allegiances, foreign affiliates, alliances, tolerance.

Reviewing Objectives
1. Approximately how many multinationals are there in the world today?
2. Give an example of a cross-border investment.
3. What are the advantages of corporate alliances?
4. What caused many foreign investors to reduce their investments in South Korea?
5. How have recent patterns of immigration to the United States increased the need for tolerance?

Readings in Economics

THE WASHINGTON POST, NATIONAL WEEKLY EDITION   JUNE 23, 1997

THE BUGS ARE COMING BACK!

by Warren Brown

Volkswagen is bringing back the Beetle, but it's not a baby boomer buggy. It's a Beetle for the boomers' babies. That's the view of some U.S. auto industry analysts and dealers awaiting the reintroduction of the Beetle, the first import car widely accepted by the American public. . . .

The first Beetle introduced into the United States in 1949 helped define a generation. With its bug-like body and rear-mounted, air-cooled engine, it was the automotive counter-statement to the Age of Chrome—an era ruled by Detroit with big cars, big engines and enough ornamental "britework" to reflect the sun, moon and stars. . . .

The new car, built on a Volkswagen Golf platform, will be bigger, which means it will have more headroom and legroom than the earlier version. The new car also will be safer, incorporating all of the crash-protection and collision-avoidance items such as air bags, side-crash protection beams and antilock braking systems. . . .

"Ideally, the new Beetle will appeal to singles under 30, the Generation Xers who are in the next major consumer wave behind their boomer parents," says Susan Jacobs, president of Jacobs & Associates, an auto marketing research firm in Rutherford, N.J.

"Hooking the Xers with the Beetle—and keeping them hooked with excellent customer service—would give Volkswagen an ample group of buyers for future products," Jacobs says. . . .

The company will first offer a two-door hard-top Beetle, and if that one hits the spot in consumers' hearts, it will roll out a Beetle convertible.

Nostalgia will play a role in all of this, but it'll be a decidedly secondary part.

"The new Beetle," VW says in a promotional statement, "is a demonstration of its owner's philosophy on life: individual, unhampered, youthful and relaxed.

• THINK ABOUT IT •

1. **When was the original Beetle introduced in the United States?**

2. **Why is the new Beetle targeted at Generation Xers?**

ECONOMICS IN ACTION

Global Economic Challenges

Setting up the Video

With your classmates, view "Global Economic Challenges" on the videodisc *Economics in Action.* The video focuses on the challenges and opportunities of a global economy. A news report describes McDonald's expansion into 101 countries. The video also suggests that a global economy can encourage companies to be socially responsible in response to boycotts.

 **Chapter 29
Disc 2, Side 2**

View the video by scanning the bar code or by entering the chapter number on your keypad and pressing Search. *(Also available in VHS format.)*

Hands-On Activity

Clip out two articles from a recent newspaper or magazine. One article should describe a foreign business that has established a company in the United States. If possible, choose an article about a company that has affairs in your community. The other article should describe an American business that has established a company in a foreign country. Compare the two articles and prepare a brief oral report summarizing each article. Present your report to your classmates.

SURFING THE "NET"

Global Demand for Resources

In this chapter you learned about the growing concerns about the rapid depletion of nonrenewable energy sources. Many Americans became acutely aware of this depletion in the 1970s after the countries of the Middle East started an oil embargo. The embargo encouraged Americans to seek alternative energy sources. These renewable resources include solar power, hydroelectric power, wind power, and nuclear energy. You can learn more about renewable energy sources on the Internet.

Getting There

1. Use a search engine. Type in the words *alternative energy sources.*
2. After typing in *alternative energy sources,* enter words like the following to focus your search: *solar power, wind power, nuclear energy,* and *hydroelectric power.*
3. The search engine will provide you with a number of links to follow. Links are "pointers" to different sites on the Internet and often appear as blue, underlined words.

What to Do When You Are There

Click on the links to navigate through the pages of information. Gather your findings. Using the findings, write several paragraphs describing several of the alternatives to nonrenewable resources that are currently being investigated.

CHAPTER 22 Review

Identifying Key Terms

Use terms from the following list to fill in the blanks in the paragraph below.

global integration (p. 532)
telecommunications (p. 532)
direct foreign investment (p. 537)
foreign affiliates (p. 543)
multinationals (p. 543)
allegiances (p. 543)
tolerance (p. 547)

　　(1)　 has increased over the past several decades, in part due to the rapid spread of cheap 　(2)　. There has been 　(3)　 in the United States and elsewhere for hundreds of years. Much of this has been undertaken by 　(4)　, which are companies that do business and have offices and factories in many countries. Such large businesses apparently do not have any single national 　(5)　. They do have almost 200,000 　(6)　. When dealing with other people with different cultures, the watchword is 　(7)　.

Recalling Facts and Ideas

Section 1

1. Why have improved telecommunications led to increased global integration?
2. What happened elsewhere when the stock market crashed in the United States in 1987?
3. What language is the leading second language in the world and why?

Section 2

4. What foreign nation's investors own much of the office space in downtown Los Angeles?
5. Why do foreigners purchase United States government securities?

6. Has Japan had to spend very much money on its national defense since World War II? Explain your answer.
7. What is the United States share of worldwide direct investment?

Section 3

8. How can multinationals help developing countries throughout the world?
9. What four countries own about half of the 37,000 multinationals that exist today?
10. In geographic terms, where do most companies invest?
11. Why do firms in different countries form alliances with one another?

Critical Thinking

Section 1

Making Generalizations While cheap telecommunications are widespread in the United States, they are not so widespread in Africa and South America. What will happen to global integration as the rest of the world catches up with the United States?

Section 2

Drawing Conclusions The Japanese government does not spend much money on defense. Explain how this would affect foreign investment.

Section 3

Evaluating Information "Because multinational firms have no allegiance to any one country's government, they are dangerous to every country's stability." What is your opinion of this statement?

550　*Unit 6 The International Scene*

Applying Economic Concepts

Investment Incentives While the popular press may refer to "foreigners" as if they were different types of people when they invest in the United States, just about everybody makes each investment for one reason—to earn the highest rate of return possible on that investment. Consequently, Americans should not be afraid of the British, the French, the Germans, the Japanese, the Dutch, or anybody else owning "too much" of America. Make a list of the reasons that people sometimes give for why they are afraid of direct foreign investment in this country. For each reason, present a one-sentence counter argument.

Chapter Projects

1. **Individual Project** Choose a country other than the United States and investigate how much direct foreign investment occurs there each year. Try to establish the dollar volume of such direct foreign investment, what percentage of total investment this represents, and the major foreign countries that do the investing. Write a summary of your results. (United Nations and World Bank publications are useful sources.)
2. **Cooperative Learning Project** Working in groups of four, study the following innovations:
   - the fax machine
   - overnight delivery service (e.g., Federal Express and Airborne)
   - plain-paper copy machines
   - high-speed computer modems
   - satellite television
   - portable cellular phones
   - the Internet

   Each team member will be responsible for one or more of the following:
   - Explaining what the innovation involves
   - Information on when it was first used and how much it cost then
   - How the innovation changed the way business is done
   - The future of the innovation

Reviewing Skills

Making Inferences

1. **Understanding Symbols** What can you infer from the content of the cartoon?
2. **Recognizing Point of View** Examine the cartoon and determine the cartoonist's point of view.

3. **Analyzing Information** In Jamaica about 5,000 people work in offices connected to the United States by satellite signals. Skilled workers in Jamaica earn far less than their counterparts in the United States. Based on this, what inference can you draw about the global workforce?

Technology Activity

Developing a Multimedia Presentation

Refer to the list of businesses that you compiled in Your Economics Journal on page 531. Choose one of these businesses to investigate further. Use library resources or the Internet or visit the business and ask for information about the history of the business, its size, its organization, and its plans for the future. Then use this information to prepare a multimedia presentation about the business.

Professional Specialty

Occupation	Salaries	Training	Job Outlook	Working Conditions
Architect	$24,700-$110,000	ACD, L	average	office, deadlines
Actuary	$36,000-$96,000	CD, L	favorable	office, some travel
Biological Scientist	$16,300-$67,000	CD, ACD	favorable	laboratory, vary
Chemical Engineer	$53,100 median	CD, L	average	40 hour week, some stress
Computer Systems Analyst	$25,100-$69,400	CD or TS	favorable	40+ hour week, office
Economist	$25,400-$94,000	CD, ACD	favorable	deadlines, some travel
Lawyer	$29,200-$115,000	ACD, L	favorable	long hours, some travel
Meteorologist	$18,700-$41,100	CD	below average	irregular hours
Psychologist	$24,000-$58,300	ACD, L	favorable	vary with type of practice
Social Worker	$17,500-$44,000	CD, L	favorable	some stress
Statistician	$56,890 average	CD, ACD	below average	office, regular hours
Surveyor	$17,680-$49,400	CD or Tr, L	very unfavorable	office and field work
Teacher, Secondary School	$36,900 average	CD, ACD	favorable	long hours, some stress
Technical Writer	$42,469 median	CD	favorable	deadlines

Medical Professional

Occupation	Salaries	Training	Job Outlook	Working Conditions
Chiropractor	$28,000-$150,000	ACD, L	favorable	average workweek
Dentist	$100,000 median	ACD, L	below average	vary, some weekends
Optometrist	$80,000 median	ACD, L	average	office
Physician Assistant	$37,639-$57,005	CD, L	favorable	vary greatly
Recreational Therapist	$31,472 average	CD	favorable	physically demanding
Veterinarian	$59,188 average	ACD, L	average	vary, long hours

Medical Technical

Occupation	Salaries	Training	Job Outlook	Working Conditions
Dental Hygienist	$21.10 per hour average	CD or TS, L	very favorable	some part time
Dispensing Optician	$19,400-$30,400	Tr or AD	favorable	standing
Emergency Medical Technician	$19,919-$37,690	Tr, L	very favorable	physically demanding
Licensed Practical Nurse	$16,432-$33,072	Tr, L	favorable	irregular hours, stress
Medical Records Technician	$36,700 median	Ad, L	very favorable	office, some stress
Radiologic Technologist	$20,700-$49,036	Tr, AD	favorable	emotional stress

Technical

Occupation	Salaries	Training	Job Outlook	Working Conditions
Broadcast Technician	$16,400-$53,600	CD	average	irregular schedule
Computer Programmer	$22,000-$60,600	Tr or CD	average	long hours at times
Drafter	$16,400-$50,200	AD	below average	some eyestrain
Engineering Technician	$16,590-$51,060	Tr or AD	below average	40 hour week
Paralegal	$31,700 average	AD	very favorable	some overtime
Pilot, airline	$13,000-$200,000	Flight Tr, L	below average	irregular schedule

Marketing and Sales

Occupation	Salaries	Training	Job Outlook	Working Conditions
Insurance Agent	$15,500-$69,990	HS or CD, L	below average	long hours, travel
Manufacturing Sales Representative	$15,500-$69,200	Tr or CD	favorable	travel
Real Estate Agent	$10,296-$75,244	Tr, L	below average	long hours, travel
Sales Representative	$28,800 median	HS or CD	very favorable	competitive, stress
Securities Agent	$17,600-$120,700	CD, L	very favorable	vary
Travel Agent	$13,000-$38,400	Tr	favorable	office

Clerical and Administrative Support

Occupation	Salaries	Training	Job Outlook	Working Conditions
Bank Teller	$9,900-$24,200	HS	below average	some part time
Computer Operator	$12,800-$39,500	Tr or CD	well below average	hours vary
Dispatcher	$12,000-$37,000	HS	below average	stress, sitting long hours
Insurance Claims Examiner	$21,700 median	CD or Tr	average	office, some travel
Mail Carrier	$25,240-$35,604	HS, exam	below average	early hours
Word Processor	$22,900 average	HS, Tr	below average	stress, some part time

Services

Occupation	Salaries	Training	Job Outlook	Working Conditions
Barber	$14,800 median	Tr, L	below average	standing, long hours
Chef	$12,500-$40,000	HS, Tr	average	vary
Flight Attendant	$12,700-$40,000	HS, Tr	favorable	nights, weekends
Groundskeeper	$9,600-$26,400	HS	average	weather, some part time
Nurse's Aide	$9,100-$25,000	Tr	favorable	hours vary
Police Officer	$17,900-$56,100	HS, Tr, Exam	above average	hazardous, irregular hours
Security Guard	$5-$12 per hour	Tr	very favorable	night and irregular hours

Construction Trades, Repair, Mechanic

Occupation	Salaries	Training	Job Outlook	Working Conditions
Automotive Body Repairer	$13,000-$41,000	Tr	average	strenuous
Carpenter	$13,100-$40,800	3-4 yr. Tr	below average	outdoors
Diesel Mechanic	$30,400 median	Tr/AD	average	physically demanding
Electrician	$15,650-$50,500	4-5 yr. Tr	below average	strenuous, dangerous
Heating, Air Conditioning Technician	$14,900-$42,500	Tr/AD	above average	vary, some outdoors
Plumber	$14,800-$50,400	4-5 yr. Tr	below average	strenuous
Roustabout	$13,700-$50,400	Tr/AD	very unfavorable	strenuous, outdoors

Agriculture, Forestry, Transportation

Occupation	Salaries	Training	Job Outlook	Working Conditions
Bus Driver	$11,800-$39,400	Tr, L	average	stress, varying hours
Farm Manager	$9,000-$30,900	Tr/CD	below average	vary from long hours to part time
Ship captain, Mate	$22,000-$57,800	Tr, L	below average	irregular hours, travel
Timber Cutter, Logger	$8,200-$41,000	Tr	below average	dangerous
Truck Driver	$8-$16 per hour	Tr, L	average	long hours, stress

A

ability-to-pay principle: principle of taxation in which those with higher incomes pay more taxes than those with lower incomes, regardless of the number of government services they use (p. 428).

absolute advantage: ability of one country, using the same quantity of resources as another country, to produce a particular product at less cost (p. 464).

accounts receivable: money owed to a business by its customers (p. 266).

agency shop: company in which employees are not required to join the union, but must pay union dues (p. 313).

aggregate (A-grih-guht) demand: total quantity of goods and services in the entire economy that all citizens will demand at any one time (p. 342).

aggregate demand curve: a graphed line showing the relationship between the aggregate quantity demanded of all goods and services by all people and the average of all prices, measured by the implicit GDP deflator (p. 343).

aggregates: summation of all the individual parts in the economy (p. 342).

aggregate supply: real domestic output of producers based on the rise and fall of prices (p. 345).

aggregate supply curve: a graphed line showing the macroeconomic measure of aggregate supply based on real domestic output using the implicit GDP deflator as the price index (p. 345).

allegiances: loyalties to countries, people, or causes (p. 543).

alliances: joint ventures formed by firms in different countries; often between firms from industrialized countries (p. 545).

annual percentage rate (APR): cost of credit expressed as a yearly percentage (p. 93).

antitrust legislation: laws passed by federal and state governments to prevent new monopolies from forming and to break up those that already exist (p. 244).

arbitration (AHR-buh-TRAY-shuhn): stage of negotiation process in which union and management submit the issues they cannot agree on to a third party for a final decision. Both sides agree in advance to accept the arbitrator's decision (p. 319).

articles of incorporation: document filed with the state establishing a corporation within a state; these articles include basic information about the corporation, the board of directors, and the stock being issued (p. 221).

assembly line: production system in which the good being produced moves on a conveyor belt past workers who perform individual tasks in assembling it (p. 275).

assets: items of value such as houses, cars, jewelry, and so on (p. 214).

authoritarian socialism: system that supports revolution as the means to overthrow capitalism and bring about socialist goals; the entire economy is controlled by a central government; also called communism (p. 484).

automated teller machines (ATMs): units that allow consumers to do their banking without the help of a teller (p. 372).

automation: production process in which machines do the work and people oversee them (p. 275).

B

bait and switch: deceptive advertising practice in which a store attracts consumers with an ad offering a product at a low price, then tries to sell a similar product but at a higher price (p. 65).

balanced-budget amendment: proposal to reduce the federal government budget deficits by amending the Constitution (p. 426).

balance of trade: difference between the value of a nation's exports and its imports (p. 469).

bankruptcy: the inability to pay debts based on the income received; a condition in which debtors give up most of what they own for distribution to creditors (p. 100).

barriers to entry: obstacles to competition that prevent others from entering a market (p. 238).

barter: exchange of goods and services for other goods and services (p. 362).

base year: year used as a point of comparison for other years in a series of statistics (p. 340).

benefits-received principle: system of taxation in which those who use a particular government service support it with taxes in proportion to the benefit they receive; those who do not use a service do not pay taxes for it (p. 428).

blue-collar: category of workers employed in crafts, manufacturing, and nonfarm labor (p. 306).

bond: certificate issued by a company or the government in exchange for borrowed money; a bond promises to pay a stated rate of interest over a stated period of time and to repay the borrowed amount in full at the end of that time (p. 155).

boom: period of prosperity in a business cycle in which economic activity is at its highest point; also called peak (p. 347).

boycott: economic pressure exerted by unions urging the public not to purchase the goods or services produced by a company (p. 320).

brand name: word, picture, or logo on a product that helps consumers distinguish it from similar products (p. 66).

broker: person who acts as a go-between for buyers and sellers of stocks and bonds (p. 157).

bureaucracies: offices and agencies of the government that deal with a specific area (p. 517).

business cycle: irregular changes in the level of total output measured by real GDP (p. 347).

business fluctuations: ups and downs in an economy (p. 347).

capital: all property—machines, buildings, tools, and money—used in the production of other goods and services (p. 10).

capital gain: increase in value of an asset from the time it was bought to the time it was sold (p. 157).

capitalism: economic system in which private individuals own the factors of production and decide how to use them within the limits of the law (p. 37); also called market economic system (p. 33), free enterprise system (p. 38).

capital loss: decrease in value of an asset or bond from the time it was bought to the time it was sold (p. 158).

cartel: arrangement among groups of industrial businesses, often in different countries, to reduce international competition by controlling the price, production, and distribution of goods; international form of monopoly (p. 239).

certificates of deposit (CDs): time deposits that state the amount of the deposit, maturity, and rate of interest being paid; CDs earn more interest than savings accounts, but there is a penalty for early withdrawal; also called savings certificates (p. 148).

channels of distribution: routes by which goods are moved from producers to consumers (p. 293).

charge account: credit extended to a consumer allowing the consumer to buy goods or services from a particular company and to pay for them later (p. 89). *See also* installment charge account; regular charge account; revolving charge account.

checkable deposits: money deposited in a bank that can be withdrawn at any time by presenting a check; formerly called demand deposits (p. 377).

check clearing: method by which a check that has been deposited in one depository institution is transferred to the depository institution on which it was written (p. 396).

checking account: account in which deposited money can be withdrawn at any time by writing a check (p. 376).

circular flow of income: economic model that pictures income as flowing continuously between businesses and consumers; income flows from businesses to households as wages, rent, interest, and profits; income flows from households to businesses as payments for consumer goods and services (p. 443).

civilian labor force: total number of people 16 years or older who are either employed or actively seeking work (p. 306).

closed shop: company in which only union members may be hired; outlawed in 1947 (p. 313).

closing costs: fees involved in arranging for a mortgage or in transferring ownership of property; can include fees for title search, legal costs, loan application, credit report, house inspections, and taxes (p. 129).

coincident indicators: economic indicators whose changes in activity seem to happen at the same time as changes in overall business activity (p. 355)

collateral (kuh-LA-tuh-ruhl): something of value that a borrower lets the lender claim if a loan is not repaid (p. 95).

collective bargaining: process by which unions and employers negotiate the conditions of employment (p. 318).

command economic system: system in which the government controls the factors of production and makes all decisions about their use; also called controlled economy (p. 33).

commercial bank: bank offering wide range of services; main functions are to accept deposits, lend money, and transfer funds among banks, individuals, and businesses (p. 86).

commodity money: mediums of exchange such as cattle and gems that have value as a commodity, or a good, aside from their value as money (p. 365).

communism: term used by Karl Marx for his ideal society in which no government is necessary; has come to mean any authoritarian socialist system that supports revolution as a means to overthrow capitalism and bring about socialist goals; a central government controls the entire economy (p. 484).

comparative advantage: ability of a country to produce a product at a lower opportunity cost than another country (p. 465).

comparison shopping: getting information on the types and prices of products available from different stores and companies (p. 66).

competition: rivalry among producers or sellers of similar goods to win more business by offering the lowest prices or better quality (p. 39).

competitive advertising: advertising that attempts to persuade consumers that a product is different from and superior to any other (p. 64).

complementary good: one product often used with another product; as the price of the second product decreases, the demand for the first product will increase; as the price of the second product increases, the demand for the first product will decrease (p. 188).

condominium: separately owned single unit in an apartment building or a series of townhouses; common areas such as hallways and the land on which the building is built are owned in common (p. 126).

conglomerate merger: buying out of unrelated businesses (p. 245).

conglomerates: large corporations made up of smaller corporations dealing in unrelated activities (p. 245).

consumer: any person or group that buys or uses goods and services to satisfy personal needs and wants (p. 58).

consumer durables: manufactured items that people use for long periods of time before replacement (p. 80).

consumer finance company: company that makes loans directly to consumers at high rates of interest (p. 88).

consumer goods: goods produced for individuals and sold directly to the public to be used as they are (p. 271).

consumerism: movement to educate buyers about the purchases they make and to demand better and safer products from manufacturers (p. 68).

consumer price index (CPI): government measure of the change in price over time of a specific group of goods and services used by the average household (p. 339).

contraction: part of the business cycle during which economic activity is slowing down; leading to a trough (p. 347).

convenience stores: stores open from 16 to 24 hours a day, carrying a limited selection of items generally at higher prices than supermarkets or warehouse stores (p. 109).

cooperative (co-op): apartment whose owner owns equal shares in the company that owns the building and the land on which the building stands; the owner does not own his or her own apartment but rather holds a lease on it (p. 126).

corporate charter: license to operate granted to a corporation by the state where it is established (p. 221).

corporation: organization owned by many people but treated by the law as though it were a person; it can own property, pay taxes, make contracts, and sue and be sued (p. 219).

cosigner: person who signs a loan contract along with the borrower and promises to repay the loan if the borrower does not (p. 96).

cost-benefit analysis: a financial process in which a business estimates the cost of action and compares it with the benefits of that action (p. 258).

cost-of-living adjustment (COLA): union contract or other provision providing for an additional wage increase each year if the general level of prices in the economy rises beyond a certain level (p. 319).

cost-push inflation: theory that the wage demands of labor unions and the excessive profit motive of large corporations push up prices resulting in stagflation (p. 441).

craft union: union made up of skilled workers in a specific trade or industry (p. 312).

credit: receipt of money either directly or indirectly to buy goods and services in the present with the promise to pay for them in the future (p. 80).

credit bureau: private business that investigates a person's income, current debts, personal life, and past history of borrowing and repaying debts to determine the risk involved in lending money to that person (p. 94).

credit card: credit device that allows a person to make purchases at many kinds of stores, restaurants, hotels, and other businesses without paying cash (p. 90).

credit check: investigation of a person's income, current debts, personal life, and past history of borrowing and repaying debts (p. 94).

credit limit: maximum amount of goods or services a person or business can buy on the promise to pay in the future (p. 89).

credit rating: rating of the risk involved in lending money to a specific person or business (p. 94).

credit union: depository institution owned and operated by its members to provide savings accounts and low-interest loans to its members only (p. 87).

debit card: credit device used to make cashless purchases of goods and services; money is electronically withdrawn from the consumer's checkable account and transferred directly to the store's bank account (pp. 91, 377).

debt financing: raising money for a business through borrowing (p. 265). *See also* intermediate-term financing; long-term financing; short-term financing.

deficit financing: spending by the government that exceeds the money it takes in through taxation (p. 423).

deflation: prolonged decline in the general price level (p. 339).

demand curve: line plotted on a graph showing the quantity demanded of a good or service at each possible price (p. 183).

demand deposits: money deposited in a bank that can be withdrawn at any time; now called checkable deposits (p. 377).

demand-pull inflation: theory that prices rise as the result of excessive business and consumer demand; demand increases faster than total supply resulting in shortages leading to higher prices (p. 440).

demerit goods: goods such as gambling and injurious drugs that the government has deemed socially undesirable; use is discouraged through taxation, regulation, or prohibition of the manufacture, sale, and use of such goods (p. 417).

democratic socialism: system that works within the constitutional framework of a nation to elect socialists to office; the government usually controls only some areas of the economy (p. 484).

depreciate (di-PREE-shee-AYT): decline in value over time; occurs as an item wears out or becomes outdated (p. 126).

depreciation (goods): loss of value because of wear and tear to consumer durables, such as cars: also applies to producer goods—machines and equipment (p. 334).

depreciation (monetary): fall in price of a currency through the action of supply and demand; often improves a country's competitive edge in trade (p. 469).

depression: major slowdown of economic activity during which millions are out of work, many businesses fail, and the economy operates at far below capacity (p. 348).

deregulation: gradual reduction of government regulation and control over business activity (p. 246).

devaluation: lowering a currency's value in relation to other currencies by government order (p. 468).

developed nations: nations with relatively high standards of living and economies based more on industry than on agriculture (p. 504).

developing nations: nations with little industrial development and low standards of living (p. 504).

direct foreign investment (DFI): purchase by foreigners of real estate and businesses in another country (p. 537).

direct-mail advertising: type of promotion using a mailer that usually includes a letter describing the product or service and an order blank or application form (p. 291).

discount rate: interest rate the Fed charges on loans to banks (p. 401).

discretionary (dis-KREH-shuh-NEHR-ee) income: money income a person has left to spend on extras after necessities have been bought (p. 58).

disposable income: income remaining for people to spend or save after all taxes have been paid (p. 58).

disposable personal income (DI): income remaining for people to spend or save after all taxes have been paid (p. 336). *See* disposable income.

distribution of income: money payment for work, the amount of health care, education, food, and so on, that each person receives; distribution of goods and services among all members of an economic system (p. 31).

diversification: spreading of investments in several different types of accounts to lower overall risk (p. 164).

dividends: money return a stockholder receives on the amount he or she originally invested in the company by purchasing stock (p. 155).

division of labor: breaking down of a job into small tasks; each task may be performed by a different worker (p. 275).

double coincidence of wants: situation resulting when each party to a transaction wants exactly what the other person has to offer, allowing a direct exchange of goods; this is a requirement for bartering (p. 364).

durability: ability of an item to last a long time (p. 115).

E

economic assistance: loans and outright grants of money or equipment to other nations to add to their capital resources (p. 513).

economic efficiency: wise use of available resources so that people will be confortable given the amount and their need of available resources (p. 45).

economic growth: expansion of the economy to produce more goods, jobs, and wealth (p. 45).

economic indicators: statistics that measure variables in the economy (p. 355).

economic model: simplified representation of the real world which shows people's reactions to changes in the economy; theory (p. 18).

economics: study of how individuals and nations make choices about ways to use scarce resources to fulfill their needs and wants (p. 8).

economic system: way in which a nation uses its resources to satisfy its people's needs and wants (p. 30).

economy: all activity in a nation that affects the production, distribution, and use of goods and services (p. 18).

elastic demand: situation in which the rise or fall in price of a product greatly affects the amount of that product which people are willing to buy; if the prices of certain products rise, consumers will buy cheaper substitutes (p. 185).

elasticity: economic concept dealing with consumers' responsiveness to an increase or decrease in prices; price responsiveness (p. 185).

electronic funds transfer (EFT): system of putting onto computers all the various banking functions that in the past were handled on paper (p. 369).

embargo: complete restriction on the import or export of a particular good (p. 473).

entrepreneur: person who starts a business to gain profits and is willing to take the risks involved (p. 208).

entrepreneurship (AHN-truh-pruh-NUHR-SHIP): ability to start new businesses, to introduce new products and techniques, and to improve management techniques (p. 11).

equilibrium price: price of a product or service at which the amount producers are willing to supply is equal to the amount consumers are willing to buy. On a graph, the equilibrium price is where the supply curve and the demand curve intersect (p. 197).

equity (E-kwuh-tee): amount of money invested in a property minus the debt, such as the mortgage payments that are still owed (p. 130).

equity (value): that which is fair and just (p. 45).

equity financing: raising money for a company by selling stock in the company (p. 267).

ethical behavior: acting in accordance with moral and ethical convictions about right and wrong (p. 71).

excise (EK-SYZ) tax: tax on the manufacture, sale, or use within the country of specific products, such as liquor, gasoline, and automobiles (p. 136).

expansion: portion of the business cycle in which economic activity slowly increases; also called a recovery (p. 348).

exports: goods sold to other countries (p. 462).

F

factors of production: resources of land, labor, capital, and entrepreneurship used to produce goods and services (p. 11).

Fed, the: Federal Reserve System created by Congress in

1913 as the nation's central banking organization; functions include processing checks, serving as the government's banker, and controlling the rate of growth of the money supply (p. 388).

Federal Open Market Committee (FOMC): 12-member committee in the Federal Reserve System which meets approximately eight times a year to decide the course of action that the Fed should take to control the money supply (p. 394).

fiat (FEE-uht) money: money that has value because a government fiat, or order, has established it as acceptable for payment of debts (p. 366).

finance charge: cost of credit expressed in dollars and cents (p. 91).

finance company: company that takes over contracts for installment debts from stores and adds a fee for collecting the debt; also make loans directly to consumers (p. 87).

fiscal policy: federal government's use of taxation and spending policies to affect overall business activity (p. 443).

fiscal year: year by which accounts are kept; for the federal government, October 1 to September 30 of the next year (p. 421).

five-year plans: centralized planning system that was the basis for China's economic system; eventually was transformed to a regional planning system leading to limited free enterprise (p. 487).

fixed rate of exchange: system under which a national government sets the value of its currency in relation to a single standard then it establishes equivalents between its currency and that of other countries (p. 467).

flexible exchange rates: arrangement in which the forces of supply and demand are allowed to set the price of various currencies (p. 468).

foreign affiliates: branches of multinational firms (p. 543).

foreign aid: money, goods, and services given by governments and private organizations to help other nations and their citizens (p. 512).

foreign exchange markets: markets dealing in buying and selling foreign currency for businesses that want to import goods from other countries; some currency trading takes place through banks (p. 467).

form utility: the conversion of raw materials to finished goods to satisfy consumer wants (p. 284).

fractional reserve banking: system in which only a fraction of the deposits in a bank is kept on hand, or in reserve; the remainder is available to lend to borrowers or is otherwise invested (p. 389).

franchise: contract in which one business (the franchiser) sells to another business (the franchisee) the right to use the franchiser's name and sell its products (p. 222).

free enterprise system: system in which individuals own the factors of production and decide how to use them within legal limits. Also called capitalism (p. 38).

full employment: condition of the economy when the un-

employment rate is lower than a certain number established by economists' studies (p. 439).

General Agreement on Tariffs and Trade (GATT): trade agreement under which countries meet periodically to negotiate tariff reductions that are mutually advantageous to all members; in effect since January 1, 1948 (p. 474).

generalization (JEN-ruh-luh-ZAY-shuhn): statement that pulls together common ideas among facts and is true in most cases (p. 21).

generic (juh-NER-ihk) brands: general name for a product rather than a specific brand name given by the manufacturer (p. 66).

geographic monopolies: market situations occurring when an individual seller has control over a market because of the location (p. 239).

global integration: interdependency among the countries of the world, especially within financial markets and telecommunications (p. 532).

goods and services: end results of factors of production; goods are the things people buy; services are the activities done for others for a fee (p. 11).

government monopolies: market situations created by the government and protected by legal barriers to entry; activity exclusive to government (p. 239).

gross domestic product (GDP): total dollar value of all *final* goods and services produced in the nation in a single year (p. 332).

horizontal merger: buy-out of a company by one in the same business (p. 245).

hypotheses: educated guesses or predictions, used as starting points for investigations (p. 19).

![I]

imperfect competition: market situation in which individual or group buys or sells a good or service in amounts large enough to affect price; includes monopoly, oligopoly, and monopolistic competition (p. 237).

implicit GDP price deflator: price index that removes the effect of inflation from GDP so that the overall economy in one year can be compared to another year (p. 341).

import quota: restriction imposed on the value of or on the number of units of a particular good that can be brought into the country (p. 473).

imports: goods bought from other countries for domestic use (p. 462).

income redistribution: government activity that takes income from some people through taxation and uses it to help citizens in need (p. 417).

Individual Retirement Account (IRA): private retirement plan that allows individuals or married couples to save a certain amount of their earnings per year, dependent on total income; also depending on income, the contribution is not taxed and the interest is tax deferred (p. 162).

industrial union: union made up of all the workers in an industry regardless of job or skill level (p. 312).

inelastic demand: situation in which a price change of a product has little impact on the quantity demanded by consumers (p. 186).

infant mortality: death rate of infants who die during first year of life (p. 506).

inflation: prolonged rise in the general price level of goods and services (p. 338).

informative advertising: advertising that benefits consumers by giving information about a product (p. 64).

injunction: court order preventing some activity (p. 320).

innovations: inventions and new production techniques (p. 352).

inside information: information available to a broker that no one else has; it is illegal for a broker to give out this information and illegal for a client to profit from it (p. 159).

installment charge account: credit extended to a consumer allowing the consumer to buy major items such as furniture, televisions, and refrigerators from a particular store and to pay for them in equal payments, or installments, spread over a period of time (p. 90).

installment debt: type of loan repaid with equal payments, or installments, over a specific period of time (p. 80).

interest: amount of money the borrower must pay for the use of someone else's money (p. 80). Payment people receive when they lend money, allowing someone to use their money (p. 146).

interlocking directorate: situation occurring when the majority of members of the boards of directors of competing corporations are the same; in effect, having one group of people manage both companies (p. 244).

intermediate-term financing: borrowing money by a business for 1 to 10 years (p. 265).

International Monetary Fund (IMF): agency whose member governments are obligated to keep their foreign exchange rates more or less fixed (p. 467).

inventory: supply of whatever items are used in a business, such as raw materials or goods for sale (p. 210).

invisible hand: term used by Adam Smith to describe the effect of competition in guiding individuals toward working for their own self-interest, thereby achieving the maximum good for society (p. 37).

joint venture: temporary partnership set up between individuals or companies for a specific purpose and for a short period of time (p. 217).

Keogh (KEE-oh) Plan: retirement plan that allows self-employed individuals to save a maximum of 15 percent of their income up to a specified amount each year and to deduct that amount from their yearly taxable income (p. 161).

labor: work people do; often called a human resource (p. 10).

labor union: association of workers organized to improve wages and working conditions for its members (p. 311).

lagging indicators: indicators that seem to lag behind changes in overall business activity (p. 355)

land: in economics, term used to refer to natural resources and surface land; all things found in nature, on or in the water and earth. Economically, the most important are surface land and mineral deposits (p. 10).

law of demand: economic rule which states that the quantity demanded and price move in opposite directions; as price goes up, quantity demanded goes down; as price goes down, quantity demanded goes up. There is an inverse, or opposite, relationship between demand and price (p. 177).

law of diminishing marginal utility: economic rule stating that the additional satisfaction a consumer gets from purchasing one more unit of a product will lessen with each additional unit purchased (p. 177).

law of diminishing returns: economic rule stating that after some point, adding units of a factor of production (such as labor) to all the other factors of production (such as equipment) increases total output for a time; after a certain point, the extra output for each additional unit will begin to decrease (p. 192).

law of supply: economic rule stating that as the price rises for a good, the quantity supplied rises. As the price falls, the quantity supplied also falls (p. 191).

leading indicators: statistics that point to what will happen in the economy (p. 355)

lease: long-term agreement describing the terms under which property is rented (p. 126).

leasing: renting rather than buying such items as equipment, housing, and cars (p. 266).

legal tender: money that must by law be accepted for payment of public and private debts (p. 366).

liability insurance: insurance that pays for bodily injury and property damage; required by many states before licensing an automobile (p. 139).

limited liability: situation in which an owner's responsibility for a company's debts is limited to the size of the owner's investment in the firm (p. 220).

limited partnership: special form of partnership in which the partners are not equal; the general partner(s) assumes responsibility for all management duties and debts; the other partner(s) contributes money or property and has no voice in management (p. 217).

line of credit: maximum amount of money a company can borrow from a bank during a period of time, usually one year, without having to reapply for a loan (p. 266).

local union: members of a union in a particular factory, company, or geographic area; the local deals with a company by negotiating a contract and making sure contract terms are kept (p. 313).

lockout: situation which occurs when management prevents workers from returning to work until they agree to a new contract (p. 320).

long-term financing: money borrowed by a business for a period of more than 10 years (p. 265).

loose money policy: monetary policy that makes credit inexpensive and abundant, possibly leading to inflation (p. 389).

Ⓜ

M1: narrowest definition of the money supply; consists of moneys that can be spent immediately and against which checks can be written; includes all the paper bills and coins in circulation including currency, travelers checks, and checkable deposits (p. 378).

M2: broader definition of the money supply; includes all of M1, plus such near moneys as money market mutual fund balances and Eurodollars; includes all paper bills and coins in circulation (p. 378).

market: freely chosen activity between buyers and sellers of goods and services in which business is done with those who best satisfy the needs and wants of those involved (p. 33).

market economic system: system in which individuals own the factors of production and make economic decisions through free interaction while looking out for their own best interests; the government does not intervene; capitalism (p. 33).

marketing: all the activities needed to move goods and services from the producer to the consumer; includes market research, advertising and promotion, and distribution (p. 282).

market research: gathering, recording, and analyzing data about the types of goods and services that people want (p. 284).

market survey: survey in which researchers gather information about possible users of a product based on such characteristics as age, sex, income, education, and location; written questionnaires and personal interviews are often used (p. 284).

maturity: period of time at which time deposits will pay a stated rate of interest (p. 148).

mechanization: combined labor of people and machines; originally, machines were combined with unskilled workers to replace skilled handwork (p. 274).

mediation (MEE-dee-AY-shuhn): stage in contract negotiations between union and management, in which a neutral person steps in and tries to get both sides to reach an agreement (p. 318).

Medicaid: state and federal public-assistance program that provides free health care for low-income and disabled persons (p. 417).

Medicare: government program that provides health care for the aged (p. 415).

medium of exchange: use of money in exchange for goods or services (p. 362).

merger: situation occurring when one corporation buys more than half the stock of another corporation (p. 244). *See also* conglomerate merger; horizontal merger; vertical merger.

merit good: any good or service that the government has deemed socially desirable such as museums, ballets, and classical music concerts; often subsidized by government so that all people may enjoy it (p. 416).

military assistance: either economic or technical assistance to a nation's armed forces (p. 513).

minimum wage law: federal, state, or city law which sets the lowest legal hourly wage rate that may be paid to certain types of workers (p. 309).

mixed economy: system combining characteristics of more than one type of economy with others so that the mix varies and the economic system created leans more toward one pure type than another (p. 34).

monetarism (MAH-nuh-te-RIH-zuhm): theory that deals with the relationship between the amount of money the Federal Reserve places in circulation and the level of activity in the economy (p. 448).

monetarists: supporters of the theory of monetarism, often linked with Milton Friedman (p. 448).

monetary policy: policy that involves changing the rate of growth of the supply of money in circulation to affect the amount of credit and, therefore, business activity in the economy (p. 388).

monetary rule: monetarists' policy that the Fed should allow the money supply to grow at a specified rate (perhaps 3 to 5 percent) per year and not use monetary policy to stimulate or slow the economy (p. 449).

monetary standard: manner in which a nation assigns value to its money (p. 370).

money: anything customarily used as a medium of exchange, a unit of accounting, and a store of value (p. 362).

money market deposit account (MMDA): account that pays relatively high rates of interest, requires a minimum balance, and allows immediate access to money (p. 148).

money market fund: type of mutual fund that uses investors' money to make short-term loans to businesses and banks; most allow investors to write checks against their investments in the fund (p. 158).

monopolistic competition: market situation in which a large number of sellers offer similar but slightly different products and each has some control over price (p. 240).

mortgage: installment debt owed on real property—houses, buildings, or land (p. 81).

multinationals: firms that do business and have offices or factories in many countries (p. 543).

mutual fund: investment company that pools the money of many individuals to buy stocks, bonds, or other investments (p. 158).

N

national debt: total amount of debt outstanding for the federal government; public debt (p. 425).

national income (NI): total income earned by everyone in the economy (p. 335).

national income accounting: measurement of the national economy's performance, dealing with the overall economy's income and output as well as the interaction of consumers, businesses, and governments (p. 332).

nationalization: placement of railroads, businesses, and so on, under government ownership (p. 519).

natural monopolies: market situations resulting when one company forces its competitors out of business by producing goods or services at the lowest cost; usually found in industries that need large investments to get started and when it is more efficient to have one company rather than several (p. 239).

near moneys: assets, such as savings accounts, that can be turned into money or into a means of payment relatively easily and without the risk of loss of value (p. 378).

net domestic product (NDP): value of nation's total output (GDP) minus total value lost through wear and tear on machines and equipment (p. 335).

net exports: difference between what the nation sells to other countries (exports) and what it buys from other countries (imports). (p. 334).

North American Free Trade Agreement (NAFTA): trade agreement designed to reduce tariff barriers among Mexico, Canada, and the United States; approved in 1993 (p. 475).

O

oligopoly (AH-luh-GAH-puh-lee)**:** industry dominated by a few suppliers that exercise some control over price (p. 240).

open-market operations: buying and selling of United States securities by the Fed to affect the money supply by changing depository institution reserves or by putting money into or taking it out of circulation in the economy (p. 402).

opportunity cost: value of the next best alternative given up for the alternative that was chosen (p. 14).

over-the-counter market: purchase and sale of stocks and bonds, often of smaller, lesser-known companies, which takes place outside the organized stock exchanges; most over-the-counter stocks are quoted in the National Association of Securities Dealers Automated Quotations (NASDAQ) listings (p. 157).

overdraft checking: checking account that allows a customer to write a check for more money than exists in his or her account (p. 369).

ownership utility: utility created by assuring orderly transfer of ownership of desired goods (p. 284).

partnership: business that two or more individuals own and operate (p. 217).

passbook savings account: account for which a depositor receives a booklet in which deposits, withdrawals, and interest are recorded; also called a regular savings account (p. 147).

past-due notices: reminders sent by businesses and lending institutions that debt payments are overdue (p. 96).

patent: right granted by the government to exclusively manufacture an invention for a specified number of years (p. 239).

peak: period of prosperity in a business cycle in which economic activity is at its highest point; also called a boom (p. 347).

penetration pricing: selling a new product at a low price to attract customers away from an established product (p. 290).

pension plans: company plans that provide for retirement income (p. 161).

perfect competition: market situation in which there are numerous buyers and sellers, and no one buyer or seller can affect price (p. 232).

personal income (PI): total income individuals receive before personal taxes are paid (p. 336).

picketing: activity in which striking workers walk up and down in front of a workplace carrying signs that state their disagreement with the company (p. 320).

place utility: utility created by having a good available where a consumer wants to buy it (p. 284).

points: fee paid to a lender and computed as percentage points of a loan (p. 129).

price elasticity of demand: economic concept that deals with how much demand varies according to changes in price (p. 185).

price leadership: practice of setting prices close to those charged by other companies selling similar products; found especially in oligopolies (p. 289).

price system: system of pure capitalism that allows prices to seek their own level as determined by the forces of supply and demand (p. 482).

prime rate: rate of interest banks charge on loans to their best business customers (p. 401).

principal: amount of money originally borrowed in a loan (p. 80).

private-labeled products: store-brand products carried by some supermarket chains and club wholesale chains as a lower cost alternative to national brands (p. 110).

private property: whatever is owned by individuals or groups rather than the federal, state, or local governments (p. 38).

private property rights: rights of individuals or groups to own goods; these rights are enforced by the government (p. 482).

privatization: change from state ownership of business, land, and buildings to private ownership (p. 492).

producer goods: goods produced for businesses to use in making other goods (p. 271).

producer price index (PPI): measure of the change in price over time of a specific group of goods used by businesses; formerly wholesale price index (p. 340).

product differentiation: manufacturers' use of minor differences in quality and features to try to differentiate between similar goods and services (p. 240).

production: process of changing resources into goods that satisfy the needs and wants of individuals and businesses (p. 271).

production possibilities: all the combinations of goods and services that can be produced from a fixed amount of resources in a given period of time (p. 15).

productivity: ability to produce greater quantities of goods and services in better and faster ways (p. 10).

product life cycle: series of stages that a product goes through from first introduction to complete withdrawal from the market; a cycle has no fixed number of months or years (p. 291).

professionals: highly educated individuals with college degrees and usually additional education or training (p. 307).

profit: money left after all the costs of production—wages, rent, interest, and taxes have been paid (p. 39).

profit incentive: desire to make money that motivates people to produce and sell goods and services that others want to buy (p. 39).

progressive tax: tax that takes a larger percentage of higher incomes than lower incomes; justified on the basis of the ability-to-pay principle (p. 430).

proletariat (PROH-luh-TER-ee-uht)**:** term used by Karl Marx to mean workers (p. 484).

promissory (prah-muh-SOHR-ee) **note:** written agreement to repay a loan by a specified time and with a specified rate of interest (p. 266).

promotion: use of advertising and other methods to inform consumers that a new or improved product or service is available and to persuade them to purchase it (p. 290).

property rights: protection of private property; the govern-ment may not legally take private property without paying fair market value (p. 523).

proportional tax: tax that takes the same percentage of all incomes; as income rises, the amount of tax paid also rises (p. 430).

proprietor: owner of a business; from the Latin word *proprietas*, meaning "property" (p. 213).

protectionists: people who argue for trade restrictions (p. 474).

protective tariff: tax on imports used to raise the cost of imported goods and thereby protect domestic producers (p. 472).

public-assistance programs: government programs that make payments based on need; also called welfare (p. 418).

public goods: goods or services that government sometimes supplies to its citizens; can be used by many individuals at the same time without reducing the benefit each person receives (p. 416).

public-works projects: publicly-used facilities such as schools and highways, built by federal, state, or local governments with public money (p. 413).

purchasing power: the real goods and services that money can buy; determines the value of the money (p. 338).

pure monopoly: most extreme market form of imperfect competition in which a single seller controls the supply of a good or service and thus has control over price (p. 237). *See also* geographic monopolies; government monopolies;natural monopolies; technological monopoly.

Ⓡ

rational choice: involves choosing the alternative that has the greatest value from among comparable quality products (p. 61).

real estate taxes: taxes paid on land and buildings (p. 125).

real GDP: figure resulting when the GDP is adjusted for inflation by applying the price deflator (p. 341).

real income effect: economic rule stating that individuals cannot keep buying the same quantity of a product if its price rises while their income stays the same; this works in reverse direction also—if the price of a product decreases and income remains the same, purchasing power is increased and the amount of product purchased will likely be increased (p. 179).

recession: portion of the business cycle in which the nation's output, the real GDP, does not grow for at least two quarters (six months) (p. 348).

recovery: portion of the business cycle in which economic activity increases; also called an expansion (p. 348).

registration fee: licensing fee, usually annual, paid to a state for the right to use a car (p. 137).

regressive tax: tax that takes a larger percentage of lower incomes than higher incomes (p. 430).

regular charge account: credit extended to a consumer

allowing the consumer to buy goods or services from a particular store and to pay for them later. Interest is charged on that part of the account not paid within a certain period of time. Also known as a 30-day charge (p. 89).

representative money: money not valuable in itself for nonmoney uses which can be exchanged for some valuable commodity such as gold or silver (p. 366).

reregulation: federal government regulation and control over business activity of formerly heavily-regulated industries (p. 246).

reserve requirements: regulations set by the Fed, requiring banks to keep a certain percentage of their deposits as cash in their own vaults or as deposits in their district Federal Reserve Bank (p. 389).

resource: anything that people can use to make or obtain what they need or want (p. 8).

retailers: businesses that sell consumer goods directly to the public (p. 294).

revenue tariff: tax on imports used primarily to raise income without restricting imports (p. 472).

revolving charge account: credit extended to a consumer allowing the consumer to buy goods or services from a particular store and to pay for them later. Usually a certain portion of the balance must be paid each month; interest is charged on the amount not paid (p. 89).

right-to-work laws: state laws forbidding union shops and closed shops; workers are allowed to continue working in a particular job without joining a union (p. 313).

robotics: sophisticated computer-controlled machinery that operates an assembly line (p. 275).

S

saving: nonuse of income for a period of time so that it can be used later (p. 146).

savings and loan association (S&L): depository institution that, like a commercial bank, accepts deposits and lends money. Originally established to lend money for home building, federal laws in the 1980s permitted S&Ls to provide some of the same services as banks (p. 86).

savings banks: depository institutions originally set up to serve small savers overlooked by commercial banks; most of their business comes from savings accounts and home loans (p. 86).

savings bonds: bonds issued by the federal government as a way of borrowing money; bonds are purchased at half the face value and then increase in value every six months until full face value is reached (p. 155).

scarcity: state in which people do not and cannot have enough income, time, or other resources to satisfy their every desire (p. 9).

secondary market: process through which owners of securities sell the securities to other investors for cash (p. 493)

secured loan: loan that is backed up by collateral (p. 95).

security deposit: money a renter lets an owner hold; if the rent is not paid or an apartment is damaged, the owners may keep all or part of the deposit (p. 130).

semiskilled workers: people whose jobs require some training, in job-related skills, often using modern technology (p. 307).

service flow: amount of use a person gets from an item over time and the value a person places on this use (p. 115).

service workers: people who provide services directly to individuals (p. 307).

shortages: situations occurring when, at the going price, the quantity demanded is greater than the quantity supplied (p. 198).

short-term financing: money borrowed by a business for any period of time less than a year (p. 265).

skilled worker: person who has learned a trade or craft either through a vocational school or as an apprentice to an experienced worker (p. 307).

small business incubator: a business that helps small businesses develop by providing such forms of assistance as a low-rent building, management advice, and computers; often operated with state and federal funds (p. 215).

social insurance programs: government programs that pay benefits to retired and disabled workers, their families, and the unemployed; financed by taxes paid into programs by workers and employers (p. 418).

Social Security: federal program that provides monthly payments to people who are retired or unable to work (p. 417).

sole proprietorship: business owned by one person; most basic type of business organization (p. 213).

special economic zones: designated geographic areas in the People's Republic of China which, since 1979, have been moving toward restricted decentralized capitalism (p. 488).

specialization (SPE-shuh-luh-ZAY-shuhn): concept that it is profitable for a nation to produce and export a limited assortment of goods for which it is particularly suited (p. 464).

stabilization (STAY-buh-lih-ZAY-shuhn) **policies:** attempt by the federal government to keep the economy healthy and to make the future more predictable for planning, saving, and investing; includes monetary and fiscal policies (p. 438).

stagflation: combination of inflation and low economic activity (p. 441).

standard of living: material well-being of an individual, group, or nation measured by the average value of goods and services used by the average citizen during a given period of time (p. 45).

start-ups: newly-established businesses; business advice and assistance are available from the federal and state governments, colleges, and universities (p. 214)

statement savings account: account similar to a passbook savings account except that instead of a passbook, the depositor receives a monthly statement showing all transactions (p. 147).

stock: share of ownership in the corporation issuing the stock; entitles the buyer to a certain part of the future profits and assets of the corporation (p. 154).

stockholders: people who have invested in a corporation and own stock; stockholders hold a claim against a certain part of the profits (p. 155).

store of value: use of money to store purchasing power for later use (p. 364).

strike: deliberate work stoppage by workers to force an employer to give in to their demands (p. 312).

subsistence agriculture: raising of just enough food by a family to take care of its own needs; no crops are available for export or to feed an industrial work force (p. 505).

substitution effect: economic principle stating that if two items satisfy the same need and the price of one rises, people will buy the other (p. 179).

Supplemental Security Income: federal programs that include food stamps, veterans' benefits, and payments to the aged, blind, and disabled (p. 417).

supply curve: line plotted on a graph that shows the quantities supplied of a good or service at each possible price (p. 194).

surplus: situation occurring when supply is greater than demand (p. 198).

T

tariff: tax on imports; most commonly used barrier to free trade (p. 472). *See also* protective tariff; revenue tariff

tax-exempt bonds: bonds sold by local and state governments; interest paid on the bond is not taxed by the federal government (p. 155).

technical assistance: aid, in the form of professionals such as engineers, teachers, and technicians, supplied by nations to teach skills to individuals in other nations; strengthens a nation's human resources (p. 513).

technological monopoly: market situation resulting when a seller develops a product or production process for which it obtains a patent; company holds exclusive rights to the new invention for a specified number of years (p. 239).

technology: any use of land, labor, and capital that produces goods and services more efficiently. Today, generally means the use of science to develop new products and new methods for producing and distributing goods and services (pp. 11, 197).

telecommunications: long-distance communications, usually electronic, using communications satellites, and fiber-optic cables (p. 532).

Temporary Assistance to Needy Families: state-run public-assistance program that provides money to needy parents raising young children (p. 417).

test marketing: offering a product for sale in a small area for a limited period of time to see how well it sells before offering it nationally (p. 285).

three *P's*: prices, profits, and private property—the basis of market capitalism (p. 482).

thrift institutions: mutual savings banks, savings and loan associations (S&Ls), and credit unions that offer many of the same services as commercial banks (p. 377).

tight money policy: monetary policy which makes credit expensive and in short supply in an effort to slow the economy (p. 389).

time deposits: savings plans that require savers to leave their money on deposit for certain periods of time (p. 148).

time lags: periods between the time fiscal policy is enacted and the time it becomes effective (p. 450).

time utility: utility created by having a good available when a consumer wants to buy it (p. 284).

tolerance: fair, objective, and permissive attitude toward the opinions, and practices of other religions, races, and nationalities (p. 547).

trade-off: exchanging one thing for the use of another; often making unavoidable choices because of the problem of scarcity (p. 13).

trade credit: credit extended by a seller to a business buying goods; allows a buyer to take immediate possession of goods to pay for them at some future date (p. 266).

traditional economic system: system in which economic decisions are based on customs, beliefs, and ways of doing things that have been handed down from generation to generation (p. 32).

transfer payments: welfare and other supplementary payments, such as unemployment compensation, Social Security, and Medicaid, that a state or the federal government makes to individuals, adding to an individual's income even though the payments are not in exchange for any current productive activity (p. 336).

Treasury bills: certificates issued by the U.S. Treasury in exchange for borrowed money in minimum amounts of $10,000 and maturing during a period ranging from three months to one year (p. 156).

Treasury bonds: certificates issued by the U.S. Treasury in exchange for borrowed money in minimum amounts of $1,000 or $5,000 and maturing in 10 or more years (p. 156).

Treasury notes: certificates issued by the U.S. Treasury in exchange for borrowed money with minimum amounts of $1,000 or $5,000 and maturing in 2 to 10 years (p. 156).

trough: lowest portion of the business cycle in which the downward spiral of the economy levels off (p. 348).

U

underground economy: transactions by people who do not follow federal and state laws with respect to reporting earnings; includes tax avoiders, gamblers and drug traffickers, and those illegally receiving unemployment benefits (p. 439).

unemployment rate: percentage of the civilian labor force that is without jobs but that is actively looking for work (p. 438).

union shop: company that requires that new company employees to join a union after a specific period of time, usually three months (p. 313).

unit of accounting: use of money as a yardstick for comparing the values of goods and services in relation to one another (p. 364).

unlimited liability: requirement that an owner is personally and fully responsible for all losses and debts of a business (p. 214).

unsecured loan: loan guaranteed only by a promise to repay it (p. 95).

unskilled workers: people whose jobs require no specialized training (p. 307).

usury law: law restricting the amount of interest that can be charged for credit (p. 99).

utility: ability of any good or service to satisfy consumer wants (pp. 177, 282). *See also* form utility; ownership utility; place utility; time utility.

values: beliefs or characteristics that an individual or group considers important, such as religious freedom, and equal opportunity (p. 20).

vertical merger: a merger in which a business that is buying from or selling to another business merges with that business (p. 245).

vicious cycle of poverty: trap in which a less-developed country with low per-capital incomes cannot save and invest enough to achieve acceptable rates of economic growth (p. 524).

voluntary exchange: principle that is the basis of activity in a market economy; a buyer and a seller exercise their economic freedoms by working out their own terms of exchange (p. 176).

W

wants: economists' term for everything people desire beyond basic goods and services that meet their needs (p. 9).

warehouse food store: store that carries a limited number of brands and items; less expensive than supermarkets; goods are often available only in large quantities (p. 109).

warranty: promise made by a manufacturer or a seller to repair or replace a product within a certain period of time if it is found to be faulty (p. 60).

welfare: public-assistance programs that make payments based on need; includes Supplemental Security Income, Temporary Assistance to Needy Families, and Medicaid (p. 418).

welfare state: country that is a blend of capitalism and socialism, combining private ownership of the means of production and competitive allocation of resources with the goal of social equality for its citizens (p. 494).

white-collar: category of workers employed in offices, sales, or professional positions (p. 307).

wholesalers: businesses that purchase large quantities of goods from producers for resale to other businesses (p. 293).

Workers' Compensation: government program that extends payments for medical care to workers injured on the job; people who have lost jobs can receive payments through unemployment insurance (p. 417).

World Trade Organization: trade agreement among 117 nations that constitutes the world's largest trade agreement (p. 474).

ability-to-pay principle/principio de capacidad de pago principio de tributación el cual prescribe que aquellos que tengan ingresos más altos paguen más impuestos que aquellos que tengan ingresos más bajos, irrespectivamente del número de servicios gubernamentales que usen (p. 428).

absolute advantage/ventaja absoluta capacidad de un país, que usa la misma cantidad de recursos que otro, para producir un determinado producto a menos costo. (p. 464).

accounts receivable/cuentas por cobrar dineros que le deben los clientes a un negocio (p. 266).

agency shop/empresa con cotización sindical obligatoria compañía en la cual no se les exige a los empleados pertenecer al sindicato, pero deben pagarle cuotas a éste (p. 313).

aggregate demand/demanda total cantidad total de bienes y servicios en la totalidad de la economía que todos los ciudadanos demandan en un momento dado (p. 342).

aggregate demand curve/curva de demanda total línea gráfica que demuestra la relación entre la cantidad total que demandan todos los ciudadanos y el promedio de todos los precios, medidos mediante el índice implícito de deflación del PNB (p. 343).

aggregates/agregados suma de todas las partes que individualmente componen la economía (p. 342).

aggregate supply/oferta total producción nacional real basada en la subida y caída de los precios (p. 345).

aggregate supply curve/oferta total, curva de línea gráfica que demuestra la relación entre la demanda total cuando ésta se mide basándola en la producción nacional real y usando el índice implícito de deflación del PNB como índice de precios (p. 345).

allegiances/lealtades fidelidad a causas, países y personas (p.543).

alliances/alianzas negocios en conjunto formados por firmas en distintos países; a menudo entre firmas de países industrializados (p. 545).

annual percentage rate (APR)/índice de porcentaje anual costo del crédito expresado en términos de porcentaje anual (p. 93).

antitrust legislation/leyes antimonopolistas leyes promulgadas por el gobierno federal y estatal para impedir la formación de nuevos monopolios y para romper los que ya existan (p. 244).

arbitration/arbitraje etapa en un proceso de negociación en la cual el sindicato y la gerencia plantean a un tercero los asuntos sobre los cuales no se pueden poner de acuerdo para que éste dé una decisión final. Ambas partes aceptan por adelantado la decisión del árbitro (p. 319).

articles of incorporation/escritura de constitución documento que establece en un estado una sociedad; dicho documento abarca cierta información básica sobre la sociedad, la junta directiva y las acciones que se emiten (p. 221).

assembly line/cadena de montaje sistema de producción en la cual al artículo que se fabrica lo lleva una banda transportadora a los trabajadores que a su vez lo ensamblan (p. 275).

authoritarian socialism/socialismo autoritario sistema que respalda la revolución como medio para derribar al capitalismo y lograr metas socialistas; un gobierno central controla toda la economía; también llamado comunismo (p. 484).

automated teller machines/cajeros automáticos unidades que les permiten a los clientes realizar sus transacciones bancarias sin la ayuda de un cajero (p. 372).

automation/automatización proceso de producción en el cual las máquinas realizan el trabajo y el personal humano lo fiscaliza (p. 275).

B

bait and switch/publicidad con cebo práctica publicitaria engañosa mediante la cual una tienda atrae a los consumidores con un anuncio de un producto a bajo precio, y entonces trata de venderles un producto similar a precio superior (p. 65).

balanced budget amendment/enmienda del presupuesto equilibrado propuesta para reducir los déficits del gobierno federal mediante enmiendas a la Constitución (p. 426).

balance of trade/balanza comercial diferencia entre el valor de las exportaciones y las importaciones de una nación (p. 469).

bankruptcy/bancarrota incapacidad de pagar deudas con los ingresos percibidos; condición en la cual los deudores renuncian a la mayor parte de sus propiedades para distribuir éstas a sus acreedores (p. 100).

barriers to entry/barreras para entrar en un mercado obstáculos a la competencia para impedir que otros tengan acceso al mercado (p. 238).

barter/trueque intercambio de bienes y servicios por otros bienes y servicios (p. 362).

base year/año base año utilizado como punto de comparación para los demás años en una serie estadística (p. 340).

benefits-received principle/principio de beneficios recibidos sistema tributario en el cual los que hacen uso de un cierto servicio que preste el gobierno mantienen al mismo con impuestos en proporción a los beneficios que reciban; los que no usen dicho servicio no pagan impuestos por el mismo (p. 428).

blue-collar/obreros categoría de trabajadores que se desempeñan en artesanías, fábricas y trabajo no agrícola (p. 306).

bond/bono certificado emitido por una compañía o el gobierno a cambio de un préstamo de dinero; el bono promete pagar un cierto tipo de interés durante un cierto plazo de tiempo y devolver la suma prestada en su totalidad al final de dicho plazo (p. 155).

boom/período de auge período de prosperidad en un ciclo comercial en el cual la actividad económica está en su más elevado punto; llamado también máximo o cumbre (p. 347).

boycott/boicot presión económica ejercida por los sindicatos que le urgen al público que no adquieran los bienes y servicios que produzca una compañía (p. 320).

brand name/marca de fábrica palabra, imagen o logotipo en un producto que ayuda a los consumidores a distinguirlo de otros productos similares (p. 66).

broker/corredor persona que actúa como intermediario entre los compradores y vendedores de bonos y acciones (p. 157).

bureaucracies/burocracias oficinas y agencias del gobierno que se desempeñan en su propio y específico campo en la administración del gobierno (p.517).

business cycle/ciclo económico cambios irregulares en el nivel de la producción total medida por el PNB real (p. 347).

business fluctuations/fluctuaciones económicas sube-y-bajas en la economía (p. 347).

capital/capital todas las propiedades: máquinas, edificios, herramientas y dinero—que se usen en la producción de otros bienes y servicios (p. 10).

capital gains/ganacias de capital aumento en el valor bienes desde el momento en que se compran hasta el momento en que se vendan (p. 157).

capitalism/capitalismo sistema económico en el cual personas particulares son dueñas de los factores de producción y deciden cómo utilizarlos dentro del margen de la ley; también llamado sistema de mercado; sistema de libre empresa (p. 37).

capital loss/pérdidas de capital disminución en el valor bienes desde el momento en que se compran hasta el momento en que se vendan (p. 158).

cartel/cartel convenio entre grupos de negocios industriales, a menudo en distintos países, de reducir la competencia internacional controlando el precio, producción y distribución de bienes; una forma internacional de monopolio (p. 239).

certificates of deposit/certificados de depósito depósitos a plazo que declaran la cantidad del depósito, el vencimiento y el tipo de interés que paga; los CD ganan más interés que las cuentas de ahorro, pero tienen penalidad por retirar fondos antes de tiempo; se les llama también certificados de ahorro (p. 148).

channels of distribution/canales de distribución rutas mediante las cuales se distribuyen los bienes de los productores a los consumidores (p. 293).

charge account/cuenta de crédito crédito extendido a un consumidor que le permite a éste comprarle bienes y servicios a cierta compañía y pagarlos luego. (p. 89). *Vea también* cuenta de crédito a plazos (installment charge account); cuenta de crédito regular (regular charge account); cuenta de crédito rotativa (revolving charge account).

checkable deposits/depósitos verificables dinero depositado en un banco que se puede extraer en cualquier momento presentando un cheque; anteriormente llamados *demand deposits* (depósitos disponibles o extraíbles a la vista) (p. 377).

check clearing/compensación de cheques bancarios método medante el cual un cheque que ha sido depositado en una institución depositaria se transfiere a la institución depositaria en la que fue hecho (p. 396).

checking account/cuenta corriente bancaria cuenta en la cual el dinero depositado se puede extraer en cualquier momento haciendo un cheque (p. 376).

circular flow of income/flujo circular de ingresos modelo económico que representa a los ingresos como si fluyeran contínuamente entre los negocios y los consumidores; los ingresos fluyen de los negocios a los domicilios como sueldos, alquileres, intereses y ganancias; los ingresos fluyen de los domicilios a los negocios como pagos por los bienes y los servicios de consumo (p. 443).

civilian labor force/fuerza laboral civil número total de personas de 16 años o más que estén bien empleadas o procurando activamente trabajo (p. 306).

closed shop/empresa con sindicación obligatoria compañía en la cual sólo pueden trabajar los que pertenezcan al sindicato; prohibido en 1947 (p. 313).

closing costs/costos de cierre costos en que se incurre al tramitar una hipoteca o transferir el título de una propiedad; puede incluir gastos por concepto de investigación del título, costos jurídicos, solicitud del préstamo, informe de crédito, inspecciones de la casa e impuestos (p. 129).

collateral/garantía algo de valor que el prestatario permite que el prestamista reclame para sí si no se devuelve el préstamo (p. 95).

collective bargaining/convenio colectivo proceso mediante el cual los sindicatos y los empleadores o patronos negocian las condiciones de empleo (p. 318).

command economic system/sistema de economía dirigida sistema en el cual el gobierno controla los factores de producción y toma todas las decisiones con respecto a su uso; también llamado de economía controlada (p. 33).

commercial bank/banco comercial banco que ofrece una amplia gama de servicios; sus principales funciones son aceptar depósitos, prestar dinero y transferir fondos entre bancos, individuos y negocios (p. 86).

commodity money/dinero mercancía medios de intercambio tales como ganado o joyas que tienen valor como artículo o bien comerciable, fuera de su valor como dinero (p. 365).

communism/comunismo término usado por Carlos Marx para describir su sociedad ideal en la cual no hace falta gobierno; ha venido a significar cualquier tipo de sistema social-ista autoritario que respalda la revolución como medio para derrocar al capitalismo y lograr metas socialistas; un gobierno central controla toda la economía (p. 484).

comparative advantage/ventaja comparativa capacidad de un país de producir un producto a un costo de oportunidad menor que otro país (p. 465).

comparison shopping/comparación de las condiciones de venta obtener información sobre los tipos y precios de los productos que hay en distintos comercios y compañías (p. 66).

competition/competencia rivalidad entre los productores o vendedores de artículos similares para conseguirse más negocio ofreciendo los precios más bajos o de mejor calidad (p. 39).

competitive advertising/publicidad competidora publicidad que intenta persuadir a los consumidores de que un producto es distinto y superior a cualquier otro (p. 64).

complementary good/bien complementano producto que a menudo se utiliza con otro; al disminuir el precio del segundo producto, la demanda por el primero aumenta; al aumentar el precio del segundo producto, la demanda por el primero disminuye (p. 188).

condominium/condominio unidades, cada cual con su dueño por separado, en un edificio de apartamentos o en una serie de *townhouses;* las áreas comunes tales como los pasillos y el terreno en el cual está construído el edificio son propiedad en común de todos (p. 126).

conglomerate merger/fusión de conglomerados adquisición de negocios que no están relacionados entre sí (p. 245).

conglomerates/conglomerados grandes compañías compuestas de compañías más pequeñas que se desempeñan en actividades que no están relacionadas entre sí (p. 245).

consumer/consumidor cualquier persona o grupo que compre o utilice bienes y servicios para satisfacer necesidades o deseos personales (p. 58).

consumer durables/bienes duraderos de consumo artículos fabricados que usan las personas durante largo tiempo antes de reemplazarlos (p. 80).

consumer finance company/compañía financiera para el consumidor compañía que le hace préstamos directamente al consumidor a altas tasas de interés (p. 88).

consumer goods/bienes de consumo bienes producidos para personas y vendidos directamente al público para que los usen tal como están (p. 271).

consumerism/consumo movimiento para educar a los compradores acerca de la compras que hacen y demandar productos mejores y más seguros a los fabricantes (p. 68).

consumer price index/índice de precios al consumidor medida usada por el gobierno del cambio en precios durante cierto tiempo de un grupo específico de bienes y servicios que utiliza el domicilio promedio (p. 339).

contraction/contracción parte del ciclo comercial durante el cual la actividad económica está más lenta; llamada también punto bajo ("trough") (p. 347).

convenience stores/tiendas de artículos de consumo frequente tiendas que abren de 16 a 24 horas al día, y que tienen una selección limitada de artículos, por lo general a un precio más elevado que los supermercados o las tiendas almacenes (p. 109).

cooperative/cooperativas apartamento cuyo dueño tiene intereses por partes iguales en la compañía que es propietaria del edificio y del terreno sobre el cual está éste; el dueño no es propietario exclusivo del apartamento en sí sino que más tiene un arrendamiento por el mismo (p. 126).

corporate charter/escritura de constitución licencia para funcionar que le concede a la sociedad el estado en el cual se ha establecido ésta (p. 221).

corporation/corporación organización propiedad de muchas personas la cual, sin embargo, la ley la trata como si fuera una persona; puede tener propiedad, pagar impuestos, hacer contratos y demandar y ser demandada (p. 219).

cosigner/cosignatario persona que firma un contrato de préstamo junto con el prestatario y promete devolver el préstamo si este último no lo hace (p. 96).

cost-benefit analysis/análisis de costo-beneficio proceso financiero mediante el cual un negocio calcula el costo de una acción y la compara con los beneficios de ésta (p. 258).

cost-of-living adjustment (COLA)/ajuste por costo de vida contrato sindical o disposición de algún otro tipo que prescribe un aumento adicional en los salarios si el nivel general de los precios en la economía sube más allá de cierto nivel (p. 319).

cost-push inflation/inflación con estancamiento teoría que las demandas salariales de los sindicatos laborales y el excesivo afán de lucro de las grandes compañías empujan hacia arriba los precios, lo cual resulta en "estanca-inflación" (p. 441).

craft union/gremio sindicato compuesto por obreros calificados en un oficio o industria específico (p. 312).

credit/crédito lo que permite a una persona recibir dinero directamente o indirectamente para comprar bienes y servicios en el presente con la promesa de pagarlos en el futuro (p. 80).

credit bureau/agencia de informes de crédito negocio particular que investiga los ingresos, deudas actuales, vida personal e historial de préstamos y pago de deudas de una persona para determinar el riesgo en prestarle dinero a dicha persona (p. 94).

credit card/tarjeta de crédito dispositivo de crédito que le permita a una persona hacer compras en muchos tipos de tiendas, restaurantes, hoteles y demás negocios sin pagar en efectivo (p. 90).

credit check/investigación de crédito investigación de los ingresos, deudas actuales, vida personal e historial de préstamos y pago de deudas de una persona (p. 94).

credit limit/límite del crédito máxima cantidad de bienes y servicios que una persona o negocio puede adquirir bajo promesa de pagarlos en el futuro (p. 89).

credit rating/evaluación de crédito evaluación del riesgo en prestarle dinero a un cierto negocio o persona (p. 94).

credit union/unión de crédito institución depositaria que es propiedad de y está administrada por sus miembros para proporcionarles exclusivamente a éstos cuentas de ahorro y préstamos de bajos intereses (p. 87).

D

debit card/tarjeta de débito dispositivo de crédito que se utiliza para hacer compra de bienes y servicios sin usar efectivo; el dinero se extrae electrónicamente de la cuenta corriente del consumidor y se transfiere directamente a la cuenta bancaria de la tienda (pp. 91, 377).

debt financing/financiamiento mediante créditos a la emisión de obligaciones recaudación de dinero para un negocio con préstamos (p. 265). *Vea también* financiamiento a mediano plazo; a largo plazo; y a corto plazo.

deficit financing/financiamiento del déficit gastos del gobierno que exceden lo que éste recauda a través de impuestos (p. 423).

deflation/deflación declinación prolongada en el nivel general de precios (p. 339).

demand curve/curva de demanda línea gráfica que demuestra la cantidad que se demanda de un bien o servicio a cada precio posible (p. 183).

demand deposits/depósitos a la vista dinero depositado en un banco y que se puede extraer en cualquier momento; llamados ahora depósitos extraíbles por cheque (checkable deposits) (p. 377).

demand-pull inflation/inflación de demanda teoría que dice que los precios suben como resultado de demanda excesiva por parte de los negocios y el consumidor; la demanda aumenta más rápido que la oferta total lo cual resulta en insuficiencias de oferta que causan precios más elevados (p. 440).

demerit goods/bienes de demerito bienes tales como juegos al azar y drogas peligrosas que el gobierno considera son socialmente indeseables; se desalienta su uso mediante impuestos, regulaciones o prohibición de la fabricación, venta y uso de dichos bienes (p. 417).

democratic socialism/socialismo democrático sistema que funciona dentro del contexto constitucional de una nación para elegir socialistas a cargos públicos; el gobierno usualmente controla solamente algunas áreas de la economía (p. 484).

depreciate/depreciar declinar en valor con el pasar del tiempo; ocurre al irse gastando un artículo o al quedarse obsoleto (p. 126).

depreciation (goods)/sobregiro pérdida de valor a causa de desgaste y deterioro de bienes duraderos de consumo, tales como automóviles; también se aplica a los bienes de producción, tales como maquinaria y equipos (p. 369).

depreciation (monetary)/depreciación (monetaria) caída del precio de una divisa a causa de la acción de la oferta y la demanda (p. 469).

depression/depresión declinación de importancia en la actividad económica durante la cual millones de personas se quedan sin trabajo, fracasan numerosos negocios y la economía funciona muy por debajo de su capacidad (p. 348).

deregulation/desregulación reducción gradual en la regulación y control gubernamentales de las actividades comerciales (p. 246).

devaluation/devaluación baja del valor de una moneda en relación con otras por orden del gobierno (p. 468).

developed nations/naciones desarrolladas naciones con niveles relativamente altos de vida basados más en la industria que en la agricultura (p. 504).

developing nations/naciones en vías de desarrollo naciones de poco desarrollo industrial y bajos niveles de vida (p. 504).

direct foreign investment (DFI)/inversión extranjera directa compra por parte de extranjeros de cosas tales como bienes raíces y negocios en otro país (p. 537).

direct-mail advertising/publicidad directa por correo tipo de promoción que utiliza un anuncio postal, el cual por lo general contiene una carta que describe el producto o servicio y un pedido o solicitud en blanco (p. 291).

discount rate/tasa de descuento tasa de interés que la Reserva Federal carga sobre los préstamos a los bancos (p. 401).

discretionary income/ingreso discrecional ingreso monetario que queda para gastarlo en cosas adicionales después de haber adquirido lo necesario (p. 58).

disposable income/ingreso disponible ingreso que queda para gastarlo o ahorrarlo después de haber pagado todos los impuestos (p. 58).

disposable personal income/ingreso disponible personal ingreso personal que queda para gastarlo o ahorrarlo después de haber pagado todos los impuestos (p. 336).

distribution of income/distribución de ingresos pago monetario por el trabajo, para cuidados a la salud, para la educación, para alimentos, etc., que cada persona recibe; distribución de bienes y servicios a través de todos los miembros de una economía (p. 31).

diversification/diversificación distribución de las inversiones a varios diferentes tipos de cuentas para reducir el riesgo general (p. 164).

dividends/dividendos créditos monetarios que el accionista recibe sobre la suma que invirtiera en la compañía al comprar las acciones (p. 155).

division of labor/división de trabajo reparto de una labor en varias tareas más pequeñas; cada una la puede realizar un obrero distinto (p. 275).

double coincidence of wants/doble coincidencia de necesidades situación que resulta cuando cada participante en una transacción desea exactamente lo que la otra parte tiene que ofrecer, permitiendo así un intercambio directo de bienes; es un requisito para los trueques (p. 364).

durability/durabilidad capacidad de un artículo de durar largo tiempo (p. 115).

E

economic assistance/asistencia económica préstamos y francas donaciones de dinero o equipos a otras naciones para aumentar sus recursos de capital (p. 513).

economic efficiency/eficiencia económica uso sabio de los recursos disponibles para que el pueblo salga bien económicamente (p. 45).

economic growth/crecimiento económico expansión de la economía para producir más bienes, empleos y riqueza (p. 45).

economic model/modelo económico representación simplificada del mundo real que demuestra las reacciones de las personas a cambios en la economía; teoría (p. 18).

economics/economía (disciplina) estudio de cómo los individuos y las naciones toman decisiones en cuanto a las maneras de utilizar los escasos recursos para satisfacer sus deseos y necesidades (p. 8).

economic system/sistema económico manera en la cual una nación utiliza sus recursos para satisfacer los deseos y necesidades de su pueblo (p. 30).

economy/economía la suma de las actividades de una nación que afectan la producción, distribución y uso de los bienes y servicios (p. 18).

elastic demand/demanda elástica situación en la cual la subida o caída en el precio de un producto afecta grandemente la cantidad de ese producto que el público está dispuesto a comprar; si los precios de ciertos productos aumentan, los consumidores compran sustitutos más baratos (p. 185).

elasticity/elasticidad concepto económico que tiene que ver con la respuesta del consumidor a los aumentos o disminuciones en precios; sensibilidad a los precios (p. 185).

electronic funds transfer (EFT)/transferencia electrónica de fondos sistema para realizar en computadoras todas las diversas funciones bancarias que en el pasado se hacían con papel (p. 369).

embargo/embargo restricción total sobre la exportación o importación de determinado artículo (p. 473).

entrepreneur/empresario persona que comienza un negocio para obtener ganancias y está dispuesto a afrontar los riesgos que esto implica (p. 208).

entrepreneurship/espíritu empresarial la facultad de empezar nuevos negocios, introducir nuevos productos y técnicas y mejorar las técnicas de administración (p. 11).

equilibrium price/precio de equilibrio precio de un producto o servicio al cual la cantidad del mismo que los productores están dispuestos a suministrar es igual a la cantidad que los consumidores están dispuestos a adquirir. En una gráfica, el precio de equilibrio queda donde la curva de la oferta y la de la demanda se intersectan (p. 197).

equity (financial)/equidad cantidad de dinero que se invierte en una propiedad menos las deudas, tales como pagos de hipoteca, que se deban (p. 130).

equity (value)/equidad lo que es equitativo y justo (p. 45).

equity financing/financiamiento por venta de participación recaudación de dinero para una compañía vendiendo acciones de ésta (p. 267).

ethical behavior/comportamiento ético conducta de acuerdo con convicciones éticas y morales acerca del bien y del mal (p. 71).

excise tax/impuesto interno sobre el consumo impuesto sobre la fabricación, venta o uso dentro del país de determinados productos, tales como licores, gasolina y automóviles (p. 136).

expansion/expansión porción del ciclo comercial durante el cual la actividad económica lentamente aumenta; se le llama también recuperación (p. 348).

exports/exportaciones artículos que se venden a otros países (p. 462).

factors of production/factores de producción recursos de tierras, mano de obra, capital y capacidad emprendedora para producir bienes y servicios (p. 11).

"Fed, the"/El "Fed" sistema creado por el Congreso en 1913 como la organización central bancaria de la nación; entre sus funciones se encuentran el procesamiento de cheques, servir como banquero del gobierno, y control de la tasa de crecimiento del suministro de dinero (p. 388).

Federal Open Market Committee (FOMC)/Comisión Federal de Mercado Abierto comité de doce miembros del Sistema de la Reserva Federal que se reúne aproximadamente ocho veces al año para decidir el curso de acción que la Reserva debe seguir para controlar el suministro del dinero en circulación (p. 394).

fiat money/moneda de curso legal dinero que tiene valor a causa de orden o decreto del gobierno que establece que es aceptable para el pago de deudas. También *moneda fiduciaria* (p. 366).

finance charge/gasto financiero costo del crédito expresado en dólares y centavos (p. 91).

finance company/compañía financiera compañía que asume los contratos de las ventas a plazos de las tiendas y les añade un honorario por cobrar la deuda; también hace préstamos directamente a los consumidores (p. 87).

fiscal policy/política fiscal uso de los impuestos y de las políticas de gastos por parte del gobierno federal para afectar la actividad general del comercio (p. 443).

fiscal year/año fiscal año durante el cual se llevan las cuentas; para el gobierno federal, desde el 1 de octubre al 30 de septiembre del año entrante (p. 421).

five-year plans/planes quinquenales sistema de planificación central que formó la base para el sistema económico chino; finalmente terminó por transformarse en un sistema de planificación regional que condujo a un sistema limitado de libre empresa (p. 487).

fixed rate of exchange/tipo de cambio fijo sistema bajo elcual un gobierno nacional fija el valor de su moneda en relación a una norma exclusiva; el gobierno establece los equivalentes entre su moneda y las de otros países (p. 467).

flexible exchange rates/tipos de cambio flexibles situación en la cual se permite que las fuerzas de la oferta y la demanda impongan los precios de las distintas monedas (p. 468).

foreign affiliates/filiales extranjeras sucursales de firmas multinacionales (p. 543).

foreign aid/ayuda exterior dinero, bienes y servicios que dan los gobiernos e instituciones particulares para ayudar a otras naciones y los ciudadanos de éstas (p. 512).

foreign exchange markets/los mercados de divisas bolsas que negocian con la compra y venta de divisas extranjeras para los negocios que quieran importar productos de otros países; algún cambio de monedas tiene lugar a través de los bancos (p. 467).

form utility/utilidad de forma la conversión de materia prima en productos terminados para satisfacer los deseos de los consumidores (p. 284).

fractional reserve banking/reserva parcial bancaria sistema en el cual sólo una fracción de los depósitos de un banco se mantiene a mano, o en reserva; el resto está disponible para prestárselo a los prestatarios o para invertirlo en otra cosa (p. 389).

franchise/franquicia contrato en el cual un negocio (el otorgante) le vende a otro negocio (el concesionario) el derecho a usar el nombre del otorgante y vender sus productos (p. 222).

free enterprise system/sistema de libre empresa sistema en el cual los particulares son dueños de los factores de producción y deciden cómo usarlos dentro de los márgenes de la ley; llamado también capitalismo (p. 38).

full employment/pleno empleo condición de la economía cuando la tasa de desempleo está por debajo de cierto número establecidos por estudios de los economistas (p. 439).

General Agreement on Tariffs and Trade (GATT)/Acuerdo General sobre Aranceles Aduaneros y Comercio acuerdo de comercio con el cual los distintos países se reúnen periódicamente para negociar reducciones arancelarias que convienen mutuamente a todos los miembros; en efecto desde el 1 de enero de 1948 (p. 474).

generalization/generalización frase que unifica ideas comunes entre los distintos datos y que es acertada en la mayoría de los casos (p. 21).

generic brands/nombres genéricos nombres generales para productos en vez de para nombres específicos de marca dado por los fabricantes (p. 66).

geographic monopolies/monopolios geográficos situaciones de mercado que ocurren cuando un vendedor controla individualmente un mercado a causa de la ubicación del vendedor (p. 239).

global integration/integración mundial interdependencia entre los países del mundo, especialmente en los mercados financieros y las telecomunicaciones (p. 532).

goods and services/productos y servicios resultados finales de los factores de producción; los bienes son lo que el público compra; los servicios son las actividades que se hacen por los demás a cambio de honorarios (p. 11).

government monopolies/monopolios estatales situaciones de mercado creadas por el gobierno y protegidas por barreras legales al acceso; actividad exclusiva al gobierno (p. 239).

gross domestic product (GDP)/producto nacional bruto (PNB) valor total en dólares de todos los productos y servicios finales en la nación durante un solo año (p. 332).

horizontal merger/fusión horizontal compra total de una compañía por otra en el mismo giro (p. 245).

hypotheses/hipótesis opiniones o predicciones basadas en información, que se utilizan como puntos de partida para iniciar investigaciones (p. 19).

imperfect competition/competencia imperfecta situación de mercado en la cual un particular o grupo compra o vende un bien o un servicio en cantidades lo suficientemente grandes como para afectar el precio; abarca monopolio, oligopolio y la competencia monopolística (p. 237).

implicit GDP price deflator/índice implícito de deflación precios del PNB índice de precios que le quita el efecto de la inflación al PNB para que la economía general de un año se pueda comparar con la de otro (p. 341).

import quota/cuota de importación restricción impuesta al valor o al número de unidades de un artículo en particular que se pueda traer al país (p. 473).

imports/importaciones artículos que se traen de otros países para uso nacional (p. 462).

income redistribution/redistribución del ingreso actividad gubernamental que toman los ingresos de ciertas personas mediante los impuestos y los usan para ayudar a los ciudadanos necesitados (p. 417).

Individual Retirement Account (IRA)/Cuenta de Retiro Individual (IRA) plan privado de retiro que les permite a individuos o a parejas casadas ahorrar cierta cantidad de sus ingresos al año, dependiendo del total de los ingresos; dependiendo también de los ingresos, no se le gravan impuestos a esta cantidad y se difiere el impuesto sobre los intereses (p. 162).

industrial union/sindicato industrial sindicato compuesto por todos los trabajadores en una industria irrespectivamente del puesto o del nivel de capacitación (p. 312).

inelastic demand/demanda inelástica situación en la cual la subida o caída de precios de un producto tiene poco impacto en la cantidad que demandan los consumidores (p. 186).

infant mortality/mortalidad infantil índice de mortalidad de lactantes que mueren durante el primer año de vida (p. 506).

inflation/inflación aumento prolongado en el nivel general de precios de los bienes y servicios (p. 338).

informative advertising/publicidad de información publicidad que beneficia a los consumidores al darles información sobre un producto (p. 64).

injunction/interdicción laboral orden judicial que prohíbe cierta actividad (p. 320).

inside information/información interior de un empresa información disponible a un corredor de bolsa pero que no posee nadie más; es ilegal que un corredor dé esta información a alguien de afuera y que un cliente se beneficie de ésta (p. 159).

installment charge account/cuenta de crédito a plazos crédito que se extiende al consumidor permitiéndole a éste comprar artículos de cierto valor, tales como sofás, televisores y refrigeradores a una tienda y pagarlos en pagos, o plazos, iguales que se distribuyen a lo largo de cierto período de tiempo (p. 90).

installment debt/préstamo a plazos tipo de préstamo que se devuelve con pagos iguales, o plazos, que se distribuyen a lo largo de cierto período de tiempo (p. 80).

interest/interés cantidad de dinero que el prestatario debe pagar por el uso del dinero ajeno (p. 80). Pago que se percibe cuando se presta dinero, permitiendo a otra persona hacer uso de éste (p. 146).

interlocking directorate/consejo de administración coincidente situación que ocurre cuando la mayoría de los miembros de juntas directivas de compañías competidoras son los mismos en efecto haciendo que un solo grupo de personas administre ambas compañías (p. 244).

intermediate-term financing/financiamiento a medio plazo préstamo a un negocio durante de uno a diez años (p. 265).

International Monetary Fund (IMF)/Fondo Monetario Internacional (FMI) agencia cuyos gobiernos miembros están obligados a mantener sus tasas de cambio más o menos fijas (p. 467).

inventory/inventario suministro de cualquier tipo de artículos que se usan en un negocio, tales como materias primas o mercancías a la venta (p. 210).

invisible hand/mano invisible término usado por Adam Smith para describir el efecto de la competencia en guiar a los individuos a trabajar para su propio interés, y por ese medio lograr el máximo bien de la sociedad (p. 37).

joint venture/sociedad de personas asociación temporal que se establece entre individuos o compañías con un fin específico y durante un breve período de tiempo (p. 217).

Keogh Plan/Plan Keogh plan de retiro que le permite al que trabaja por su cuenta ahorrar cada año un máximo del 15 por ciento de sus ingresos hasta llegar a cierta cantidad específica y descontarle esa cantidad a sus ingresos anuales gravables (p. 161).

labor/trabajo tareas que la gente realiza; a menudo llamado un recurso humano. También llamado *mano de obra* (p. 10).

labor union/sindicato asociación de trabajadores que se organizan para mejorar los sueldos y condiciones de trabajo para sus miembros (p. 311).

land/tierra en economía, término que se usa para referirse a los recursos naturales y los terrenos superficiales; todas las cosas que se encuentran en la naturaleza, en las aguas y en la tierra. Económicamente, lo más importante son los terrenos de la superficie y los depósitos minerales (p. 10).

law of demand/ley de la demanda regla económica que declara que la cantidad que se demanda y el precio se mueven en direcciones opuestas; al subir el precio, la cantidad demandada baja; al bajar el precio, la cantidad demandada sube. Existe una relación inversa, u opuesta, entre el precio y la demanda (p. 177).

law of diminishing marginal utility/ley de la utilidad marginal decreciente regla económica que declara que la satisfacción adicional que deriva un consumidor de comprar una unidad más de un producto irá disminuyendo con cada unidad adicional que éste adquiera (p. 177).

law of diminishing returns/ley de rendimientos decrecientes regla económica que declara que después de cierto punto, el añadir una unidad de un factor de producción (tal como la mano de obra) a todos los demás factores de producción (tales como equipos) aumenta el rendimiento total por cierto tiempo; después de cierto punto, el rendimiento adicional por cada unidad añadida empieza a decrecer (p. 192).

law of supply/ley de la oferta regla económica que declara que al subir el precio de un producto, la cantidad que se ofrece del mismo aumenta; al caer el precio, la oferta del producto también disminuye (p. 191).

lease/arrendamiento contrato a largo plazo que describe los términos y condiciones bajo los cuales una propiedad se arrienda (p. 126).

leasing/arrendar alquilar en vez de comprar ciertos artículos como equipos, viviendas y automóviles (p. 266).

legal tender/moneda de curso legal moneda que por ley se tiene que aceptar como pago de deudas públicas y privadas (p. 366).

liability insurance/seguro de responsabilidad civil seguro que paga lesiones corporales y daños a la propiedad; lo exigen muchos estados antes de otorgar la matrícula para automóviles (p. 139).

limited partnership/sociedad de personas con responsabilidad limitada forma especial de sociedad en la cual no todos los socios son iguales; los socios generales asumen responsabilidad de todas las deudas y tareas administrativas; los demás socios contribuyen dinero o propiedades y no tienen voz en la gerencia (p. 217).

line of credit/línea de crédito máxima cantidad de dinero que una compañía puede pedirle prestado a un banco durante un período de tiempo, por lo general un año, sin tener que solicitar de nuevo un préstamo (p. 266).

local union/sindicato local miembros de un sindicato en una cierta fábrica, compañía o zona geográfica; el sindicato local tiene tratos con la compañía para negociar contratos y asegurarse de que los términos y condiciones de éste se cumplan (p. 313).

lockout/cierre patronal situación que ocurre cuando la gerencia les impide a los trabajadores volver a su trabajo sino hasta que éstos hayan aceptado un nuevo contrato (p. 320).

long-term financing/financiamiento a largo plazo dinero que se le presta a un negocio durante un período de más de diez años (p. 265).

loose money policy/política de dinero disponible política monetaria que da crédito abundante y barato, y que posiblemente conduce a la inflación (p. 389).

M

M1: definición más estricta del suministro de dinero; consisten en dineros que se pueden gastar inmediatamente y contra los cuales se pueden hacer cheques; abarca todas las demás letras o documentos en papel y monedas en circulación incluyendo moneda, cheques de viajero y depósitos extraíbles por cheque (p. 378).

M2: definición más amplia del suministro de dinero; abarca a toda la M1, más aquellos bienes convertibles en dinero tales como los mercados monetarios, saldos de fondos mutualistas y Eurodólares; abarca todas las letras y documentos en papel y monedas en circulación (p. 378).

market/mercado actividad libremente escogida entre compradores y vendedores de bienes y servicios en la cual se hacen negocios con aquéllos que puedan satisfacer mejor las necesidades y deseos de los participantes (p. 33).

market economic system/sistema de economía de mercado sistema en el cual los particulares son dueños de los factores de producción y toman las decisiones económicas a través de la libre interacción mientras que al mismo tiempo protegen sus propios intereses; el gobierno no interviene; capitalismo (p. 33).

marketing/mercadeo todas las actividades necesarias para trasladar bienes y servicios del productor al consumidor; abarca la investigación de mercados, publicidad y promoción, y la distribución (p. 282).

market research/investigación de mercado recolección, registro y análisis de datos acerca de los tipos de bienes y servicios que desea el público (p. 284).

market survey/encuesta de mercado encuesta en la cual los investigadores reúnen datos acerca de posibles usuarios de un producto basado en tales características como la edad, el sexo, ingresos, educación y ubicación; a menudo se usan cuestionarios escritos y entrevistas personales (p. 284).

maturity/vencimiento período de tiempo durante el cual los depósitos pagan una determinada tasa de interés (p. 148).

mechanization/mecanización trabajo combinado de personas y máquinas; originalmente, se combinan las máquinas con obreros no calificados para reemplazar a los calificados (p. 274).

mediation/mediación etapa en las negociaciones de contratos entre el sindicato y la gerencia en la cual una persona neutral intercede y trata que las dos partes lleguen a un acuerdo (p. 318).

Medicaid/Medicaid programa de asistencia pública estatal y federal que les proporciona a personas incapacitadas o de bajos ingresos cuidados gratis a la salud (p. 417).

Medicare/Medicare programa gubernamental que proporciona cuidados a la salud a personas de edad avanzada (p. 415).

medium of exchange/medios de cambio uso del dinero a cambio de bienes o servicios (p. 362).

merger/fusión situación que ocurre cuando una sociedad compra más de la mitad de las acciones de otra (p. 244). *Vea también* fusión de conglomerados (conglomerate merger), fusión horizontal (horizontal merger), fusión vertical (vertical merger).

merit good/bien preferente cualquier bien o servicio que el gobierno haya socialmente deseable, tal como os museos, el ballet y conciertos de música clásica; a menudo subvencionados por el gobierno para que el público general pueda disfrutarlos (p. 416).

military assistance/asistencia militar asistencia económica o técnica a las fuerzas armadas de una nación (p. 513).

minimum wage law/ley de salario mínimo ley federal, estatal o municipal que fija el salario legal más bajo por hora que se le puede pagar a ciertos tipos de trabajadores (p. 309).

mixed economy/economía mixta sistema que combina las características de más de un tipo de economía variando la mezcla para que el sistema se incline más hacia un tipo puro que al otro (p. 34).

monetarism/monetarismo teoría que trata la relación entre la cantidad de dinero que la Reserva Federal pone en circulación y el nivel de actividad en la economía (p. 448).

monetarists/los monetaristas personas que apoyan la teoría del monetarismo, a menudo vinculados con Milton Friedman (p. 448).

monetary policy/política monetaria política que trata de cambiar la tasa de crecimiento del dinero en circulación para afectar la cantidad de crédito y, por lo tanto, la actividad comercial en la economía (p. 388).

monetary rule/principio monetario política monetarista que insiste que la Reserva Federal debe permitir el suministro del dinero en circulación crecer a una tasa especificada (quizá del 3 al 5 por ciento) al año y no usar la política monetario para estimular ni desacelerar la economía (p. 449).

monetary standard/patrón monetario manera en que una nación asigna valor a su moneda (p. 370).

money/dinero toda cosa de uso general como medio de intercambio, unidad contable y acopio de valor (p. 362).

money market deposit account (MMDA)/cuenta de depósito en el mercado monetario cuenta que paga tasas relativamente altas de interés, requiere un saldo mínimo y permite extraer fondos en persona en cualquier momento (p. 148).

money market fund/fondos mutuos tipo de fondo mutualista que usa el dinero de los inversionistas para hacer préstamos a corto plazo a negocios y bancos; la mayor parte les permite a los inversionistas hacer cheques contra sus inversiones en el fondo (p. 158).

monopolistic competition/competencia monopolista situación de mercado en la cual un gran número de vendedores ofrecen productos similares pero ligeramente diferentes y cada uno tiene cierto control sobre los precios (p. 240).

mortgage/hipoteca préstamo a plazos que se debe sobre bienes raíces: casas, edificios o terreno (p. 81).

multinationals/empresas transnacionales firmas que hacen negocios y tienen oficinas o fábricas en muchos países (p. 543).

mutual fund/fondo mutuo compañía inversionista que reúne los dineros de muchos individuos para comprar acciones, bonos u otras inversiones (p. 158).

N

national debt/deuda pública cantidad total de la deuda pendiente del gobierno federal; deuda pública (p. 425).

national income/renta nacional total de rentas o ingresos que ganará todo el mundo en la economía (p. 335).

national income accounting/contabilidad de la renta nacional medición del rendimiento de la economía nacional, que trata sobre los ingresos y producción de la economía en general así como la interacción entre los consumidores, los negocios y los gobiernos (p. 332).

nationalization/nacionalización colocación de los ferrocarriles, los negocios, etc., bajo propiedad del estado (p. 519).

natural monopolies/monopolios naturales situaciones de mercado que resultan cuando una compañía lleva a sus competidores a la quiebra produciendo bienes y servicios en costo más bajo; por lo general se encuentra en industrias que necesitan grandes inversiones para empezar, y cuando es más eficiente tener una sola compañía que varias (p. 239).

near moneys/cuasidinero activo, tal como cuentas de ahorro, que se puede convertir en dinero o medio de pago con relativa facilidad y sin el riesgo de perder valor (p. 378).

net domestic product (NDP)/producto neto nacional (PNN) valor total del producto nacional (PNB) menos el valor total perdido a causa de desgaste y deterioro de la maquinaria y equipos (p. 335).

net exports/exportaciones netas diferencia entre lo que la nación le vende a otros países (exportaciones) y lo que le compra a éstos (importaciones) (p. 334).

North American Free Trade Agreement (NAFTA)/Tratado de Libre Comercio para América del Norte acuerdo comercial diseñado para reducir las barreras arancelarias entre México, Canadá y los Estados Unidos; aprobado en 1993 (p. 475).

O

oligopoly/oligopolio industria dominada por unos pocos suministradores que ejercen cierto control sobre los precios (p. 240).

open-market operations/operaciones de mercado abierto compra y venta por parte de la Reserva Federal de obligaciones del gobierno de los Estados Unidos para afectar el suministro de dinero cambiando las reservas institucionales de depósito o colocando o sacando dinero de la circulación en la economía (p. 402).

opportunity cost/costo de oportunidad valor de la segunda mejor alternativa después de haber renunciado a la que se escogiera (p. 14).

over-the-counter market/mercado de valores no oficial compra y venta de acciones y bonos, con frecuencia de compañías más pequeñas y menos conocidas, que tiene lugar fuera de las bolsas de valores organizadas; la mayor parte de los valores "no vendidos en la Bolsa" se cotizan en los listados de la National Association of Securities Dealers Automated Quotations (NASDAQ) (p. 157).

overdraft checking/sobregiro cuenta corriente que permite a un cliente hacer un cheque por más dinero de lo que existe en ésta (p. 369).

ownership utility/utilidad de la transferibilidad del título utilidad creada al asegurar la transferencia ordenada del título de los bienes deseados (p. 284).

P

partnership/sociedad de personas con responsabilidad limitada negocio propiedad de dos o más individuos que lo hacen funcionar (p. 217).

passbook savings account/cuenta de ahorro con libreta cuenta para la cual el depositante recibe una libreta en la cual se llevan los depósitos, extracciones e intereses; también llamada cuenta de ahorro regular (p. 147).

past-due notices/notificaciones de vencimiento recordatorios que envían los negocios e instituciones de préstamo que los pagos están ya sobrevencidos y morosos (p. 96).

patent/patente derecho otorgado por el gobierno para fabricar con exclusividad un invento durante un número específico de años (p. 239).

peak/cumbre período de prosperidad en un ciclo comercial en el cual la actividad económica está en su más elevado punto; llamado también de auge (boom) (p.347).

penetration pricing/precios de penetración vender un nuevo producto a un precio bajo para sustraerle clientes a un producto establecido (p. 290).

pension plans/planes de pensiones planes de compañía que hacen provisiones para tener ingresos en la jubilación o retiro (p. 161).

perfect competition/competencia perfecta situación de mercado en la que existen numerosos compradores y vendedores, y ningún comprador ni vendedor puede afectar el precio (p. 232).

personal income (PI)/renta personal total de rentas o ingresos que reciben los individuos antes de pagar sus impuestos personales (p. 336).

picketing/piquetes laborales actividad en la cual los huelguistas marchan de un lado a otro en frente al centro de trabajo portando letreros que declaran su desacuerdo con la compañía (p. 320).

place utility/utilidad de lugar utilidad creada al hacer que un artículo esté disponible donde el consumidor desea adquirirlo (p. 284).

points/puntos porcentuales honorario que se paga a un prestamista y se computa como puntos de porcentaje de un préstamo (p. 129).

price elasticity of demand/elasticidad de precios de la demanda concepto económico que versa sobre cuánto varía la demanda dependiendo de los cambios en el precio (p. 185).

price leadership/liderazgo en precios práctica de fijar precios muy cercanos a los de las demás compañías que vendan productos similares; se encuentra especialmente en los oligopolios (p. 289).

price system/sistema de precios sistema de capitalismo puro que permite que los precios encuentren su propio nivel, tal como lo determinen las fuerzas de la oferta y la demanda (p. 482).

prime rate/tasa mínima de interés tipo o tasa de interés que los bancos cobran sobre los préstamos a sus mejores clientes comerciales (p. 401).

principal/principal suma de dinero que se pidiera prestado originalmente en un préstamo (p. 80).

private-labeled products/productos con etiquetas de la casa productos con la marca de la tienda que tienen algunas cadenas de supermercados y de asociaciones de mayoristas como alternativas de bajo costo a las marcas nacionales (p. 110).

private property/propiedad privada bienes de los que son propietarios individuos o grupos en vez de los gobiernos federales, estatales o locales (p. 38).

private property rights/derechos de propiedad privada los derechos de individuos o grupos a ser propietarios de bienes; el gobierno pone en vigor y hace valer estos derechos (p. 482).

privatization/privatización cambio de la propiedad estatal de los negocios, terrenos y edificios a la propiedad privada (p. 492).

producer goods/bienes de producción bienes producidos para que los negocios los usen en producir otros artículos (p. 271).

producer price index (PPI)/índice de precio de producción medida del cambio en precio al pasar el tiempo de un grupo específico de productos utilizados por negocios; anteriormente llamado índice de precios mayoristas (p. 340).

product differentiation/diferenciación de productos uso por parte del fabricante de pequeñas diferencias en características y calidad para intentar diferenciar entre bienes y servicios que son similares (p. 240).

production/producción proceso de convertir los recursos en bienes que satisfagan los deseos y necesidades de comercios e individuos (p. 271).

production possibilities/posibilidades de producción todas las combinaciones de bienes y servicios que se puedan producir con una cierta cantidad fija de recursos en un determinado período de tiempo (p. 15).

productivity/productividad capacidad de producir mayores cantidades de bienes y servicios mejor y más rápidamente (p. 10).

product life cycle/ciclo de vida de un producto serie de etapas por las que atraviesa un producto desde su primera introducción hasta su completo retiro del mercado; el ciclo no tiene un número fijo de meses ni años (p. 291).

professionals/profesionales individuos altamente educados con títulos universitarios y usualmente educación o capacitación adicional (p. 307).

profit/utilidades dinero que queda después que se hayan pagado todos los costos de producción: salarios, alquiler, intereses e impuestos (p. 39). También llamado *ganacia* y *lucro*.

profit incentive/incentivos para obtener utilidades deseo de hacer dinero que motiva a las personas a producir y vender bienes y servicios que los demás quieran comprar (p. 39).

progressive tax/impuesto progresivo impuesto que grava un porcentaje superior de los ingresos más altos en comparación con los más bajos; se le justifica en base al principio de la capacidad económica (p. 430).

proletariat/el proletariado término usado por Carlos Marx para denominar a los trabajadores (p. 484).

promissory note/pagaré convenio escrito para la devolución de un préstamo en determinado momento y a una tasa específica de interés (p. 266).

promotion/promoción uso de la publicidad y demás métodos para informar a los consumidores que un nuevo o mejorado producto o servicio está a su disposición y persuadirlos a que lo compren (p. 290).

property rights/derechos de propiedad privada protección de la propiedad privada; el gobierno no puede legalmente tomar propiedad privada sin pagar por ella el justo valor en el mercado (p. 523).

proportional tax/impuesto proporcional impuesto que toma el mismo porcentaje de todos los ingresos; al aumentar los ingresos, la cantidad de impuesto que se paga también aumenta (p. 430).

proprietor/propietario dueño de un negocio; de la palabra en latín proprietas, que significa "propiedad" (p. 213).

protectionists/proteccionistas aquellos que abogan a favor de restricciones comerciales (p. 474).

protective tariff/arancel proteccionista impuesto sobre las importaciones que se utiliza para aumentar los costos de los bienes importados y de esa manera proteger los productores nacionales (p. 472).

public assistance programs/programas de asistencia pública programas gubernamentales que hacen pagos basados en la necesidad; llamados también de bienestar social (p. 418).

public goods/bienes públicos bienes y servicios que el gobierno a veces suministra a sus ciudadanos; los pueden utilizar muchos individuos al mismo tiempo sin reducir el beneficio que recibe cada cual (p. 416).

public works projects/proyectos de obras públicas instalaciones de uso público tales como escuelas y carreteras, construidas por los gobiernos federales, estatales o locales con dineros públicos (p. 413).

purchasing power/poder adquisitivo los bienes y servicios que el dinero puede realmente comprar; determina el valor que tiene el dinero (p. 338).

pure monopoly/monopolio puro la forma más extrema de competencia imperfecta en la cual un solo vendedor controla la oferta de un bien o servicio y de esa manera controla el precio (p. 237). *Vea también* monopolios geográficos; monopolios gubernamentales; monopolios naturales; monopolio tecnológico.

R

rational choice/selección racional la selección de la alternativa que tenga el mayor valor de entre productos que tienen una calidad comparable (p. 61).

real estate taxes/impuestos sobre bienes inmuebles impuestos que se pagan por concepto de terrenos y edificios (p. 125).

real GDP/PNB real cifra que resulta cuando se compensa la inflación en el Producto Nacional Bruto aplicando el índice de deflación de precios (p. 341).

real income effect/efecto de ingreso real regla económica que declara que el público no puede seguir comprando la misma cantidad de un producto si el precio de éste sube mientras que sus ingresos se mantienen igual; esto tiene efecto en la dirección opuesta también: si el precio de un producto disminuye y los ingresos permanecen igual, el poder adquisitivo aumenta y la cantidad del producto que se compra probablemente aumentará también (p. 179).

recession/recesión porción del ciclo comercial en la cual la producción nacional, el PNB real, no crece durante al menos dos trimestres (seis meses) (p. 348).

recovery/recuperación porción del ciclo comercial en la cual la actividad económica aumenta; llamada también expansión (p. 348).

registration fee/derecho de registro derecho o cargo de matriculación que cobra el estado, por lo general anualmente, por el derecho de usar un auto (p. 137).

regressive tax/impuesto regresivo impuesto que toma un porcentaje mayor de los ingresos más bajos que de los más altos (p. 430).

regular charge account/cuenta de crédito regular crédito que se le extiende a un consumidor y que le permite comprar bienes y servicios a cierta tienda y pagarlos luego. El interés se cobra por la porción de la cuenta que quede sin pagar en el plazo de cierto período de tiempo. Conocido también como el cargo de 30 días (p. 89).

representative money/dinero en cuenta dinero sin valor de por sí para usos no monetarios que se puede intercambiar por algún artículo comerciable valioso tal como el oro o la plata (p. 366).

reregulation/nueva regulación regulación y control del gobierno federal sobre la actividad comercial de las industrias que eran antiguamente fuertemente reguladas (p. 246).

reserve requirements/reserva obligatoria regulaciones impuestas por la Reserva Federal, que exigen a los bancos que mantengan en efectivo en sus cajas fuertes un cierto porcentaje de sus depósitos o que lo depositen en el Banco de la Reserva Federal de su distrito (p. 389).

resource/recurso cualquier cosa que las personas puedan usar para hacer u obtener lo que deseen o necesiten (p. 8).

retailers/detallistas negocios que le venden bienes de consumo directamente al público (p. 294).

revenue tariff/arancel financiero impuesto sobre las importaciones usado principalmente para recaudar rentas sin restringir las importaciones (p. 472).

revolving charge account/cuenta de crédito rotativa crédito que se le extiende a un consumidor y que le permite comprar bienes y servicios a cierta tienda y pagarlos luego. Por lo general cierta porción del saldo se tiene que pagar cada mes; el interés se cobra sobre la cantidad no pagada (p. 89).

right-to-work laws/ley sobre libertad laboral leyes estatales que prohíben los talleres donde los obreros tienen que pertenecer al sindicato y los talleres cerrados; a los trabajadores se les permite seguir trabajando en cierto puesto sin tener que hacerse miembros del sindicato (p. 313).

robotics/robótica maquinaria con control por computadora altamente sofisticado que funciona en las líneas de montaje (p. 275).

saving/ahorro el no usar los ingresos durante cierto tiempo para poder usarlos después (p. 146).

savings and loan association (S&L)/asociación de ahorro y préstamo institución depositaria que, como un banco comercial, acepta depósitos y presta dinero. Originalmente se establecieron para hacer préstamos para construir casas, pero las leyes federales de la década de 1980 les permitieron prestar algunos de los mismos servicios que los bancos (p. 86).

savings banks/bancos de ahorro instituciones depositarias originalmente establecidas para servir a los pequeños ahorradores dejados al margen por los bancos comerciales; la mayor parte del negocio de estas instituciones proviene de cuentas de ahorro y préstamos para casas (p. 86).

savings bonds/bonos de ahorro bonos emitidos por el gobierno federal a manera de pedir dinero prestado; los bonos se compran a mitad de su valor nominal y aumentan entonces de valor cada seis meses hasta llegar a su pleno valor nominal (p. 155).

scarcity/escasez condición en la cual el público no tiene ni puede tener suficientes ingresos, tiempo y demás recursos para satisfacer todas sus necesidades (p. 9).

secondary market/mercado secundario proceso a través del cual los dueños de valores las venden a otros inversionistas a cambio de efectivo (p. 493).

secured loan/préstamo garantizado préstamo que está respaldado por una garantía (collateral) (p. 95).

security deposit/depósito de garantía dinero que el inquilino que alquila deposita con el dueño; si el alquiler no se paga o el apartamento queda dañado, el dueño puede quedarse con todo o parte del depósito (p. 130).

semiskilled workers/obreros semicualificados personas cuyos trabajos requieren algún entrenamiento en técnicas relacionadas con el trabajo, a menudo utilizando tecnología moderna (p. 307).

service flow/flujo de servicio cantidad de uso que una persona le saca a un artículo durante cierto tiempo y el valor que dicha persona le da a ese uso (p. 115).

service workers/trabajadores en el área de servicios personas que le proporcionan servicios directamente a los demás (p. 307).

shortages/falta situaciones que ocurren cuando, al precio existente, la cantidad que se demanda es mayor que la oferta disponible (p. 198).

short-term financing/financiamiento a corto plazo dinero que pide prestado un negocio por cualquier período de tiempo que sea menos de un año (p. 265).

skilled worker/profesionales persona que ha aprendido una ocupación u oficio bien a través de una escuela de capacitación o como aprendiz de un obrero con experiencia (p. 307).

small business incubator/incubador de pequeños negocios negocio que ayuda a negocios pequeños a desarrollarse proporcionándoles tales formas de ayuda como edificios de bajo alquiler, asesoría administrativa y computadoras; frecuentemente funcionan con fondos estatales y federales (p. 215).

social insurance programs/programas de seguro social programas gubernamentales que pagan beneficios a los trabajadores retirados e incapacitados, a sus familias y los desempleados; financiados con impuestos que pagan a estos programas los trabajadores y los patronos (p. 418).

Social Security/Seguro Social programa federal que proporciona pagos mensuales a personas que están retiradas o que no pueden trabajar (p. 417).

sole proprietorship/propietario único de empresada negocio propiedad de una sola persona; el tipo más básico de organización de negocios (p. 213).

special economic zones/zonas económicas especiales zonas geográficas designadas en la República Popular China las cuales, a partir de 1979, se han estado moviendo hacia un capitalismo descentralizado restringido (p. 488).

specialization/especialización concepto según el cual le es beneficioso a una nación producir y exportar un surtido limitado de bienes para los cuales está particularmente bien dotada (p. 464).

stabilization policies/políticas de estabilización intento por parte del gobierno federal de mantener la economía saludable y hacer que el futuro sea más predecible para la planificación, el ahorro y las inversiones; abarca las políticas monetarias y fiscales (p. 438).

stagflation/inflación con estancamiento combinación de inflación y estancamiento económico (p. 441).

standard of living/nivel de vida bienestar material de un individuo, grupo o nación medido por el valor promedio de los bienes y servicios que usa el ciudadano promedio durante un cierto período de tiempo (p. 45).

start-ups/negocios recién establecidos nuevos negocios; hay asesoría y ayuda disponibles de parte de los gobiernos estatales y federal, así como de las universidades y facultades (p. 214).

statement savings account/cuenta de ahorros con estado de cuenta cuenta similar a la cuenta de ahorro de libreta, excepto que en vez de la libreta, el depositante recibe un estado de cuenta mensual donde se ven todas las transacciones (p. 147).

stock/acciones participación propietaria en la sociedad que emite las acciones; éstas le dan el derecho al comprador a cierta parte de las futuras ganancias y bienes de la sociedad (p. 154).

stockholders/accionistas personas que han invertido en una sociedad y poseen acciones; los accionistas pueden reclamar cierta parte de las ganancias (p. 155).

store of value/reserva de valor uso del dinero para guardarlo y así hacer acopio de poder adquisitivo para usarlo más adelante (p. 364).

strike/huelga paro deliberado de los trabajadores para forzar a un patrono a ceder a sus demandas (p. 312).

subsistence agriculture /agricultura de subsistencia cultivar para una familia sólo suficiente comida para satisfacer sus propias necesidades; no hay cultivos para la exportación ni para alimentar a una fuerza laboral industrial (p. 506).

substitution effect/efecto de sustitución principio económico que dice que si dos artículos satisfacen la misma necesidad y el precio de uno aumenta, el público comprará el otro (p. 179).

Supplemental Security Income/Ingreso de Seguridad Suplementario programas federales que abarcan los cupones de alimentos, los beneficios a los veteranos y los pagos a las personas ciegas, de edad o incapacitadas (p. 417).

supply curve/curva de oferta línea trazada en una gráfica que demuestra las cantidades ofrecidas de un bien o un servicio a cada precio posible (p. 194).

surplus/superávit situación que ocurre cuando la oferta es mayor que la demanda (p. 198). También llamado *excedente*.

tariff/arancel impuesto sobre las importaciones; la barrera más comúnmente usada para liberar el comercio (p. 472). *Vea también* arancel protector; arancel para rentas

tax-exempt bonds/bonos exentos de impuesto bonos vendidos por gobiernos locales y estatales; el gobierno federal no grava el interés que pagan los bonos (p. 155).

technical assistance/asistencia técnica ayuda, en la forma de profesionales tales como ingenieros, maestros y técnicos que suministran naciones para enseñar conocimientos y técnicas a individuos en otras naciones; fortalece los recursos humanos de una nación (p. 513).

technological monopoly/monopolio tecnológico situación de mercado que resulta cuando un vendedor desarrolla un producto o proceso de producción para el cual obtiene una patente; la compañía posee los derechos exclusivos a la nueva invención por un cierto número de años (p. 239).

technology/tecnología todo uso de terrenos, mano de obra o capital que produzca bienes y servicios con más eficiencia. Hoy, por lo general, significa el uso de la ciencia para desarrollar nuevos productos y métodos para producir y distribuir bienes y servicios (pp. 11, 197).

telecommunications/telecomunicaciones comunicaciones a larga distancia, por lo general electrónicas, que usan satélites de comunicación y cable de fibra óptica (p. 532).

Temporary Assistance to Needy Families/Asistencia Temporal a Familias Necesitadas: programa de asistencia pública administrado por el estado que provee dinero a padres necesitados con niños pequeños (p. 417)

test marketing/mercadeo de prueba ofrecer un producto a la venta en una zona pequeña por un período limitado de tiempo para ver qué tal se vende antes de ofrecerlo nacionalmente (p. 285).

three P's/las tres "P's" del inglés "prices, profits and private property", o sea, precios, ganancias o lucro y propiedad privada, las tres bases del capitalismo de mercado (p. 482).

thrift institutions/instituciones de ahorro bancos de ahorro mutualistas, asociaciones de ahorro y préstamo ("S&L's") y uniones de crédito que ofrecen muchos de los mismos servicios que ofrecen los bancos comerciales (p. 377).

tight money policy/política de dinero escaso política monetaria que hace que haya poco suministro de crédito y que éste sea caro en un esfuerzo por desacelerar la economía (p. 389).

time deposits/depósitos a plazo planes de ahorros que requieren que los ahorradores dejen sus dineros en depósito por cierto tiempo (p. 148).

time lags/desface cronológico períodos entre el momento que la política fiscal se promulga y el momento en que entra en efecto (p. 450).

time utility/utilidad de tiempo utilidad creada al poner un artículo a la disposición del consumidor cuando éste quiere adquirirlo (p. 284).

tolerance/tolerancia actitud justa, objetiva y permisiva con las opiniones y prácticas de otras religiones, razas y nacionalidades (p. 547).

trade-off/compensación de factores alternativos cambiar una cosa por el uso de otra, a menudo tomando decisiones inevitables y difíciles a causa del problema de la escasez (p. 13).

trade credit/crédito comercial crédito que extiende un vendedor a un negocio que le compra artículos; le permite al comprador tomar posesión inmediata de éstos y pagarlos en algún momento en el futuro (p. 266).

traditional economic system/sistema económico tradicional sistema en el cual las decisiones económicas se basan en las costumbres, creencias y maneras de hacer las cosas que se han pasado de generación en generación (p. 32).

transfer payments/pagos de transferencia pagos de bienestar social y demás pagos suplementarios, tales como compensación por desempleo, *Social Security* y *Medicaid*, que el gobierno federal o estatal les hacen a individuos, lo cual aumenta el ingreso del individuo aunque los pagos no se hagan a cambio de ninguna actividad productiva actualmente (p. 336).

Treasury bills/pagarés del Tesoro certificados emitidos por la Tesorería Federal de los Estados Unidos en cantidades mínimas de $10,000 a cambio de dinero prestado y que vencen durante un período que abarca desde tres meses hasta un año (p. 156).

Treasury bonds/bonos del Tesoro a largo plazo certificados emitidos por la Tesorería Federal de los Estados Unidos en cantidades mínimas de $1,000 ó $5,000 a cambio de dinero prestado y que vencen en diez o más años (p. 156).

Treasury notes/bonos del Tesoro a corto plazo certificados emitidos por la Tesorería Federal de los Estados Unidos en cantidades mínimas de $1,000 o $5,000 a cambio de dinero prestado y que vencen en el plazo de dos a diez años (p. 156).

trough/punto bajo porción más baja del ciclo comercial en el cual la caída en espiral de la economía empieza a nivelarse (p. 348).

U

underground economy/economía sumergida transacciones que hace la gente que no obedecen las leyes federales y estatales con respecto a declarar sus ingresos; abarca a los que evitan pagar impuestos, los jugadores y los narcotraficantes y aquéllos que ilegalmente reciben beneficios de desempleo (p. 439).

unemployment rate/índice de desempleo porcentaje de la fuerza laboral civil que está sin trabajo pero que está activamente buscando empleo (p. 438).

union shop/empresa con sindicación eventual obligatoria compañía en la que se exige que los nuevos empleados se hagan miembros del sindicato después de cierto tiempo, por lo general tres meses (p. 313).

unit of accounting/unidad de contabilidad uso del dinero como punto de comparación de los valores que tienen los bienes y servicios entre sí (p. 364).

unsecured loan/préstamo no garantizado préstamo garantizado solamente por la promesa de devolverlo (p. 95).

unskilled workers/obreros no cualificados personas cuyos empleos no exigen capacitación especializada (p. 307).

usury law/ley antiusura ley que restringe la cantidad de interés que se le puede cargar al crédito (p. 99).

utility/utilidad capacidad de cualquier bien o servicio de satisfacer los deseos del consumidor (pp. 177, 282). *Vea también* utilidad de la forma (form utility); utilidad de la transferibilidad de título (ownership utility); utilidad de lugar (place utility); utilidad de tiempo (time utility).

values/valores (morales) creencias o características que un individuo o grupo considera importante, tales como la libertad religiosa y la oportunidad igualitaria (p. 20).

vertical merger/fusión vertical fusión en la que un negocio que le compra o vende a otro negocio se fusiona con éste (p. 245).

vicious cycle of poverty/ciclo vicioso de la pobreza trampa en la que cae un país menos desarrollado con bajos ingresos *per cápita* y que no puede ahorrar e invertir lo suficiente como para lograr tasas aceptables de crecimiento económico (p. 524).

voluntary exchange/intercambio voluntario principio que forma la base de la actividad en una economía de mercado; el comprador y el vendedor ejercen sus libertades económicas resolviendo sus propios términos y condiciones de intercambio (p. 176).

wants/necesidades término de los economistas para todo lo que el público desea que va más allá de los bienes y servicios básicos que satisfacen sus necesidades (p. 9).

warehouse food store/almacén para compra de alimentos tienda que dispone de un número limitado de marcas y artículos; menos cara que los supermercados; los artículos frecuentemente están disponibles sólo en grandes cantidades (p. 109).

warranty/garantía promesa que hace un fabricante o vendedor que reparará o reemplazará un producto dentro de un cierto período de tiempo si se determina que tiene fallas (p. 60).

welfare/bienestar social programas de asistencia pública que hacen pagos basados en la necesidad; abarca el *Ingreso Suplementario de Seguridad* (Supplemental Security Income), *Asistencia Temporal a Familias Necesitadas* (Temporary Assistance to Needy Families), y *Medicaid* (p. 418).

welfare state/estado de bienestar país que es una mezcla de capitalismo y socialismo, que combina la propiedad privada de los medios de producción y la asignación competitiva de los recursos con la meta de lograr la igualdad social de sus ciudadanos (p. 494).

white-collar/empleados de oficina categoría de empleados que trabajan en oficinas, ventas o cargos profesionales (p. 307).

wholesalers/mayoristas negocios que compran grandes cantidades de artículos a los productores para revenderlos a otros negocios (p. 293).

workers' compensation/indemnización por accidente de trabajo programa gubernamental que hace pagos para el cuidado médico de obreros lesionados en el trabajo; las personas que han perdido sus empleos pueden recibir pagos a través del seguro contra desempleo (p. 417).

World Trade Organization/Organización Mundial de Comercio: acuerdo comercial entre 117 países que constituye el mayor acuerdo comercial del mundo (p. 474).

1 Puntos destacados

Los problemas básicos en Economía

Términos claves:

economía (p. 8)
recursos (p. 8)
escasez (p. 9)
necesidades (p. 9)
tierra (p. 10)
trabajo (p. 10)
capital (p. 10)
productividad (p. 10)

espíritu empresarial (p. 11)
factores de producción
  (p. 11)
productos y servicios (p. 11)
tecnología (p. 11)

Resumen

La escasez es el problema básico en economía. La economía es el estudio de cómo los individuos y las naciones deciden utilizar los recursos escasos para satisfacer sus necesidades. La tierra, el trabajo, el capital y la iniciativa son factores de producción. Algunos economistas incluyen la tecnología.

Compensación de factores alternativos ("Trade-Offs")

Términos claves

compensación de factores
  alternativos (p. 13)
costo de oportunidad (p. 14)
posibilidades de producción
  (p. 15)

Resumen

Cuando un bien o actividad debe ser abandonado para ser sustituido por otro, ha ocurrido una compensación de factores alternativos. Lo que debe ser sustituido es el costo de oportunidad (o de sustitución) de una acción. Una curva de posibilidades de producción muestra la máxima cantidad de bienes que pueden ser producidos con los recursos de la nación en un período determinado. Cuando una nación opera de acuerdo con la curva de posibilidades de producción, está produciendo de una manera eficiente.

¿Qué hacen los economistas?

Términos claves

economía (p. 18)
modelo económico (p. 18)
hipótesis (p. 19)
valores (p. 20)
generalización (p. 21)

Resumen

Los economistas observan la información proveniente del mundo real para probar los modelos económicos que ellos han formulado sobre el comportamiento de los individuos y las empresas. Los modelos económicos son representaciones de la realidad que sólo toman en consideración los factores más importantes que pueden influir en un problema. Los modelos económicos y los economistas no dicen si determinadas políticas son buenas o malas, debido a que tales juicios dependen de los valores de cada individuo.

CAPÍTULO

2 *Puntos destacados*

Sección 1

Sistemas económicos

Términos claves

sistema económico (p. 30)
distribución de ingresos (p. 31)
sistema económico tradicional (p. 32)
sistema de economía dirigida (p. 33)

sistema de economía de mercado (p. 33)
mercado (p. 33)
economía mixta (p. 34)

Resumen

Todos los sistemas económicos responden a cuatro preguntas básicas que determinan el uso de los recursos. En un sistema tradicional las decisiones económicas son dictadas por lo que se hizo en el pasado. El gobierno controla los factores de producción en un sistema de economía dirigida. En un sistema de mercado, los individuos de acuerdo con sus propios intereses deciden las respuestas a las cuatro preguntas básicas. Una economía dirigida contiene elementos de los sistemas de economía dirigida y de mercado.

Sección 2

Características de la Economía de los Estados Unidos

Términos claves

mano invisible (p. 37)
capitalismo (p. 37)
sistema de libre empresa (p. 38)
propiedad privada (p. 38)

utilidades (p. 39)
incentivos para obtener utilidades (p. 39)
competencia (p. 39)

Resumen

La decisión de los consumidores es la clave del uso de los recursos en un sistema de libre empresa. Libre empresa significa que los individuos privados son dueños de las empresas, compiten en mercados libres y obtienen utilidades. El papel del estado en una economía de mercado es objeto de debates públicos.

Sección 3

Los objetivos de la nación

Términos claves

eficiencia económica (p. 45)
crecimiento económico (p. 45)
equidad (p. 45)
nivel de vida (p. 45)

Resumen

Una nación fija sus objetivos económicos en base a su sistema de valores. Algunos objetivos del sistema económico de los Estados Unidos son la eficiencia, el crecimiento, la seguridad, la equidad, la estabilidad y la libertad individual. La libertad personal, la diversidad en los estilos de vida y un alto nivel de vida son beneficios de un sistema de libre empresa.

CAPÍTULO 3 Puntos destacados

Sección 1

Consumo, ingreso y la toma de decisiones

Términos claves
consumidor (p. 58)
ingreso disponible (p. 58)
ingreso discrecional (p. 58)
garantía (p. 60)
selección racional (p. 61)

Resumen
Parte del ingreso disponible es discrecional y no tiene que ser gastado en necesidades básicas. Un consumidor inteligente considera varios factores antes de hacer una compra.

Sección 2

Principios de compra o estrategias

Términos claves
publicidad competitiva (p. 64)
publicidad de información (p. 64)
publicidad con cebo ("bait and switch") (p. 65)
comparación de las condiciones de venta (p. 66)
nombres genéricos (p. 66)
marcas de fábrica (p. 66)

Resumen
El valor del tiempo y los esfuerzos de un consumidor para obtener información no deben exceder el valor obtenido al haber hecho la mejor decisión con respecto a un producto. Cierta publicidad tiene fines de información, otra es esencialmente competitiva. Antes de comprar los consumidores deben comparar las condiciones de venta de un producto.

Sección 3

Consumismo

Términos claves
consumismo (p. 68)
comportamiento ético (p. 71)

Resumen
Los consumidores tienen importantes derechos y fuentes de ayuda. Agencias privadas y estatales ofrecen información y ayuda al consumidor. Los consumidores tienen también varias responsabilidades incluyendo la responsabilidad de comportarse con ética.

4 *Puntos destacados*

Sección 1

Los estadounidenses y el crédito

Términos claves
crédito (p. 80)
capital de un préstamo (p. 80)

interés (p. 80)
deuda a plazos (p. 80)
bienes de consumo duraderos (p. 80)
hipoteca (p. 81)

Resumen
El pago de una deuda a largo plazo brinda algunas ventajas al prestatario. Las personas compran al crédito por varias razones. No obstante, los consumidores deben siempre decidir con cuidado si han de tomar dinero a préstamo y el monto del mismo.

Sección 2

Fuentes de préstamos y créditos

Términos claves
banco comercial (p. 86)
institución de ahorro y préstamo (p. 86)
banco de ahorro (p. 86)
cooperativa de crédito (p. 87)
compañía financiera (p. 87)
compañía de créditos personales (p. 88)
cuenta de crédito (p. 89)
cuenta crédito regular (p. 89)

límite de crédito (p. 89)
cuenta corriente rotativa (p. 89)
cuenta corriente a plazo (p. 90)
tarjeta de crédito (p. 90)
tarjeta de débito (p. 91)
cargo de financiamiento (p. 91)
tasa de porcentaje anual (p. 93)

Resumen
Los consumidores que desean tomar dinero a préstamo pueden escoger entre seis tipos de instituciones financieras. Los consumidores que quieren abrir una cuenta corriente pueden seleccionar entre una cuenta regular, una cuenta rotativa o una cuenta a plazo. En todos los casos, los consumidores deben tener en cuenta que la tasa de porcentaje anual no es igual al cargo de financiamiento convenido.

Sección 3

Solicitud de crédito

Términos claves
agencia de crédito (p. 94)
cheque de crédito (p. 94)
clasificación crediticia (p. 94)

garantía (colateral) (p. 95)
préstamo con garantía (p. 95)
préstamo sin garantía (p. 95)
cosignatario (p. 96)
notificaciones de vencimiento (p. 96)

Resumen
Varios factores se toman en cuenta cuando las instituciones financieras evalúan la solvencia de una persona. Una vez que a una persona se le otorga un crédito, tiene la responsabilidad de usarlo con inteligencia.

Sección 4

Regulación del crédito por el gobierno

Términos claves
leyes sobre usura (p. 99)
quiebra (p. 100)

Resumen
La Ley de Iguales Oportunidades de Crédito ("Equal Credit Opportunity Act") prohíbe la discriminación en el otorgamiento de préstamos en base a varios factores. Muchos estados tienen leyes sobre la usura que también protegen a los prestatarios. Los prestatarios que agotan su capacidad de crédito pueden declararse en quiebra.

5 Puntos destacados

Comprando alimentos

Términos claves

almacén para compra de alimentos (p. 109)

tiendas de artículos de consumo frecuente (p. 109)

productos con etiquetas de la casa (p. 110)

Resumen

Los consumidores deben conocer las muchas sugerencias útiles que se obtienen comparando las condiciones de venta de un bien o producto antes de hacer una compra. Existen tres clases importantes de tiendas de comestibles; cada una ofrece sus ventajas.

Selección de ropa

Términos claves

durabilidad (p. 115)

flujo de servicio (p. 115)

Resumen

Los valores de cada persona influyen en su elección de ropa. El valor de la ropa es determinado por el estilo, la durabilidad y el costo de mantenimiento. Reconocer el momento oportuno es un factor importante en la venta de ropa.

CAPÍTULO 6

Puntos destacados

Sección 1

Necesidades y preferencias de vivienda

Términos claves
impuestos sobre bienes inmuebles (p. 125)
condominios (p. 126)
cooperativas (p. 126)
arrendamiento (p. 126)
depreciar (p. 126)

Resumen
Existen cinco tipos diferentes de viviendas disponibles a los consumidores. Los arrendatarios deben tomar en cuenta los pros y los contras de compartir un apartamiento o una casa antes de firmar un contrato de arrendamiento.

Sección 2

Arrendar o comprar

Términos claves
costos de cierre (p. 129)
puntos porcentuales (p. 129)
equidad (p. 130)
depósito de garantía (p. 130)

Resumen
Al tomar una decisión sobre su vivienda, se debe considerar las ventajas y desventajas de arrendar y comprar una casa. Existen normas que determinan cuánto se debe gastar en una casa. Tanto el arrendatario como el arrendador tienen derechos y responsabilidades.

Sección 3

Compra y manejo de un automóvil

Términos claves
impuesto interno sobre el consumo (p. 136)
derecho de registro (p. 137)
seguro de responsabilidad civil (p. 139)

Resumen
La compra de un automóvil implica varios gastos. El dueño de un auto debe también hacer gastos relacionados con el manejo y el mantenimiento del mismo.

7 Puntos destacados

¿Para qué ahorrar?

Términos claves

ahorro (p. 146)
interés (p. 146)
cuenta de ahorro con libreta (p. 147)
cuenta de ahorro con estado de cuenta (p. 147)
cuenta de depósito en el mercado monetario (p. 148)

depósito a plazo (p. 148)
vencimiento (p. 148)
certificados de depósito (p. 148)

Resumen

Toda persona debe decidir el momento más oportuno para ahorrar e invertir. Los inversionistas principiantes deben comparar las cuentas de ahorro con libreta, con estado de cuenta y en el mercado monetario. Las cuentas de depósito a plazo brindan asimismo algunas ventajas.

Las inversiones: corriendo riesgos con sus ahorros

Términos claves

acciones (p. 154)
accionistas (p. 155)
dividendos (p. 155)
bonos (p. 155)
bonos exentos de impuesto (p. 155)
bonos de ahorro (p. 155)
bonos del Tesoro a corto plazo (p. 156)
pagarés del Tesoro (p. 156)
bonos del Tesoro a largo plazo (p. 156)

mercado de valores no oficial (p. 157)
ganancias de capital (plusvalía) (p. 157)
corredor (p. 157)
pérdidas de capital (minusvalía) (p. 158)
fondos mutuos (p. 158)
fondo de inversión a corto plazo en el mercado de dinero (p. 158)
información interior de una empresa (p. 159)

Resumen

Las acciones y los bonos ofrecen al inversionista opciones con ventajas distintas. Algunos fondos de inversión disponibles en los mercados de acciones y bonos implican menos riesgos que las acciones y los bonos individuales. Los consejos especulativos no ayudan a los inversionistas a hacerse ricos de la noche a la mañana en el mercado de valores.

Planes especiales de ahorro y objetivos

Términos claves

planes de pensiones (p. 161)
Plan Keogh (p. 161)
Cuenta de Retiro Individual o IRA (p. 162)
diversificación (p. 164)

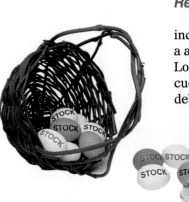

Resumen

Los planes de pensiones patrocinados por individuos o empresas ayudan a las personas a ahorrar para el momento de su jubilación. Los intereses y el riesgo deben tomarse en cuenta antes de decidir la cantidad que se debe ahorrar e invertir.

8 Puntos destacados

La demanda

Términos claves

intercambio voluntario (p. 176)
ley de la demanda (p. 177)
utilidad (p. 177)
ley de la utilidad marginal decreciente (p. 177)

efecto de ingreso real (p. 179)
efecto de sustitución (p. 179)

Resumen

En una economía de mercado, el principio de intercambio voluntario ayuda a determinar el precio que los consumidores están dispuestos a pagar por un producto o servicio determinado. La ley de la demanda, según es afectada por la utilidad marginal decreciente, el efecto de ingreso real y el efecto de sustitución, explica cómo reaccionan los consumidores ante las variaciones de precios.

Curva de demanda y elasticidad de la demanda

Términos claves

curva de demanda (p. 183)
elasticidad (p. 185)
elasticidad de precios de la demanda (p. 185)

demanda elástica (p. 185)
demanda inelástica (p. 186)
bienes complementarios (p. 188)

Resumen

Los economistas con frecuencia dibujan la curva de demanda para entender mejor la dinámica de los precios. La elasticidad de precios de la demanda influye en las variaciones del precio de un producto. Además de esta elasticidad, otros factores determinan la demanda en una economía de mercado.

La ley de la oferta y la curva de oferta

Términos claves

ley de la oferta (p. 191)
ley de los rendimientos decrecientes (p. 192)

curva de oferta (p. 194)

Resumen

En el sistema de mercado libre, el incentivo de obtener mayores ganancias afecta la cantidad de productos que los fabricantes están dispuestos y en capacidad de ofrecer. Igual que la curva de demanda, la curva de oferta muestra la relación entre el nivel de la oferta y los precios.

Equilibrio de la oferta y la demanda

Términos claves

precio de equilibrio (p. 191)
tecnología (p. 197)
falta (p. 198)
superávit (p. 198)

Resumen

Cuatro factores determinan la oferta en una economía de mercado. Un cambio en la oferta puede, con frecuencia, producir cambios significativos en los precios. Tanto la falta como el superávit afectan el precio en una economía de mercado. Algunas veces este cambio adopta la forma de un cambio en el precio de equilibrio. Aunque la oferta y la demanda influyen conjuntamente en los precios, las fuerzas que se ocultan detrás de la oferta y la demanda pueden asimismo alterar el precio de un producto o servicio.

9 Puntos destacados

Resumen
Poner en marcha un negocio requiere dos etapas. Una vez que las etapas esten completadas, los empresarios deben considerar detenidamente los cuatro elementos claves de todo negocio.

Resumen
La forma de organización empresarial más común en los Estados Unidos es la de propietario único, que tiene sus ventajas y desventajas. Las sociedades de dos o más personas tienen también sus ventajas y desventajas. Las sociedades de personas con responsabilidad limitada tienen que seguir directrices específicas.

Resumen
Muchas personas comparten la propiedad de las corporaciones, lo que tiene ventajas y desventajas diferentes de las de otras formas de organización empresarial. Las franquicias, por medio de las cuales el franquiciador vende a otro negocio el derecho de usar su nombre y vender sus productos, son comunes en algunas industrias.

10 *Puntos destacados*

Competencia perfecta

Término clave
competencia perfecta
(p. 232)

Resumen
La competencia perfecta tiene cuatro condiciones que conducen a que las empresas no tengan control de los precios. En los Estados Unidos la agricultura es la rama que se acerca más a cumplir con estas condiciones. Aunque ideal de sí, la competencia perfecta casi no existe en el mundo real.

Monopolio, oligopolio y la competencia monopolista

Términos claves
competencia imperfecta
(p. 237)
monopolio puro (p. 237)
barreras para entrar en un
mercado (p. 238)
monopolios naturales
(p. 239)
monopolios geográficos
(p. 239)
monopolio tecnológico
(p. 239)

patente (p. 239)
monopolios estatales (p. 239)
cartel (p. 239)
oligopolio (p. 240)
diferenciación de productos
(p. 240)
competencia monopolista
(p. 240)

Resumen
Tres condiciones conducen a que un negocio llegue a tener control casi total de los precios en el mercado (monopolio puro). Las cuatro condiciones que producen un oligopolio dan a los vendedores control limitado sobre los precios. La competencia monopolista es el tipo de estructura de mercado más común en los Estados Unidos.

Políticas gubernamentales hacia la competencia

Términos claves
leyes antimonopolistas
(p. 244)
consejo de administración
coincidente (p. 244)
fusión (p. 244)
fusión horizontal (p. 245)

fusión vertical (p. 245)
conglomerados (p. 245)
fusión de conglomerados
(p. 245)
desregulación (p. 246)
nueva regulación (p. 246)

Resumen
Las leyes federales prohíben los consejos de administración coincidentes, pero permiten las fusiones de empresas siempre que no signifiquen la formación de un monopolio. Para promover la competencia y proteger a los consumidores el gobierno ha creado muchas agencias federales regulativas. Muchos de los reglamentos emitidos por estas agencias han sido eliminados, pero algunas personas están a favor de una nueva regulación.

11 Puntos destacados

Sección 1

La inversión en el sistema de libre empresa

Términos claves
análisis de costo-beneficio
(p. 258)

Resumen

Las personas y las empresas invierten sus ahorros en muchos lugares incluyendo diferentes bancos, fondos mutuos y planes de pensiones. Financiando sus inversiones, las personas esperan ganar interés. Las empresas recurren a estas inversiones para financiar la expansión. Este financiamiento de la expansión es una forma de determinar la asignación de recursos en un sistema de mercado libre.

Sección 2

Tipos de financiamiento de las operaciones comerciales

Términos claves
financiamiento mediante créditos o la emisión de obligaciones (p. 265)
financiamiento a corto plazo (p. 265)
financiamiento a medio plazo (p. 265
financiamiento a largo plazo (p. 265)

crédito comercial (p. 266)
pagaré (p. 266)
cuentas por cobrar (p. 266)
línea de crédito (p. 266)
arrendamiento (p. 266)
financiamiento por venta de participación (p. 267)

Resumen

Cuando las empresas toman dinero prestado, el plazo para pagar la deuda es un factor importante que debe ser tomado en cuenta. Las empresas que toman dinero prestado consideran la tasa de interés, las condiciones del mercado y su capacidad para hacer frente a la carga de la deuda. Algunas veces las empresas consiguen capital financiero vendiendo acciones o bonos.

Sección 3

El proceso de producción

Términos claves
producción (p. 271)
bienes de consumo (p. 271)
bienes de producción (p. 271)
mecanización (p. 274)

cadena de montaje (p. 275)
división del trabajo (p. 275)
automatización (p. 275)
robótica (p. 275)

Resumen

El proceso de producción implica diseño del producto, planificación, compra, control de calidad y control de existencias. La tecnología ha aumentado la productividad. La mecanización, la cadena de montaje, la división del trabajo, la automatización y la robótica se han combinado para hacer más eficiente la producción.

---

12  *Puntos destacados*

Sección 1

El papel cambiante de la mercadotecnia ("marketing")

Términos claves

mercadotecnia (p. 282)
utilidad (p. 282)
utilidad por la forma (p. 284)
utilidad de tiempo (p. 284)
utilidad de emplazamiento (p. 284)
utilidad de la posesión (p. 284)

investigación de mercado (p. 284)
informe de mercado (p. 284)
comercialización de prueba (p. 285)

Resumen

El desarrollo de la mercadotecnia en los Estados Unidos ha tenido cuatro etapas, que han conducido a la soberanía del consumidor. Mediante una serie de preguntas elaboradas de antemano, los estudios de mercados tratan de descubrir la calidad, las características y los estilos que los consumidores desean en un producto, el tipo de embalaje que atraerá a los consumidores y el precio que los moverá a comprar.

Sección 2

Los componentes básicos de la mercadotecnia

Términos claves

liderazgo en la fijación de precios (p. 289)
fijación de precios de penetración (p. 290)
publicidad (p. 290)

publicidad directa por correo (p. 291)
ciclo de vida del producto (p. 291)

Resumen

Los cuatro componentes básicos de mercadotecnia son el producto, el precio, el lugar y la publicidad. Al fijar el precio de un producto, una empresa debe tomar en cuenta los costos de producción, publicidad, venta y distribución, así como las utilidades que desea obtener y el precio que los competidores están cobrando por el mismo producto. El precio es usado también en las estrategias de mercadotecnia. El lugar donde se vende el producto y el tipo de publicidad usada ayudan a determinar el éxito de ese producto.

Sección 3

Canales de distribución

Términos claves

canales de distribución (p. 293)
mayoristas (p. 293)
vendedores al por menor (p. 294)

Resumen

Los mayoristas compran grandes cantidades de productos de los fabricantes para venderlos a otros negocios. Los vendedores al por menor venden bienes de consumo directamente al público. Como parte del proceso de distribución, las mercancías pueden ser almacenadas por el fabricante, el mayorista o el vendedor al por menor para su futura venta. Los aumentos más significativos en la distribución de productos se han logrado por medio de los club-almacenes ("club-warehouses") y la publicidad directa por correo.

13 Puntos destacados

La fuerza laboral en los Estados Unidos

Términos claves

fuerza laboral civil (p. 306)
obreros (p. 306)
profesionales (p. 307)
empleados de oficina (p. 307)
trabajadores en el área de
　servicios (p. 307)

obreros no cualificados
　(p. 307)
obreros semicualificados
　(p. 307)
obreros cualificados (p. 307)
ley del salario mínimo
　(p. 309)

Resumen

Los trabajadores pueden ser clasificados por categorías según el tipo de trabajo. Los trabajadores también pueden ser clasificados como no cualificados, semicualificados, cualificados y profesionales. En el mercado de trabajo, la oferta viene de los trabajadores que ofrecen sus servicios y la demanda de los empleadores que necesitan trabajadores. Tres factores determinan cómo la oferta y la demanda afectan los salarios: la capacidad, el tipo de trabajo y el lugar.

Trabajo organizado

Términos claves

sindicato (p. 311)
huelga (p. 312)
gremio (p. 312)
sindicato industrial
　(p. 312)
sindicato local (p. 313)
empresa con sindicación
　obligatoria ("closed shop")
　(p. 313)

empresa con sindicación
　eventual obligatoria
　("union shop") (p. 313)
empresa con cotización
　sindical obligatoria
　("agency shop") (p. 313)
ley sobre libertad laboral
　(p. 313)

Resumen

En el siglo XIX, los sindicatos atraían a los trabajadores porque parecían ofrecer un medio para obligar a los empleadores a mejorar las condiciones de trabajo. No obstante, el sindicalismo encontró mucha resistencia durante la mayor parte del siglo XIX y principios del XX. Los sindicatos lograron en el siglo XX establecer empresas donde los trabajadores tienen que estar sindicados, sindicarse transcurrido cierto tiempo o cotizar al sindicato.

Convenio colectivo

Términos claves

convenio colectivo (p. 318)
mediación (p. 318)
ajuste por coste de vida
　(p. 319)
arbitraje (p. 319)

piquetes laborales (p. 320)
boicot (p. 320)
cierre patronal ("lockout")
　(p. 320)
interdicción laboral (p. 320)

Resumen

Los asuntos más importantes tratados usualmente en las negociaciones colectivas de trabajo son los salarios, las horas de trabajo, los beneficios complementarios, las condiciones de trabajo, la seguridad en el trabajo y los procedimientos de presentación de agravios. Cuando se rompen las negociaciones colectivas, el arbitraje o la mediación, puede surgir una huelga en la que piquetes de huelguistas pueden hacer guardia alrededor de las instalaciones de la empresa y organizar un boicot exhortando al público a no comprar los productos o servicios fabricados por dicha empresa. La administración puede responder declarando un cierre patronal u obteniendo una interdicción judicial contra los trabajadores.

Resumen

El producto interior bruto (PIB) es el valor total en dólares de todos los bienes finales de consumo, de producción y estatales, las exportaciones netas y los servicios producidos en la nación durante un año. El ingreso personal se encuentra restando del ingreso nacional los impuestos sobre la renta de las corporaciones, las utilidades y las contribuciones de los empleadores al Seguro Social.

Resumen

Cuando hay inflación, el dinero pierde su poder adquisitivo. Las tres formas de medir los cambios en los precios promedios son el índice de precios al consumidor (IPC), el índice de precios al productor (IPP) y el deflactor de precios del PIB implícito.

Resumen

La suma total de la oferta y la demanda de bienes y servicios representa el total de la economía. La intersección de las curvas de demanda global y de oferta total determina el nivel de precios de equilibrio y el PIB real (producción nacional).

Resumen

Las fluctuaciones económicas se miden de un período de prosperidad a otro. Un "ciclo" típico comienza con el punto máximo (auge); luego la economía comienza a contraerse, período durante el cual puede darse una recesión (punto mínimo) seguida de una recuperación.

Resumen

La economía estudia muchas posibles causas de los ciclos económicos. Los economistas usan indicadores anticipados, coincidentes y de retardo para medir la actividad de algunas variables en la economía.

Puntos destacados

Funciones y características del dinero

Términos claves

dinero (p. 362)
medios de cambio (p. 362)
trueque (p. 362)
doble coincidencia de necesidades (p. 364)
unidad de contabilidad (p. 364)

reserva de valor (p. 364)
dinero mercancía (p. 365)
dinero en cuenta (p. 366)
papel moneda (p. 366)
moneda de curso legal (p. 366)

Resumen

Se considera dinero todo lo que es usado como medio de cambio, unidad de contabilidad y reserva de valor. Actualmente, todo el dinero de los Estados Unidos es papel moneda. Es portátil, divisible, de valor estable y aceptado. No obstante, el papel moneda no es muy duradero.

Historia del dinero y la banca en los Estados Unidos

Términos claves

sobregiro (p. 369)
transferencia electrónica de fondos (EFT) (p. 369)
patrón monetario (p. 370)
cajeros automáticos (ATMs) (p. 372)

Resumen

La historia del dinero y la banca del país ha sido un proceso de ordenamiento gradual de un sistema desordenado. El Congreso dio el primer paso en esta dirección en 1792 cuando estableció el dólar como la unidad básica de cambio y estableció la primera casa de la moneda. Los servicios bancarios modernos incluyen muchos servicios además de las cuentas de cheques y ahorro.

Tipos de dinero en los Estados Unidos

Términos claves

cuenta corriente bancaria (p. 376)
depósitos a la vista (p. 377)
depósitos verificables (p. 377)
instituciones de ahorro (p. 377)

tarjetas de débito (p. 377)
cuasidinero (p. 378)
M1 (p. 378)
M2 (p. 378)

Resumen

Actualmente la oferta monetaria de los Estados Unidos se compone de dinero en circulación, depósitos verificables y cuasidinero. La definición M1 de la oferta monetaria incluye el dinero en circulación, los cheques viajeros y los depósitos verificables en los bancos comerciales y las instituciones de ahorro. La definición de dinero M2 incluye la definición M1 más algunos activos fácilmente convertibles en dinero (cuasidinero).

16 *Puntos destacados*

La oferta monetaria y la economía

Términos claves

El "Fed" (p. 388)
política monetaria (p. 388)
política de dinero disponible
  (p. 389)
política de dinero escaso
  (p. 389)
reserva parcial bancaria
  (p. 389)
reserva obligatoria (p. 389)

Resumen

Una política de dinero disponible significa que el crecimiento de la oferta monetaria ha aumentado y hay dinero en abundancia y es barato de tomar prestado. Con una política de dinero escaso ocurre lo contrario. Con el sistema de reserva parcial bancario, sólo una fracción de los depósitos en un banco se mantiene disponible. El resto es dado en préstamo o invertido. Debido al sistema de reserva parcial bancario, cualquier cambio en el dinero nuevo en circulación producirá un cambio múltiple en la oferta monetaria.

Organización y funciones del Sistema de la Reserva Federal

Términos claves

Comisión Federal de
  Mercado Abierto (FOMC)
  (p. 394)
compensación de cheques
  bancarios (p. 396)

Resumen

La Junta Directiva del Sistema de la Reserva Federal dirige las operaciones del Sistema de la Reserva Federal y establece políticas con respecto a asuntos como la reserva obligatoria y las tasas de descuento. El Sistema de la Reserva Federal ejerce muchas funciones además de compensar cheques para los bancos y reglamentar la oferta monetaria.

Regulación de la oferta monetaria

Términos claves

tasa de descuento (p. 401)
tasa mínima de interés
  (p. 401)
operaciones de mercado
  abierto (p. 402)

Resumen

Para regular la oferta monetaria, el Fed emplea cambios en la reserva obligatoria, la tasa de descuento y las operaciones de mercado abierto. Algunas veces resulta difícil diseñar políticas monetarias porque el gobierno no tiene siempre información correcta sobre las definiciones M1 y M2. Además, el Fed no es la única fuerza que afecta la economía.

17 *Puntos destacados*

Sección 1

Aumento en las dimensiones del gobierno

Términos claves
proyectos de obras públicas (p. 413)
Medicare (p. 415)

Resumen
El gobierno de los Estados Unidos ha crecido de cerca de 3 millones de empleados en 1929 a cerca de 19 millones actualmente. Varios factores explican este gran crecimiento del aparato estatal.

Sección 2

Las funciones del gobierno

Términos claves
bienes públicos (p. 416)
bienes preferentes (p. 416)
Seguro Social (p. 417)
indemnización por accidente de trabajo (p. 417)
Ingreso de Seguridad Suplementario (p. 417)

Asistencia Temporal a Familias Necesitadas (p. 417)
Medicaid (p. 417)
bienes de demérito (p. 417)
redistribución del ingreso (p. 417)
programas de seguro social (p. 418)
programas de asistencia pública (p. 418)
bienestar social (p. 418)

Resumen
Cuatro funciones importantes del gobierno son: (1) proporcionar bienes públicos, (2) redistribuir el ingreso y asegurar el bienestar público, (3) regular la actividad económica y (4) asegurar la estabilidad económica. El gobierno facilita los bienes públicos a todos los ciudadanos. El gobierno usa los programas de seguro social y los programas de asistencia pública para redistribuir el ingreso. Al mismo tiempo, el gobierno trabaja para promover la estabilidad económica.

Sección 3

El presupuesto nacional y la deuda pública

Términos claves
año fiscal (p. 421)
financiamiento del déficit (p. 423)

deuda pública (p. 425)
enmienda del presupuesto equilibrado (p. 246)

Resumen
El proceso de elaboración del presupuesto federal incluye varios pasos que involucran a los poderes ejecutivo y legislativo. Aun con restricciones para salvaguardar la balanza de pagos e intentos de reducir el déficit, la deuda pública sigue creciendo a un ritmo alarmante.

Sección 4

Impuestos

Términos claves
principio de beneficios recibidos (p. 428)
principio de capacidad de pago (p. 428)

impuesto progresivo (p. 430)
impuesto regresivo (p. 430)
impuesto proporcional (p. 430)

Resumen
Dos principios tributarios son el principio de imputación basado en los beneficios recibidos y el principio de imputación basado en la capacidad de pago. Los impuestos son clasificados de acuerdo con la forma en que distribuyan la carga tributaria entre los contribuyentes, mientras algunos impuestos son gravados para afectar la actividad económica.

18 *Puntos destacados*

Desempleo e inflación

Términos claves
políticas de estabilización (p. 438)
índice de desempleo (p. 438)
pleno empleo (p. 439)
economía sumergida (p. 439)
inflación de demanda (p. 440)
inflación con estancamiento (p. 441)
inflación de costes (p. 441)

Figure 18.5 Cost-Push Inflation

Large Unions
Receive wage increases

Workers
Demand higher wages to balance decline in their purchasing power

Businesses
Pay higher wages and their costs increase

Consumers
Pay higher prices for goods

Businesses
Raise prices to maintain profits

Resumen
Medir el desempleo es difícil porque los economistas no están de acuerdo sobre el nivel de pleno empleo. Las investigaciones sobre desempleo son inexactas debido a la economía sumergida. La inflación de demanda ocurre generalmente en tiempos de pleno empleo. La inflación de costos ocurre con frecuencia cuando los índices de inflación y desempleo son altos.

Política fiscal y estabilización

Términos claves
política fiscal (p. 443)
flujo circular de ingresos (p. 443)

Resumen
Los economistas usan un modelo para explicar el flujo circular de ingresos. Los economistas keynesianos creen que la política fiscal (los impuestos y los gastos del gobierno) debe ser usada para regular el nivel global de la actividad económica. Quieren que el gobierno use la política fiscal para reducir la inflación.

El monetarismo y la economía

Términos claves
monetarismo (p. 448)
los monetaristas (p. 448)
principio monetario (p. 449)
desface cronológico (p. 450)

Resumen
Los monetaristas creen que el Sistema de la Reserva Federal cometió errores que profundizaron la Gran Depresión. Sus teorías influyeron en las políticas gubernamentales a partir de la década de los 1980. Los monetaristas cuestionan la capacidad de la política fiscal para resolver los problemas de la inflación y el desempleo.

Puntos destacados

Los beneficios del comercio mundial

Términos claves
importaciones (p. 462)
exportaciones (p. 462)
ventaja absoluta (p. 464)
especialización (p. 464)
ventaja comparativa (p. 465)

Resumen

Las naciones se benefician del comercio mundial porque los factores de producción disponibles en cada nación son diferentes. La ventaja absoluta es la capacidad de un país de producir más cantidad de un producto determinado que otra nación, usando la misma cantidad de recursos. Si un país tiene al menos una ventaja comparativa con respecto a un producto, es ventajoso para ese país especializarse en la producción de dicho producto. Puede entonces establecer relaciones de intercambio con otros países para obtener los productos que desea.

El financiamiento del comercio mundial

Términos claves
los mercados de divisas (p. 467)
tipo de cambio fijo (p. 467)
Fondo Monetario Internacional (FMI) (p. 467)

devaluación (p. 468)
tipos de cambio flexibles (p. 468)
depreciación (p. 469)
balanza comercial (p. 469)

Resumen

Con un tipo de cambio fijo, el gobierno nacional fija el valor de su moneda con relación a un solo patrón. Con un tipo de cambio flexible, las fuerzas de la oferta y la demanda de bienes determinan los precios de las monedas. Cuando el valor de nuestras exportaciones excede el valor de nuestras importaciones, tenemos un superávit en nuestra balanza comercial.

Restricciones del comercio mundial

Términos claves
arancel (p. 472)
arancel financiero (p. 472)
arancel proteccionista (p. 472)
cuota de importación (p. 473)
embargo (p. 473)
proteccionistas (p. 474)

Acuerdo General sobre Aranceles Aduaneros y Comercio (GATT) (p. 474)
Organización Mundial de Comercio (p. 474)
Tratado de Libre Comercio para América del Norte (NAFTA) (p. 475)

Resumen

Las restricciones legales al comercio mundial tratan de proteger a las industrias y a los trabajadores del país. Los pros y los contras de las restricciones al comercio son con frecuencia objeto de intensos debates. La mayor parte del comercio mundial se rige por el GATT y varios tratados comerciales regionales.

Comparación entre el capitalismo y el socialismo

Términos claves

Resumen

El capitalismo de mercado puro puede ser descrito en base a las llamadas tres "P": precios ("prices"), utilidades ("profits") y propiedad privada ("private property"). Los derechos de propiedad privada existen y son legales; se permite a los precios alcanzar sus propios niveles de acuerdo con la oferta y la demanda; los recursos son dirigidos a las áreas que producen mayores utilidades. En el socialismo puro, el estado fija la mayoría de los precios, el estado es dueño de los principales factores de producción, las decisiones económicas son tomadas por el estado por medio de sus agencias de planificación centralizada y el movimiento de los recursos está estrictamente controlado. La planificación en el capitalismo está descentralizada. El capitalismo ofrece libertad personal y premia la iniciativa individual.

Cambios en el socialismo autoritario: el caso de China

Términos claves

Resumen

Después de la Segunda Guerra mundial, los chinos establecieron una serie de planes quinquenales, ninguno de los cuales dio los resultados esperados. A partir de 1979, se designaron zonas económicas especiales. El índice de crecimiento en estas zonas económicas especiales ha sido muy alto.

Las naciones se dirigen al sistema de mercado

Términos claves

Resumen

La tendencia en Rusia, en las otras repúblicas de la antigua Unión Soviética y en la Europa oriental es hacia una privatización cada vez mayor. Suecia, que ha sido un estado de bienestar durante muchos años, ha avanzado recientemente hacia la privatización y a una menor participación del estado en la satisfacción de las necesidades básicas del individuo. Empezando con los cambios en México a mediados de la década de los 1980, un número cada vez mayor de países en América Latina están privatizando las compañías pertenecientes al estado.

21 *Puntos destacados*

Características de las naciones en vías de desarrollo

Términos claves

naciones desarrolladas (p. 504)

naciones en vías de desarrollo (p. 504)

agricultura de subsistencia (p. 505)

mortalidad infantil (p. 506)

Resumen

Tres de cada cuatro personas en el mundo viven en naciones en vías de desarrollo. Cuando los economistas miden el desarrollo de una nación consideran varios factores. Varias naciones asiáticas han demostrado un crecimiento rápido y estable en años recientes.

El proceso de desarrollo económico

Términos claves

ayuda exterior (p. 512)

asistencia económica (p. 513)

asistencia técnica (p. 513)

asistencia militar (p. 513)

Resumen

El desarrollo económico de una nación puede ser financiado por medio de una combinación de ahorros domésticos e inversiones y ayuda exterior. La ayuda exterior se compone de asistencia económica, técnica y militar. Muchas naciones industriales brindan ayuda exterior por razones humanitarias, económicas y políticas y de seguridad nacional.

Obstáculos al crecimiento en las naciones en vías de desarrollo

Términos claves

burocracias (p. 517)

nacionalización (p. 519)

Resumen

Las naciones en vías de desarrollo tienen que hacer frente a varios obstáculos que dificultan su crecimiento. La falta de desarrollo económico de Indonesia nos enseña que el solo hecho de proporcionar dinero a una nación en desarrollo no garantiza el crecimiento económico. La ayuda exterior debe ser usada con sabiduría, junto con los ahorros domésticos, la inversión extranjera y políticas gubernamentales que aseguren la estabilidad económica.

La industrialización y el futuro

Términos claves

derechos de propiedad privada (p. 523)

ciclo vicioso de la pobreza (p. 524)

Resumen

La rápida industrialización no es necesariamente la solución para las naciones en vías de desarrollo que no tienen una ventaja comparativa en la producción de determinados bienes que deciden fabricar. Mientras más seguridad existe con respecto a los derechos de propiedad privada, mayor será la inversión tanto doméstica como extranjera.

22 Puntos destacados

Causas y resultados de la integración mundial

Términos claves
integración mundial (p. 532)
telecomunicaciones (p. 532)

Resumen

Una de las razones más importantes de la mayor integración mundial ha sido las mejoras en las telecomunicaciones debidas a las reducciones considerables de los costos de los "chips" (plaquetas) de computadoras. En la actualidad, muchos instrumentos financieros se venden en los mercados internacionales. Los acontecimientos en un mercado nacional repercuten en otros mercados por todo el mundo.

¿Debe preocuparnos la inversión extranjera directa?

Términos clave
inversión extranjera directa (p. 537)

Resumen

Los extranjeros han invertido siempre en los Estados Unidos y lo siguen haciendo actualmente. Pero la inversión extranjera directa es una parte relativamente pequeña de nuestra economía considerada en su totalidad. No obstante, el objetivo último de la inversión extranjera directa por parte de naciones como el Japón es aumentar al máximo las utilidades.

Las empresas transnacionales y la competencia económica

Términos claves
empresas transnacionales (p. 543)
lealtades (p. 543)
filiales extranjeras (p. 543)
alianzas (p. 545)
tolerancia (p. 547)

Resumen

La inversión fuera de las fronteras nacionales corre a cargo de 35,000 empresas transnacionales por todo el mundo. La mayoría de las transnacionales invierten en regiones que están cerca de casa. Por ejemplo, las compañías de los Estados Unidos invierten principalmente en los Estados Unidos, Canadá, México y América del Sur. Las corporaciones pueden formar alianzas con antiguos competidores por muchas razones. La competencia internacional por los fondos de inversión extranjera significa que cuando las complicaciones de las burocracias estatales y los altos impuestos se vuelven un problema en un determinado país, los extranjeros invierten en otros países con un clima más favorable para la inversión.

TEXT DESIGN: Martucci Studio
COVER DESIGN: Martucci Studio, PHOTOS (l) Suzanne and Nick Geary/Tony Stone/Worldwide (r) Martucci Studio.
ILLUSTRATION: Martucci Studio/Jerry D. Malone
PHOTO RESEARCH: Susan Van Etten
PHOTO CREDITS: i, (l) Susan and Nick Geary/Tony Stone, Worldwide, (r) Martucci Studio. iv, (b) Pictor/Uniphoto v, ©Martucci Studio vi, ©Martucci Studio (bl) Courtesy, Ramsey & Muspratt Collections vii, (t) Courtesy, Charles B. Wang/Computer Associates (m) The Granger Collection (b) ©Martucci Studio viii, (tl&br) The Granger Collection (tr&bl) ©Martucci Studio ix, (tr) ©Martucci Studio (m) Vince Streano/Tony Stone Images/Chicago Inc. (br) David Austen/Stock Boston (bm) Barrie Rokeach/The Image Bank (bl) ©Susan Van Etten x, (t) David Hiser/Tony Stone Images/Chicago Inc. (m) © Martucci Studio (b) Uniphoto xi, (tl) ©Martucci Studio (l) ©Moore & Associates (m) Wide World (b) ©Martucci Studio 4–5, Jake Rais/The Image Bank 6–7, ©Martucci Studio 8, ©Martucci Studio 9, (t) Arnold J. Kaplan/The Picture Cube (b) Wide World 10, Gary Cralle/The Image Bank 11, (l) Guido Alberto Rossi/The Image Bank (r) Don Carroll/The Image Bank 13, (l) Cindy Lewis Photography, (r) Arthur Tilley/FPG; 14, D.D. Morrison/The Picture Cube 14–15, Chris Hackett/The Image Bank 16, ©Paul Conklin 17, Courtesy, New School for Social Research 18, Jeff Greenburg/The Picture Cube 19, ©Martucci Studio 20, Jay Freis/The Image Bank 20–21, ©Martucci Studio 22, (t) Brian Smith/Outline, (b) U.S. Postal Service/Archive Photos 23, Mark Burnett 24, ©Martucci Studio 26, Bob Daemmrich/Stock Boston 26–27, Jim Karageorge 27, Bob Daemmrich/Stock Boston 28–29, Tom McCarthy/The Picture Cube 31, (tr) Alvis Upitis/The Image Bank (l) Pete Turner/The Image Bank 30–31, Pictor/Uniphoto 32, D. C. Clegg/FPG 33, ©Susan Van Etten 34, ©Martucci Studio 35, (t) Pamela Zully/The Image Bank (b) Owen Franken/Stock Boston 37, ©Martucci Studio 38, (l) Bob Daemmrich/Stock Boston (r) Tony Freeman/Photo Edit 39, (r) ©Susan Van Etten (b) ©Paul Conklin 41, The Granger Collection 42–43, ©Martucci Studio 45, (tr) Larry Lawfer/The Picture Cube (tl) Richard Ustinich/The Image Bank (mr) Fotographia, Inc. Stock Boston (br) Eddie Hironaka/The Image Bank 44–45, Bob Daemmrich/Stock Boston 46, (t) ©Susan Van Etten (m) ©Susan Van Etten (b) Steve Dunwell/The Image Bank 48, (l) ©Martucci Studio (t&m) Courtesy, Southwest Airlines/Pam Francis 49, Mark Burnett 50, Tom McCarthy/The Picture Cube 54–55, ©Mark Thayer 56–57, Mike Kagan/Monkmeyer Press Photos 59, ©Susan Van Etten 60, 61, ©Martucci Studio 62, TLC Beatrice 63, ©Susan Van Etten 64, ©Martucci Studio 65, ©Susan Van Etten 66, 68, ©Martucci Studio 69, (r) Michael Newman/Photo Edit (l) ©Martucci Studio 70–71, 72, ©Martucci Studio 73, Mark Burnett 74, Mike Kagan/Monkmeyer Press Photos 76, Steve Dunwell/The Image Bank 76–77, Ross H. Horowitz/Stockphotos 77, ©Susan Van Etten 78–79, ©Martucci Studio 81, Gerard Champlong/The Image Bank 82, (l) ©Susan Van Etten (r) ©Martucci Studio 83, ©Martucci Studio 84, Courtesy, Ronal Homer/Boston Bank of Commerce 86, (l) Rob Crandall/Stock Boston (b) Karl Gehring/Gamma-Liaison 87, (l) David Young-Wolff/Photo Edit (tr) ©Susan Van Etten 88, ©Benson, Arizona Republic, 8/89, Reprinted by permission of Tribune Media Services. 89,

Jeff Smith/The Image Bank 90–91, 92, ©Martucci Studio 94, Tony Freeman/Photo Edit 94–95, ©Susan Van Etten 95, Costa Manos/Magnum 96, David Young-Wolff/Photo Edit 98, Robert V. Eckert, Jr./Stock Boston 99, Vera Kelly/FPG 101, ©Martucci Studio 102, (l) ©Susan Van Etten (c) Jane Art/The Image Bank (b) ©Susan Van Etten 103, Mark Burnett 104–105, ©Martucci Studio 106–107, Gary Gladstone/The Image Bank 108–109, ©Martucci Studio 108–109, Stephen McBrady/Photo Edit 109, (m) Mark Richards/Photo Edit (r) ©Susan Van Etten 110–111, ©Martucci Studio 112, The Bettmann Archive 114, (l) Kevin Forest/The Image Bank (c) Nancy Brown/The Image Bank (r) Mel DiGiacomo/The Image Bank 115, (l) David Browell/The Image Bank (c) Nancy Brown/The Image Bank (r) Eric Wheater/The Image Bank 116, (t) ©Susan Van Etten (b) ©Martucci Studio 118, (tc) Donna Binder/Impact Visuals, (b) R. W. Jones/Westlight 119, Mark Burnett 120, Gary Gladstone/The Image Bank 121, Nancy Brown/The Image Bank 112–123, ©Susan Van Etten 125, (t) Frank Siteman/Monkmeyer Press Photos (b) Marc Romanelli/The Image Bank 126, (t) ©Susan Van Etten (b) Tony Freeman/Photo Edit 127, (r) Amy Etra/Photo Edit (l) ©Susan Van Etten 128, The Bettmann Archive 130–133, ©Martucci Studio 135, Stephen Frisch/Stock Boston 136, ©Martucci Studio 137, Lisa J. Goodman/The Image Bank 138, ©Susan Van Etten 139, ©Martucci Studio 140, (t) Reggie Parker/FPG (b) Elizabeth Zuckerman/Photo Edit 141, Mark Burnett 142, ©Susan Van Etten 144–145, George Ombremski/The Image Bank 146–147, 148, ©Martucci Studio 148, (b) Murray Alcosser/The Image Bank 151, Matt Mendelsohn/Corbis 152–153, 154, 155, 156, ©Martucci Studio 157, David Jeffery/The Image Bank 160, ©Susan Van Etten 161, Larry Pierce/The Image Bank 164, ©Martucci Studio 166, (t) Michael Grecco, (c) Glencoe photo, (b) Thomas Veneklasen 167, Mark Burnett 169, George Ombremski/The Image Bank 172–173, Jook Leung/FPG 174–175, Mark Burnett 176, Michael Newman/Photo Edit 177, Bob Daemmrich/Stock Boston 178, 180–181, 184–185, 186, 188, ©Martucci Studio 190, The Granger Collection 191, ©Martucci Studio 192, Steve Allen/The Image Bank 193, ©Martucci Studio 195, Mark Burnett 196, ©Martucci Studio 198–199, Bill Varie/The Image Bank 200, Dorothy Littell/Stock Boston 201, ©Martucci Studio 202, (tr) courtesy Toshiba, (l) Telegraph Color Library/FPG 203, Mark Burnett 204, ©Martucci Studio 206–207, Don Swetzer/Tony Stone Images/Chicago, Inc. 209, Peter M. Miller/The Image Bank 211, Lawrence Migdale/Stock Boston 212, Wide World 213, ©Susan Van Etten 214, 215, 216, ©Martucci Studio 217, Lawrence Migdale/Stock Boston 220, ©Martucci Studio 223, David Young-Wolff/Photo Edit 224, (t) courtesy Yahoo! Inc., (l) James D. Wilson/Gamma Liaison, (r) Aaron Haupt 225, Mark Burnett 226, Don Swetzer/Tony Stone Images/Chicago, Inc. 228, Benn Mitchell/The Image Bank 228–229, Pete Turner/The Image Bank 229, Spencer Grant/Stock Boston 230–231, George Goodwin/Monkmeyer Press Photos 232–233, ©Susan Van Etten 234, Grafton Smith/The Image Bank 235, (l) Steve Proehl/The Image Bank (r) James Carmichael/The Image Bank 236, Mark Burnett 237, ©Susan Van Etten 239, (tr) ©Martucci Studio (lr) Tennessee Valley Authority (tl&bl) ©Susan Van Etten 240, ©Susan Van Etten 242, ©Martucci Studio 243, Courtesy, Ramsey & Muspratt

Collection 244, The Granger Collection 246, Michael R. Schneps/The Image Bank 248, (tl tr) Focus on Sports, (b) Michael Neveux/Westlight 249, Mark Burnett 250, George Goodwin/Monkmeyer Press Photos 254–255, FPG 256–257, Stacy Pick/Stock Boston 260, David Young-Wolff/Photo Edit 261, ©Susan Van Etten 262, Gabriel Covian/The Image Bank 263, David Hamilton/The Image Bank 265, 266, 267, ©Martucci Studio 269, Greg Pease/Tony Stone Images/Chicago, Inc. 270, M. Gerber/Corbis 271, Erik Leigh Simmons/The Image Bank 272, (l) Les Wollam (r) Jaime Villaseca/The Image Bank 273, Schneps/The Image Bank 274, (t) Michael Melford/The Image Bank (b) The Bettmann Archive 275, (bl) The Bettmann Archive (tl) Ellis Herwig/The Picture Cube (tr) Steve Dunwell/The Image Bank 276, (t) Juice Club, Inc., (cl) Ruth Dixon, (cr) Doug Martin, (b) Daniel A. Erickson 277, Mark Burnett 278, Stacy Pick/Stock Boston 279, Michael Melford/The Image Bank 280–281, ©Martucci Studio 283, (l) The Granger Collection (r) U. of Louisville Photo Archives, Caufield & Shook Collection/Susan Van Etten Historical Files (ll&lr) The Granger Collection 284, (l) Steve Dunwell/The Image Bank (r) Lincoln Russell/Stock Boston (m) Christopher Johnson/Stock Boston (ll) ©Susan Van Etten 288–289, ©Martucci Studio 292, Courtesy, Charles B. Wang/Computer Associates 293, ©Susan Van Etten 294–295, Mark Richards/Photo Edit 295, (ll) © Martucci Studio (lr) ©Susan Van Etten 296, ©Martucci Studio 297, Mark Burnett 298, (ll) ©Martucci Studio (l) Marc Solomon/The Image Bank (r) ©Susan Van Etten 299, Mark Burnett 300, ©Martucci Studio 302, Lou Jones/The Image Bank 302–303, Lawrence Fried/The Image Bank 303, Alvis Upitis/The Image Bank 304–305, David Young-Wolff/Photo Edit 309, Larry Keenan Associates/The Image Bank 311, 312–313, The Granger Collection 314–315, ©Martucci Studio 316, (l) Bob Daemmrich/Stock Boston (r) ©Susan Van Etten 317, 318, Wide World 319, ©Martucci Studio 320, Rick Browne/Stock Boston 322, (t) Ron Chapel/FPG, (others) Claudio Vazquez 323, Mark Burnett 324, David Young-Wolff/Photo Edit 328–329, Hunter/Freeman Studio, San Francisco 330–331, Hans Wolf/The Image Bank 332–333, ©Susan Van Etten 335, David Brownell/The Image Bank 340, ©Martucci Studio 342–343, ©Jim Pickerell/FPG 344, Louis Padilla/The Image Bank 346, UPI/The Bettmann Archive 349, The Granger Collection 350, Library of Congress/Susan Van Etten Historical Files 351, Bryan F. Peterson/The Stock Market 352, (l) Alvis Upitis/Stock Boston (r) Steve Gottlieb/FPG 353, (t) Susan Van Etten Historical Files (b) Mark Richards/Photo Edit 354, ©Martucci Studio 356, (l) Shawn C. Henry, (r) Ken Frick, (b) courtesy MacTemps 357, Mark Burnett 358, Hans Wolf/The Image Bank 360–361, 362–363, ©Martucci Studio 364, Frank Siteman/Stock Boston 365–366, ©Martucci Studio 367, Courtesy, Ariel Capital Management 368, The Granger Collection 370–371, ©Martucci Studio 372, R. Rathe/FPG 374, 375, ©Martucci Studio 377, (l) Andy Caulfield/The Image Bank (t) Gerald French/FPG (r) Jay Freis/The Image Bank 378, (r) ©Susan Van Etten (l) ©Martucci Studio 380, (l&r) ©Susan Van Etten (b) ©Martucci Studio 381, Mark Burnett 382, R. Rathe/FPG 383, ©Martucci Studio 384, ©Susan Van Etten 384–385, John Lei/Stock Boston 385, Bernard Roussel/The Image Bank 386–387, Al Satterwhite/The Image